Projecting the Holocaust
into the Present

Projecting the Holocaust into the Present

The Changing Focus of Contemporary Holocaust Cinema

Lawrence Baron

ROWMAN & LITTLEFIELD PUBLISHERS, INC.
Lanham • Boulder • New York • Toronto • Oxford

ROWMAN & LITTLEFIELD PUBLISHERS, INC.

Published in the United States of America
by Rowman & Littlefield Publishers, Inc.
A wholly owned subsidiary of The Rowman & Littlefield Publishing Group, Inc.
4501 Forbes Boulevard, Suite 200, Lanham, Maryland 20706
www.rowmanlittlefield.com

PO Box 317
Oxford
OX2 9RU, UK

British Library Cataloguing in Publication Information Available

Library of Congress Cataloging-in-Publication Data
Baron, Lawrence.
  Projecting the Holocaust into the present: the changing focus of contemporary Holo-
caust cinema / Lawrence Baron.
     p. cm.
  Includes bibliographical references and index.
  ISBN 0-7425-4332-3 (cloth : alk. paper)—ISBN 0-7425-4333-1 (pbk. : alk. paper)
  1. Holocaust, Jewish (1939–1945), in motion pictures. I. Title.
  PN1995.9.H53B37 2005
  791.43'658—dc22   2005012519

Printed in the United States of America

♾ ™ The paper used in this publication meets the minimum requirements of
American National Standard for Information Sciences—Permanence of Paper
for Printed Library Materials, ANSI/NISO Z39.48-1992.

Contents

Preface

*F*or twelve years, I have taught a course on the depiction of twentieth-century Jewish history in feature films. A substantial number of the movies I assign my students to watch are about the Holocaust or its impact on postwar Jewish identity. The deep impression motion pictures like *Schindler's List* and *The Quarrel* made on class members prompted me to offer a course on Holocaust cinema. As I selected books for the reading list, I was surprised to discover that the last survey of this field, the second edition of Annette Insdorf's *Indelible Shadows,* had been published in 1989. Thus, I started in 2002 to fill this gap by authoring an overview of key Holocaust films produced between 1990 and the present. While I was working on this project, updated editions of Insdorf's book and Judith Doneson's *The Holocaust in American Film* were released. Since neither discussed many of the newer pictures I used in my course, I proceeded with my undertaking. Caroline Picart's new *Holocaust Film Sourcebook* is too expensive and long to require as a course textbook, but it does provide the first extensive, although hardly comprehensive, filmography of Holocaust cinema.[1]

As I proofread my manuscript, I marvel at the divergence between the book I planned to write and the one I did. One reason for the difference is that I derived the movies I analyzed from the trends revealed by the movie database I compiled. I originally anticipated including a generational saga like *Sunshine*, a courtroom drama like *The Kastner Trial*, and a thriller about tracking Nazi war criminals like *The Man Who Captured Eichmann*, but the statistics I gathered pointed in other directions, providing indexes of which genres and themes filmmakers thought would be the most appealing and meaningful to contemporary audiences. Rowman & Littlefield's reasonable limitation on the length of my book necessitated my dropping sections on *Hamsun, My Heart Is*

Mine Alone, and *Mother's Courage.* I hope that delving deeper into fewer films stimulates readers to watch other recent movies that I have included in the filmography. I particularly recommend several recent films that have introduced significant new topics to the corpus of Holocaust cinema: *Divided We Fall* (2000), *The Believer* (2001), *Taking Sides* (2001), *The Last Letter* (2002), *Amen* (2002), *Birch Tree Meadow* (2003), *Out of the Ashes* (2003), *Rosenstrasse* (2003), and *The Ninth Day* (2004).

The database gave me a historical perspective on how public memory of the Holocaust has changed over time. I am by training a cultural and intellectual historian. I have spent my career interpreting how artistic styles, philosophical systems, and religious beliefs influence and reflect the economic, national, political, and social forces that were rising, dominant, or declining when the former were in vogue. In this regard, movies are not simply a form of mass entertainment or purely the aesthetic visions of their directors but expressions of a particular mind-set, place, and era in history. They do not merely reenact the event they are depicting; they alter it to render it relevant to the audiences they hope to attract to watch it at theaters or in their homes.

While I was confident in my skills to explain the historical context and impact of how the Holocaust has been represented in movies, I needed to ground myself in the extensive literature on the casting, editing, filming, scripting, scoring, and marketing of movies. I gravitated to genre theorists like Rick Altman and Steve Neale and reception theorists like Judith Mayne and Janet Staiger. I tend to be eclectic in my application of theoretical insights and to avoid relying on any one approach to deal with such a diverse body of films. Moreover, I employ language that nonspecialists can understand rather than the theoretical terminology of film criticism. As much as possible, I have kept the theoretical framework for the book in the footnotes so that the text will read more smoothly and comprehensibly.

I also found a kindred spirit in Robert Rosenstone, whose articles and books on cinema have challenged professional historians to study feature films as an alternative version of history capable of imparting a more tangible sense of how past events were experienced than most academic histories can achieve. The resistance to this idea seems even more entrenched among Holocaust scholars, who insist that the memory of this terrible event be represented only with the utmost realism and reverence. I respect their commitment but doubt whether an event as multifaceted as the Holocaust should be represented in a monolithic way. Different directors dealing with various topics naturally use diverse modes of representation and degrees of verisimilitude to render their films visually effective, emotionally moving, or thought provoking. Their movies should not be judged by whether they are historically, politically, or theoretically "correct" but by whether they figuratively or literally evoke a sense of the collective and individual choices and historical circumstances that enabled Hitler to persecute or liquidate millions of civilians he designated as asocial, deviant, ideological, racial, or religious enemies.

Although my observations are anecdotal, I perceive generational differences in the responses of the community and campus audiences to the Holocaust films I have shown them. Older viewers who lived during the Holocaust or were born in the immediate postwar period usually prefer historically realistic movies about the persecution and genocide of the Jews during World War II. They generally dislike comedies like *Life Is Beautiful* or wishful endings like the closing scene of *Korczak*. Conversely, people born after 1960 seem to be more receptive to films that are more creative than literal in their portrayals of the Holocaust. They also are less offended by the inclusion of characters from other persecuted groups, like Gypsies and homosexuals, in films about the Nazi era. They want to learn why the Holocaust is relevant today instead of why it was unique. Directors and studios have started to accommodate this shift because the profitability of their creations depends on attracting young adults and teens into buying tickets to see them in theaters or renting or buying them to view at home. While historical movies remain popular, particularly biographies of figures from the Holocaust, chronological distance from World War II explains the increased production of humorous and children's films about the Shoah and the new prominence of neo-Nazi and second-generation themes in recent Holocaust cinema.

If it takes a village to raise a child, it takes a community of colleagues to birth a book. I have been fortunate to get critical feedback and cordial support from Alan Berger, Michael Berkowitz, David Brenner, Robert Cherry, Steve Colston, June Cummins, Judith Doneson, Richard Freund, Esther Fuchs, Oddvar Hoidal, Yariv Kohn, Yvonne Kozlovsky Golan, Sam Lehman-Wilzig, Andrea Liss, Hemamalimi Ramachandran, Lynn Rapaport, Peter Rollins, Robert Rosenstone, Anna Rosmus, Alyssa Sepinwall, Naomi Sokoloff, Liliane Targownik, Cynthia Walk, Mary Wauchope, and David Weinberg. Although they have not always shared my interpretations of particular films, they have shared their erudition. I also am grateful for the sabbatical and minigrant awarded to me by San Diego State University's College of Arts and Letters to work on this book. I thank Brian Romer of Rowman & Littlefield for accepting my manuscript, Erin McKindley and Jen Kelland for editing it, and Mark Fein for fixing computer glitches that seemed intent on deleting it.

I deeply mourn the recent deaths of my dear friends Judith Doneson, Diane Goldberg, Liz Kahn, and Tom O'Shaughnessy. Judy taught me that movies are as valuable a historical source as written texts; Tom showed me that kindness and whimsy are more effective than rudeness and solemnity in personal and professional interactions; Liz embodied the art of living with gusto; Diane exemplified how to die with dignity and grace.

My beautiful Siamese cat, Geraldine, presided over the writing of this book by nestling atop my monitor every day. She died at the ripe old age of eighteen the morning I completed the first draft. She has been reincarnated in the quixotic kitten Mercury, who now supervises me from the same warm spot. Our other pets exhibit no interest in my research.

I greatly appreciate the patience and love of my son, Ari, and my wife, Bonnie. Throughout the last four years, I cannot count how many times they excused me from attending meetings and parties and respected my need not to be disturbed while I was writing. I dedicate this book to Bonnie for staying married to me for over thirty-five years and to Ari for showing me how to watch movies through a child's eyes. He wonders why anyone would read such a long book with so few pictures. I also dedicate this book to my mother-in-law, Gert Rubin, and recently deceased father-in-law, Phil Rubin, for their encouragement of my academic career ever since I became a member of their family.

NOTE

1. Caroline Joan Picart, *The Holocaust Film Sourcebook*, Vols. 1 and 2 (Westport, CT: Praeger, 2004). I cross-checked my filmography against Picart's. Although her entries are generally useful, some are placed in the wrong categories. For example, she considers the comedy *Mendel* a documentary (2:110–11) and the 1962 biopic *Hitler* a propaganda film (2:372–73). She also omits many significant pictures, including ones I have selected to analyze, like *The Empty Mirror, Bonhoeffer: Agent of Grace, Jew Boy Levi, Genghis Cohn, Alan and Naomi, Swing Kids, Rosenzweig's Freedom, Max, Hitler: The Rise of Evil,* and *Nowhere in Africa.* She also overlooks some landmark films, like *The Last Stop, Hell 24 Doesn't Answer, Verboten, One Day, Madame Rosa, Malou, Reunion, Sidonie, Three Days in April, Les Misérables, Lucie Aubrac, All My Loved Ones,* and *Amen.*

The Holocaust: A Cinematic Cataclysm?

The question inexorably asserts itself: Does there exist another way, another language, to say what is unsayable? The image perhaps? Can it be more accessible, more malleable, more expressive than the word? Can I admit it? I am as wary of one as of the other. Even more of the image. Of the filmed image, of course. One does not imagine the unimaginable. And in particular, one does not show it on screen.[1]

—Elie Wiesel

Film changes the rules of the historical game, insisting on its own sort of truths, truths which arise from a visual and aural realm that is difficult to capture adequately in words. This new historical past on film is potentially much more complex than any written text, for on the screen, several things can occur simultaneously—image, sound, language, even text—elements that support and work against each other to render a realm of meaning as different from written history as written was from oral history.[2]

—Robert Rosenstone

𝒯he images and sounds linger. In the midst of a crowd of Jews who are being systematically massacred by Schutzstaffel (SS) troops, a young girl named Genia meanders nonchalantly as if the killings were not occurring. She would be inconspicuous but for the contrast of her bright red coat with the black-and-white figures of uniformed soldiers firing their pistols and rifles at unarmed victims. The staccato volleys of gunfire interrupt the soothing melody of a Yiddish lullaby sung by children. The audience hears and sees this scene from atop a hill where Oskar Schindler sits upon his horse, realizing that Germany plans to slaughter all the Jews in Krakow, Poland, including children like Genia, whose red coat has caught his eye too. He is visibly shaken but remains speechless. This central scene in *Schindler's List* enables the audience to understand that the "Final Solution" entails the eradication of anyone who is Jewish, regardless of age or gender.[3]

The images and sounds linger. In Roberto Benigni's *Life Is Beautiful*, Guido shields his son Giosuè from the harsh realities of concentration camp incarceration by pretending that survival is a game. Searching for his barracks at night, he carries the boy in his arms and walks into a shrouded patch of dark blue fog. When he treads into a clearing, the wind howls ominously. He gazes in horror at a heap of entangled corpses that resembles the sculpture of twisted bodies on display at Dachau and Yad Vashem. Backing away from this grisly monument, he is dwarfed by its height. After hiding Giosuè in a utility box, a German guard arrests Guido and takes him behind a building. A round of bullets pierces the silence. As the next day dawns, Giosuè believes he has won the game when Allied tanks liberate the camp. The audience knows his victory is incomplete because his father lies dead in the compound.[4]

These scenes touch us emotionally because the images and sounds do not require intellectual reflection to construe their meanings. Despite the magnitude of the mass executions, Genia's composure and individuality stand out as much as the color of her coat in a frame populated by efficient executioners, terrified victims, and fresh corpses. The loss of a parent is a universal experience made infinitely more devastating during the Holocaust, when it was part of a plan to eradicate all Jewish families. Guido dies alone, but we surmise that the Germans will dump his cadaver onto the pile of bodies he had stumbled upon earlier. He perished protecting his son's innocence.

Schindler's List and *Life Is Beautiful* garnered many of the most prestigious awards bestowed upon motion pictures in the United States and the rest of the world. Many movie critics reviewed them favorably. The two movies fared extremely well at the box office.[5] To achieve their fame and fans, did these films desecrate or trivialize the memory of the Holocaust? Did they imagine the unimaginable?

Many Holocaust scholars have tended to share Elie Wiesel's skepticism about the ability of popular feature films to depict the Holocaust without rendering it photogenic, resorting to generic formulas of epic struggles between good heroes and evil villains, or imposing edifying endings on an unmitigated tragedy. Ilan Avisar's criticism of *Schindler's List* typifies this line of reasoning: "The message implied in Spielberg's project is one that focuses on exhilarating qualities of courage and moral strength at the expense of an excruciating recognition of the genocidal evil that prevailed over a period of years and at the cost of millions of lives."[6] Similarly, Omer Bartov maintains that Schindler's story fosters a distorted perspective of history "because within the context of the Holocaust, it was so unique as to be untrue in the sense of not reflecting (or even negating) the fate of the vast majority of victims who were in turn swallowed up in a unique and unprecedented and therefore (as least as far as Hollywood conventions are concerned) unrepresentable murder machine."[7] In other words, even though Oskar Schindler really saved more than a thousand Jews, a film about his deed is "untrue" because it misleads viewers into thinking that most Jews were rescued. In his scathing denunciation of *Schindler's List*, Claude Lanzmann declared, "Fiction is a transgression. I deeply believe that there are some things that cannot and should not be represented."[8]

Although positive reviews of *Schindler's List* far outnumbered negative ones, Benigni's irreverent combination of slapstick gags and filial melodrama elicited more vituperative condemnations because he eschewed any pretext of realism and found humor in the dire circumstances of a concentration camp. As one journalist observed, "The film [*Life Is Beautiful*] has become a sort of metal detector whose alarm bell signals ideas, defects, goodness, hypocrisy or wickedness in people's DNA."[9] Richard Schickel of *Time Magazine* loathed Benigni's manipulation of emotions because "sentimentality is a kind of fascism too, robbing us of judgment and moral acuity."[10] *Salon's* film critic Charles Taylor denounced the film's "attempt to give a heartwarming, life-affirming cast to an event that exists outside of human meaning."[11] David Denby of the *New Yorker* decried the picture's happy ending as tantamount to Holocaust denial.[12]

The criticisms leveled at *Schindler's List* and *Life Is Beautiful* are premised on two assumptions. The first asserts that since the Holocaust is "unique" and "exists outside of human meaning," it can never be accurately represented in cinema or literature. Lanzmann extrapolates this opinion to its most radical conclusion. The second assumption concedes that even though it might be possible to approximate what the Holocaust was like in feature films and novels, such portrayals must mirror the reality that "most of the Jews died, most of the Germans collaborated with the perpetrators or remained passive bystanders, and most of the victims sent to the showers were gassed."[13]

Both of these caveats bother me as a Holocaust educator and historian. Human beings planned, implemented, condoned, perished in, resisted, and survived the Final Solution. Consequently, it should not be regarded as a supernatural phenomenon beyond human comprehension and representation.[14] For almost thirty years, I have attended conferences on the Holocaust and listened to renowned scholars preface their remarks with an obeisance to the inexplicability of the Shoah. Then, they deliver lectures that demonstrate a brilliant grasp of whatever aspect of the event they analyzed.

Commercially distributed films, even those based on historical events, always run the risk of becoming too boring or depressing if they inundate their audiences with excessive brutality, overwhelm them with copious amounts of factual detail, or prevent them from identifying with main characters. If a director hopes to capture a semblance of the atrocities, sights, and sounds of the Holocaust effectively on the screen, then he or she must be skilled as a storyteller and filmmaker rather than as an academic historian. Scholars should not dismiss the potential of feature films to convey a sense of the catastrophe that befell European Jewry. Financial considerations and the standard length of films require that directors condense the chronology of events to insure dramatic narrative flow, embody impersonal historical forces in representative characters, invent compelling dialog that concisely delineates the traits and values of those who utter it, simplify complex historical interactions into struggles between good and evil, and resolve these conflicts with uplifting endings that vindicate the protagonist, usually as an exception to the tragic rule of mass complicity, passivity, or victimization. As Robert Brent Toplin has advised historians in general, "In sum we need a sensitive effort to judge integrity and an informed view of film that balances the defense of artistic liberties with the recognition that some dramatic flourishes can be problematic."[15]

A growing number of cultural and media scholars have challenged the injunctions against either representing the Holocaust in feature films or restricting its depictions to documentaries and meticulously accurate docudramas. The late Judith Doneson always appreciated the potential of American Holocaust films to "make the Holocaust meaningful to an audience for whom the Final Solution remains a foreign event."[16] Although initially fearful that Hollywood might trivialize the Holocaust, Annette Insdorf now considers this "a lesser evil than having the memory of the Shoah disappear from cultural attention."[17] While cognizant of the shortcomings of television programs about the Shoah, Jeffrey Shandler recognizes that the medium "has emerged over the course of the second half of the twentieth century as the most pervasive and diverse source of Holocaust mediations in America."[18]

Other cinema and literature experts question why directors must adhere to the dictum of portraying the Holocaust realistically as a debacle in which the majority of Jews were killed and the majority of Gentiles were killers, collaborators, or bystanders. They champion the latitude of the filmmaker to use cinematic styles appropriate to the subject matter they have chosen and the audience reaction they intend to evoke. Defending Schindler's List against charges of being overly theatrical, Marcia Landy retorts that melodrama "is preoccupied with questions of discernment and judgment" and "strikes an affective chord in the viewer in its appeal to the necessity of a moral response."[19] Dismayed by the vitriolic attacks on Benigni's comedic fable about concentration camp survival, Hilene Flanzbaum asserts "that words like 'truth,' 'verisimili-tude,' 'reality' as the preeminent categories upon which we make aesthetic judgments about the representations of the Holocaust need to fall by the way-side." In her opinion, filmmakers should be accorded the artistic license to em-ploy more creative narrative and visual strategies to "compel viewers (and es-pecially large numbers of them) to take another look, a deeper look, a more thoughtful look at the event."[20]

Another school of Holocaust scholars argues that since the Holocaust constituted a traumatic rupture in the personal memories of those who en-dured it and in the collective history of humankind in the twentieth century, it must be represented by radical breaks with cinematic conventions. Instead of being linear, time should be fragmented by shifts to traumatic memories that unexpectedly surface in the present. Rather than maturing from overcoming adversities, characters continually confront the deformation of their psyches by the Nazi assault on their humanity. The victory of the Allies and the demise of Hitler do not provide closure for shattered lives and relationships that cannot be healed by therapy or restored by forging new bonds. Joshua Hirsch cites pi-oneering movies like *Night and Fog* and *The Pawnbroker* as models of posttrau-matic witnessing that convey, respectively, the profound shock liberators felt upon finding the evidence of Nazi atrocities and the disturbing memories that intrude into a survivor's mind through flashbacks.[21]

Michael Rothberg believes that the historicity and extremity of the Holocaust require a hybrid of artistic styles that he dubs "traumatic realism" to bridge the chasm between the factual basis of the event and the inconceivabil-ity of something like it happening in an advanced industrialized society. Trau-matic realist texts seek "a form of documentation beyond direct reference and coherent narrative, but do not fully abandon the possibility for some kind of reference and some kind of narrative." Put another way, they "attempt to pro-duce the traumatic event as an object of knowledge" and force its viewers to "acknowledge their relationship to posttraumatic culture."[22]

Yet, can trauma really serve as the basis for the aesthetics of a mass medium? Trauma denotes the sense of degradation, impotence, or suffering ex-perienced personally by survivors, victims, and witnesses of a terrible tragedy.[23] The vast majority of people living today are "nonwitnesses," to use Gary Weissmann's term.[24] They have learned about the Holocaust through artworks, cinema, fictional narratives, history books, memoirs, museums, and survivor testimonies. These sources communicate an artificially constructed approxima-tion of how it might have felt to experience the Holocaust as a bystander, lib-erator, perpetrator, or victim. While some docudramas like *Amen,* debate films like *The Quarrel,* and trial films like *Judgment at Nuremberg* may yield intellec-tual insights into the Holocaust and its repercussions, most movies affect their viewers emotionally by enabling them to empathize with the feelings of people swept into the murderous vortex of the Holocaust.[25]

I align myself with the scholars who value both the accomplishment of feature films in popularizing the Holocaust and the unique capacity of the medium to make history come alive. I concur with Robert Rosenstone's recognition that even though feature films based on historical events simplify their subject matter and alter or invent characters and incidents to make for a more coherent and dramatic plotline, they are not inherently "poor history" but rather an alternative form of history that informs us about the past through different means. In Rosenstone's opinion, "Film lets us see landscapes; hear sounds; witness strong emotions as they are expressed with body and face, or physical conflict between individuals and groups." For a mass audience, he continues, "film can most directly render the look and feel of all sorts of historical particulars and situations."[26] Similarly, Alison Landsberg argues that motion pictures can serve as "prosthetic memories" that can "bridge the temporal chasms that separate individuals from the meaningful and potentially interpellative events of the past."[27]

While a few filmmakers have experimented with the cinematic forms Hirsch and Rothberg suggest to mirror the traumatic impact of the Holocaust, most have employed traditional genres and assumed audience familiarity with Holocaust cinema, images, and symbols. What has changed over time is which genres and themes are the most commonly used by filmmakers to make the Holocaust relevant to audiences who are removed in time, and often place, from the genocide perpetrated against European Jewry during World War II. By choosing film as a measure of popular perceptions of the Holocaust, I am not implying that the written word is no longer an important tool for raising public awareness, but I am recognizing that the visual media play an increasingly larger role in that process. In a Roper Poll of American adults conducted in 1994, 58 percent of the respondents cited television as a source of their knowledge about the Holocaust, compared to 48 percent and 43 percent who credited school and books, respectively, with educating them about it. A third of those queried mentioned movies as one source of their information on the topic, roughly the same proportion as those who learned about it from newspapers and magazines.[28]

My decision to concentrate on the 1990s is not an arbitrary one. Not only did the numbers of Holocaust feature films produced then remain at the peak postwar level achieved in the 1980s, but these films as a group achieved more critical and popular acclaim than their predecessors. Since this book is intended for laypeople and students in Holocaust courses, it concentrates on films that are easily accessible to these readers.

A cursory survey of some of the best-known films from the 1990s reveals the caliber of this body of work. *The Nasty Girl* (1990), directed by Michael

Verhoeven, unmasks the antagonism and obstructionism of a German city toward a teenager conducting research into local complicity in executing Nazi policies during the Nazi era. *Korczak* (1990), directed by Andrzej Wajda, portrays the ultimately futile efforts of the famed Jewish-Polish educator to shield the orphans under his care from the deprivations of the Warsaw ghetto and prevent their deportation to Treblinka. *Europa, Europa* (1991), directed by Agnieszka Holland, traces the incredible survival of a Jewish boy whose Gentile appearance and knowledge of foreign languages gained him entry into the Soviet Young Communists League and German Hitler Youth. *Schindler's List* (1993), directed by Steven Spielberg, portrays the transformation of a war profiteer into a rescuer of Jews amid the backdrop of the decimation of the Jewish community of Krakow. *Under the Donim Tree* (1994), directed by Eli Cohen, delves into the mind-set of Israeli children whose parents perished in the Holocaust. *Les Misérables* (1995), directed by Claude Lelouche, imagines how a modern Jean Valjean would have reacted to the plight of Jews in Vichy, France. *Shine*, directed by Scott Hicks, records how the son of a survivor escapes his abusive father and becomes a celebrated pianist. *The Harmonists* (1997), directed by Joseph Vilsmaier, recalls the formation and dissolution of a German singing group comprising Jewish and Gentile musicians. *Life Is Beautiful* (1998), directed by Roberto Benigni, uses humor to show the touching devotion of an Italian Jew to his wife and son in a concentration camp. *Sunshine* (1999), directed by Istvan Szabó, spans the twentieth century to follow the attenuation and recovery of Jewish identity of several generations of Hungarians during the Hapsburg Empire, interwar period, German occupation, Soviet occupation, and postcommunist era.

When I started to write this book in 2001, the last surveys of Holocaust feature films dated back to the 1980s. The most recent, the second edition of Insdorf's *Indelible Shadows,* appeared in 1989[29]; Avisar's *Screening the Holocaust* was published in 1988,[30] and Doneson's *The Holocaust in American Film* came out in 1987.[31] In 2002 and 2003, revised editions of the books by Doneson and Insdorf were released. Doneson, whose untimely death robbed us of a pioneer in this field, appended one chapter on *Schindler's List* to her book.[32] Insdorf included six new chapters and an updated filmography. Only three short chapters deal with feature films produced since 1989. While Insdorf and I devote chapters to the conspicuous emergence of Holocaust comedies in this period, the only other movies we both analyze are *Korczak, The Nasty Girl,* and *Schindler's List.* As will become apparent, we differ over the criteria for defining a Holocaust movie, over the genres and themes we have selected to organize our books, and over the depiction of survivors and their children in contemporary feature films.[33] Other recent monographs limit their focus to representations of the Holocaust in specific countries, to a single movie like *Schindler's List* or *Life Is Beautiful,* to a particular medium like television, as in

Shandler's fine book, or to a distinct analytical approach like the expression of trauma in Holocaust cinema as explored in Hirsch's monograph.[34]

While I am indebted to the insights of the scholars who have preceded me in this field, I am not merely trying to update their work. My approach focuses on the most common genres and themes in recent Holocaust films as determined by a statistical coding of these films for each decade since 1945. I seek to situate each movie within the history of Holocaust feature films that preceded it and to contextualize it within the remembrance of the Holocaust in the country that produced it. Next, I review the plots and cinematic techniques used to depict them. Finally, I discuss the reception of the movie by critics and audiences to ascertain whether it communicated the intent of its director.

Since movies often mix genres and themes, I have singled out what I considered the predominant genre and theme in each film, recognizing that there can be honest disagreements over my classifications.[35] One genre I do not discuss in this book is the documentary. There are several reasons for my decision. One is purely practical: the number of documentaries made about the Holocaust in the last decade surpasses the number of Holocaust feature films released in this period. A survey of documentaries deserves a volume of its own, and Insdorf does an admirable job of analyzing the most important ones.[36] I do question the extent to which documentaries influence collective memory about the Holocaust. Their distribution tends to be limited to Jewish and independent film festivals, art theaters, the Public Broadcasting System, and cable stations like the Arts and Entertainment Network and the History Channel. Only a few documentaries that win Oscars or receive rave reviews from nationally syndicated film columnists ever land on the shelves of major video-store chains.[37]

Nevertheless, Holocaust scholars tend to prefer the authenticity of documentaries over feature films because the former rely on movies taken by the Nazis themselves, newsreel footage, photographs shot by journalists and soldiers when the camps were liberated, photos preserved by the survivors and perpetrators, and interviews with eyewitnesses to the event.[38] The usage of these "actualities" should not mask the intensive editing of material to substantiate the stance directors assume when they interpret what they have compiled. Lanzmann's *Shoah* merits the accolades it has received for revealing the bureaucratic nature of the Final Solution, the widespread hostility of Poles toward Jews, and the psychological wounds that burden the minds of Jewish survivors. To shorten *Shoah* to its final 9-hour length, Lanzmann cut out over 340 hours of film. He staged situations simulating experiences survivors had endured during the Holocaust to force them to "relive" the moment. The most insensitive example of this practice involved the interview with Abraham Bomba, a barber assigned by the Germans to shear the hair of Jewish women about to be gassed. To jar Bomba's memory of this gruesome task, Lanzmann posed Bomba in the act of trimming the hair of a customer in his shop. When, in the documentary, Bomba refuses to speak because it is too painful, Lanzmann relentlessly prods him until he tearfully admits that he saw his wife and sister waiting to be gassed. By questioning the appropriateness of Lanzmann's methods, I am not denying the searing impression *Shoah* leaves on its viewers but merely pointing out that making documentaries involves directorial abridgement and emplotment.[39]

I omit movies made before 1945 in my database because they predate public awareness that the Third Reich mandated the systematic "extermination" of European Jewry. As Charlie Chaplin retrospectively remarked about his parody of Hitler in *The Great Dictator*, "Had I known of the actual horrors of the German concentration camps, I could not have made fun of the homicidal insanity of the Nazis."[40]

I do not share Insdorf's earlier generalizations about the "Hollywood version of the Holocaust." She doubted whether Hollywood directors could portray the event in "sufficiently complex terms and resist relying on epic effects, melodrama, and stars whose previous roles often undermine their credibility as characters trapped in the maelstrom of Nazi genocide." She qualified this by asserting that a "film does not have to be made in or by America to be considered a Hollywood film." She discounted some serious foreign films like *The Assault* and *For Those I Loved* for their obeisance to Hollywood conventions and lost her critical bearings when praising a formulaic action movie like *Hanna's War* simply because so few Holocaust movies highlight Zionist resistance to Nazism.[41] On the other hand, she inconsistently included Hollywood productions like *Cabaret, The Pawnbroker*, and *Sophie's Choice* within her original canon of serious representations of the Holocaust.[42]

Avisar's bashing of American Holocaust cinema exceeds Insdorf's. He excoriates the American film industry for its failure to condemn Nazi anti-Jewish measures before the United States entered World War II, its stereotypical portrayals of Jewish characters, its universalization of Holocaust themes, its depictions of Holocaust survivors as insane or vindictive, and its placement of the Holocaust within a Christian framework of crucifixion and rebirth. He doubts whether American directors ever can grapple with the uniqueness of the Holocaust and the Jewish particularity of its victims because the Final Solution happened in Europe. Thus, he maintains, "Unlike the personal drives of west and east European filmmakers, who deal with the Holocaust in order to explore and express their own national traumas, the American interest in the subject is motivated by other considerations which are not necessarily rooted in a genuine concern with the disturbing truth of the historical tragedy."[43]

Most historians believe that American public awareness of the Holocaust developed as a response to Israel's trial of Adolf Eichmann at the beginning of the 1960s.[44] Yet, the American film industry accounted for 40 percent of the movies about the Holocaust produced between 1945 and the 1960s.[45] Avisar lumps all Hollywood productions under one rubric to bolster his contention that only European filmmakers can relate the Holocaust to the histories of their respective nations. The United States, however, fought Germany during World War II, even if it did not liberalize its immigration policies or mount a concerted refugee relief effort until 1944.[46] American troops witnessed the macabre sights of emaciated survivors and decomposing human remains in the camps they liberated.[47] Magazine photographs and newsreel footage of the dead and living found in the camps soon achieved the status of visual icons for the calamity the Jews had suffered under Hitler.[48] The pivotal role of the United States in the Nuremberg Trials established the German crime of the liquidation of European Jewry as part of American historical consciousness.[49] Even before blockbusters like *The Diary of Anne Frank, Exodus,* and *Judgment at Nuremberg* attracted mass audiences, Americans heard about the Final Solution from Jewish inmates in the displaced persons camps and the 140,000 Jewish survivors who settled in the United States. American television broadcast dramatic and documentary television programs about the subject throughout the 1950s.[50]

The blanket criticism of American films about the Holocaust also fails to take into account significant changes over the last twenty years in how movies get produced and distributed. First, there is the resurgence of independent filmmaking.[51] Second, venues for screening films have proliferated with the advent of cineplexes, film festivals, network television movies, premium movie cable stations, and VCR and DVD players. Finally, the size of the audience reached by films has grown with the use of new communications technologies like the Internet.[52] Globalization not only extends the influence of the Hollywood image of the Holocaust abroad but also enriches Hollywood productions with the perspectives of foreign actors, crews, and directors recruited to work on American films.[53] Steven Spielberg hired many cast and crew members who were Croatian, English, German, Israeli, and Polish and viewed classic foreign films about the Holocaust to imbue *Schindler's List* with a European look.[54]

Indeed, the internationalization of the Holocaust as a symbol of evil and the production of movies by countries with minimal connections to the event call for explications that go beyond analyzing feature films as expressions of national collective memory.[55] In the 15 years following World War II, 14 countries produced 119 feature films about the Holocaust. In the 1990s, thirty-one countries produced more than two hundred Holocaust movies. Of these nations, China, Iceland, Japan, Mexico, and South Africa had at best a tenuous connection to the travail of the Jews who fell under the yoke of the Third Reich. A film like *Red Cherry* (1995), a harrowing account of the suffering of two Chinese exchange students trapped in the Soviet Union during the German invasion of it, may be more preoccupied with Nazi racism as a pernicious manifestation of fascist ideology than with the Holocaust, but the influence of *Schindler's List* is evident in several of its scenes.[56]

Multinational collaborations make it difficult to ascertain what the country of origin is for some films. *Europa, Europa* was a joint Franco-German production, directed by a half-Jewish Pole who coscripted the story with a German Jew who had immigrated to Israel and on whose memoir it was based. The movie struck a more responsive chord with American audiences than with German ones. Although many movie critics expected *Europa, Europa* to be the official German entry for the Academy Award for Best Foreign Language Film, Germany refused to nominate it. Around 20 percent of the Holocaust films made in the 1990s were multinational endeavors, and that rate has climbed to nearly 40 percent for movies released between 2000 and 2004.[57]

Nevertheless, globalization has not diminished nationalistic preoccupations with the meaning of the Holocaust in the postwar cinema of countries that fell within the Nazi sphere of power. The interpretive model that Alan Mintz applies to explicating American feature films about the Holocaust is equally valid for other national cinemas, namely that "meaning is constructed by communities of interpretation—differently by different communities—out of the their own motives and needs."[58] Directors and studios in many countries often adapt stories that are part of their history into feature films.

The watershed events of the late 1980s that changed the political landscape of Europe—the reunification of Germany and the fall of the Soviet Union—have renewed European interest in the Holocaust. Recent German "heritage" movies reinstate Jews as lead characters in motion pictures about the Weimar Republic and the Third Reich.[59] Alarmed by contemporary parallels to the forces that allowed Hitler to become chancellor of Germany in 1933, German directors have produced films criticizing the postunification neo-Nazi and skinhead backlash against Americanization, asylum seekers, foreign laborers, and high unemployment in films like *Rosenzweig's Freedom*.[60]

Since the end of World War II, Eastern European countries have been prolific producers of films about the Holocaust because their predominantly Slavic populations suffered terribly under German rule too. Depicting the epic struggles between the Soviet Union and the Third Reich and of local partisans against native collaborators was politically permissible at certain times. During periods of liberalization in Czechoslovakia and Hungary, the fate of the Jews received more attention in films produced in these countries.[61] Usually, the treatment of Jews in films from the Soviet Bloc adhered to narrow ideological parameters set by Moscow, namely, courageous communist partisans fighting bourgeois Nazi collaborators. The Jewish characters in these movies either remained passive victims or underwent a transformation into communist activists like the Jewish hero of Wajda's *Samson*.[62] The death of Tito in 1980 and the disintegration of the Soviet Union after 1989 liberated filmmakers in formerly communist countries to handle the subject of the Holocaust in a less ideological manner. Films from former communist states often show how the Nazi reign of terror was followed by Soviet despotism, as is the case in the generational saga *Sunshine* (1999). Emir Kusterica's comedy *Underground* (1995) satirizes the motives for partisan aid to Jews, the communist glorification of wartime resistance, and the "Balkanization" of Yugoslavia after Tito's death.[63]

My inclusion of movies like *Bent* and *Red Cherry* as Holocaust films marks another difference between my criteria for what constitutes a Holocaust film and those formulated by Avisar and Insdorf. Avisar excludes films that refuse "to acknowledge . . . that the main victims were Jews" as this essentially "ignor[es] the crucial facts of history."[64] Insdorf defines the Holocaust as the genocide of European Jews, who "unlike their fellow victims of the Nazis . . . were stripped not only of life and freedom, but of an entire culture."[65]

Concurring with Michael Burleigh and Wolfgang Wippermann, I view the Third Reich as a "racial state."[66] I consider any group that experienced discrimination, incarceration, liquidation, or sterilization because it supposedly posed a biological, cultural, political, or social threat to the Aryan race as victimized by Nazism. Without broaching the whole debate over whether the Jewish genocide was unique, I perceive more similarities than differences in cinematic depictions of the eugenics and euthanasia programs, the imprisonment and torment of homosexuals in concentration camps, the liquidation of gypsies in death camps, and the "extermination" of European Jewry by gassing, mass shootings, starvation, and overwork.[67] The belated appearance of these groups in movies about the Nazi era reflects several developments: (1) new research on hitherto neglected victims of Nazism, (2) the lobbying by these groups to document their suffering and gain legal restitution for it, and (3) the rise of the multicultural model to accommodate ethnic, gender, racial, or religious diversity in democratic societies.

I also broaden the spectrum of what is deemed a Holocaust film to include movies that depict the postwar displacement and immigration of groups the Germans and their allies victimized on ideological and racial grounds. Films featuring the capture, trial, and punishment of the perpetrators of wartime atrocities also belong in this category. Another type of Holocaust film explores the continuing impact of the event on the collective memory of states like France, Germany, Israel, Poland, and other nations directly or indirectly affected by Nazi crimes against humanity. Character studies of how the Holocaust shaped the personalities and values of perpetrators, survivors, and their children fall under the rubric of Holocaust cinema, as do motion pictures about postwar white supremacists who embrace Nazi ideas and symbols.

What ideas and images do audiences associate with the Holocaust? I have examined the most frequently used genres and themes in Holocaust movies made in the 1990s to yield a rough approximation of the events, images, and issues most commonly associated with the Holocaust by those who currently produce or watch such films. *Genre* is a term "used to describe the way in which groups of narrative conventions (involving plot, character, and even locations and set design) become organized into recognizable types of narrative entertainment."[68] Often what draws audiences to watch a movie is not the movie itself but a favorite genre or star they are familiar with and have enjoyed in the past.[69] Even when survivors write memoirs about their experiences, they employ the narrative conventions of autobiography to impose conventional meanings and structures on stories of senseless suffering.[70]

The advertising tagline for a movie provides the viewer with a clue about whether a film will live up to his or her expectations associated with a particular genre. The video box for *Life Is Beautiful* informs browsers in the store that the film is "an unforgettable fable that proves love, family, and imagination conquer all." While the notes on the back of the box indicate that World War II places Guido in a situation where he must "save his beloved wife and son from an unthinkable [and I should add unnamed] fate," those thinking of renting this video are assured that it will lift their "spirits and capture their hearts." Notwithstanding the recurring images of Jews being executed in *Schindler's List*, the tagline for the film is more upbeat: "Whoever saves one life, saves the world entire."

I do not agree with Insdorf's recent assertion that Holocaust movies "constitute a veritable genre."[71] Filmmakers still plot and promote these motion pictures as traditional genres or hybrids of genres with which audiences can identify and assume will fulfill their emotional and intellectual expectations. Rick Altman attributes genre mixing to "increasing a film's marketability." He observes that mixing is "facilitated by the use of easily recognizable semantic genre cues, parallel or sequential deployment of cues based on differing aspects of the film, a tendency to base genre identification on a small fraction of a film, and the fact that certain types of scenes fit easily into multiple different genres."[72]

Consider the diverse constituencies that might be enticed to see *Europa, Europa* because ads described it as an "incredible adventure on an epic canvas with a wonderful combination of realistic drama and ironic humor." In my book, I classify it as a biopic since it is based on the memoir of a Holocaust survivor. Yet, I admit that the film follows the format of a road movie and employs the plot device of mistaken identity.

Since the directors of feature films about the Holocaust package their creations as familiar genres, there is often a tension between the discomforting collapse of morality during the Holocaust and the comforting platitudes often peddled in popular films. *Schindler's List* neatly balances scenes of relentless brutality with the moral redemption of its hero. It follows a common pattern in Holocaust movies, employing a double narrative in which the main characters escape execution while secondary ones do not.[73] *Triumph of the Spirit* subverts its title and the trite plotline of the protagonist's becoming stronger and wiser for his struggles. Instead, the final shot of the Jewish boxer who survives Auschwitz by knocking out (and thereby condemning to death) other prisoners to win bets for SS guards tracks a dazed and partially nude man hobbling down the road into the distance, wondering how human beings can be so cruel to each other. As I analyze how notable exemplars of the most popular genres of Holocaust movies work as films, I will draw attention to the double-narrative structure or the rarer contradiction between the unsettling endings of some Holocaust movies and the sanguine endings audiences expect from motion pictures belonging to particular genres.

In the second chapter, I examine the evolution of Holocaust films from the immediate postwar period until the 1980s. I contend that classics like *The Search*, *The Diary of Anne Frank*, and *The Shop on Main Street* prefigure the double-narrative structure that characterizes many subsequent Holocaust films. These films introduce the Jewish genocide into their narratives and imagery more candidly than contemporary scholars have acknowledged. Their optimism and universalism reflect the politics of the period when they were released. The NBC miniseries *Holocaust* marked and influenced the shift toward the production of historical docudramas, graphic representations of the atrocities committed against the Jews, and the portrayal of Jews as complete characters rather than faceless victims of Nazi mass murder.

The third chapter explores thematic changes in the most popular genre of Holocaust films since the 1980s, the biopic. Biographical pictures convey the limits and possibilities of the individual to affect the outcome of an event of this magnitude. Over the decades, different types of individuals assume more prominence than others in Holocaust biopics. Although movies about Hitler (*The Empty Mirror*) and Nazi fellow travelers (*Hamsun*) continue to be made, Gentile rescuers and resisters and Jewish victims and survivors have replaced perpetrators and their accomplices as the favored subjects of such films. This shift has been an international phenomenon rather than a consequence of the "Americanization" of the Holocaust, as Alvin H. Rosenfeld has asserted.[74] *Bonhoeffer: Agent of Grace* is one of a spate of movies about religiously motivated Christian resistance to Nazism. Wayda dramatizes Janusz Korczak's gentle courage as a means to promote contemporary Jewish-Polish reconciliation.

While *Europa, Europa* dwells primarily on Solomon Perel's masquerade as a Hitler Youth, it also presents the Soviet alternative to Hitler's rule in a critical light. *Triumph of the Spirit* deals with the amoral choices made by those who survived Auschwitz, but it clearly blames the German perpetrators for constructing an environment that necessitated a Darwinian struggle for survival among its inmates.

The fourth chapter is devoted to love stories about Jews and Gentiles separated by Nazi racial policies. In earlier films, the Gentile partner had to decide whether to abandon or remain loyal to his or her Jewish lover or spouse. This Holocaust version of the *Romeo and Juliet* scenario remains popular, as evidenced in *The Harmonists* and *Jew Boy Levi*. In many films from the 1990s, however, the proactive member of the couple is as likely to be the Jew, who either resists persecution as in *Aimée and Jaguar* or attempts to spare his or her mate further suffering by encouraging divorce as in *Martha and I*. Moreover, the partners in these couples are not necessarily heterosexuals. The persecution of homosexuals drives the plotlines of Holocaust movies like *Aimée and Jaguar* and *Bent*.

The fifth chapter analyzes how well-known Holocaust comedies like *Life Is Beautiful* and *Jakob the Liar* and lesser known ones like *Train of Life, Genghis Cohn*, and *Mendel* have managed to succeed or fail at blending humor and pathos. Since liquidation rarely is a topic treated with levity, what themes and approaches can best combine the two? In *Genghis Cohn*, the murdered Jew gets the last laugh as a ghost who haunts the German who killed him. The downtrodden Jews of *Jakob the Liar* elevate Jakob into a hero because he has overheard a radio broadcast about the impending liberation of his ghetto. Seeing how this raises their morale, he fabricates more stories, even though he owns no receiver to confirm them. The father in *Life Is Beautiful*, to prevent his son from succumbing to despair, pretends the deadly purpose of a concentration camp is really an elaborate game. *Train of Life* invokes the stock characters and harebrained schemes found in much Yiddish literature about the shtetl to enable a village of doomed Jews to evade their oppressors. The young lead character of *Mendel* naively imagines what secrets his survivor parents have been concealing from him and eventually summons the courage to fight against injustice as the resistance fighters of his adopted homeland of Norway did. Although not all of these films are equally effective as comedies, they employ humor in ways that respect the victims and censure the perpetrators without trivializing the suffering of the former or exonerating the latter.

Can films made for children replicate the horrors of the Holocaust without traumatizing their target audience? The sixth chapter looks at this recently popular genre of film that has evolved along with the incorporation of the Holocaust into the public school curriculum and the concomitant demand for age-appropriate movies on this topic. These films are often based on best-selling children's books. *Alan and Naomi* uses the buddy genre to depict the experiential gulf between an American boy and a girl who witnessed the Nazis' murder of her father. *Swing Kids* provides an object lesson in how political and peer pressure dissolve friendships among a cohort of adolescent jazz enthusiasts. *The Island on Bird Street* and *The Devil's Arithmetic* transplant the plots of children's classics into the Holocaust and thereby transform an event that is remote into something familiar. Lois Lowry's book *Number the Stars* demonstrated that the rescue of the Jews in Denmark appealed to young readers since it resolved a dangerous situation with a happy ending. Disney's *Miracle at Midnight* follows this same formula.

In chapter 7, I look at films whose plots revolve around the four most commonly recurring themes in the movies produced in the 1990s. Movies about neo-Nazis and skinheads comprise the most numerous group of films from the 1990s that refer to the Holocaust. These exposés of contemporary, right-wing extremism usually fall outside the academic purview of Holocaust cinema.[75] Yet, they consciously forge a link between the Third Reich and today's racist movements. Political neo-Nazis and skinheads make more than a fashion statement when they decorate their bodies with swastika tattoos, hang Nazi banners and pictures of Hitler on the walls of their rooms, and espouse white supremacist doctrines. They seriously believe that the Final Solution should serve as a model for a future race war conducted against the minorities they stigmatize as aliens or inferiors. That the neo-Nazis and skinheads portrayed in movies produced in different parts of the world vary so little in the clothes they wear and the viewpoints they articulate is a symptom of the globalization of neo-Nazism. Thus, *Rosenzweig's Freedom* underscores the similarities between Hitler's goals and tactics and neo-Nazi violence against asylum seekers and immigrants in reunified Germany.

Since the end of World War II, the rescue of Jews has afforded filmmakers with inspiring plotlines about righteous heroes saving innocent Jews from arrest and deportation. In the 1950s, Bruno Bettelheim attributed the popular appeal of *The Diary of Anne Frank* as a play and movie to its implicit confirmation of Anne's faith in human goodness by failing to depict Anne's suffering at Auschwitz and death in Bergen-Belsen.[76] As *Schindler's List* amply attests, contemporary movies about rescuers of Jews neither idealize their protagonists nor spare their viewers from seeing the terrible fate that awaited the majority of Jews who never found someone like Schindler to protect them.[77]

In the first decades after World War II, movies like *The Juggler*, *The Pawnbroker*, and *Sophie's Choice* fixated on the mental instability of survivors forever scarred by their experiences of deprivation, dehumanization, and loss. As a teenager whose bar mitzva coincided with the thirteenth anniversary of the state of Israel's existence, I recall being invited with other Jewish boys of my age to a screening of *Exodus*. Even now, I empathize with the sadness of Karen when she is reunited with her father who has been reduced to an empty hulk vacantly staring into space. The television broadcasts of *Holocaust* in 1978 and *Skokie* in 1981, as well as the increasing prominence of Elie Wiesel, which culminated in his receiving the Nobel Peace Prize in 1986, recast the image of the survivor in a more positive light.[78] The survivor has become "emblematic of Jewish suffering, Jewish memory, and Jewish endurance."[79]

Recent films about survivors encompass a greater range of characterizations of those who lived through the Third Reich's attempt to eradicate them.[80] Their brush with death can intensify their faith in Judaism or their atheism as is evident in the fierce debate between the two protagonists of *The Quarrel*.

The flurry of movies about the children of perpetrators and victims mirrors the maturation of the postwar generation. The offspring of parents who were either implicated in Germany's commission of genocide or managed to survive are now authoring books, memoirs, and screenplays or are directing movies about how these events have left an imprint on their lives, too. The denial of the past or hypocrisy about it can drive an inquisitive adolescent literally up a tree if she rattles the skeletons in her town's past, as *The Nasty Girl* vividly illustrates. *Left Luggage* illustrates that covering or digging up the past can be a source of alienation or intimacy between survivors and their offspring. Movies about second-generation children are the fictionalized counterparts of the documentaries Alan Berger discusses in his book *Children of Job*. Both kinds of films confront "issues such as the survivors 'conspiracy of silence,' parents who wanted either to micromanage their children's lives or who, conversely, were emotionally unavailable, and feelings of being unworthy."[81]

The last chapter analyzes several notable Holocaust films released since 2000. The biopic is still the most popular genre of Holocaust film. *Max* speculates about how Hitler ultimately chose to pursue a career in politics rather than in art. *Hitler: The Rise of Evil* reenacts how he emerged from obscurity as an embittered war veteran to become chancellor of Germany. I speculate about why the plots and settings of *The Pianist* and *Nowhere in Africa* received critical acclaim and commercial success, whereas *The Grey Zone*'s visceral realism repelled audiences. The percolation of the Holocaust into the mainstream of pop culture is evidenced in *X-Men*. Therein the audience witnesses how the villain's loss of his parents in the Holocaust fuels his fears that humanity will persecute mutants like himself.

Through increasingly accessible technologies and the recollections of previously watched films, movies enable contemporary audiences to bridge the distance to the past and become vicarious witnesses to it. The verbal and visual power of cinema resembles the vividness of legends and myths in preliterate communities, whose beliefs, origins, and social structures were encapsulated in these tales. According to Jan Vansina, the leading scholar of African oral traditions, "Images have the property of expressing what may be complex relationships, situations, or trains of thought in a dense, concrete form, immediately grasped on an emotional and concrete level."[82] In this regard, Rosenstone's notion that "film is a postliterate equivalent of the preliterate way of dealing with the past" rings true.[83] Serious feature films about the Holocaust refract a vision of the past and the concerns of the present through a prism that has the potential to illuminate our hearts and minds, as well as the silver screen.

NOTES

1. Elie Wiesel, foreword to Annette Insdorf, *Indelible Shadows: Film and the Holocaust*, 3rd ed. (New York: Cambridge University Press, 2003), xi. Unless noted, citations refer to this edition.

2. Robert A. Rosenstone, *Visions of the Past: The Challenge of Film to Our Idea of History* (Cambridge, MA: Harvard University Press, 1995), 15.

3. *Schindler's List,* directed by Steven Spielberg (United States, 1993).

4. *Life Is Beautiful*, directed by Roberto Benigni (Italy, 1997).

5. For award and box office information, see www.imdb.com (accessed June 3, 2005).

6. Ilan Avisar, "Holocaust Movies and the Politics of Collective Memory," in *Thinking about the Holocaust after Half a Century*, ed. Alvin H. Rosenfeld (Bloomington: Indiana University Press, 1997), 53.

7. Omer Bartov, "Spielberg's Oskar: Hollywood Tries Evil," in *Spielberg's Holocaust: Critical Perspectives on Schindler's List*, ed. Yosefa Loshitzky (Bloomington: Indiana University Press, 1997), 46–47. Also see Omer Bartov, *The "Jew" in Cinema: From the Golem to Don't Touch My Holocaust* (Bloomington: Indiana University Press, 2005), 162–64.

8. Claude Lanzmann, "Why Spielberg Has Distorted the Truth," *Guardian Weekly* (April 9, 1994): 14–15.

9. E. Gruber, cited in Maurizio Viano, "*Life Is Beautiful*: Reception, Allegory, and Holocaust Laughter," *Jewish Social Studies: The New Series* 5, no. 3 (1999): 48.

10. Richard Schickel, "Fascist Fable," *Time* (November 9, 1998): 116–17.

11. Charles Taylor, "The Unbearable Lightness of Benigni," *Salon* (October 30, 1998), at www.salon.com/ent/movies/reviews/1998/10/30reviewa.html (accessed October 26, 2001).

12. David Denby, "Life Is Beautiful," *New Yorker* (March 15, 1999): 96–99. "Boy Freed from Buchenwald," http://english.gfh.org/il/boy-freed-from-buchenwald.htm.

13. Bartov, "Spielberg's Oskar," 46.

14. Yedhua Bauer, *Rethinking the Holocaust* (New Haven, CT: Yale University Press, 2001), 34–38.

15. Robert Brent Toplin, *Reel History: In Defense of Hollywood* (Lawrence: University of Kansas Press, 2002), 58–62.

16. Judith Doneson, *The Holocaust in American Film*, 2nd ed. (Syracuse, NY: Syracuse University Press, 2002), 8. Unless noted, citations to Doneson's book will be to this edition.

17. Insdorf, *Indelible Shadows*, 249.

18. Jeffrey Shandler, *While America Watches: Televising the Holocaust* (New York: Oxford University Press, 1999), 256.

19. Marcia Landy, "Cinematic History, Melodrama, and the Holocaust," in *Humanity at the Limit: The Impact of the Holocaust Experience on Jews and Christians*, ed. Michael A. Signer (Bloomington: Indiana University Press, 2000), 387; Miriam Bratu Hansen, "*Schindler's List* Is Not *Shoah*: Second Commandment, Popular Modernism, and Public Memory," in Loshitzky, *Spielberg's Holocaust*, 77–103.

20. Hilene Flanzbaum, "But Wasn't It Terrific: A Defense of Liking *Life Is Beautiful*," *Yale Journal of Criticism* 14, no. 1 (Spring 2001): 285.

21. Joshua Hirsch, *Afterimage: Film, Trauma, and the Holocaust* (Philadelphia: Temple University Press, 2004). Also see Janet Walker, *Trauma Cinema: Documenting Incest and the Holocaust* (Berkeley: University of California Press, 2005).

22. Michael Rothberg, *Traumatic Realism: The Demands of Holocaust Representation* (Minneapolis: University of Minnesota Press, 2000), 1–15, 99–106.

23. Dominick LaCapra, *Representing the Holocaust: History Theory Trauma* (Ithaca, NY: Cornell University Press, 1994).

24. Gary Weissman, *Fantasies of Witnessing: Postwar Efforts to Experience the Holocaust* (Ithaca, NY: Cornell University Press, 2004), 18–24, 131–39.

25. Amy Hungerford, *The Holocaust of Texts: Genocide, Literature, and Personification* (Chicago: University of Chicago Press, 2003), 1–23, 97–121.

26. Rosenstone, *Visions,* 31–32; Toplin, *Reel History,* 119–23, 189–96; Orly Lubin, "Teaching Cinema, Teaching the Holocaust," in *Teaching the Representation of the Holocaust*, ed. Marianne Hirsch and Irene Kacandes (New York: Modern Language Association, 2004), 220–33.

27. Alison Landsberg, "Prosthetic Memory: The Ethics and Politics of Memory in an Age of Mass Culture," in *Memory and Popular Film*, ed. Paul Grange (Manchester, UK: Manchester University Press, 2003), 148.

28. Tom W. Smith, *Holocaust Denial: What the Survey Data Reveal* (New York: American Jewish Committee, 1995), 46.

29. Insdorf, *Indelible Shadows.*

30. Ilan Avisar, *Screening the Holocaust: Cinema's Images of the Unimaginable* (Bloomington: Indiana University Press, 1988).

31. Doneson, *Holocaust in American Film.*

32. Doneson, *The Holocaust*, 199–215.

33. Insdorf, *Indelible Shadows,* 245–355.

34. Andre Colombat, *The Holocaust in French Film* (Metuchen, NJ: Scarecrow Press, 1993); Thomas C. Fox, *Stated Memory: East Germany and the Holocaust* (Rochester, NY: Camden House, 1999); Alan Mintz, *Popular Culture and the Shaping of Holocaust Memory in America* (Seattle: University of Washington Press, 2001); Robert C. Reimer and

Carole J. Reimer, *Nazi-Retro Film: How German Narrative Cinema Remembers the Past* (New York: Twayne, 1992); Kobi Niv, *Life Is Beautiful, but Not for Jews* (Lanham, MD: Scarecrow Press, 2003).

35. On the mixing of contemporary genres, see Geoff King, *New Hollywood Cinema: An Introduction* (New York: Columbia University Press, 2002), 116–46.

36. "Special Focus: The Holocaust on Film (Part 1)," *Film and History* 32, no. 1 (2002); Insdorf, *Indelible Shadows,* 199–241, 300–12; Caroline Joan Picart, *Documentary and Propaganda,* Vol. 2 of *The Holocaust Film Sourcebook.* Westport, CT: Praeger, 2004.

37. *One Survivor Remembers,* directed by Kary Antholis (United States, 1995); *The Long Way Home,* directed by Mark Jonathan Harris (United States, 1997); *The Last Days,* directed by James Moll (United States, 1998). For a critique of *The Last Days,* see Walker, *Trauma Cinema,* 138–44.

38. Avisar, *Screening,* 6–32; Insdorf, *Indelible Shadows,* 211–52.

39. Michael Bernard-Donals and Richard Glejzer, *Between Witness and Testimony: The Holocaust and the Limits of Representation* (Albany: State University of New York Press, 2001), 111–19; Walker, *Trauma Cinema,* 130–37.

40. Charles Chaplin, *My Autobiography* (New York: Simon and Schuster, 1964), 426.

41. Insdorf, *Indelible Shadows,* 3–25.

42. Insdorf, *Indelible Shadows,* 27–31, 34–36, 47–49, 59–70, 170–73, 258–67.

43. Avisar, *Screening,* 90–133.

44. Peter Novick, *The Holocaust in American Life* (Boston: Houghton Mifflin Co., 1999); Tim Cole, *Selling the Holocaust: From Auschwitz to Schindler, How History Is Bought, Packaged, and Sold* (New York: Routledge, 1999); Norman G. Finkelstein, *The Holocaust Industry: Reflections on the Exploitation of Jewish Suffering* (New York: Verso, 2000).

45. Avisar, *Screening,* 116.

46. Henry L. Feingold, *Bearing Witness: How America and Its Jews Responded to the Holocaust* (Syracuse, NY: Syracuse University Press, 1995); W. D. Rubinstein, *The Myth of Rescue: Why the Democracies Could Not Have Saved More Jews from the Nazis* (New York: Routledge, 1997); David S. Wyman, *The Abandonment of the Jews: America and the Holocaust, 1941–1945* (New York: Pantheon Books, 1984).

47. Robert Abzug, *Inside the Vicious Heart: America and the Liberation of the Nazi Concentration Camps* (New York: Oxford University Press, 1985).

48. Andrea Liss, *Trespassing through Shadows: Memory, Photography, and the Holocaust* (Minneapolis: University of Minnesota Press, 1998); Barbie Zelizer, *Remembering to Forget: Holocaust Memory through the Camera's Eye* (Chicago: University of Chicago Press, 1998), 16–164.

49. Lawrence Douglas, *The Memory of Judgment: Making Law and History in the Trials of the Holocaust* (New Haven, CT: Yale University Press, 2001), 1–94; Michael R. Marrus, "The Holocaust at Nuremberg," *Yad Vashem Studies* 26 (1998): 40–41.

50. William B. Helmreich, *Against All Odds: How the Survivors of the Holocaust Succeeded in the United States* (New York: Summit Books, 1992); Shandler, *While America Watches,* 27–79.

51. Emanuel Levy, *Cinema of Outsiders: The Rise of the American Independent Film* (New York: New York University Press, 1999).

52. Charles R. Acland, *Screen Traffic: Movies, Multiplexes, and Global Culture* (Durham, NC: Duke University Press, 2003); Tino Balio, ed., *Hollywood in the Age of Television* (Boston: Unwin Hyman, 1990); Mark Jancovich and Lucy Faire, *The Place of the Audience: Cultural Geographies of Film Consumption* (London: BFI Publishing, 2003); Elvis Mitchell, "Everyone's a Film Geek Now," *New York Times*, August 17, 2003, at www.nytimes.com/2003/08/17Elvi.html (accessed August 21, 2003).

53. Zygmunt Bauman, *Globalization: The Human Consequences* (New York: Columbia University Press, 1998).

54. Frank Manchel, "A Reel Witness: Steven Spielberg's Representation of the Holocaust in *Schindler's List*," *Journal of Modern History* 65 (March 1995): 83–100.

55. Avisar, *Screening,* 52–89; Insdorf, *Indelible Shadows,* 187–207.

56. David Brenner, "Working through the Holocaust Blockbuster: *Schindler's List* and *Hitler's Willing Executioners,* Globally and Locally," *Germanic Review* 75, no. 4 (Fall 2000): 296–316; Picart, *Holocaust Film Sources,* 1:167–68.

57. Alan Williams, ed. *Film and Nationalism* (New Brunswick, NJ: Rutgers University Press, 2002); Angus Finney, *The State of European Cinema: A New Dose of Reality* (New York: Cassell, 1996).

58. Mintz, *Popular Culture,* 39–41.

59. Lutz Koepnick, "Reframing the Past: Heritage Cinema and Holocaust in the 1990s," *New German Critique* 87 (Fall 2002): 47–83.

60. Daniel Levy and Nathan Sznaider, *Erinnerung im globalen Zeitalter: der Holocaust* (Frankfurt: Suhrkamp, 2001).

61. Avisar, *Screening,* 52–89; John Cunningham, *Hungarian Cinema: From Coffeehouse to Multiplex* (London: Wallflower Press, 2004), 171–82.

62. Insdorf, *Indelible Shadows,* 152–60; Sean Allan and John Sandford, eds., *DEFA, East German Cinema, 1946–1992* (New York: Berghahn Books, 1999).

63. Marek Haltof, *Polish National Cinema* (New York: Berghahn Books, 2001); Dina Iordanova, *Cinema of the Other Europe: The Industry and Artistry of East Central European Film* (London: Wallflower Press, 2003).

64. Avisar, *Screening,* 90–91.

65. Insdorf, *Indelible Shadows,* xvi–xvii.

66. Michael Burleigh and Wolfgang Wippermann, *The Racial State: Germany, 1933–1945* (New York: Cambridge University Press, 1991).

67. Steven T. Katz, *The Holocaust in Historical Context* (New York: Oxford University Press, 1994); Alan S. Rosenbaum, ed., *Is the Holocaust Unique? Perspectives on Comparative Genocide* (Boulder, CO: Westview Press, 1996).

68. Graeme Turner, *Film as Social Practice*, 2nd ed. (New York: Routledge, 1993), 38.

69. See the chapter on "Star Power," in King, *New Hollywood,* 147–77.

70. Andrea Reiter, *Narrating the Holocaust*, trans. Patrick Camiller (New York: Continuum, 2000), 50–83.

71. Compare to Insdorf, *Indelible Shadows,* 245–49.

72. Rick Altman, *Film/Genre* (London: British Film Institute, 1999), 142–43; also see Steve Neale, *Genre and Hollywood* (New York: Routledge, 2000),

73. Adrienne Kertzer, *My Mother's Voice Children, Literature, and the Holocaust* (Peterborough, Canada: Broadview Press, 2002), 74–75.

74. Alvin H. Rosenfeld, "The Americanization of the Holocaust," in Rosenfeld, *Thinking about the Holocaust*, 135–47.

75. Andrea Slane, *A Not So Foreign Affair Fascism, Sexuality, and the Cultural Rhetoric of American Democracy* (Durham, NC: Duke University Press, 2001). Also see Lawrence Baron, "Holocaust Iconography in American Feature Films about Neo-Nazis," *Film and History* 32, no. 2 (2002): 38–47.

76. Bruno Bettelheim, "The Ignored Lesson of Anne Frank," *Harper's Magazine* (November 1960): 45–46.

77. Lawrence L. Langer, *Admitting the Holocaust: Collected Essays* (New York: Oxford University Press, 1995), 9–11; Stephen J. Whitfield, *In Search of American Jewish Culture* (Hanover, NH: University Press of New England, 1999), 186–90.

78. Shandler, *While America Watches,* 183–210.

79. Novick, *The Holocaust*, 272–76.

80. Insdorf, *Indelible Shadows,* 293–99.

81. Alan L. Berger, *Children of Job: American Second-Generation Witnesses to the Holocaust* (Albany: State University Press of New York, 1997), 120–82.

82. Jan Vansina, *Oral Tradition as History* (Madison: University of Wisconsin Press, 1985), 138.

83. Rosenstone, *Visions*, 78.

• 2 •

Picturing the Holocaust
in the Past: 1945–1979

For the constructivist model, the point of departure is the assumption that beyond their factual core, historical events, even the Holocaust, possess no inscribed meanings; meaning is constructed by communities of interpretation—differently by different communities—out of their own motives and needs.[1]

—Alan Mintz

*W*hen the victorious Allied troops entered the gates of hastily abandoned German concentration, extermination, and labor camps, they surveyed the remnants of the Third Reich's ideological and racial war. The stench and sight of rotting corpses scattered on the spots where they had died or been stacked before they could be buried or burned overwhelmed even the most battle-hardened veterans. The ashes in the crematoria and the instruments once plied in medical experiments and torture sessions testified to the fate of victims who left no remains. The bony bodies and vacant gazes of the survivors made them look like phantoms returned from the netherworld. As Robert Abzug has observed, "The liberations made horrified believers out of the skeptics and brought a new and hideous sense of reality even to those who never doubted the worst."[2]

Documentary films, newsreels, and photographs disseminated these appalling scenes.[3] By May 1945, 84 percent of Americans polled believed that Germany had slaughtered many civilians in its camps and wartime operations.[4] The prosecution team at the Nuremberg Trials submitted a compilation of footage of the atrocities discovered at the liberated camps as evidence of German "crimes against humanity." The gaunt survivors, crematoria chimneys, barbed wire fences, gas chambers, mass graves, railway cars, SS insignia, Star of David armbands, striped camp clothing, swastikas, warehouses full of personal items and human hair, and Zyklon-B canisters became commonly recognized symbols of Nazi inhumanity.[5] According to David Wyman, "the news reports from Nuremberg . . . catalogued the scope and enormity of the extermination, and impressed them, along with the number six million, on the world's consciousness."[6]

Many scholars maintain that the initial shock over the revelations of the decimation of European Jewry was short-lived. International awareness of the Final Solution allegedly dissipated as Jewish losses were subsumed under the staggering casualty statistics for World War II as a whole and overshadowed by subsequent events like the dropping of atomic bombs on Japan, the onset of the cold war, and dealing with domestic problems neglected during wartime. Most countries occupied by or allied with Germany concealed their records of collaboration in implementing anti-Semitic policies or indifference to the arrest and deportation of their fellow Jewish citizens. The Soviet Union pressured the states it "liberated" to interpret the ordeal of World War II in doctrinaire communist terms. It perceived Nazis as agents of monopoly capitalists who crushed communism and distracted the masses with wars and racism.[7]

Jews supposedly fostered this historical amnesia too. Those who survived the camps, ghettoes, and massacres or evaded capture by fleeing, hiding, or living incognito as Aryans suppressed their traumatic memories. Psychologists hypothesized that survivors were wracked with guilt for escaping death while their loved ones had perished.[8] Jewish immigrants to Palestine found themselves embroiled in a struggle first against the British and then against the Arabs.[9] Jewish citizens of Western democracies downplayed their concern about the annihilation of European Jewry and support for Israel to dispel suspicions of dual loyalties. With hindsight, they felt they had not heeded the warnings of a Jewish bloodbath in Europe and failed to save their doomed coreligionists.[10] Jews under Soviet rule dared not memorialize their slain brethren in anticipation of persecution as reactionary nationalists.[11]

Yet, forty-four movies on Holocaust themes appeared in the four-year period following the cessation of hostilities in Europe. The memories of those whose lives had been imperiled by the Nazis were still fresh[12] (see table 2.1). The Kremlin's claim that Jews, along with communists and Slavs, were merely the scapegoats of fascist regimes went unchallenged. The Red Army, after all, had defeated Germany on the eastern front, thereby sparing the remaining Jews there from liquidation.[13] Although highlighting the plight of the Jews might generate diplomatic and popular sympathy for Zionism, the Soviet Union temporarily supported the creation of a Jewish state in Palestine to provide a haven for Jewish refugees, undermine British dominance in the Middle East, and win the gratitude of the socialist leaders of the new Jewish state.[14]

Table 2.1.   Holocaust Movie Database, 1945–1999

	Years					
	1945–1949	*1950–1959*	*1960–1969*	*1970–1979*	*1980–1989*	*1990–1999*
Number of Films	44	76	135	124	227	222
Bulgaria	0	0	1	0	1	1
Czech.	1	1	13	0	2	2
East Germany	5	5	5	2	7	N/A
France	4	4	6	11	12	15
Hungary	1	1	5	4	7	3
Israel	1	4	3	2	6	6
Italy	3	2	5	16	6	2
Poland	4	6	15	5	12	11
United Kingdom	2	0	10	10	12	6
United States	13	33	33	25	63	66
Soviet Union/Russia	1	1	3	1	2	5
West Germany/Germany	3	11	14	17	27	24
Yugoslavia	0	2	3	5	5	1
Multinational	4	6	14	20	38	49
Other	Belgium 1 Switzerland 1	0	Austria 1 Belgium 2 Greece 1 Netherlands 1 Sweden 1	Austria 1 Japan 1 Mexico 1 Netherlands 1 Spain 1 Switzerland 1	Argen. 2 Australia 2 Austria 4 Belgium 1 Canada 4 Finland 1 Ireland 1 Netherlands 9 Norway 1 Pakistan 1 Spain 1	Australia 2 Austria 4 Belgium 1 Canada 6 China 1 Denmark 2 Iceland 1 Japan 2 Mexico 2 Netherlands 3 Norway 3 South Africa 1 Spain 1 Sweden 4 Switzerland 1

In this window of opportunity between 1945 and 1949, the states comprising the Soviet Bloc produced twelve motion pictures about the persecution and slaughter of European Jews during World War II. These films possess a sense of authenticity resulting from their proximity in time and place to the stories they portray. Director Wanda Jakubowska and screenwriter Gerda Schneider had been inmates at Auschwitz. They drew on their own experiences as the basis for *The Last Stop* (1947), a realistic depiction of the tribulations of female prisoners at Auschwitz.[15] Not only was the film shot on location, but it was cast primarily with concentration camp survivors. In spite of its ideological glorification of communist resistance and conventional heroic ending in which a Jewish member of the camp underground martyrs herself, *The Last Stop* reenacts, in Annette Insdorf's words, "overwhelming events with effective simplicity."[16]

Jewish director Aleksander Ford spent the war in the Soviet Union, where he served as the chief of the Polish Army's cinema unit. In *Border Street* (1948), he dramatized the chronic brutality, epidemics, and starvation that ravaged the Jews trapped in the Warsaw ghetto. He originally intended to make Polish anti-Semitism a central element of the plot but watered the story down under government pressure to present instances of Polish solidarity with the Jews. The final version closes with a scene of Christian and Jewish children descending together into the sewers of Warsaw after German troops have crushed the uprising of 1943. In the early 1950s, Stalin rebuked Ford for devoting too much attention to the Jewish characters rather than the working-class ones.[17]

The postwar cinema from other communist countries occupied by Germany similarly mirrored the Nazi assault against Jews. The Czech picture *Distant Journey* chronicles the arrest and separation of a Jewish wife from her Gentile husband and her subsequent internment at Theresienstadt.[18] In late 1943, Germany temporarily reduced the overcrowding at the camp and spruced it up with building facades and greenery to convince a Red Cross delegation that the former fortress was a model ghetto where Jews enjoyed a decent standard of living and rich cultural life. Following this propaganda coup, the Nazis released a documentary about the visit to validate the deception.[19] Born into a marriage between a Christian man and Jewish woman, director Alfred Radok knew about Theresienstadt because his Jewish father had died in captivity there. He filmed *Distant Journey* to reveal that the reputed haven actually served as a transit camp where a steady flow of fresh internees replaced the dwindling ranks of prisoners who succumbed to disease, hard labor, malnutrition, and physical punishments or disappeared regularly on trains bound for Auschwitz. Radok previewed the fate of the deportees by showing the construction of a gas chamber and the herding of a panic-stricken group of children into it. The movie climaxes with the liberation of Theresienstadt by the Soviet Army and a chaotic celebration of freed prisoners overwhelmed by anguish and elation. Radok quickly fell into disfavor with the Stalinist regime imposed on his country.[20]

Most German filmmakers in the early postwar era shied away from offending their audiences with the gory details of the Final Solution. The stories from movies produced in both the American and Russian occupation zones were typically set in the bombed-out landscape of the cities of the vanquished Third Reich. These "rubble" films often elicited sympathy for the innocent majority of Germans coping with the devastation brought upon their nation by Nazi fanaticism. Harald Braun's *Between Yesterday and Tomorrow* (1947) uses flashbacks to show why the Jewish owner of a necklace found in the rubble of a hotel had committed suicide. A Nazi officer of the Gestapo had stalked her so relentlessly that she felt her only escape was to take her own life. As Robert Shandley has commented, the message of *Between Yesterday and Tomorrow* was an exculpatory one: "The Nazis are the bad guys. Everyone else is a victim of circumstances."[21]

German films made in the Russian occupation zone confronted the guilt for Nazi crimes against humanity more candidly because the German Communist Party and the Soviet Union had been Hitler's archenemies. The title of Wolfgang Staudte's *The Murderers Are among Us* (1946) announces that the purge of Nazis from German society still must be undertaken.[22] Amid the wreckage of buildings and disabled tanks, a train pulls into Berlin's central station. Susanna Wallner, a concentration camp survivor, disembarks. She returns to her old apartment to find a squatter named Hans Mertens residing there. He too is a camp survivor. While Susanna exhibits no mental or physical symptoms of her incarceration, Hans anesthetizes himself by drinking heavily and plans to assassinate Ferdinand Brückner, who accrued postwar wealth by recycling army helmets into kitchen pots, a Marxist metaphor for the interchangeability of fascism and capitalism. Brückner has concealed his wartime record as a Nazi who ordered the execution of the inhabitants of a Polish village. In one scene, he eats a sandwich wrapped in a newspaper that carries the headline, "2,000,000 People Gassed." Susanna stops Hans from shooting Brückner with the admonishment, "We don't have the right to be judge and hangman!" Given the early date of its release, *The Murderers Are among Us* represented a bold statement indicting ordinary Germans for condoning mass murder and absolving war criminals in West Germany. From today's vantage point, the movie seems timorous for not specifying Jews as the victims of gassing and depicting Susanna as unaffected by her captivity in a concentration camp.[23]

Contrary to the scholarly consensus that the only effect of the Holocaust on Hollywood was the tackling of the issue of domestic anti-Semitism in films like *Crossfire* (1947) and *Gentleman's Agreement* (1947),[24] the United States produced more motion pictures dealing with Holocaust themes than any other country between 1945 and 1949. These movies were characterized by their focus on postwar problems arising from Hitler's racial war, like hunting Nazi fugitives (*The Stranger*, 1946), conducting trials for war crimes (*Sealed Verdict*, 1948), or thwarting plots by obdurate Nazis to undermine the Allied occupation and regain power (*Berlin Express*, 1948).[25] The Holocaust provided a rationale for why escaped Nazis remained a clear and present danger to the free world. Public distrust of Germans as culturally militaristic, racist, or totalitarian lingered in cinematic representations after the Third Reich fell.[26]

Orson Welles's *The Stranger* illustrates how the Final Solution served as a plot device in a postwar American movie.[27] Franz Kindler, the villain of the piece, relies on his fluency in English and forged papers to procure a position as a professor of German history at a Connecticut college. Detective Wilson of the Allied War Crimes Commission stages a jailbreak of a convicted camp commandant, Konrad Meinike, hoping that tailing him will lead to Kindler. Meinike approaches Kindler's guileless fiancé, Mary, to establish contact with her prospective groom. To eliminate any trace of his past, Kindler murders

Meinike. At a dinner party that Wilson attends, Kindler maintains that the German people innately obey military leaders and lack any concept of freedom. When his future brother-in-law cites Karl Marx to disprove this generalization, Kindler scoffs that Marx was a Jew and not a German. To pressure Mary to admit Meinike had contacted her, Wilson shows her atrocity footage of the liberated concentration camps. In a darkened room, images of strewn corpses, a gas chamber, a limed burial pit, and a skeletal survivor flicker on the screen and across Mary's face. Wilson tells Mary that Kindler "conceived of the theory of genocide, the mass depopulation of conquered countries."[28]

While *The Stranger*'s explanation of Nazi racial policies leaves much to be desired, the movie holds the distinction of being the first American feature film to include clips of films introduced as evidence at the Nuremberg Trials.[29] Wilson's assertion that Hitler's goal was the liquidation all non-Aryans in Europe exceeds Hitler's plan to exterminate European Jewry. In retrospect, the detective's pursuit of Kindler glosses over how the cold war dampened the American zeal to de-Nazify Germany in favor of containing Soviet expansion.[30] Yet, in 1946, the use of atrocity footage, the mention of genocide, a term coined only two years earlier,[31] and the anti-Semitic clue planted in Kindler's verbal slip revealed an incipient consciousness of the Final Solution.

Displaced persons (DPs) symbolized the most vulnerable victims of the upheaval resulting first from the German and Soviet occupations of central and Eastern Europe. Approximately seven million DPs flocked to the American, British, and French zones in Germany upon Germany's surrender in May 1945. Jews constituted a minority of this amalgamation, which comprised foreigners conscripted or enlisted to work in wartime Germany, fugitives from persecution, prisoners of war, survivors of German camps, and immigrants fleeing postwar communist rule. Millions of ethnic Germans forcibly expelled from Czechoslovakia and Poland soon joined this flood of refugees. By September, the Allied military authorities had repatriated nearly six million DPs.[32]

Most Jewish DPs under Allied or U.N. guardianship refused to return to their native countries, where few Gentiles had protested Nazi anti-Semitic policies and some had collaborated in their implementation. Panicked by the outbreak of pogroms in postwar Poland, Polish Jews compounded the overcrowding in the DP camps under American, British, or French control in 1946.[33] Compared to Gentile DPs, Jews usually spent longer periods in confinement or hiding, had lost more members of their families, and had suffered greater psychological and physical harm as acknowledged by the American Harrison Commission in September 1945.[34] Many yearned to settle in Palestine, and the commission and President Truman recommended that one hundred thousand be admitted to that country. England balked, worried that a large influx of Jews would ignite the volatile tensions between Arabs and Jews in the area.[35]

Several postwar directors turned their cameras on the predicament of the DPs as a portal into the calamities that had robbed these refugees of their families, homelands, and sanity. This approach lent itself to three cinematic genres. Psychodramas traced the traumatic source of the behaviors exhibited by DPs. Natan Gross's *Our Children* (1948) opens with newsreel footage of the deportation of Jews to Auschwitz to contextualize the frightened reactions of Jewish orphans to a performance of a Yiddish comedy about a fire in the shtetl. The play reminds the children of their own memories of the burning of the Warsaw ghetto.[36] The road movie provided an apt genre for stories about DPs who wandered through Europe searching for lost relatives and a safe haven to restore meaning to their lives. *Long Is the Road* (1947) follows the odyssey of David, who sneaks off a transport headed for Auschwitz, hides in the Polish countryside, joins a band of Jewish partisans, marries a concentration camp survivor, locates his mother in a DP hospital, and presumably emigrates to Palestine.[37] Filmmakers who were either Zionists before the war or sympathizers after 1945 produced movies about DPs going to Israel to participate in the establishment of the new Jewish state of Israel.[38]

Between 1945 and 1948, a congruence of American and Zionist interests emerged, with the former preferring to channel Jewish DPs away from the United States and toward Palestine and the latter welcoming American pressure on England to admit more Jewish settlers into Palestine and relinquish its mandate there. Directors concerned about the DPs perceived the melodramatic potential of the situation of the Jewish refugees in Allied or U.N. camps and produced movies that projected an image of the United States as a benevolent country caring for the dispossessed Jewish victims of Nazism and supporting their aspirations to return to the Holy Land. *Sword in the Desert* (1949) was the first of several war films, like *Exodus* (1960) and *Cast a Giant Shadow* (1966), to feature an American character getting involved in the struggle against the English or Arabs to attain Israeli independence. These films sometimes portrayed the Arabs as enlisting ex-Nazis as military advisors or mercenaries. This discredited Arab opposition to Jewish statehood by associating it with Nazi anti-Semitism.[39]

THE GI AND THE DP: *THE SEARCH*
Directed by Fred Zinnemann
(Switzerland, United States: Praessens Film Swiss and MGM, 1948)

> I do not know where the stateless Jews will be given a permanent home. It is my aim until that time to make it possible for them to lead a normal and useful life.[40]

—Dwight David Eisenhower

Although *The Search* has been praised as a landmark movie, it has at best received a short synopsis and at worst a filmographic citation in books on Holocaust cinema.[41] Yet, it was the first mainstream American film shot on location in the shambles of heavily bombed German cities and devoted to the shattered lives of DPs. The main plotline is an exercise in unabashed sentimentality. An American soldier befriends a young escapee from a DP camp and reunites the boy with his mother in a contrived happy ending. The background details reveal the political oppression that cruelly separated the son and mother and the mistreatment that left such deep psychological scars on the boy and his peers in the camp. In style and substance, *The Search* was a fictionalized version of the documentaries about the survivors in the liberated concentration camps.

For those unfamiliar with Fred Zinnemann's early films, the neorealistic look of *The Search* bears little resemblance to his polished classics like *High Noon, From Here to Eternity, Oklahoma,* and *Julia*.[42] As a Jew growing up in Austria, Zinnemann recalled the pervasive anti-Semitism, hunger, and unemployment that ensued after the defeat and dissolution of the Austro-Hungarian Empire in World War I. Drawn to a career in filmmaking, he apprenticed in Berlin and Paris before immigrating to Los Angeles in 1929. In 1934, Mexico's Department of Fine Arts commissioned him to direct a semidocumentary entitled *The Wave* about the grinding poverty and strenuous work of fishermen in a small village. This experience encouraged his predilections to film on site, cast amateurs to play themselves, and tackle socially significant themes. Under contract for MGM, Zinnemann primarily received assignments to direct shorts and B films. *The Seventh Cross* (1944) represents a notable exception. It concerns a political prisoner who escapes from a Nazi concentration camp and approaches a variety of characters for help. Most lack the courage or conviction to shelter him, but a few help him. Zinnemann's direction of *The Wave* and *The Seventh Cross* prepared him for the documentary style and social theme that informed *The Search*. The death of his parents in the Holocaust impelled him to make movies about the catastrophe that had befallen Europe.[43]

Impressed by *The Seventh Cross* and moved by Thérèse Bonney's photography book *Europe's Children,* Swiss producer Lazar Wechsler approached Zinnemann to direct a semidocumentary that would convey to American audiences the fear, loss, and suffering experienced by the "unaccompanied" children languishing in DP camps. Both Wechsler and screenwriter Richard Schweizer had collaborated on *The Last Chance* (1945), a pioneering film about Allied soldiers shepherding a group of refugees to safety in neutral Switzerland. They recruited Bonney to serve as technical advisor for *The Search*. The U.N. Relief and Rehabilitation Administration (UNRRA) granted Wechsler and Bonney permission to visit DP camps in Germany, interview staff and inmates, and read the files of DP children. The two combined their own observations with incidents recorded in the interviews and files to fashion a story that dramatized the adversities DP children encountered. For all but the leading roles in the film, they cast DP children, after initially hiring Swiss children whose attempts to act scared and traumatized proved unconvincing. Zinnemann filmed the outdoor scenes in the rubble of Munich and Nuremberg. This bleak backdrop mirrored the themes of desolation and displacement.[44]

The Search starts with the image of a train screeching to a halt at night in a heavily damaged railway station. A narrator describes the plight of DP children, fostering the impression that the viewer is watching a documentary. When the door slides open, the sleeping children look like corpses piled upon one another. UNRRA personnel shine flashlights on the motionless figures, some of whom are still wearing concentration camp uniforms. The awakening of the dazed boys and girls figuratively signals their rebirth. The narrator establishes the magnitude of the crisis: "This is but a handful, a tiny handful, of the millions of orphaned, homeless, bewildered children, children who had a right to better things—a right taken from them by the war." They march from the station to the UNRRA compound. The youngsters initially fail to comprehend that the shelter is not another concentration camp and that "those now in charge of them want to help." They filch extra bread, move mechanically, obey orders, remain taciturn, and stretch their arms out after meals expecting to be frisked for stolen items. A partially effaced swastika and German eagle painted on a wall loom as reminders of their persecution under Nazism.

The camera assumes the point of view of the UNRRA caretakers as they debrief the new arrivals. Prior to this scene, the children blend into the group. Only when each is called upon to relate his or her story does the range of their nationalities and ordeals emerge. The children speak in their native languages, which are then translated by their social workers. A parentless French Catholic boy discloses that he had been interned at Mauthausen. A Polish girl and her little brother reveal that their mother and father died at Bergen-Belsen. A Hungarian girl named Miriam says her parents were gassed at Dachau, where she recalls seeing her mother's blouse in the clothing she sorted.

A blond boy with an identification number from Auschwitz tattooed on his arm steps up. At first he remains mute. When he finally replies to questions about his identity, he repeats, "I don't know" in German. A narrated flashback divulges the boy's repressed secret—that his parents were Czech intellectuals who had been arrested by the Gestapo. Although he never saw his father or sister again, the boy, whose name is Karel, stayed with his mother in a concentration camp until one day he saw her carrying an umbrella and being marched away on the other side of a barbed wire fence. His amnesia and silence serve as a metaphor for the survivors' repression of traumatic memories.[45]

Zinnemann places Karel and his mother, Hannah, in settings and situations that epitomize the destruction of family ties and basic trust. Karel's caseworker decides to transfer him to another center for intensive therapy. An ambulance drives into the camp to pick up Karel and other severely troubled youngsters. To them, the ambulance resembles German gas vans. Suspecting the worst, the children panic and escape from the vehicle. Karel and a companion leap into a river. While Karel conceals himself in reeds, his friend is carried away by the swift current and drowns. Meanwhile, Hannah treks along the abandoned autobahn, where she passes collapsed bridges. She has been seeking her lost son in DP centers in the Allied occupation zones. Approaching the center where Karel had been detained, she notices a cemetery. These juxtapositions illustrate how Nazi policies tainted the meaning of objects and institutions used to save lives.[46]

Karel roams like a wild animal through the wasteland of splintered boards, shattered bricks, and twisted steel. Stevenson, the GI affably played by Montgomery Clift, coaxes the hungry boy out of hiding by tossing him a sandwich. Then, he grabs Karel and drives him to his home. Karel tries to escape and accidentally knocks over a goldfish bowl. The sight of fish flapping helplessly on the floor provides a projection of how Karel feels. Stevenson finally unlocks the door and gate and lets Karel leave. Only then does Karel realize that Stevenson is his friend and not his warden. The soldier teaches Karel to speak English, but the boy always forgets what the word umbrella means. A model bridge represents Stevenson's efforts to communicate with Karel. To Americanize Karel, Stevenson shows him a picture of a fawn, which Karel dubs Bambi. Postwar audiences probably knew that Bambi's mother was killed by hunters. This precedes the scene where Stevenson informs Karel of his plan to adopt him since his mother is presumably dead. Karel sketches horizontal and vertical lines that look like a fence. He runs away to hunt for his mother at a local factory surrounded by a fence.

Although Karel and Hannah are not Jewish, Zinnemann does not overlook the Jewish dimension of the DP crisis. When Hannah inquires whether her son is living at the camp, she is introduced to a choirboy who claims to be Karel. Of course, she immediately recognizes the child is not her son. His real name turns out to be Joel Markowsky. Joel has pretended to be Catholic and usurped Karel's name because his mother had warned him never to let anyone know he was Jewish. Joel wistfully glances at Hannah in several shots, longing for her to replace his dead mother. The chief social worker mentions that most of the DP children at the shelter are Jewish. Many have chosen to settle in Palestine. Zinnemann depicts the Zionist youth as better adjusted and more optimistic than other kids in the camp. Toward the end of the movie, a group of children celebrates its departure for Palestine. The background props for this scene include a Jewish star, portraits of Herzl and Henrietta Szold, and a Hebrew placard with the number six million on it.[47]

Unfortunately, the ending of *The Search* is as maudlin as it is predictable. Hannah boards a train to resume her search, while Stevenson leaves the boy he calls Jimmy at the UNRRA shelter until the adoption is finalized. As Stevenson relates the details of how and when he met Jimmy, the social worker realizes that Jimmy is Karel. She rushes to the train station to stop Hannah from departing but ostensibly arrives too late. Much to her surprise, Hannah has decided to stay to care for the new group of orphans who have disembarked from the train. At the shelter, Karel and Hannah embrace in a tearful reunion. A reviewer for *Variety* aptly remarked, "By putting a saccharine finale on a single case, there's an undue submergence of the fact that other millions of these pitiable youngsters are still in camps and have still failed to find their mothers and security."[48]

Nevertheless, it would be a mistake to accuse Zinnemann of glossing over the horrors of the Holocaust by reuniting Karel and Hannah and stressing that many Jewish children settled in Israel.[49] Within *The Search*'s visual and verbal references to the troubled memories of the DP children, there is a subtext about death, dislocation, and trauma that tempers the joy of the film's ending. Zinnemann sought to educate the public about "a vital modern problem" while entertaining them sufficiently so that they would see the movie. The shocking interviews with the children, their frightened reactions to the routines in the camp, and the intrusion of the past into Karel's present circumstances discomfort the viewer. This double narrative, a characteristic in subsequent Holocaust films, wraps a sugar coating around a bitter pill. Zinnemann admitted as much when he told an interviewer, "All of us realized, of course, that it would be necessary to soften the truth to a certain extent, because to show things as they really were would have meant—at least in our sincere opinion—that the American audience would have lost any desire to face it, used as they have been through the years to seeing a sentimentalized world."[50]

Although it depicts the Holocaust more obliquely than the Eastern European films discussed earlier in this chapter, *The Search* surpassed them all in the honors bestowed on it. It received five Academy Award nominations and won Oscars for best screenplay and Ivan Jandl's performance as Karel. It garnered awards from the United Nations, the British Academy of Film and Television Arts, and the Golden Globes for its script and promotion of international understanding.[51] Eleven years would pass before a Holocaust movie earned more critical acclaim. Unlike Karel, its heroine was not reticent.

THE DECADE OF THE DIARY: *THE DIARY OF ANNE FRANK*
Directed by George Stevens
(United States: Twentieth Century Fox, 1959)

> Anne Frank died because her parents could not get themselves to believe in Auschwitz. And her story found wide acclaim because for us too, it denies implicitly that Auschwitz ever existed. If all men are good, there was never an Auschwitz.[52]

> —Bruno Bettelheim

> *The Diary of Anne Frank*, however, derives its shattering impact as much from what is left unsaid as from the candid simplicity of its prose. Each entry is framed, as it were, by the black silence into which its author disappeared.[53]

> —Ernst Pawel

The Holocaust did not entirely vanish in the plotlines of feature films produced in the 1950s. When it appeared, however, it usually loomed in the background as an ominous fate awaiting Jewish characters if arrested or deported, as a traumatic experience affecting their personalities in the present, as a cause for anti-Nazi resistance, or as grounds for postwar trials of German war criminals. Only the Italian movie *Kapo* (1959) dealt exclusively with survival in a death camp.[54] Some directors followed Orson Welles's precedent of inserting atrocity footage of the liberated camps into their movies. The screening of these shocking images in the television version of *Judgment at Nuremberg* (1959) and in Samuel Fuller's *Verboten* (1958) discredited the rationales for supporting Nazism raised by the defense attorney in the former and the neo-Nazi brother of the German wife of an American occupation official in the latter.[55]

While documentary clips heightened the pretence of realism in fictional films about the Holocaust, they could not foster audience empathy with Jewish victims. The dead in the newsreels formed an anonymous mass, and the survivors appeared more like fleeting ghosts than living human beings. Understanding how demeaning and enervating the conditions in the camps and ghettos were required a leap of imagination that few Americans were willing or able to make. Of all the Holocaust memoirs published in the United States during the 1950s, *The Diary of Anne Frank* most successfully overcame the disparity between the personal security Americans took for granted and the constant vulnerability European Jews felt after Germany occupied their countries. The American public could identify with Anne's idealism and interactions with her family and comrades in hiding, if not with their protracted confinement. Readers of the diary and audiences who saw the play or movie knew that the girl who authored it had perished in a German camp, but the book's cover photo of Anne's cheerful face remained in their minds.[56]

In 1952, the American edition of *The Diary of a Young Girl* became an instant bestseller. Soon thereafter, it was adapted into a television drama that was broadcast on the Sunday morning religious series *Frontiers of Faith*. The final scene began with the narrator announcing that Anne had died in Bergen-Belsen but ended with Anne thanking God for giving her the opportunity to achieve immorality through her writing.[57] A radio play by Meyer Levin aired the same year. Otto Frank, Anne's father, originally granted Levin's request to author a play based on the diary, but then opted to let the husband-wife team of Frances Goodrich and Albert Hackett write it because they had a record of churning out successful scripts for movies like Frank Capra's *It's a Wonderful Life*. Levin bitterly suspected that his manuscript was rejected because it was too overtly Jewish. The universal and optimistic message of the Goodrich and Hackett version contributed to the play's long run on Broadway following its premier in 1955 and earned Otto Frank's approval. Frank minced no words about his aversion to Levin's interpretation of Anne as a Jewish martyr: "It is not a Jewish book either, though Jewish sphere, sentiment and surrounding, is the background. It is (at least here) read and understood more by gentiles than in Jewish circles."[58] By 1958, Ernst Schnabel's biography of Anne and a children's edition of her diary were published in the United States.[59] Details about Anne's arrest and deportation appeared in *Reader's Digest* and *Life* in the years prior to the film's release.[60]

Stevens obtained the movie rights for the diary in 1956. He possessed excellent credentials for transforming the diary into a poignant motion picture. During the 1950s, he had directed several of the most highly acclaimed films of the decade, like *A Place in the Sun* (1951), *Shane* (1953), and *Giant* (1956). More pertinently, he had served in the U.S. Army Signal Corps for the Allied Expeditionary Forces in Europe toward the end of World War II and supervised the filming of the liberated Nazi concentration and prison camps. He edited the footage for the documentary that the Allied prosecution team entered as evidence at the Nuremberg Trials.[61] As his son recalls, *The Diary of Anne Frank* finally gave his father a chance to make a "war film" that drew on his unique military service. Stevens met with Otto Frank, who personally guided him through the Amsterdam building on Prinsengracht where his family and friends had hidden. Stevens meticulously recreated their quarters as the claustrophobic setting for the film. He revisited Dachau to revive his memory of the gruesome sights he had photographed there.

While retaining Goodrich and Hackett as screenwriters and casting Joseph Schildkraut to reprise his stage role as Otto Frank, Stevens and his associates conducted thousands of interviews in Europe and the United States to find a girl who physically resembled Anne but lacked professional acting experience. They eventually picked Millie Perkins, an attractive nineteen-year-old model. Stevens hoped audiences would identify her solely as Anne since they could not associate her with any previous roles.[62]

The reviews of *The Diary of Anne Frank* were positive, if not always glowing. Although it is difficult today to envision Anne without conjuring up the looks and mannerisms of Millie Perkins, some critics felt that her performance was the film's major flaw. Bosley Crowther of the *New York Times* considered her appearance too mature and acting too amateurish to be convincing. Yet, he still commended Stevens for his brilliant reenactment of the "harrowing ordeal" and "brave behavior of eight Jews" confined in an attic in "Nazi-occupied Amsterdam."[63] The critic for *Variety* faulted Stevens for not shortening the film's running time of almost three hours: "Unlike the play, the picture leaves too little to the imagination."[64] *Time* deemed the movie "a masterpiece" and kept it on its list of recommended films for over three months.[65] Similarly, *The Diary of Anne Frank* received many nominations for Oscars, Golden Globes, and other cinema awards but consistently lost in the most prestigious categories of best director and picture to William Wyler's gladiator epic *Ben Hur* (1959).[66] Notwithstanding this mixed reception, the movie stimulated more international interest in the diary itself.[67]

As awareness of the Nazi determination to eradicate European Jewry has grown, the play and movie have fallen into disfavor among many Holocaust scholars. They judge the dramatization of Anne's diary by Goodrich and Hackett as irreparably deficient on three counts.[68] First, it obscures Anne's realization that Jews have been perennial scapegoats in Christian Europe by presenting Jews as one of many groups victimized throughout history.[69] Thus, she tells Peter in the final version of the play and movie, "We're not the only people that've had to suffer. Right down through the ages there have been people that have had to suffer. Sometimes one race . . . sometimes another."[70] Second, it minimizes Anne's consciousness of being Jewish. Although a central scene in the play and movie highlights the celebration of Chanukah, this scene is now perceived as a token of assimilation since the prayers and songs are not in Hebrew. Third, ending the play and movie with a voice-over of Anne affirming her belief that "people are really good at heart" diminishes the tragedy of the Nazis' storming the attic and Otto Frank returning there as a shattered man grieving the deaths of his family and friends.

These criticisms simply ignore other scenes that refute them or fail to take into account the cinematic and political context in which Stevens operated. An early draft of the Goodrich and Hackett script contained the line, "Right down through the ages, there have been Jews and they've had to suffer." Garson Kanin, the director of the Broadway production of the diary, urged the playwrights to delete this "embarrassing piece of special pleading" and "spread its theme into the infinite."[71]

The opening of the film makes it unmistakably clear that the Germans have targeted the Jews for persecution. Otto returns to Amsterdam and climbs down from the lorry filled with passengers still dressed in striped concentration camp outfits. As he reads the diary Miep gives him, his voice segues into Anne's. She explains that since her family was Jewish, they immigrated to Holland when Hitler came to power. After the German occupation of the Netherlands, she recalls that "things got very bad for the Jews." She lists activities the Nazis had prohibited Jews from doing. As the Frank and van Daan families enter the attic, the viewer sees the conspicuous yellow Stars of David on their coats. Anne worries when Peter removes and burns his star that the Germans will arrest him. She wonders what would happen to Miep and Kraler if the police discover they are harboring Jews. Otto replies, "They would suffer the same fate we would if caught hiding Jews." The drone of a paddy wagon siren gets closer and then fades into the distance. As the Franks and van Daans settle into their daytime routines, chants of "Sieg Heil" from a radio broadcast break the silence they maintain to prevent being detected.[72]

The feeling of Jewish entrapment manifests itself throughout the film in the alternation between tedium and tension in the action and dialog. Scenes primarily occur within the four walls of the living room, cramped bedroom nooks, or the upper loft. The camera captures the sense of confinement by surveying the vertical floors of the building in stationary tilt shots. Whenever the Franks and van Daans peer out at the street or sky, their sightlines are framed by curtains, windowpanes, or the skylight, whose perimeter eventually consists of jagged edges of glass and whose interior space becomes crisscrossed by clotheslines that look like strands of barbed wire. Anxiety mounts when the threat the Germans pose to the Jews intrudes via radio broadcasts of Hitler's speeches and threatening, external noises like jackboots clattering on the pavement, bombs exploding during air raids, and police-car sirens.

The imminent peril facing Dutch Jews is underscored when Dussel joins the group hiding in the attic. Still wearing his Star of David, he excitedly tells them that "right here in Amsterdam every day hundreds of Jews disappear." He recounts how the police round up Jews by surrounding the blocks where they reside and conducting house-to-house searches. Jews failing to report for relocation are taken to Mauthausen, which Dussel calls "a death camp." Although Mauthausen was a labor camp, Dutch Jews considered it an extermination center because the 425 Jews deported there in 1941 as a reprisal for resistance perished.[73] Anne learns from Dussel that her best girlfriend has been sent to a camp too. That night Anne has a nightmare and envisions women inmates swaying listlessly while standing at attention. Anne recognizes her girlfriend among them. Gunshots awaken Anne who cries out, "Save me! Save me! Don't take me!"[74]

The charge that the play and movie minimized Anne's Jewish identity is predicated on an exaggeration of what her religiosity entailed. Anne simply hated the unfairness of anti-Semitism and believed that Jewish suffering and survival possessed a divine meaning.[75] When she despairs over Peter's lack of faith, she quickly adds that she is "not orthodox either" and finds value in any religion that "keeps a person on the right path . . . acting in accordance with his or her conscience."[76] As Lawrence Langer has pointed out, there is little in the diary beyond the passage about Chanukah to indicate that the Frank family observed other Jewish holidays.[77]

The Chanukah celebration in the play and movie is far more elaborate than Anne's diary entry about it: "We didn't make much fuss about Chanukah. We just gave each other a few little presents and then we had the candles."[78] Although the characters recite the blessings in English, implying they were speaking Dutch rather than Hebrew, the text is quite specific about the Jewish meaning of the holiday: "We kindle the Chanukah light to celebrate the great and wonderful deeds wrought through the zeal with which God filled the hearts of the heroic Maccabees, two thousand years ago. They fought against indifference, against tyranny, and oppression, and they restored our Temple to us."[79]

Although the diary does not mention whether any Chanukah songs were sung, one scholar condemns Goodrich and Hackett for translating the Hebrew hymn "Maoz Zur" into the English "Rock of Ages."[80] Actually, the characters sing an ecumenical rendition of "Chanukah, Oh Chanukah" after being terrified by a burglar who almost stumbles upon their hiding place. This ominous juxtaposition is reinforced visually by the explosions of a bombing raid dissolving into the flickering flames of the menorah candles.[81] Anne found Christmas Eve "much more fun." The next year, Anne wrote about celebrating Christmas and did not mention Chanukah.[82]

The finale of the movie has drawn the most vehement ire from Holocaust scholars. Twice—first in a conversation with Peter and then in a voice-over in the closing scene of gulls soaring through the clouds—Anne ostensibly neutralizes the tragic impact of the betrayal of her family and friends and the torment they will endure in the concentration camps by professing, "In spite of everything, I still believe that people are really good at heart." In the diary, Anne's credo is sandwiched between her admission of how easily her ideals could be shattered by the "horrible truth" and her premonition of the "approaching thunder which will destroy us too."[83] In the film, Peter worries that they are passively awaiting their arrest, and Anne qualifies her idealism by acknowledging "how difficult it is to have any faith, when people are doing such terrible things." When she tries to assure Peter that this turbulent phase in human history will pass, albeit after centuries, Peter finds little solace in her words: "I want to see something now. . . . Not a thousand years from now!" The menacing sound of the police siren momentarily drowns out the melodramatic background music. German soldiers pound on the door, ring the buzzer, and demolish the concealed entrance to the attic. Shouts of "Wo sind die Juden?" (Where are the Jews?) are heard. Otto Frank stoically counsels his family and friends to stop living in fear and start living in hope. The last image of the diary belies any happy outcome as the wind flips its pages from written sections to blank ones, which will remain empty because Anne will never return.[84]

Even if a particularly obtuse viewer had not comprehended that everyone died in the camps except for Anne's father, Otto's soliloquy in the ransacked attic establishes that he is the only survivor. Sheltered first between Miep and Kraler and then appearing alone in a close-up, Otto occupies the center of the screen. He relates how the men were sent to Auschwitz and the women to Belsen. In January 1945, he was liberated with the few "who were left." From there, he embarked on a journey back to Amsterdam.

Along the way, he queried former camp inmates about what happened to his loved ones. He gradually learned of their deaths. The day before his return to Amsterdam, he met a woman who confirmed that Anne had perished in Belsen. At this point, Anne's voice-over brightens the mood. Yet, the only light in this scene initially emanates from the skylight in the loft where Miep, Kraler, and Otto remain shrouded in shadows before the camera zooms in on the flying gulls and billowing clouds. The ending exhibits the dichotomy that runs through the movie, of Anne's optimism counterpoised with the death sentence that hung over Dutch Jews like her during World War II.[85]

Instead of judging Stevens's film on the basis of the kind of graphic realism expected in recent movies about the Holocaust, it needs to be compared to how American films produced between 1945 and 1959 handled the topic. From this vantage point, it stacks up well. From *The Stranger* and *The Search* in the late 1940s to *The Juggler* and *Singing in the Dark* in the 1950s, American directors explored the postwar problems resulting from the Holocaust like the prosecution of war criminals, the resettlement of displaced persons, and the psychological impact on survivors. *The Diary of Anne Frank* placed the dangers of Jewish existence in wartime Europe at the center of its narrative. It individualized a collective tragedy by embodying the fate of millions in a precocious teenager with whom audiences could identify.

Stevens did more than verbally or symbolically allude to the ordeal that awaited deported Jews. For the nightmare sequence, he inserted footage taken by the Germans in Auschwitz to foreshadow Anne's incarceration there. He initially considered ending the movie with a shot of Anne standing at attention with other inmates in a concentration camp but decided against this finale because he wanted to confine the action to the attic and the contents of the diary.[86]

Stevens's use of black and white endowed the film with a gloomy look that subliminally reminded the audience of newsreel documentaries and portended the dangers that encircled and eventually doomed the Franks and their friends. Ironically, he sometimes used color stock to photograph the liberation of the concentration camps. His reliance on black and white to convey a sense of documentary authenticity and avoid beautifying an ugly reality anticipated the aesthetic choice that many directors of Holocaust movies subsequently would make.[87]

The Diary of Anne Frank began the process of globalizing the Holocaust. It appeared in numerous translations, and the play was staged throughout the world. In Japan, Anne has become a beloved symbol of World War II, who conveniently overshadows that nation's tarnished record in the conflict.[88] The diary lends itself to various interpretations. Goodrich, Hackett, Kanin, and Stevens accentuated its perceptive portrayal of adolescence and condemnation of prejudice. Judith Doneson argued that the play and movie functioned as an allegory about McCarthyism and the human damage done by informers.[89] In 1958, East Germany released a semidocumentary entitled *A Diary for Anne Frank*, wherein the story of an actress rehearsing for Anne's role frames an exposé of West German corporations and politicians who had supported Hitler.[90] More than half of the subsequent movies about Anne are American productions, but British, Dutch, French, Irish, Japanese, and Yugoslavian studios have made renditions of the diary too.[91]

THE VENALITY OF EVIL: *THE SHOP ON MAIN STREET*
Directed by Ján Kadár and Elmar Klos
(Czechoslovakia: Filmové Studio Barrandov, 1965)

> The basis of violence consists for the most part of harmless, kind people who are indifferent toward brutality. Sooner or later these people may overcome their indifference, but then it is usually too late.[92]
>
> —Ján Kadár

The cinematic honors bestowed on *The Diary of Anne Frank* and its modest success demonstrated that a movie dealing with the Holocaust did not have to be so depressing that it would repel critics and audiences alike. The grisly details of genocide could loom in the background and be referenced verbally or visually in flashbacks and premonitions. The Holocaust presented a worst-case scenario of state discrimination, a message that resonated with audiences in a decade when the civil rights, antiwar, and student movements were at their peak. This helps account for the near doubling of the number of Holocaust films during this period (see table 2.1)

Many historians attribute the new American interest in the Holocaust during the 1960s to the extensive publicity surrounding Israel's trial of Adolf Eichmann in the first three years of the decade. The popularity of other books wholly or partially devoted to the Holocaust, like John Hersey's *The Wall* (1950), Leon Uris's *Exodus* (1958), and William Shirer's *The Rise and Fall of the Third Reich* (1960), indicate that the American public began gravitating toward this subject in the previous decade. To be sure, the Holocaust assumed a higher public profile due to the Eichmann trial, Rolf Hochhuth's controversial play *The Deputy* (1963), which accused Pope Pius XII of suppressing reports about the liquidation of deported Jews, and the West German trial of Auschwitz guards between 1963 and 1965. These accordingly sparked debates over the motivations of Nazi perpetrators, their guilt under international law, and the moral duty of leaders like the pope and ordinary citizens to defend innocent victims of oppression.[93]

The two most famous American Holocaust films of the 1960s continued the universalizing narrative strategies of their predecessors. Stanley Kramer's *Judgment at Nuremberg* (1961) employs the courtroom parrying between the defense and prosecution lawyers to present the American and German perspectives on individual culpability for abetting Hitler's crimes against humanity. The American attorney makes his case against several German judges by demonstrating how their rulings sanctioned the execution of a Jewish man convicted of making sexual advances to an Aryan girl and the sterilization of a feebleminded man incapable of forming a sentence out of three words. The extermination of "two-thirds of the Jews of Europe" is mentioned only to identify which groups comprised the victims seen in the atrocity footage screened during the trial. The German lawyer casts the burden of guilt more broadly by noting that the Soviet Union and Vatican signed treaties with the Third Reich, Winston Churchill admired Hitler's early accomplishments, and the United States practiced eugenic sterilization and dropped atomic bombs on Japan. Although the American judges convict the defendants, the epilogue reveals how quickly these sentences were commuted.[94]

Sidney Lumet's *The Pawnbroker* (1965) dared to reenact a Holocaust survivor's tormented memories of being in a deportation train and concentration camp. The scenes from the train and camp initially appear and disappear as barely perceptible jump cuts that gradually last longer and preoccupy the thoughts of Sol Nazerman. Lumet never disguises that Nazerman is Jewish. Yet, the portrayal of Nazerman as a cynical and unfeeling figure who loathes his impoverished customers in Harlem perpetuates the traditional anti-Semitic stereotype of the Jew as an avaricious usurer. As his twenty-fifth wedding anniversary approaches, Nazerman's repressed memories resurface when he rides a subway, witnesses a mugging, and is propositioned by a prostitute. This last event is crosscut with Nazerman's remembrance of watching his wife having intercourse with SS men, an improbable occurrence given the Nazis' abhorrence of "racial" defilement.

The viewer comes away believing that survivors are emotional cripples and that their persecution under Nazi rule was analogous to the plight of disadvantaged racial minorities in the United States. When his ambitious Puerto Rican assistant, Jesús, sacrifices himself to shield Nazerman from a bullet, Nazerman impales his hand on a spindle but cannot cry. The alternatives to Nazerman's icy indifference are the companionship offered to him by a lonely social worker and the protectiveness Jesús felt toward him. *The Pawnbroker* deserves its reputation as a cinematic classic on the basis of Rod Steiger's riveting performance as Nazerman, Lumet's stark vision of personal anguish and collective poverty, and Quincy Jones's evocative jazz score. Yet, the film's response to Nazerman's detachment is an endorsement of the liberal idealism of the United States in the 1960s. Lumet's conflation of American racial discrimination and Nazi extermination distorts the historical reality of each.[95]

The Holocaust films produced by the Eastern Bloc countries in the 1960s pose more convincing parallels between the existential dilemmas confronting individuals coping explicitly with wartime German domination and implicitly with postwar Soviet rule. The sharp increase in the numbers of such movies over the decade, from one to thirteen in Czechoslovakia, one to five in Hungary, and six to sixteen in Poland, indicates that these motion pictures functioned as contemporary political protests as well as historical period pieces. The death of Stalin in 1953 and Khrushev's promulgation of a "thaw" in his predecessor's repressive policies in 1956 contributed to a liberalization of state supervision of the Czech, Hungarian, and Polish film industries.[96] Until then, World War II had been pictured as a Russian-led defensive against Western capitalists who manipulated Hitler to crush communism and wage ideological and imperialistic wars.[97]

Collaboration with, or resistance to, the German occupation, however, could be perceived subversively as symbolizing individual accommodation or opposition to Soviet puppet regimes. To devote particular attention to the plight of the Jews challenged the Marxist shibboleth that religious identity represented a diversionary social construct that subordinated economic demands and working-class solidarity to the illusionary goals of eternal salvation and supernatural beliefs and rituals. Generating sympathy specifically for the Jews clashed with the official Soviet opposition to Zionism that emerged when the Soviet Union tilted toward support of the Arab countries against Israel from the 1950s on. By dealing with how their countries treated the Jews during World War II, directors in Soviet satellite countries reclaimed their national histories from the Soviet interpretation of the war.[98] The use of the Holocaust as a subplot in Felix Máriássy's *Springtime in Budapest* (1955) or as the primary story as in Zbynek Brynch's *Transport from Paradise* (1961) and Andrzej Wajda's *Samson* (1961) coincided with the rise of movements for political reform in Hungary in the 1950s and Czechoslovakia and Poland in the 1960s.[99]

The Shop on Main Street (1965) received more national and international recognition than any other film produced by a Soviet bloc country in this period. Its codirectors, Ján Kadár and Elmar Klos, had solid credentials in the Czech state-run film industry. Kadár's parents and sister had died in Auschwitz, but he "fortunately" had been interned in a work camp by the Hungarian occupiers of the region of Czechoslovakia where he resided. Klos participated in the postwar nationalization of Czech studios because he believed that public subsidization would free directors and screenwriters from the commercial considerations that usually dictated which films got produced. As the two exercised their artistic license as filmmakers in collaborative efforts, they were repeatedly censured for criticizing the corruption of the Czech bureaucracy and the political paranoia of the communist leadership. Disillusioned by the Czech show trials of dissidents in the early 1950s, the Soviet crackdown on Hungary in 1956, and official denunciations of their films, Kadár and Klos blamed the repressiveness of communism not on the system itself but on the individual officials who ordered or condoned its unjust policies.[100]

Thus, when Kadár and Klos made a film about the disenfranchisement and deportation of Jews from fascist Slovakia during World War II, they traced how an otherwise decent man's petty motives ultimately lead to the death of an elderly Jewish woman. As Kadár succinctly put it, *The Shop on Main Street* was not about "the Six Million, but the one."[101] The opening scene situates the relationship that will develop between Tono Britko, a poor apolitical carpenter, and Rosalie Lautmann, the deaf owner of a button store, within a historical framework. Christians dressed for church and a few Hasidic Jews promenade on a Sunday afternoon along the main boulevard of a bucolic village to the melody of a waltz played by a band performing on the village square. A prologue informs the audience that the Slovakian state carved out of Czechoslovakia by the Third Reich was the first German client state to take the initiative to introduce anti-Semitic policies based on the racial criteria of the Nuremberg Laws.[102] The American distributor of the movie provided no English translation of the prologue.[103]

The movie paints Tono as an innately passive person who is content to make his daily rounds and stay aloof from the politics of his community. Yet, he cannot even take a step before a train carrying soldiers and military equipment blocks him from walking across the tracks. Tono inverts the master-pet hierarchy by pulling the wagon in which his dog Brandy is riding. When he finally arrives home, his domineering wife, Evelyna, demands that Tono give her his earnings and reprimands him for accepting pigeons as part of his payment. She nags him to ask her brother-in-law Marcus, the local fascist chief, for a better job but doubts Tono will do this because he refuses even to salute Marcus. Tono heads off to town with Brandy typically walking in front of him. He cordially greets a Jewish man and chats with a Jewish barber about not getting involved in a "filthy business" the state is planning. This refers to the Aryanization of Jewish property.

At the town square, a group of craftsmen build a wooden tower symbolizing the arrogance of dictatorships in general. Evelyna had urged her husband in vain to apply for a work assignment on this project. His antifascist friend Kuchar calls it "the tower of Babel" and likens it to the pyramids of the pharaohs. Surrounded by his lackeys, the uniformed Marcus inspects the construction site. Kuchar contemptuously dubs Marcus a "little führer." Tono avoids speaking to Marcus and skulks home. Czech audiences in the 1960s understood that this critique of tyranny applied to their Soviet overlords too.

Marcus and his wife drop in unexpectedly and ply Tono and Evelyna with fine food and liquor. Their generosity turns out to be a prelude to appointing Tono the Aryan controller of Lautmann's button shop. Tono is justifiably suspicious of Marcus because he previously had swindled Tono out of his inheritance. But the lure of prosperity and pleasing Evelyna proves too much for him to resist. His lapse in judgment precedes events that illustrate how he has relinquished control of his life to Marcus. After prodding Tono to gulp down ten shots of whiskey, Marcus coaxes him to dance. Tono blurts out, "You're calling the tune." In this state of intoxication, Tono jumps on a chair, places a comb on his upper lip, and pretends he is Hitler. Kadár considered this the pivotal scene in the film because the co-optation of Tono "seems entirely normal."[104]

Awaking from a drunken stupor, Tono recalls dreaming about a white butterfly. His wife suggests it might have been a white flag. A scene of a white stork landing upon a spire, which was the first image in the film, recurs. The first two symbols normally are associated with fragility and peace. In Slavic cultures, storks represent both new life and communal responsibility for caring for them if they nest on public buildings.[105] These meanings are personified by Rosalie Lautmann, whose hair is white and who subsequently wears white pajamas and a white dress. She is frail and unaware that a war is raging or that the

Jewish community financially supports her because the sales from her store cannot. Although Tono tells her he owns her business and shows her the Aryanization certificate, her poor hearing and eyesight prevent her from understanding what he has said. She thinks that the Jewish community has hired Tono as her assistant. Kuchar persuades Tono to humor her in return for a salary paid by the town's Jews.

Rosalie's appreciation of Tono contrasts with his wife's disparaging treatment of him. Tono repairs furniture for Rosalie, and she cooks soup for him and gives him her dead husband's suit and hat. Donning this attire, he stares at his reflection in the mirror and notices that he looks like Charlie Chaplin. The identification with Chaplin marks Tono as being capable of good and evil. When Tono imitated Hitler earlier in the film, he resembled Chaplin's portrayal of the bombastic Adenoid Hynkel addressing a rally in *The Great Dictator* (1940). Like Chaplin's character, Tono in effect plays the role of a Jew too.[106] Indeed, a rabbi thanks him for fulfilling God's will by protecting Rosalie.

Tono's friendship with Lautmann cannot withstand the radicalization of Slovakian anti-Semitic policies. Marcus advises Tono to shun Kuchar, whom the police are hunting for being "a white Jew," an Aryan who helps Jews. When the barber warns of the impending deportation of the Jews, Tono is surprised by the turn of events. The barber considers it the culmination of what happens "when the law persecutes the innocent." Kuchar is captured, beaten, and forced to wear a sign that reads, "I am a white Jew." After declaring that Jews, Bolsheviks, and Freemasons will be liquidated, an officer from the Hlinka Guard, Slovakia's equivalent of the SS, marches the patrons of the town's inn to the "Tower of Victory" and reiterates the threat to "drive out the Yids." Hoping to hide her, Tono awakens Rosalie in the middle of the night. She thinks he has come there to sleep following a quarrel with his wife. The next morning, Jews assemble for deportation. Tono implores Rosalie to flee but changes his mind, worrying that he will be punished if she fails to report. Observing Jews encircled by armed members of the Hlinka Guard, Rosalie thinks a pogrom is in progress. When she insists that Tono close the shop because it is the Sabbath, he shoves her into a closet to prevent Marcus from seeing her. The push inadvertently kills her, and Tono atones by hanging himself.

Kadár and Klos append an ethereal, slow-motion sequence to the suicide scene. It hearkens back to the film's idyllic opening and a similar dream scene in which Tono imagines himself strolling through town with a younger incarnation of Rosalie. He sports Mr. Lautmann's suit and hat, and she wears a frilly white dress. They appear to be a happily married couple. Tono confesses to Rosalie that the wooden tower frightens him, and she responds that nightmares will cease to exist "when we stop frightening each other." In the last frames, they gently dance into the future. *New York Times* critic Bosley Crowther claimed that Kadár justified tacking on this sentimental ending to provide "a balm of spiritual uplift and hope that the horrible injustices committed against innocent people may bring some realization of the need for brotherhood."[107]

While this might have been what American audiences wanted to hear, Kadár's written statement about the film is far less optimistic: "*The Shop on Main Street*, in short, is an episode of high tragedy, a concentration of the world's absurdities, in which good, ignorant, and indecisive people like Britko enable 'force' to get a firm hold."[108] In a subsequent interview, he elaborated on the fatal consequences of the apathy epitomized by Tono: "We feel that no one may be excluded from the society in which he lives, and no one may be robbed of his rights as a human being. As soon as something like that can happen, anything can happen, thanks to the indifference of the bystanders."[109]

Like *The Diary of Anne Frank, The Shop on Main Street* foregrounds Tono's relationship with Rosalie and keeps the Holocaust in the background. Much of the film is funny since it revolves around the role reversal of the Aryan boss doing the bidding of his befuddled Jewish subordinate. Yet, Tono retains the power to spare or sacrifice a life. Rosalie's death prefigures the systematic mur-

Tono (Josef Kroner) urges Mrs. Lautmann (Ida Kaminska) to hide. The Shop on Main Street. *Press Kit, courtesy of the Nostalgia Factory.*

der of Jews just as Anne's nightmare did. The defenseless Jew is embodied by Rosalie, who literally hears and sees no evil. Characters' ages, rendering them either too young or too old to resist, and their gender, stereotypically female, often signify Jewish innocence and vulnerability in Holocaust films.[110]

The casting of the veteran Yiddish actress Ida Kaminska as Rosalie gives the film more of a Jewish flavor than *The Diary of Anne Frank*. Rosalie observes the Sabbath and prays when imperiled. Yet, other Jewish characters like the barber exhibit no distinctive Jewish traits. Kadár "intentionally attempted to erect a monument to all victims of persecution." Until Czech officials criticized his film as pro-Zionist in 1967, Kadár failed to recognize how deeply rooted anti-Semitism was in his homeland. After the Soviet invasion of Czechoslovakia in 1968, he fled to the United States where Hollywood studios hired him to direct movies with Jewish themes because *The Shop on Main Street* had won the Oscar for Best Foreign Language Film in 1965.[111]

MINISERIES, MAXI-IMPACT: *HOLOCAUST*
Directed by Marvin J. Chomsky
(United States: Titus Productions, 1978)

> Perhaps art will never be able to duplicate the absolute horror of such atrocities but if it cannot re-create at least a limited authentic image of that horror—and *Holocaust* does not—then audiences will remain as deceived about the *worst* as young Anne Frank's lingering words on the essential goodness of human nature deceive us about the best.[112]
>
> —Lawrence Langer

> While its [*Holocaust's*] faults were more a matter of erroneous details—no insignificant matter since misinformation can clearly lead to misconceptions—its chief significance lay in transmitting a comprehensive picture, on a grand scale, of the overwhelming enormity of the Holocaust and presenting it undilutedly as a Jewish event to an audience unprecedented in its massiveness.[113]
>
> —Jonathan and Judith Pearl

While the Civil Rights Act of 1965 removed the legal barriers to the full equality of American Jewry, the emergence of the black-power movement, feminism, and the policy of affirmative action challenged the traditional ideal of the United States as an egalitarian melting pot that inevitably would rectify ethnic, gender, racial, and religious inequalities. For Jews, the Six Day's War of 1967 served as a source of both Jewish pride over Israel's stunning victory and concern over the prospects for its long-term survival as a tiny country surrounded by enemies. Support for Israel generated tensions with African American and various Third World radicals who embraced the cause of the Palestinian Arabs and considered Israel an agent of Western imperialism. By the end of the decade, it had become acceptable for the diverse communities in the United States to cultivate their unique customs and histories rather than minimize their distinctiveness for the sake of national unity.[114] Movies like *Fiddler on the Roof* (1971) and *Hester Street* (1975) evoked nostalgia for the Eastern European origins of many American Jews and paved the way for motion pictures that portrayed the Holocaust as the ultimate Jewish tragedy.[115]

As the multicultural paradigm for American ethnic, racial, and religious diversity developed, memoirs, novels, histories, and theological reflections about the Holocaust contemporaneously gained an increasing readership. During the 1960s, Elie Wiesel's autobiographical and fictional works grew in popularity. Scholars credit Wiesel with popularizing the term *Holocaust*, if not inventing it. By 1972, his first three novels were issued together as a trilogy.[116] Similarly, the psychological analyses of concentration camp behavior by survivors Viktor Frankl and Bruno Bettelheim merited multiple editions in the years following their release in 1959 and 1960.[117] Richard Rubenstein's *After Auschwitz* (1966) contended that the Holocaust had rendered Jewish faith in a benevolent and omnipotent God obsolete. By 1970, philosopher Emil Fackenheim formulated a 614th commandment arising from the ashes of Auschwitz that obligated Jews to assure the survival of the Jewish people and Judaism to prevent Hitler from winning a posthumous victory over both.[118] Raul Hilberg's *The Destruction of the European Jews* came out in 1961. Drawing primarily on captured German documents, Hilberg traced how the Final Solution resulted from a wartime escalation of German bureaucratic and legislative efforts to deal with the "Jewish problem" in the 1930s.[119] Seven years later, Nora Levin entitled her book about the Jewish genocide *The Holocaust*.[120] In 1975, Lucy Dawidowicz wrote the bestseller *The War against the Jews*.[121]

In the same period, new nonfiction books and documentaries about hitherto neglected aspects of the Holocaust soon inspired the plots of feature films. A few examples of this process should suffice. Between 1968 and 1974, four works exposing the failure of the United States to liberalize its immigration quotas or mount a rescue program to save Jews from Nazi persecution appeared. The last one published focused on the futile attempt of 937 German Jews on the ocean liner *St. Louis* to land first in Cuba and then in the United States rather than return to Germany in 1939. It became the basis of the British epic *Voyage of the Damned* (1976).[122] One of the few bright spots in the history of the Holocaust, the rescue of the Jews in Denmark, was the subject of two television programs and two books released in the 1960s. In 1970, a Danish

American feature-length film, *The Only Way*, depicted how several key figures organized the flotilla that ferried most of Denmark's Jews to Sweden in 1943.[123]

In France, Marcel Ophuls remarkable documentary *The Sorrow and the Pity* (1969) shattered the myth of widespread French resistance to the German occupation and collaborationist Vichy government.[124] Robert Paxton's 1972 monograph on the role of Vichy officials in drafting anti-Semitic laws and furnishing police to arrest Jews for deportation from France in the summer of 1942 corroborated charges leveled by Ophuls.[125] A string of French feature films like *Les Violons du Bal* (1973), *Lacombe Lucien* (1974), *Stavisky* (1974), *Special Section* (1975), and *Mr. Klein* (1975) followed and exposed the anti-Semitic, authoritarian, and xenophobic undercurrents in French society that the postwar consensus had dismissed as ideologies foisted on the country by Germany.[126]

The number of Italian productions about the Holocaust jumped from five during the 1960s to sixteen during the 1970s. Moreover, Italian studios teamed up with companies from other countries, particularly France, to make nine additional films dealing with Nazi oppression and Italian collaboration. Films like Luchino Visconti's *The Damned* (1969) and Bernardo Bertolucci's *The Conformist* (1971) attribute the susceptibility to obey powerful leaders and inflict violence on dissidents and minorities to an individual's psychological need to shore up a declining social status or conceal a shameful sexual deviancy.[127]

Italian memoirs, novels, and scholarship about Mussolini's promulgation of racial laws in 1938 and the participation of Italian officials and police in the German-instigated deportations of the Jews commencing in the fall of 1943 provided the impetus for the making of movies like Carlo Lizzani's *The Gold of Rome* (1961) and Vittorio De Sica's Oscar-winning *The Garden of the Finzi Continis* (1970).[128] The last film marked a return to adaptations of novels, a genre many postwar Italian directors initially avoided in favor of a semidocumentary approach that realistically portrayed contemporary events and social issues. In the 1950s, leading Italian filmmakers emulated the French auteur school, insisting on the centrality of the cinematic vision of the director rather than replicating a literary source. The revival of the adaptation in *The Garden of the Finzi Continis* proved how powerfully the verbal could be rendered in images and sounds as well as plot. The opulent garden and mansion of the upper-class Finzi Continis shield members of the family from an awareness of the threat anti-Semitism poses to their equality as Italian citizens and privileged social status afforded by their wealth. The debilitating illness of Alberto and the sexual promiscuity of his sister foreshadow the extinction of the family. The Finzi Continis consider less affluent Jews their peers only when they are forced to share a schoolroom where they await deportation. The closing scene evokes their fate with images of the withered garden, overgrown grass tennis court, and locked front gate to the villa, along with the recitation of the Jewish mourning prayer and names of Nazi death camps.[129]

The majority of the Italian Holocaust films from this period exploited the degradation and dehumanization of concentration camp prisoners pornographically, earning them the epithet "the nasties." Pornography achieved a modicum of respectability in the 1970s as a consequence of the free speech, women's liberation, and hippy movements. Although stereotypes of the German dominatrix and perverted brown-shirted storm troopers dated back to the Weimar Republic, and further in the case of the former, they inspired a genre of movies about Nazis who use concentration and death camps as brothels and laboratories for sexual experiments and torture. The best known of these "pornocaust" pictures was the American production *Ilse: She Wolf of the SS* (1974).[130] Yet, it was Italian studios that churned out most of such movies, which bore titles like *Salon Kitty* (1975), *Deported Women of the SS Special Section* (1976), *The Gestapo's Last Orgy* (1976), and *SS Bordello* (1978). The exercise of arbitrary sexual power over passive victims also appeared in the plotlines of more respectable Italian films like Liliana Cavani's *The Night Porter* (1974), which examines how a surviving inmate and her former guard compulsively repeat the coerced sexual relationship they developed in the camp. In Lina Wertmüller's black comedy *Seven Beauties* (1975), a petty crook once obsessed with defending the honor of his sisters is so dehumanized in a concentration camp that he consents to have intercourse with a repulsively obese female commandant in order to save his life.[131]

These pornocaust films share one trait with the movies adapted from literary pieces or original screenplays: they were fictional. During the 1960s and 1970s, less than a quarter of the films dealing with Holocaust themes drew on memoirs or historical accounts for their stories. *Cabaret* (1972) demonstrated how theatrical even real occurrences could become when they were reworked for the stage and screen. Christopher Isherwood's autobiographical *Berlin Stories* inspired the play and movie *I Am a Camera* back in the 1950s. Bob Fosse turned Isherwood's book into a Broadway musical and hit film. The songs and dances of *Cabaret* function as projections of the anti-Semitism, cultural backlash, militarism, and political polarization that would sweep Hitler into office in 1933. *Cabaret*'s engaging performances, flashy choreography, imaginative editing, and strong musical score made it the most honored and financially successful American feature film of the 1970s to deal with the Nazi era.[132]

One cause of the shift from fictional to factual sources in Holocaust films was the entry of the major television networks into the production of movies in the 1970s. This phenomenon resumed an older trend of adapting real Holocaust stories for the dramatic showcases and religious series broadcast on television during the 1950s and 1960s.[133] Previously, the television networks had waited a year or two after the premier of feature films before paying hefty royalties to the movie studios to air them. For budgetary reasons, the networks started making their own movies in the 1970s. The movie-of-the-week (MOW) format proved a fertile venue for docudramas about recent news stories and historical events.[134] According to Steven Lipkin, situating the actions of an individual or a group of characters within the backdrop of a real event creates "a sense of closeness to that history, an access made possible by rendering chaotic, destructive horrors understandable as essentially domestic conflicts escalated to vastly larger social scales." "Proximity to the factual," he adds, anchors the "artistic vision within the sober ground of historical actuality, suggesting at the same time that good has come out of suffering, that justice has prevailed, that as it must in melodrama, some order has been restored to a chaotic universe"[135] (see table 2.2).

Drawing upon the serial format of *Masterpiece Theatre* and television soap operas, network executives expanded the docudrama into the miniseries, a saga broadcast over several days or weeks that chronicled the impact of historical events on the fortunes of an individual, a family, or generations of their relatives. ABC's adaptation of Alex Haley's popular book *Roots* into an eight-part, twelve-hour miniseries set the standard for this genre. Beginning with the abduction and sale of an African youth named Kunta Kinte into slavery in the eighteenth century, it followed how Kinte and his descendents fared as slaves in the American South until their liberation by the Civil War. Eighty million people watched at least one of the first seven episodes, and one hundred million saw the last installment. An estimated 85 percent of television households tuned into part or all of *Roots*. It swept the Emmy Awards that year and spawned scores of high school units and college courses on slavery and its impact on African American history.[136]

NBC broadcast the nine-and-a-half-hour miniseries *Holocaust* over four consecutive nights in April 1978 to capitalize on the success of *Roots*. Although covering a span of only ten years from 1935 until 1945, the program frames

Table 2.2.   Sources of Holocaust Feature Films

Years	Factual (%)	Fictional (%)
1945–1949	29	71
1950–1959	28	72
1960–1969	26	74
1970–1979	27	73
1980–1989	40	60
1990–1999	43	57

the experiences of a German Jewish family, their Gentile relatives through in-termarriage, and a key official in the SS Department of Jewish Affairs within the context of the evolution of the Final Solution. Seeking to boost its audi-ence ratings, NBC billed the movie as a *Big Event* special. It prepared the na-tion to watch the film by distributing study guides to teachers and civic and religious organizations. Two weeks before the broadcast, an inexpensive paper-back novel based on the script hit the racks of bookstores. NBC scheduled ad-vance screenings for members of the clergy so that they could discuss the movie at services the weekend before the first installment was aired.[137] NBC hired the senior director of *Roots*, Marvin Chomsky, the producer of the tele-play *Judgment at Nuremberg*, Herbert Brodkin, and the veteran novelist Gerald Green, whose novel *The Last Angry Man* had been adapted into a feature film and television movie.[138] Green already had read extensively on the Holocaust while researching his nonfiction book about the clandestine paintings and children's drawings created in Theresienstadt.[139]

Green structured the narrative of *Holocaust* around an assimilated German Jewish family, the Weiss family, rather than a religiously orthodox Eastern Eu-ropean Jewish family, since the values and lifestyle of the former were like those of the American middle-class audience that was expected to watch the mini-series.[140] The movie opens with the Weiss family celebrating the marriage of their eldest son, Karl, to a Catholic woman, Inga Helms. Karl's father, Josef, apologizes to his brother Moses about the lack of Jewish rituals at the wedding. The men of the Helms family, particularly one wearing a swastika pin, worry about a pending ban against mixed marriages. Inga's brother Hans proudly wears his army uniform and converses with Mrs. Weiss's father, a decorated World War I veteran whose patriotic record is unimpeachable. The die is cast. Nazi anti-Semitism will obviously separate Karl and Inga and strain the ties between the Weiss and Helms families. When Karl is imprisoned in Buchenwald, Inga's fam-ily pressures her to get divorced. She remains loyal by sheltering Karl's mother and sister, prostituting herself to get letters delivered to him, and engineering her own arrest so that she can be with him after his transfer to the artist's work-shop at Theresienstadt. Rudi Weiss, Karl's younger brother, knows little about Judaism, but flees Berlin, marries an ardent Zionist, joins a Jewish partisan band, and participates in the uprising at the death camp Sobibor. The Germans de-port Josef to the Warsaw ghetto, then to Auschwitz. At both places, he is con-veniently reunited with his wife, Berta. His brother Moses reprises the liberat-ing role of his biblical namesake by joining the revolt in the Warsaw ghetto.

Green modeled the leading Nazi character, Erik Dorf, after Hilberg's study of SS bureaucrats and Hannah Arendt's characterization of Adolf Eich-mann. Dorf epitomizes Arendt's concept of the "banality of evil." He becomes mired in the mechanics of genocide not because he is a fanatical anti-Semite but because he needs a job and finds that the SS awards rapid promotions to those most adept at devising efficient methods to stigmatize, segregate, and slaughter Jews. Dorf excels in coining innocuous sounding terms to mask the murderous intent behind Germany's policies against the Jews. Although Green portrays Dorf as an opportunist, he introduces incidents that underscore Dawidowicz's thesis that the "persistent, unchanging, ultimate goal of the Nazi movement was the destruction of the Jews."[141]

Holocaust employs several hackneyed subplots designed to tug at the audience's heartstrings. As discussed in chapter 4, the *Romeo and Juliet* theme represented by Peter and Inga has a long history in Holocaust films. What better way to show the human toll of prejudice than by tearing couples apart? The marriage between Rudi and Helena is doomed from the beginning. Their marriage scene resembles the wedding from *Fiddler on the Roof* (1971), which ends in a pogrom. After Rudi and Helena exchange vows, German troops discover their partisan encampment and the newlyweds flee into the forest. Helena subsequently dies in an ambush. It is left to Rudi to fulfill Helena's Zionist dream of settling in Israel. Although Karl succumbs to illness as the Germans evacuate Auschwitz, he lives on through a son born to Inga. Neither of these developments compensates for the deaths of all the other main Jewish characters. Dorf, like Hermann Goering, commits suicide, cheating a war-crimes tribunal of the opportunity to judge him.

Despite its blatant melodramatic effects, *Holocaust* never degenerates entirely into a soap opera. The subplots remain firmly rooted in historical reality. Some characters like Erik Dorf are composites based on the lives of several historical figures. The invented characters respond to actual events and interact with the individuals who organized the Jewish resistance movements like Abba Kovner and Mordecai Anielewicz or directed the Final Solution like Adolf Eichmann, Heinrich Himmler, Reinhard Heydrich, and Ernst Kaltenbrunner. If the reenactments of events like the Babi Yar massacre or the Warsaw ghetto revolt seem too staged and sanitized to be convincing, the recurring insertion of photographs snapped either by the Germans during the war or the Allies afterward keeps reminding the viewer that the Holocaust happened, even if the miniseries bearing its name mixes fact with fiction. The concern expressed by scholars like Bill Nichols that docudramas blur the distinction between documentaries and feature films strikes me as overly alarmist. Only an extremely unsophisticated viewer could ignore the commercial interruptions, the professional quality of the acting, and the contrivances that link all of the characters together.[142]

Holocaust engaged the viewer's emotions with engrossing stories of individuals and families whose choices and loyalties are tested by momentous historical forces. Its scope included these events: the Nuremberg Laws of 1935, the *Kristallnacht* pogrom of 1938, the euthanasia program, the ghettoization of Jews, experimentation with different ways of killing Jews from carbon monoxide fumes, mass shootings, and gassings with cyanide, the massacres of Jews during the invasion of the Soviet Union, the role of the Jewish councils in enforcing German decrees, the Wannsee Conference, the Warsaw ghetto and Sobibor rebellions, the Red Cross inspection of Theresienstadt, the Jewish resistance in Eastern Europe, the Allied trials of German officials, and the immigration of many Jewish survivors to Palestine. Frank Rich observed, "Were the show exhibited in movie theaters, no one would sit still for its 9½-hour running time. Were it produced for PBS [public television], *Holocaust* would be drowned in a sea of historical minutiae. By creating their show for NBC, the authors have forced themselves to be equally responsive to the demands of both prime-time show biz and historical accuracy."[143]

One sign of the growing awareness of the Holocaust was the strident debate over whether the miniseries exploited the event to raise network profits and ratings. Nothing remotely resembling this outcry had been occasioned by the release of *The Diary of Anne Frank* in 1959. Indeed, the director of the Jewish Film Advisory Board commended Stevens for rendering Anne's story more "universal" than the play and preventing it from becoming "an outdated Jewish tragedy by less creative or more emotional handling."[144] Critics accused NBC of trivializing the Holocaust by committing factual errors, disrupting the narrative with inappropriate commercials, rationalizing Dorf's complicity, and transforming, as Elie Wiesel put it, "an ontological event into soap-opera."[145]

The defenders of *Holocaust* praised the program for reaching an audience estimated at 120 million Americans who would have remained uninformed about the history of the Holocaust.[146] The results of a poll conducted by the American Jewish Committee indicated that 60 percent of the respondents felt watching *Holocaust* enabled them to better understand Hitler's treatment of the Jews. More Christian than Jewish viewers, and younger than older viewers, answered this question affirmatively. Three-quarters of interviewed viewers believed that the series provided "an accurate picture of Nazi anti-Semitic policies." Although scholars and survivors criticized the sanitized depictions of the violence perpetrated against the Jews, 46 percent of the viewers polled found parts of the movie "difficult and disturbing" to watch. The only negative finding in the poll was that almost half of those questioned blamed the Jewish victims for not resisting German policies sufficiently. These viewers focused on scenes of Jewish compliance with Nazi orders and overlooked the segments about Jewish partisans, the Warsaw Ghetto Uprising, and the Sobibor escape.[147] If anything, *Holocaust* showcased a greater range of Jewish responses to persecution than had *The Diary of Anne Frank* and *The Shop on Main Street*.

The favorable reception to *Holocaust* influenced President Jimmy Carter's decision to establish a Holocaust commission, which eventually recommended the building of the U.S. Holocaust Memorial Museum.[148] In West Germany, the broadcast of the series in 1979 turned public opinion against the pending abolition of the statute of limitations on murder. Without this shift, the country would have rejected the measure that authorized continued prosecutions of Nazi war criminals.[149] The capitalized term *Holocaust* has since become synonymous with the genocide of European Jewry. When written with a small "h," it implies terrible human rights abuses.[150] By popularizing images and events from the Shoah, the miniseries enabled future filmmakers to depict it more graphically, as Steven Spielberg did in *Schindler's List*, or less realistically, as Roberto Benigni would do in *Life Is Beautiful*. In the recent French comedy *God Is Great and I'm Not*, a woman earnestly rejects her boyfriend's insistence that she use the term *Shoah* instead of *Holocaust* by declaring, "That series was called *Holocaust*. TV is serious stuff."[151]

NOTES

1. Alan Mintz, *Popular Culture and the Shaping of Holocaust Memory* (Seattle: University of Washington, 2001), 40.

2. Robert H. Abzug, *Inside the Vicious Heart: Americans and the Liberation of Nazi Concentration Camps* (New York: Oxford University Press, 1985).

3. Barbie Zelizer, *Remembering to Forget: Holocaust Memory through the Camera's Eyes* (Chicago: University of Chicago Press, 1998), 1–85.

4. David Wyman, *The Abandonment of the Jews: America and the Holocaust, 1941–1945* (New York: Pantheon Books, 1985), 326.

5. Lawrence Douglas, *The Memory of Judgment: Making Law and History in the Trials of the Holocaust* (New Haven, CT: Yale University Press, 2001), 11–37; Zelizer, *Remembering*, 86–140; Caroline Joan Picart and Jason Grant McKahan, "Visualizing the Holocaust in Gothic Terms: The Ideology of the U.S. Signal Corps Cinematography," in Caroline Joan Picart, *Documentary and Propaganda*, Vol. 2 of *The Holocaust Film Sourcebook* (Westport, CT: Praeger, 2004), 508–15.

6. David S. Wyman, "The United States," in *The World Reacts to the Holocaust*, ed. Charles H. Rosenzveig and David S. Wyman (Baltimore: Johns Hopkins University Press, 1996), 716. Also see Michael Marrus, "The Holocaust at Nuremberg," *Yad Vashem Studies* 26 (1998): 5–41.

7. Rosenzveig and Wyman, *The World Reacts*; Judith Miller, *One by One: Facing the Holocaust* (New York: Simon and Schuster, 1990).

8. Henry Greenspan, *On Listening to Holocaust Survivors: Recounting and Life History* (Westport, CT: Praeger, 1998); Aaron Hass, *The Aftermath: Living with the Holocaust* (New York: Cambridge University Press, 1995); Lawrence Langer, *Holocaust Testimonies: The Ruins of Memory* (New Haven, CT: Yale University Press, 1991).

9. Judith Tydor Baumel, *Kibbutz Buchenwald: Survivors and Pioneers* (New Brunswick, NJ: Rutgers University Press, 1996); Tom Segev, *The Seventh Million: The Israelis and the Holocaust*, trans. Haim Watzman (New York: Hill and Wang, 1993); Judith Zertal, *From*

Catastrophe to Power: Holocaust Survivors and the Emergence of Israel (Berkeley: University of California Press, 1997).

10. Lucy Dawidowicz, *The Holocaust and the Historians* (Cambridge, MA: Harvard University Press, 1981), 4–19; Mintz, *Popular Culture,* 3–16; Peter Novick, *The Holocaust in American Life* (Boston: Houghton Mifflin, 1999), 63–102.

11. Zvi Gitelman, ed., *Bitter Legacy: Confronting the Holocaust in the USSR* (Bloomington: Indiana University Press, 1997); Joshua D. Zimmerman, ed., *Contested Memories: Poles and Jews during the Holocaust and Its Aftermath* (New Brunswick, NJ: Rutgers University Press, 2003).

12. Mordechai Altshuler, "Jewish Holocaust Commemoration Activity in the USSR under Stalin," *Yad Vashem Studies* 30 (2002): 271–95.

13. Ilya Ehrenburg and Vasily Grossman, eds. *The Black Book: The Ruthless Murder of Jews by German-Fascist Invaders throughout the Temporarily-Occupied Regions of the Soviet Union and in the Death Camps of Poland during the War of 1941–1945,* trans. John Glad and James S. Levine (New York: Holocaust Publications, 1981).

14. Arnold Krammer, *The Forgotten Friendship: Israel and the Soviet Bloc, 1947–1953* (Urbana: University of Illinois Press, 1974).

15. *The Last Stop* (a.k.a. *The Last Stage*), directed by Wanda Jakubowska (Poland, 1947); Hanno Loewy, "The Mother of All Holocaust Films? Wanda Jacubowska's Auschwitz Triology," *Historical Journal of Film, Radio, and Television* 24, no. 2 (June 2004): 179–204.

16. Annette Insdorf, *Indelible Shadows: Film and the Holocaust,* 3rd ed. (New York: Cambridge University Press, 2003), 144–48; Ilan Avisar, *Screening the Holocaust* (Bloomington: Indiana University Press, 1988), 35–38.

17. *Border Street,* directed by Aleksander Ford (Poland, 1948). Avisar, *Screening the Holocaust,* 38–41.

18. *Distant Journey,* directed by Alfred Radok (Czechoslovakia, 1949).

19. H. G. Adler, *Theresienstadt 1941–1945,* (Tübingen: Mohr, 1955); Zdenck Lederer, *Ghetto Theresienstadt,* trans. K. Weisskopf (London: E. Goldston, 1953); Norbert Troller, *Theresienstadt: Hitler's Gift to the Jews,* trans. Susan E. Cernyak-Spatz (Chapel Hill: University of North Carolina Press, 1991).

20. Alfred Radok, quoted in Antonín J. Liehm, *Closely Watched Films: The Czechoslovak Experience* (White Plaines, NY: International Arts and Sciences Press, Inc., 1974), 35–52.

21. *Between Yesterday and Tomorrow,* directed by Harald Braun (Germany, 1947); Robert R. Shandley, *Rubble Films: German Cinema in the Shadow of the Third Reich* (Philadelphia: Temple University Press, 2001), 64–71.

22. *The Murderers Are among Us,* directed by Wolfgang Staudte (Germany, 1946).

23. Shandley, *Rubble Films,* 25–46; Robert C. Reimer and Carol J. Reimer, *Nazi-Retro Film: How German Narrative Cinema Remembers the Past* (New York: Twayne, 1992), 15–18; Ulrike Weckel, "The *Mitläufer* in Two German Postwar Films: Representation and Critical Reception," *History and Memory* 15, no. 2 (Fall/Winter 2003): 64–93.

24. Judith E. Doneson, *The Holocaust in American Film,* 2nd ed. (Syracuse, NY: Syracuse University Press, 2001), 49–56; Mintz, *Popular Culture,* 3–10. This viewpoint is also

articulated in the documentary *Imaginary Witness: Hollywood and the Holocaust*, directed by Daniel Anker (United States, 2004).

25. *Sealed Verdict,* directed by Lewis Allen (United States, 1948); *Berlin Express*, directed by Jacques Tourneur (United States, 1948).

26. Benjamin L. Alpers, *Dictators, Democracy, and American Public Culture: Envisioning the Totalitarian Enemy, 1920s–1950s* (Chapel Hill: University of North Carolina Press, 2003), 188–219.

27. *The Stranger,* directed by Orson Welles (United States, 1946).

28. Orson Welles and Peter Bogdanovich, *This Is Orson Welles*, ed. Jonathan Rosenbaum (New York: Harper Collins, 1992), 186–90; Palmer R. Barton, "The Politics of Genre in Welles' *The Stranger*," *Film Criticism* 9, no. 2 (Winter 1984–1985), 2–14; Peter Conrad, *Orson Welles: The Stories of His Life* (London: Faber and Faber, 2003), 223–28.

29. Rosenbaum, *This Is Orson Welles,* 189.

30. Marchael Barson and Steven Heller, *Red Scared! The Commie Menace in Propaganda and Popular Culture* (San Francisco: Chronicle Books, 2001); Ronnie D. Lipschutz, *Cold War Fantasies: Film, Fiction, and Foreign Policy* (Lanham, MD: Rowman & Littlefield, 2001).

31. Raphael Lemkin, *Axis Rule in Occupied Europe* (Washington, DC: Carnegie Endowment for International Peace, Division of International Law, 1944); Samantha Power, *"A Problem from Hell": America and the Age of Genocide* (New York: Basic Books, 2002), 17–65.

32. Mark Wyman, *DP: Europe's Displaced Persons, 1945–1951* (Philadelphia: Balch Institute Press, 1989).

33. Angelika Königseder and Juliane Wetzel, *Waiting for Hope: Jewish Displaced Persons in Post-World War II Germany*, trans. John A. Broadwin (Evanston, IL: Northwestern University Press, 2001), 9–53.

34. Leonard Dinnerstein, *America and the Survivors of the Holocaust* (New York: Columbia University Press), 39–99.

35. Yehuda Bauer, *Flight and Rescue: Brichah* (New York: Random House, 1970); Arieh J. Kochavi, *Post-Holocaust Politics: Britain, the United States, and Jewish Refugees, 1945–1948* (Chapel Hill: University of North Carolina Press, 2001); Abram Leon Sachar, *The Redemption of the Unwanted: From the Liberation of the Death Camps to the Founding of Israel* (New York: St. Martin's Press, 1983).

36. *Our Children*, directed by Natan Gross (Poland, 1946); Ira Konigsberg, *"Our Children* and the Limits of Cinema: Early Jewish Responses to the Holocaust," *Film Quarterly* 52, no. 1 (1998): 11–18; Lawrence Langer, *Preempting the Holocaust* (New Haven, CT: Yale University Press, 1998), 157–65.

37. *Long Is the Road*, directed by Herbert Fredersdorf, Marek Goldstein, and Israel Becker (U.S. Occupation Zone of Germany, 1947). Eric A. Goldman, *Visions, Images, and Dreams: Yiddish Film Past and Present* (Teaneck, NJ: Ergo Media, Inc., 1979), 143–46.

38. *My Father's House*, directed by Herbert Kline (Palestine and United States, 1946); *The Great Promise*, directed by Joseph Lejtes (Palestine, 1947); *The Illegals*, directed by Meyer Levin (United States, 1947); *Tomorrow's a Wonderful Day*, directed by Helmar Lerski (Israel and United States, 1948).

39. *Sword in the Desert*, directed by George Sherman (United States, 1949); *Exodus*, directed by Otto Preminger (United States, 1960); *Cast a Giant Shadow*, directed by Melville Shavelson (United States, 1966); Omer Bartov, *The "Jew" in Cinema: From the Golem to Don't Touch My Holocaust* (Bloomington: Indiana University Press, 2005), 188–204; Michelle Mart, "Tough Guys and American Cold War Policy: Images of Israel," *Diplomatic History* 20, no. 3 (Summer 1996): 357–80. Also see Caroline Joan Picart and Jeneen K. Surrency, "Documenting the DP Camp," in Picart, *Holocaust Film Sourcebook*, 2:94–100.

40. Dwight David Eisenhower, quoted in Sachar, *Redemption of the Unwanted*, 165.

41. Insdorf, *Indelible Shadows*, 347–48; Avisar, *Screening the Holocaust*, 202. Anker features a clip from it in *Imaginary Witness*.

42. Neil Sinyard, *Fred Zinnemann: Films of Character and Conscience* (Jefferson, NC: McFarland and Co., 2003), 171–78.

43. Sinyard, *Fred Zinnemann*, 1–30; Fred Zinnemann, *A Life in the Movies: An Autobiography* (New York: Charles Scribner's Sons, 1992), 7–55.

44. Sinyard, *Fred Zinnemann*, 31–32; Zinnemann, *A Life*, 56–73; Thérèse Bonney, *Europe's Children* (New York: Plantin Press, 1943).

45. Sara R. Horowitz, *Voicing the Void: Muteness and Memory in Holocaust Fiction* (Albany: State University of New York Press, 1997).

46. Claudia Sternberg, "Real Life References in Four Fred Zinnemann Films," in *The Films of Fred Zinnemann: Critical Perspectives*, ed. Arthur Nolletti Jr. (Albany: State University of New York Press, 1999), 200–204.

47. See the photograph of the filming of this scene in *Zinnemann, A Life*, 71.

48. Herb, "*The Search*," *Variety* (March 24, 1948).

49. Jeffrey C. Alexander, "On the Social Construction of Moral Universals: The 'Holocaust' from War Crime to Trauma Drama," in *Cultural Trauma and Collective Identity*, ed. Jeffrey Alexander et al. (Berkeley: University of California Press 2004), 219–20.

50. Fred Zinnemann, "Different Perspective," *Sight and Sound* 17, no. 67 (Autumn 1948): 113. Zinnemann's next film, *Act of Violence* (United States, 1948), was about the attempt of a former POW to exact revenge from a fellow POW who had betrayed him during their captivity in a German camp.

51. "Awards," *The Search*, at www.imdb.com/title/tt0040765/awards.

52. Bruno Bettelheim, "The Ignored Lesson of Anne Frank," *Harper's Magazine* (November 1960): 45–50.

53. Ernst Pawel, "Fiction of the Holocaust," *Midstream: A Monthly Jewish Journal* 16, no. 6 (June/July 1970): 17.

54. *Kapo*, directed by Gillo Pontecorvo (Italy, 1959); Avisar, *Screening the Holocaust*, 41–47.

55. *Judgment at Nuremberg*, directed by George Roy Hill (United States, 1959); Jeffrey Shandler, *While America Watches: Televising the Holocaust* (New York: Oxford University Press, 1999), 69–79; *Verboten*, directed by Samuel Fuller (United States, 1958); Samuel Fuller, *A Third Face: My Tale of Writing, Fighting, and Filmmaking* (New York: Alfred A. Knopf, 2002), 354–74.

56. Anne Frank, *The Diary of a Young Girl*, trans. B. M. Mooyaaart (Garden City, NY: Doubleday, 1952).

57. *Anne Frank: The Diary of a Young* Girl, directed by Martin Hoade (United States, 1952); Shandler, *While America Watches*, 62–64.

58. Lawrence Graver, *An Obsession with Anne Frank: Meyer Levin and the Diary* (Berkeley: University of California Press, 1995); Ralph Melnick, *The Stolen Legacy of Anne Frank: Meyer Levin, Lillian Hellman, and the Staging of the Diary* (New Haven, CT: Yale University Press, 1997); Judith Doneson, "The American History of Anne Frank's Diary," in *Anne Frank: Reflections on Her Life and Legacy,* ed. Hyman Aaron Enzer and Sandra Solotaroff-Enzer (Urbana: University of Illinois Press, 2000), 123–38.

59. Ernst Schnabel, *Anne Frank: A Portrait in Courage*, trans. Richard Winston and Clara Winston (New York: Harcourt, Brace, and World, 1958).

60. Louis de Jong, "The Girl Who Was Anne Frank," *Reader's Digest* 74, no. 426 (October 1957): 115–20; Ernst Schnabel, "A Tragedy Revealed: Heroine's Last Days," *Life* 45, no. 7 (August 18, 1958): 78–90.

61. *Nazi Concentration Camps*, directed by George C. Stevens (United States, 1945); *George Stevens, a Filmmaker's Journey*, directed by George Stevens Jr. (United States, 1945); *George Stevens: D-Day to Berlin* (United States and United Kingdom, 1994); Paul Cronin, ed., *George Stevens: Interviews* (Jackson, MS; 2004); Marilyn Ann Moss, *Giant: George Stevens, a Life on Film* (Madison, WI: Terrace Books, 2004), 114–18.

62. Excerpt, *George Stevens: A Filmmaker's Journey*, George Stevens Press Conference, Millie Perkins Screen Test, and Movietone newsreel clip on the selection of Millie Perkins to play Anne Frank, Side B, *The Diary of Anne Frank* DVD (United States: Twentieth Century Fox, 2004); Moss, *Giant*, 247–51.

63. Bosley Crowther, "*The Diary of Anne Frank*," *New York Times*, March 19, 1959.

64. Hift, "*The Diary of Anne Frank*," *Variety* (March 18, 1959): 6.

65. "*The Diary of Anne Frank*," *Time* 73, no. 13 (March 30, 1959): 75–76. See "Listings," *Time* 74, no. 2 (July 13, 1959): 80.

66. "Awards and Honors," *The Diary of Anne Frank* (1959), at www.imdb.com.

67. David Barnouw, "Anne Frank and Film," in Enzer and Solotaroff-Enzer, *Anne Frank*, 167–69.

68. Pascale Bos, "Reconsidering Anne Frank: Teaching the Diary in Its Historical and Cultural Context," in *Teaching the Representation of the Holocaust*, ed. Marianne Hirsch and Irene Kacandes (New York: Modern Language Association, 2004), 348–59; Tim Cole, *Selling the Holocaust: From Auschwitz to Schindler—How History Is Bought, Packaged, and Sold* (New York: Routledge, 1999), 23–46; Doneson, *The Holocaust in American Film,* 59–83; Alvin H. Rosenfeld, "Popularization and Memory: The Case of Anne Frank," in *Lessons and Legacies: The Meaning of the Holocaust in a Changing World*, ed. Peter Hayes (Evanston, IL: Northwestern University Press, 1991), 243–78; Stephen Whitfield, *In Search of American Jewish Culture* (Hanover, NH: Brandeis University Press, 171–84).

69. Frank, *The Diary*, 221.

70. Frances Goodrich and Albert Hackett, *The Diary of Anne Frank* (New York: Random House, 1956), 168.

71. Whitfield, *In Search*, 176–77.

72. Goodrich and Hackett, *The Diary*, 3–28; Scenes 2–6, *The Diary of Anne Frank* DVD.

73. Louis de Jong, *The Netherlands and Nazi Germany* (Cambridge, MA: Harvard University Press, 1990), 1–24.

74. Goodrich and Hackett, *The Diary,* 65–80; Scenes 13–14, *The Diary of Anne Frank* DVD. The nightmare is based on a diary entry. See Frank, *The Diary,* 131–33.

75. Frank, *The Diary,* 57, 139, 220–22, 252–53.

76. Frank, *The Diary,* 270–71.

77. Lawrence L. Langer, "The Uses—and Misuses—of a Young Girl's Diary: If Anne Frank Could Return from among the Murdered, She Would be Appalled," in Enzer and Solotaroff-Enzer, *Anne Frank,* 204.

78. Frank, *The Diary,* 68–69.

79. Goodrich and Hackett, *The Diary,* 84; Scene 16, *The Diary of Anne Frank,* DVD.

80. Whitfield, *In Search,* 177.

81. Goodrich and Hackett, *The Diary,* 96–108; Moss, *Giant,* 255.

82. Frank, *The Diary,* 68–69, 133–38.

83. Frank, *The Diary,* 278.

84. Scenes 30–31, *The Diary of Anne Frank,* DVD.

85. Scene 32, *The Diary of Anne Frank,* DVD.

86. Moss, *Giant,* 253–56. Moss's account is based on a 1973 interview Stevens granted to Bruce Petri. Avisar attributes the clip used in this scene to *The Last Stop.* Avisar, *Screening the Holocaust,* 118.

87. Yvonne Koslovsky Golan, "The Birth of the Holocaust in Motion Pictures: Schemes in Black and White" (unpublished paper presented at the Film and History Conference, Dallas, TX, November 11, 2004).

88. David G. Goodman and Masanori Miyazawa, *Jews in the Japanese Mind: The History and Uses of a Cultural Stereotype* (New York: Free Press, 1995), 167–73.

89. Doneson, *The Holocaust in American Film,* 2nd ed., 59–83.

90. *Ein Tagebuch für Anne Frank,* directed by Joachim Hellwig (East Germany, 1958); Barnouw, "Anne Frank and Film," 169–70.

91. *Dnevik Ane Frank,* directed by Mirjana Samardzic (Yugoslavia, 1959); *The Diary of Anne Frank,* directed by Willy van Hemert (Holland, 1962); *The Diary of Anne Frank,* directed by Alex Segal (United States, 1967); *The Diary of Anne Frank,* directed by Elji Okabe (Japan, 1979); *The Diary of Anne Frank,* directed by Gareth David (United Kingdom, 1987); *The Attic: The Hiding of Anne Frank,* directed by John Erman (United States, 1988); *Anne no nikki,* directed by Akinori Nagaoke (Japan 1995); *Anne Frank's Diary,* directed by Julian Wolff (France, Holland, Ireland, United Kingdom, 1999); *Anne Frank: The Whole Story,* directed by Robert Dornheim (United States, 2001).

92. Jan Kádár quoted in Liehm, *Closely Watched Film,* 407.

93. Lawrence Baron, "The Holocaust and American Public Memory, 1945–1960," *Holocaust and Genocide Studies* 17, no. 1 (Spring 2003): 62–88; compare to Novick, *The Holocaust,* 103–45.

94. *Judgment at Nuremberg,* directed by Stanley Kramer (United States, 1961); Doneson, *The Holocaust in American Film,* 87–107; Mintz, *Popular Culture,* 85–107.

95. *The Pawnbroker,* directed by Sidney Lumet (United States, 1965); Mintz, *Popular Culture,* 107–25; Joshua Hirsch, *Afterimage: Film, Trauma, and the Holocaust* (Philadelphia: Temple University Press, 2004), 85–110; Alan Rosen, "Teach Me Gold: Pedagogy and Memory in *The Pawnbroker,*" *Prooftexts: A Journal of Jewish Literary History* 22, nos. 1 and

2 (Winter/Spring 2002): 77–117; Wendy Zierler, "'My Holocaust Is Not Your Holocaust': Black and Jewish Experience in *The Pawnbroker, Higher Ground,* and *The Nature of Blood," Holocaust and Genocide Studies* 18, no. 1 (Spring 2004): 49–56.

96. Dina Iordanova, *Cinema of the Other Europe: The Industry and Artistry of East Central European Film* (New York: Wallflower Press, 2003), 7–19.

97. Zvi Gitelman, "Soviet Reactions to the Holocaust, 1945–1991," and Lukasz Hirszowicz, "The Holocaust in the Soviet Mirror," in *The Holocaust in the Soviet Union: Studies and Sources on the Destruction of the Jews in the Nazi-Occupied Territories of the USSR, 1941–1945,* ed. Lucjan Dobroszycki and Jeffrey S. Gurock (Armonk, NY: M. E. Sharpe, 1993), 2–27, 29–59.

98. Iordanova, *Cinema of the Other Europe,* 47–91.

99. John Cunningham, *Hungarian Cinema: From Coffee House to Multiplex* (New York: Wallflower Press, 2002), 80–83, 171–76; Avisar, *Screening the Holocaust,* 64–89; Iordanova, *Cinema of the Other Europe,* 67–82; Marek Haltof, *Polish National Cinema* (New York: Berghahn, 2001), 222–25.

100. Liehm, *Closely Watched Films,* 394–425; Peter Hames, *The Czechoslovak New Wave* (Berkeley: University of California Press, 1985), 45–55.

101. Jan Kadár, "Not the Six Million, but the One," *New York Herald Tribune* (January 23, 1966): 21, available at www.criterionco.com/asp/release.asp?id=130&eid=2028section=essay (accessed June 5, 2005).

102. Liehm, *Closely Watched Films,* 407–9.

103. *The Shop on Main Street* (United States: Films, 1966); *The Shop on Main Street* (United States: RCA Columbia Pictures Home Video, 1984); *The Shop on Main Street,* DVD (United States: Criterion, 2001).

104. Jan Kadár, quoted in Liehm, *Closely Watched Films,* 407.

105. "Bocian," *Okana's Web,* available at www.okana.org/gods.html (accessed June 5, 2005).

106. Avisar, *Screening the Holocaust,* 134–48; Doneson, *The Holocaust in American Film,* 35–43.

107. Bosley Crowther, "*The Shop on Main Street," New York Times,* January 25, 1966.

108. Kadár, "Not the Six Million," 21.

109. Kadár, quoted in Liehm, *Closely Watched Films,* 406–7.

110. Judith E. Doneson, "Feminine Stereotypes of Jews in Holocaust Films: Focus on *The Diary of Anne Frank,*" in *The Netherlands and Nazi Genocide,* ed. G. Jan Colijn and Marcia S. Littell (Lewiston, NY: Edwin Mellen Press, 1992), 139–53; Esther Fuchs, "The Construction of Heroines in Holocaust Films: The Jewess as Beautiful Soul," in *Women and the Holocaust: Narrative and Representation,* ed. Esther Fuchs (Lanham, MD: University Press of America, 1999), 97–104.

111. Kadár, interviewed in Liehm, *Closely Watched Films,* 408–11. Kadár went on to direct *The Angel Levine* (United States, 1970) and *Lies My Father Told Me* (Canada, 1975).

112. Lawrence Langer, *Admitting the Holocaust* (New York: Oxford University Press, 1995), 176.

113. Jonathan Pearl and Judith Pearl, *The Chosen Image: Television's Portrayal of Jewish Themes and Characters* (Jefferson, NC: McFarland and Co., 1999), 136.

114. See Marc Dollinger, *Quest for Inclusion: Jews and Liberalism in Modern America* (Princeton, NJ: Princeton University Press, 2000).

115. Patricia Erens, *The Jew in American Cinema* (Bloomington: Indiana University Press, 1984), 255–366; Lester D. Friedman, *The Jewish Image in American Film* (Secaucus, NJ: Citadel Press, 1987), 61–95, 161–224.

116. Elie Wiesel, *Night*, trans. Stella Rodway (New York: Hall and Wang, 1960); Elie Wiesel, *Night, Dawn, The Accident: Three Tales* (New York: Hill and Wang, 1972).

117. Bruno Bettelheim, *The Informed Heart: Autonomy in a Mass Age* (Glencoe, IL: Free Press, 1960); Viktor E. Frankl, *From Death Camp to Existentialism: A Psychiatrist's Path to a New Therapy*, trans. Ilse Lasch (Boston: Beacon Press, 1959.

118. Richard Rubenstein, *After Auschwitz* (Indianapolis: Bobbs-Merrill, 1966); Emil Fackenheim, *God's Presence in History: Jewish Affirmations and Philosophical Reflections* (New York: New York University Press, 1970).

119. Raul Hilberg, *The Destruction of the European Jews* (Chicago: Quandrangle Books, 1961).

120. Nora Levin, *The Holocaust: The Destruction of European Jewry, 1033–1945* (New York: T. Y. Crowell and Co., 1968).

121. Lucy S. Dawidowicz, *The War against the Jews, 1933–1945* (New York: Holt, Rinehart, and Winston, 1975).

122. Arthur Morse, *While Six Million Died: A Chronicle of American Apathy* (New York: Random House, 1968); Henry L. Feingold, *The Politics of Rescue: The Roosevelt Administration and the Holocaust, 1938–1945* (New Brunswick, NJ: Rutgers University Press, 1970); Saul S. Friedman, *No Haven for the Oppressed: United States Policy toward Jewish Refugees, 1938–1945* (Detroit, MI: Wayne State University Press, 1973); Thomas Gordon and Max Morgan Witts, *Voyage of the Damned* (New York: Stein and Day, 1974); *Voyage of the Damned*, directed by Stuart Rosenberg (United Kingdom, 1976).

123. Harold Flender, *Rescue in Denmark* (New York: MacFaden-Bartell, 1964); Leni Yahil, *The Rescue of Danish Jewry: A Test of Democracy* (Philadelphia: Jewish Publication Society, 1969); *The Only Way*, directed by Bent Christensen (Denmark and United States, 1970).

124. *The Sorrow and the Pity*, directed by Marcel Ophuls (France, 1969); André Pierre Colombat, *The Holocaust in French Film* (Metuchen, NJ: Scarecrow Press, 1993), 167–211; Naomi Greene, *Landscapes of Loss: The National Past in Postwar French Cinema* (Princeton, NJ: Princeton University Press, 1999), 64–73; David Weinberg, "France," in Rosenzveig and Wyman, *The World Reacts*, 20–24.

125. Joan B. Wolf, *Harnessing the Holocaust: The Politics of Memory in France* (Palo Alto, CA: Stanford University Press, 2004), 62–66.

126. Colombat, *The Holocaust in French*, 49–86, 261–97; Greene, *Landscapes*, 50–59, 73–80.

127. Angela Dalle Vacche, *The Body in the Mirror: Shapes of History in Italian Cinema* (Princeton, NJ: Princeton University Press, 1992), 57–92; Kriss Raveto, *The Unmaking of Fascist Aesthetics* (Minneapolis: University of Minnesota Press, 2001), 1–51.

128. Meir Michaelis, "Italy," in Wyman and Rosenzveig, *The World Reacts*, 524–49.

129. Milicent Marcus, *Filmmaking by the Book: Italian Cinema and Literary Adaptation* (Baltimore: Johns Hopkins University Press, 1993), 1–24, 91–110.

130. Lynn Rapaport, "Holocaust Pornography: Profaning the Sacred in *Ilsa, She-Wolf of the SS*," *Shofar: An Interdisciplinary Journal of Jewish Studies* 22, no. 1 (Fall 2003): 53–79; Marc J. Koven, "'The Film You Are About to See Is Based on Fact': Italian Nazi Sexploitation Cinema," in *Alternative Europe: Eurotrash and Exploitation Cinema Since 1945,* ed. Ernest Mathijs and Xavier Mendik (London: Wallflower Press, 2004), 19–31.

131. Ravetto, *The Unmaking,* 149–225; Slane, *A Not So Foreign Affair,* 253–86; Caroline Jean Picart and Jason Grant McKahan, "Sexuality, Power, and Holocaust Film Spectatorship in *Apt Pupil,*" in Picart, *Holocaust Film Sourcebook,* 1: 22–25.

132. Doneson, *The Holocaust in American Film,* 121–27; Insdorf, *Indelible Shadows,* 47–49.

133. Shandler, *While America Watches,* 41–79.

134. See Tom W. Hoffer and Richard Alan Nelson, "Docudrama on American Television," and Douglas Gomery, "*Brian's Song:* Television, Hollywood, and the Evolution of the Movie Made for Television," in *Why Docudrama? Fact-Fiction on Film and TV,* ed. Alan Rosenthal (Carbondale: Southern Illinois University, 1999), 64–77, 78–100.

135. Steven N. Lipkin, *Real Emotional Logic: Film and Television Docudrama as Persuasive Practice* (Carbondale: Southern Illinois University Press, 2002), 10–11.

136. *Roots,* directed by Marvin J. Chomsky, John Eman, David Greene, and Gilbert Moses (United States, 1977); Alex Haley, *Roots* (Garden City, NY: Doubleday, 1976).

137. Shandler, *While America Watches,* 159–64.

138. Doneson, *The Holocaust in American Film,* 149–55.

139. Gerald Green, *The Artists of Terezin* (New York: Hawthorn Books, 1969).

140. Doneson, *The Holocaust in American Film,* 149–51.

141. Doneson, *The Holocaust in American Film,* 156–59.

142. Bill Nichols, *Representing Reality* (Bloomington: Indiana University Press, 1991); Bill Nichols, *Blurred Boundaries* (Bloomington: Indiana University Press, 1994).

143. Frank Rich, quoted in Doneson, *The Holocaust in American Film,* 148–49.

144. John Stone, quoted in Doneson, *The Holocaust in American Film,* 72.

145. Elie Wiesel, "Trivializing the Holocaust: Semi-Fact and Semi-Fiction," *New York Times,* April 16, 1978, Section 2, 1, 29.

146. Shandler, *While America Watches,* 167–75.

147. *Americans Confront the Holocaust: A Study of the Reactions to NBC-TV's Four-Part Drama of the Nazi Era* (New York: Institute of Human Relations of the American Jewish Committee, 1978).

148. Edward T. Linenthal, *Preserving Memory: The Struggle to Create America's Holocaust Museum* (New York: Viking Press, 1995).

149. Jeffrey Herf, "The *Holocaust* Reception in West Germany: Right, Center, and Left," *New German Critique,* 19 (Winter 1980): 30–52.

150. Bartov, *The "Jew" in Cinema,* 204–23; Shandler, *While America Watches,* 211–56.

151. *God Is Great and I'm Not,* directed by Pacale Bailly (France, 2002). See Scene 8, *God Is Great and I'm Not,* DVD (Port Washington, NY: Koch-Lorber Films, 2004).

• 3 •

The Biopic: Personalizing Perpetrators, Victims, and Resisters

Film emotionalizes, personalizes, and dramatizes history. Through actors and historical witnesses, it gives us history as triumph, anguish, joy, despair, adventure, suffering, and heroism.[1]

—Robert Rosenstone

In his study of biographical movies, George Custen defines the biopic as a film "minimally composed of the life, or the portion of a life, of a real person whose real name is used."[2] Steve Neale expands upon this definition to include motion pictures that substitute fictitious names for easily identifiable historical figures or chronicle the crimes of notorious gangsters and tyrants, as well as the achievements of past or present luminaries.[3] During their heyday between the 1930s and 1950s, biopics portrayed great individuals whose extraordinary talents, innovative ideas, leadership qualities, or personal integrity prevailed over intellectual shibboleths, political opposition, or social circumstances standing in the way of their making a mark on history.[4] Custen adds that the criteria for fame shift "anew with each generation," a point particularly germane to my analysis of Holocaust biopics since the types of heroes and villains featured in these movies have changed considerably over time.[5]

The emergence of the biopic as the most popular genre of Holocaust film over the past two decades paralleled the increasing role of television in the production of docudramas. The success of *Holocaust* influenced the making of similar prime-time television movies. Many were based on memoirs by, or biographies about, collaborators, perpetrators, rescuers, or survivors. For example, CBS's *Playing for Time* (1980) dramatizes the ordeal of the French singer Fania Fénelon, whose position as a member of the women's orchestra at Auschwitz shielded her from selection for gassing.[6] NBC's *Wallenberg* (1985) follows the exploits of the Swedish diplomat to avert the deportations of Jews from Budapest. Wallenberg's name remained in the public's mind as a victim of the Soviet Union, which imprisoned him at the end of the war.[7] The British American film *The Attic: The Hiding of Anne Frank* (1988) recounts the hiding of the Franks and their friends from the perspective of their rescuer, Miep Gies[8] (see table 3.1).

The rise of subscription movie cable channels like HBO and Showtime toward the end of the 1970s contributed to the revival of the biopic too. By the 1980s, their increasing demand for new, uncut feature films prompted these networks to produce their own motion pictures. The docudrama and biopic formats appealed to executives looking for ventures that did not require expensive royalties for original scripts or advertising campaigns for films about events or figures familiar to the public. The shift of the locus of viewing from theaters to homes discouraged cable companies from making epics whose grand scope would lose their grandeur on a television screen. The biography of a single character, couple, or family was more visually suited to the nature of the medium. The rapid rise in VCR ownership in the same period provided another outlet for biopics released on videocassettes or taped directly from the cable movie channels.[9] Since cable stations could "narrowcast" to specific niche audiences, they took more risks than their broadcast competitors.[10] The Disney Channel pioneered the feature length children's movie about the Holocaust with *A Friendship in Vienna* (1988).[11] In 1997–1998, Showtime aired Barbra Streisand's three-part production of *Rescuers: Stories in Courage*. Each program consisted of two one-hour films about Christian couples, families, or women who saved Jews during the Holocaust.[12]

The biographical film staged a comeback in theatrically released features starting in the 1980s and doubled the number of the next most popular genre by the 1990s. This genre satisfied audiences' preference for personal stories rather than collective histories. Studios tried to match biopics' success in home entertainment formats. The biopic may have benefited from the individualistic values promoted by conservative leaders like Margaret Thatcher in England, Helmut Kohl in Germany, and Ronald Reagan in the United States.[13] The mounting

Table 3.1.   Most Common Genres of Holocaust Feature Films

Years	First	Second	Third	Fourth
1945–1949	Thriller (13)	Road (8)	Character (7)	Romance (5)
1950–1959	Thriller (15)	Character (14)	Biopic (11)	Romance (9)
1960–1969	Character (30)	Action (20)	Biopic (14)	Courtroom (13)
1970–1979	Action (23)	Character (20)	Porno (18)	Biopic (17)
1980–1989	Biopic (42)	Action (32)	Character (29)	Romance (26)
1990–1999	Biopic (62)	Romance (29)	Comedy (26)	Children's (22)

Table 3.2.   Venues for Holocaust Feature Films

Years	Theater	Network TV	Cable TV	Direct to Video	Fundraisers*
1945–1949	38	1	N/A	N/A	5
1950–1959	51	18	N/A	N/A	7
1960–1969	106	27	N/A	N/A	0
1970–1979	103	21	N/A	N/A	0
1980–1989	150	64	3	11	0
1990–1999	148	37	21	16	0

* Movies made for screenings sponsored by advocacy groups to raise money for their cause.

corpus of Holocaust memoirs, the intensive interviewing of survivors that began at the end of the 1970s, the awarding of the Nobel Peace Prize to Elie Wiesel in 1986, and the outpouring of nonfiction works about the Holocaust furnished the primary sources for docudramas and biopics[14] (see tables 3.2 and 3.3).

Several Holocaust memoirs like Fred Uhlman's *Reunion* (1989), Isabella Leitner's *Fragments of Isabella* (1989), and Martin Gray's *For Those I Loved* (1983) inspired movies spanning the spectrum of Jewish experiences, respectively, from the social stigmatization of Jews in Nazi Germany in 1933, to survival in a death camp, to ghettoization, revolt, and enlistment in the Soviet Army.[15] The growth in the public's fascination with Holocaust survivors coincided with the rise of a culture that admires victims who overcome hardships.[16] Other biopics concentrated on resisters from the Nazi era. German films like *The Last Five Days* (1982), *The White Rose* (1981), and *Georg Elser* (1989) indict popular German support for Hitler by demonstrating how atypical resisters like Sophie Scholl and the failed assassin of Hitler, Georg Elser, were.[17] Movies about the lives and deaths of remarkable Jewish victims of Nazi genocide like the artist Charlotte Salomon and libertarian educator Janusz Korczak highlighted the human potential squandered in Hitler's campaign to eradicate Jews.[18] National rationalization of, or retrospection about, collaboration with the Third Reich is the function served by motion pictures like *Hamsun* (1996) and *Pétain* (1993).[19]

After 1980, the number of countries producing Holocaust biopics increased dramatically. Directors from nations that never fell under German rule found stories about how some of their citizens were victims of Nazi racism or opponents of it. In *Red Cherry* (1995), Chuchu, a Chinese communist woman

Table 3.3.   Percentage of Biopics Premiered in Home Entertainment Formats (TV, Video, DVD)

	Decade				
	1950s	*1960s*	*1970s*	*1980s*	*1990s*
Percentage of Biopics	36	50	41	56	44

sent to study in Moscow, is apprehended by invading German troops while she is touring the Ukraine. An SS doctor obsessed with her unblemished skin tattoos an ornate German eagle and swastika on her back as a tribute to the system he serves. Whether *Red Cherry*'s unusual subject matter or unprecedented frontal nudity made it China's biggest domestic hit of 1996 remains unclear.[20] During the war, Japan forced consul Chiune Sugihara to resign and withheld his pension for issuing visas to Jews fleeing Lithuania before Germany invaded it. The film *The Visas That Saved Lives* (1993) rehabilitated him as a national hero.[21]

The Israeli film *Hanna's War* (1988) glorifies Zionist heroine Hanna Senesh, who volunteered for a British paratrooper mission behind German lines to assist downed Allied pilots. Instead, she headed to Budapest to save her mother. The fascist regime in Hungary arrested, tortured, tried, and executed her. In the movie based on her diary, she briefly joins a Yugoslavian partisan unit, which derails a transport carrying Jews to death camps. This suggests direct Zionist intervention to halt the Final Solution. Actually, the Zionist leadership devoted itself primarily to consolidating the institutions that could sustain a Jewish state after the war and secondarily to smuggling Jewish refugees from Europe into Palestine. Hanna's partisan band never liberated a deportation train.[22]

THE DICTATOR AS DIRECTOR: *THE EMPTY MIRROR*
Directed by Barry J. Hershey
(United States: Walden Woods Film Company, 1996)

> No representations of Hitler, highbrow or low, seem able adequately to present the man or satisfactorily to explain him. Those works that demonize him distort through tropological excess, making him into a creature altogether unlike any to be found in humankind; whereas those works that normalize him tend to minimize his wickedness and diminish or deny his destructive side.[23]
>
> —Alvin H. Rosenfeld

Although the number of biopics about Nazi perpetrators has declined sharply since the broadcast of NBC's *Holocaust*, public interest in Hitler has not diminished.[24] The first postwar biographical movie about Hitler was Georg Wilhelm Papst's *The Last Ten Days* (1955). It dramatized Hitler's retreat into a bunker in the final days of the war. An idealistic member of the Hitler Youth named Richard descends into Hitler's shelter to persuade him not to flood

Berlin's subways, where thousands, including Richard's mother and brother, are hiding from the approaching Soviet troops. He finally pleads his case to the one sane army officer in Hitler's entourage, Captain Wuest, played by Oskar Werner. Cognizant that Hitler is tottering on the edge of madness, Wuest urges Hitler to abort the plan to drown the people in the subways. His entreaty provokes Hitler's bodyguards to shoot him. Before he dies, he utters this soliloquy: "If you ever know peace, don't let them take it away. Never let them take it away. Don't say 'Jawohl.' Don't ever say 'Jawohl.' The world can get along without 'Jawohl.' Always keep faith." As Hitler's body burns following his suicide, a voice-over of Wuest's parting words is heard.

In the same year, Papst directed *It Happened on the 20th of July*, a dramatization of the 1944 assassination attempt on Hitler's life. Papst may have been trying to redeem himself for remaining in Germany during World War II. The characterization of Hitler as a demented demagogue opposed by decent Germans appealed to American audiences but had less success at the box office with Germans, who resented being portrayed as dupes of a madman. The innocent victims in Pabst's biopic are the crowds who seek refuge in the subways. Marc Silberman has concluded that although Papst did not evade the subject of the Third Reich, he "projected an imaginary resolution that helped avoid an all too precise recollection of the past that could undermine the present."[25]

The press and television coverage of Israel's audacious kidnapping and trial of Adolf Eichmann spawned a television drama, *Engineer of Death*, and an independently produced movie, *Operation Eichmann*, about Eichmann's career as the SS officer in charge of deporting Jews to the death camps. Both productions predated Hannah Arendt's book and portrayed Eichmann as an anti-Semitic zealot rather than a dutiful bureaucrat.[26] Otherwise, Hitler remained the only other Nazi who merited a biopic in the 1960s. Directed by Stuart Heisler, *Hitler* traced its antagonist's domineering personality to his doting mother and repressed sexuality. The English title *Women in Nazi Germany* reflected the film's simplistic Freudian interpretation.[27]

Most Hitler biopics are set in the besieged bunker where the sounds of exploding artillery shells and reports of the impending fall of Berlin provide a reality check for the führer's illusions that Germany still might win the war, that his political judgment was infallible, and that traitors among his own coterie had caused Germany's defeat. The bunker also serves as the backdrop for Hitler's belated marriage to Eva Braun and the suicides of the newlyweds and the Goebbels family. Rex Firkin's *The Death of Adolf Hitler* (1972) surmises that Hitler's rabid anti-Semitism developed when he was a vagrant in Vienna. In a nightmare sequence, a maniacal Jewish merchant denies Hitler bread and cake because he cannot afford them. After being propositioned by a prostitute and a pedophile, Hitler envisions rats swarming through the sewers where he sleeps. His crusade to exterminate Jewish "vermin" is linked to this memory. When Hitler asks Eva Braun to guess why he launched his war against the Jews, he replies, "Rats!" In what ranks as the worst choice of music for a death scene in a film, Eva listens to a recording of "Smoke Gets in Your Eyes" after Hitler kills himself and the bunker goes up in flames.[28]

Two subsequent bunker biopics, *Hitler: The Last Ten Days* (1973) and the television movie *The Bunker* (1980), hew more closely to eyewitness accounts of Hitler's demise. Both feature distinguished actors in the leading roles, Alec Guinness in the former and Anthony Hopkins in the latter. The first film establishes its historical credentials by opening with Hitler's personal physician requesting to be appointed head of the German Red Cross. As he recounts his gruesome résumé of killing, sterilizing, and experimenting on concentration camp inmates, atrocity footage of feeble survivors, corpses scattered on the ground, and piles of extracted teeth, shorn hair, and confiscated belongings are screened. This is followed by newsreel clips surveying Hitler's rise to power and conquest of much of Europe. A written statement by historian Hugh Trevor-Roper vouches for the authenticity of the events the film reenacts. The movie crosscuts scenes from the Nuremberg rallies, Nazi atrocities, and the fall of Berlin with Hitler's mood swings from confidence in the Aryan race, emotional outbursts against suspected conspirators, and contempt for the Germans' inability to accomplish his grandiose aims.[29]

The historicity of *The Bunker* also is affirmed in its opening scene. An American journalist enters the bunker after Germany's surrender and decides to reconstruct Hitler's final days by interviewing those who stayed by his side until he committed suicide. The Hitler who emerges from their recollections is resigned, albeit grudgingly, to defeat. As Hopkins portrays him, Hitler is physically and mentally frail from the toll exacted by military setbacks, pain pills, and injuries from the assassination attempt of 1944. Although he continues to lash out at "the scourge and pestilence" of international Jewry, he has decided to destroy Germany's infrastructure to deprive the Allies of valuable resources. Albert Speer's refusal to carry out this order provides whatever dramatic tension there is in watching the vanquished Hitler rant. The film's characterization of Hitler's vacillation between resignation and recalcitrance resembles Bruno Ganz's performance in Oliver Hirschbiegel's *The Downfall* (2004). *The Bunker*'s closing shot recalls the charismatic appeal Hitler once exuded by flashing back to an animated Hitler delivering a fiery speech.[30]

The shift away from assigning guilt for the crimes of the Third Reich to Hitler and implicating subordinates who enforced his policies is apparent in perpetrator biopics released after 1975. This change partly represented a growing body of scholarly literature on the decision-making processes that led to the Final Solution. The "functionalist" interpretation of the Holocaust articulated by prominent Holocaust historians like Martin Broszat, Christopher Browning, and Raul Hilberg stressed how the harshness of anti-Semitic policies escalated as Hitler's party paladins and governmental officials competed to devise the most efficient solution for the "Jewish problem."[31]

Reflecting this research, the Nazi perpetrators of the Final Solution assumed a greater role in Holocaust biopics. The 1977 movie *From a German Life*, whose American version was called *Death Is My Trade*, follows the career of Rudolf Hoess who started as a paramilitary assassin, became a guard at Dachau, and served as the commandant of Auschwitz. Hoess followed his orders to kill Jews punctiliously.[32] This blend of administrative meticulousness and ideological fanaticism informs the German docudrama *Reinhard Heydrich: Manager of Terror* (1977).[33] Its director, Heinz Schirk, and scriptwriter, Paul Mommertz, subsequently produced the docudrama *The Wannsee Conference* (1984), a reenactment of the fateful meeting in January 1942 when Heydrich informed state and party officials about the decision to exterminate the Jews and parceled out the tasks of each in the plan's execution.[34] In both movies, Heydrich appears more like a corporate CEO than a ruthless racist. Albert Speer, Hitler's architect and wartime economic minister, possesses similar traits in the 1982 docudrama *Inside the Third Reich*.[35]

Hans-Jürgen Syberberg's *Our Hitler: A Film from Germany* (1978) is regarded by many film historians as the most significant postwar German movie about Hitler. Hardly a traditional biopic, *Our Hitler* is an inventive pastiche of different actors articulating Hitler's opinions and puppets symbolizing the myriad of personas Germans projected onto him: the common man, the military genius, the Wagnerian hero, the tragic prince, Chaplin's Great Dictator, the purifier of the race, and the omnipotent emperor. These scenes appear amid a backdrop of documentary film footage, photographs, regalia from the Third Reich, and a soundtrack of excerpts from Hitler's speeches and Richard Wagner's music. Annette Insdorf interprets the message communicated by these cinematic devices as "reversing the idea that Hitler pulled the strings" by illustrating how his political excesses were rooted in "the collective complicity of the German people."[36]

Barry Hershey's *The Empty Mirror* (1996) returns Hitler to center stage. It probes how Hitler fabricated the myth of the führer and the superior Aryan by orchestrating political rallies, manipulating his media images, stereotyping his enemies, and waging war for chimerical objectives. He persuaded most Germans that he was the political messiah destined to deliver his nation from the throes of Western liberalism, Soviet communism, and Jewish deracination. Molding public opinion about his genius, Hershey's Hitler emerges as a precursor to today's political spin doctors. The movie invites comparisons with other American films like *Bob Roberts* (1992) and *Wag the*

Dog (1997), which satirize how the mass media falsify news and shape perceptions of public policy.[37]

Hershey cast a relatively unknown British stage actor, Norman Rodway, as Hitler because he wanted to avoid the lead's celebrity distracting the audience. The movie's opening is a succession of photographs of cadavers in concentration camps, the rubble of bombed-out German cities, and a distraught woman and child weeping. The stills dissolve into blurred and then focused footage of Hitler addressing an enraptured crowd, whose national pride is visible on people's faces and audible in their cheers. The camera pulls back to reveal that the audience is watching the projection of a newsreel on a screen in a darkened cave. Perhaps it represents the bunker, Plato's cave, Hell, or the inside of Hitler's mind. The camera pivots 180 degrees to focus on Hitler observing the movie intently. He stops the projector and runs it backward and forward to relive an intoxicating moment when admirers extended their arms to salute him. He gazes lovingly at himself in the mirror. A close-up of his head and ear is followed by an image of his eyes peering through a magnifying glass at movie frames of him rehearsing a speech.

After he looks at his reflection again, Hitler expounds upon the philosophy embodied in the visual strategies that preceded his monologue: "Film is the magician's mirror which allows the artist to project his dreams and fantasies into the inner life of the viewer." Hitler's running commentary, which often consists of direct quotes from *Mein Kampf* and his speeches, explains his propaganda theories about indoctrinating and intimidating the masses with enormity, dazzling ceremonies, and repetition of "crude simplifications" about the virtue of one's own group and the vices of one's foes. The scenes of Hitler changing the positions of buildings in an architectural model for the city of Linz reveal his compulsion to control his environment. Sigmund Freud interrupts occasionally and interrogates Hitler about the origins of his narcissistic personality.

At first, Hitler's transgressions fleetingly intrude upon his Aryan utopia, but gradually they defile all his accomplishments on behalf of Germany. He burns expressionist paintings because they constitute "the incredible fantasies of a sick people," the majority of whom are Jewish. He condemns the "effeminate" ethics of Judaism and Christianity for sapping the vitality of the Aryan race. He regards moral conscience "a blemish like a Hebrew circumcision." He brags about how his war has claimed fifty-five million casualties. "History likes round numbers," he shouts as he revises the Jewish death toll from 5.7 to 6 million and wonders why "only the Jews take their removal so personally." When he sees a frame of him sweating, he orders it cut. A Hitler Youth member approves of removing the unflattering outtakes because "these were like the Jews."

Disturbing delusions vividly illustrate the disintegration of Hitler's mind. In a tender moment, when he seems truly affectionate toward Eva Braun, she metamorphoses into a bevy of blond goddesses clad in white togas with garlands in their hair. Later, one of these sirens floats behind a glass barrier beyond Hitler's reach. In his script notes, Hershey accordingly writes, "Contact/touch destroys illusion." Wrapped in a swastika banner, Hitler proclaims, "All life is paid for in blood. I crushed the skulls of my enemies." Footage of German soldiers in retreat or slaughtered on the eastern front fills the screen. Hitler dictates the order to destroy all Jews to wrest a victory from defeat. Blood starts seeping from every corner of the bunker and floods the room. Hitler laments, "I, too, was trapped in the whirlwind. We created an empty mirror filled with hate." The movie ends with a backlit close-up of Hitler's face contorted in a horrified grimace. This image resembles the mask of tragedy or the mirror phantom in Disney's *Snow White* who tells the wicked queen she is not "the fairest one in the land."

Unlike previous Hitler biopics, with the exception of Syberberg's *Our Hitler*, *The Empty Mirror* does not employ a traditional narrative structure. With its interplay of dialog, Wagnerian and other classical music, soundtracks from newsreels, and a phantasmagoria of film clips, photographs, and Nazi symbols charting Hitler's meteoric rise to power and his precipitous downfall, it exemplifies the notion that the medium is the message. Hitler starred himself in an epic war movie about racial struggle that culminated in a cataclysm for his homeland and humanity. Hershey wanted to portray Hitler as a man trapped in his own myth.[38] Although many reviewers praised the film for its visual complexity, others claimed it was "pretentious and boring."[39] Yet, I find that it effectively communicates Alan Bullock's insight that "it's when he [Hitler] gets to that point where he no longer manipulates his image, but believes in it entirely, when he drops the manipulation, then he's destroyed."[40]

Although a theatrical flop, *The Empty Mirror* achieved some success at film festivals, on cable television, and through video rentals and sales. Premiering at the Fantasporto Film Festival in Portugal in 1997, it won the award for best cinematography and garnered more awards at American film festivals. Yet, it took two more years for the film to find an American distributor. In 1999, it was booked at only four movie houses and grossed less than $30,000 in box-office receipts during the month it played. As it had achieved critical acclaim, the film's video rights were picked up by Universal Studios the next year, when the movie appeared on HBO. This led to its release in Europe in 2001.[41]

Other 1990s movies about Hitler speculate about how he might have behaved in private or after the war. Armin Mueller-Stahl's directorial debut, *Conversation with the Beast* (1996), postulates that one of Hitler's doubles committed suicide in the bunker. The elderly Hitler lives in obscurity until an

What does Hitler (Norman Rodway) see in his reflection? The Empty Mirror. *Courtesy of Walden Woods Film Company.*

American historian confirms his identity and kills him. Mueller–Stahl strips Hitler of his power to render him "a silly, childish man trying to hurt others."[42] Aleksandr Sokurov's *Molokh* (1999) follows Hitler and Eva Braun on one of their Alpine retreats. Joseph and Magda Goebbels and Martin Bormann, who reeks of poison gas, sycophantically listen to Hitler pontificate about Aryan virtue, immortality, and vegetarianism. Cognizant of how pretentious "Adi" (Eva's nickname for Hitler) is, Eva remains obsequious until the two are in the bedroom and remarks, "Without an audience, you're nothing more than a corpse."[43]

THE CHRISTIAN AS MARTYR:
BONHOEFFER: AGENT OF GRACE
Directed by Eric Till
(Germany, Canada: NFP Teleart/Norflicks, 1999)

If your opponent has a conscience, then follow Ghandi and non-violence. But if your enemy has no conscience, then follow Bonhoeffer.[44]

—Martin Luther King Jr.

Until German reunification in 1990, German movies about the resistance to Hitler and his policies reflected the cold war loyalties of the two Germanys. East Germany perceived itself as the heir to the communist and socialist opposition to Nazism, whose leaders either fled their homeland or faced internment. The Soviet Union imposed a communist government on its occupation zone, claiming it constituted a broad-based coalition of German antifascists.[45] Deutsche Film AG (DEFA), the state-run film studio, produced pictures like *The Murderers Are among Us* (1946), *Marriage in the Shadows* (1947), *Lissy* (1957), *Professor Mamlock* (1960), *Mama, I Am Alive* (1976), and *Sansibar* (1987), which depicted the Third Reich's persecution of Jews, leftists, and Soviet prisoners of war. The Soviet Union justified its control over East German affairs by recalling its role in defeating Hitler and preventing pro-Nazi and conservative elites from returning to power.[46]

Conversely, West German films neglected communist resistance and glorified the officers, diplomats, civil servants, clergymen, and trade unionists involved in the plot to assassinate Hitler on July 20, 1944. They were depicted as defending Christian and nationalistic values and disassociated from the taint of communism or Soviet influence.[47] Historical movies like *Canaris: Master Spy* (1954) and *It Happened on the 20th of July* (1955), as well as fictional films like *The Devil's General* (1955) and *Winterspelt* (1977), characterized the conspirators as patriotic Germans who reluctantly took drastic measures to stop Hitler's strategic blunders and crimes against humanity.[48]

From the 1970s on, West German scholars devoted more research to the socialists and communists who had participated in grassroots resistance cells or emigrated to join anti-Nazi movements in other countries. Several factors raised public awareness of the contribution of these two groups to the opposition to Hitler: the formation of the first postwar social democratic government in 1969, the chancellorship of Willy Brandt, who had served in the Norwegian underground, diplomatic initiatives to normalize relations between the two Germanys, the study of local resistance activities, which revealed considerable left-wing involvement, and the appointment of a commission in 1983 to create a memorial to the German resistance to Nazism in its "whole breadth and diversity." Klaus Maria Brandauer's *Georg Elser: An Individual from Germany* (1989) revived the memory of a working-class loner who tried to kill Hitler in 1939.[49]

Although reunification encouraged the Memorial Site for German Resistance to mount exhibitions covering the gamut of opposition to Hitler, the inclusion of communists in the displays upset conservatives who equated communism with the discredited regimes in East Germany and the Soviet Union. Similarly, liberals and leftists feared that an uncritical remembrance of the July 20 plot whitewashed the initial pro-Nazi stance and authoritarian aims of many of the figures implicated in it.[50] A less controversial form of commemoration honored religiously motivated resisters whose conscientious defiance of Nazism had earned them respect among Christians throughout the world. As early as 1960, the West German government erected chapels and churches near former concentration camps to remind visitors of the Christians martyred there.[51]

In 1975, Billy Graham founded World Wide Pictures to produce *The Hiding Place,* the inspirational story of Corrie ten Boom, who, guided by her pious father, helped hide Jews in the family's house, survived internment at Ravensbrück, and traversed the globe as an evangelist, bearing witness to how her faith in Jesus prevailed over despair during her imprisonment and impelled her to forgive the Germans after the war.[52] Ten Boom's book became a perennial international bestseller. The movie based on it remains a classic example of a religious interpretation of the Holocaust as a test of Christian morality and the redemptive power of suffering and forgiveness.[53] Since 1980, there has been a steady flow of biopics about Christians who opposed Hitler or rescued Jews.[54]

As the best-known German Protestant theologian martyred for opposition to the Third Reich, Dietrich Bonhoeffer provided an obvious candidate for a German Resistance saga. His posthumous works continue to sell extremely well.[55] Biographies and documentaries about him have kept his legacy alive.[56] In 1994, his prison cell at Buchenwald was excavated and restored. The next year, the Sachsenhausen Memorial honored the two Abwehr resisters, Hans von Dohnanyi and Hans Oster, who recruited Bonhoeffer to transmit peace initiatives to the Allies, help Jews escape from Germany, and plot Hitler's murder.[57] Bonhoeffer's struggle to discard his theological prejudices against Judaism, to expand his sense of obligation beyond Christians to embrace all of Nazism's victims, to reject the Lutheran doctrine of obedience to state authority in civil matters, and to justify assassination to save the lives of others possessed the dramatic elements of a compelling biographical film with universal appeal.

Unfortunately, *Bonhoeffer: Agent of Grace* skips most of Bonhoeffer's religious maturation and starts in 1939, when Bonhoeffer decides to leave the United States and return to Germany to confront Hitler's regime. From the brightly lit opening scene in New York, he is quickly shrouded by the darkness of a Berlin church, where he articulates positions that it had taken him six years to reach: "The Nuremberg Laws are an attack on Christianity itself"; "Hitler's claim upon us is a claim a Christian can only accept from Christ himself"; "Only those who cry out for the Jews have the right to sing Gregorian chants"; "Christ himself was a Jew, and in the eyes of the Lord, we are all Jews." The Gestapo arrives, bans Bonhoeffer from teaching, and drapes the church altar with two swastika banners. Next, the film shows Bonhoeffer joining the Abwehr as a cover for his travel as a courier for the Resistance. On his first mission, he confides to the Anglican archbishop that his confederates intend to assassinate Hitler. His transformation from a proponent of nonviolence to a conspirator in an assassination plot occurs twenty-three minutes into the film.

The hectic pacing of the movie omits the intellectual stages Bonhoeffer went through to arrive at the point where he chose the lesser of two evils by colluding in the murder of Hitler. The self-assured Bonhoeffer conforms to the cinematic convention of the moral hero who always knows right from wrong. Lost, however, in the accelerated action is his evolution from champion of pacifist civil disobedience to a coconspirator in assassination. His character has no time to develop but instead spouts sound bytes more platitudinous than profound.[58]

There are two reasons why the film plays more like a trite morality play than a complex character study. The first is the shortening of the original television version of the movie by almost half to make it more commercially viable as a video.[59] The impact this had on the film can be gauged by comparing the English title of the movie to the German one. For Americans, Bonhoeffer represents "an agent of grace," essentially good from the opening scene, where he mingles with African Americans singing hymns, to the last half of the movie, where he is never discouraged by his imprisonment. There is an aura of tranquility radiating from him as he ministers to a doomed prisoner in an adjacent cell, wins the respect of his guard, and goes calmly to his hanging. The German title, *Dietrich Bonhoeffer: The Last Step*, implies that Bonhoeffer went through several phases before he took "the last step" of sanctifying murder.

The second reason for minimizing Bonhoeffer's theological qualms about joining the plot to kill Hitler is that it would detract from the religious certitude that the makers of the movie want to impart to the audience. The Aid Association for Lutherans (AAL) helped fund and produce *Agent of Grace*. It stipulated that the film had to "portray the role Christian faith played in Bonhoeffer's life and decisions." The AAL distributed copies of the film to ten thousand congregational discussion groups.[60] Gateway Films served as the American distributor for *Agent of Grace*. Gateway specializes in Christian videos and carries other Holocaust titles about Christians who opposed Hitler or helped Jews, including *The Hiding Place*, *Hill of a Thousand Children* (1994), and *Witness against Hitler* (1995).[61] As the success of Mel Gibson's *The Passion of the Christ* (2004) demonstrated, Christian groups and churches can serve as an effective distribution network for religious films.[62]

Both the director and screenwriter of *Agent for Grace* had worked on religiously oriented productions before. Canadian Eric Till had a long career directing family fare for television. Some of his TV movies include *Mary and Joseph: A Story of Faith* (1979), *The Christmas Toy* (1986), *Clarence* (1990), an updated tale about the guardian angel from *It's a Wonderful Life*, and most recently *Luther* (2003).[63] Gareth Jones, who scripted *Agent of Grace*, had previously authored screenplays for a series of movies about figures from the New Testament.[64]

Ubiquitous crucifixes hung on walls or formed by shadows or window frames accompany Bonhoeffer as he marches past his stations of the cross. When he arrives at the gallows and is asked if this is the end, Bonhoeffer serenely replies, "No." He then ascends the stairs to the noose and raises his face to heaven.

In addition to the religious universality ascribed to Bonhoeffer's fateful decision, the binational nature of the production prevented it from exerting the kind of impact it could have had in Germany. Till chose German actor Ulrich Tukur to play Bonhoeffer but had all the dialog spoken in English. When *Agent of Grace* was adapted for screening in Germany, the English was dubbed into German using the voices of the original cast members. Poor lip synchronization made the film seem like an import.[65]

Although aired in the United States by PBS, the movie primarily attracted Christian audiences. Evangelical columnist Charles Colston, who gained notoriety for his part in the Watergate scandal, appreciated the film "for exposing the myth that Christians did nothing to stop Hitler."[66] The movie never contrasts Bonhoeffer's resistance with the tacit or active support Hitler received from the majority of Protestant clergymen in Nazi Germany.[67] While most of the postings about the film on the Hollywood Jesus website are positive (hollywoodjesus.com), a few recognize that the movie offers a simplistic account of a complicated man. One blogger comments, "The biography of Dietrich Bonhoeffer is far more profound, complex, and dialectical than can be discussed in 90 minutes."[68] The editor of the Bonhoeffer Society's newsletter echoed this sentiment: "The real Bonhoeffer struggled until the very end with the irony and ambiguity of his involvement with the conspirators plotting Hitler's assassination. Questions, fears, and uncertainty were often his companions, not so much answers, confidence, certainty, and resolve."[69] In terms of Bonhoeffer's theology, his cinematic persona offers "cheap grace" instead of the costly kind attained in serious dialog with the Bible and adherence to a rigorous ideal of Christian discipleship over what constitutes good and evil behavior.

THE JEW AS MARTYR: *KORCZAK*
Directed by Andrzej Wajda
(Germany, Poland, United Kingdom: Regina Ziegler, Zespol, BBC, 1990)

> [Poles] will unavoidably encounter . . . the image of the Jew destroyed before their eyes and those of their parents and grandparents. What they will do with this memory, how it will shape Polish history and consciousness, is unpredictable. One can only hope that it will be used in the service of renewal rather than repression.[70]
>
> —Michael C. Steinlauf

Movies about the Holocaust in Poland invariably ignite the tinder of collective memories of Polish Jewish relationships during the war. Most Polish Catholics recall the German occupation as an odious regime that enslaved the Polish masses, murdered millions, and targeted for execution Polish intellectual, political, and religious elites. Polish Gentiles claim that they rendered as much assistance to their Jewish neighbors as was possible under such onerous conditions. Some Poles viewed the Jews as traitors who colluded with the Soviet occupation regime in Eastern Poland between 1939 and 1941 or collaborated with Germany by obeying the Jewish councils established to enforce German decrees in the ghettoes where Polish Jewry was segregated.[71]

The majority of Polish Jews, on the other hand, cannot forget the ferocity of prewar Polish anti-Semitism, which emanated from the Catholic Church and nationalistic political parties.[72] While a fraction of their coreligionists found refuge in Polish homes or fought the Germans in Jewish or leftist partisan cadres, many faced indifference to their plight and even betrayal by Polish informants, who extorted money from Jews in hiding and handed them over to the SS when their funds ran out.[73]

Although only 10 percent of Poland's more than three million Jews survived, their ever-dwindling, postwar presence served as a lightening rod for popular discontent against the Soviet satellite government, whose bureaucracy initially contained a disproportionate number of Jews.[74] In turn, the government pandered to local prejudices by claiming that reform movements that challenged its authority in 1956 and 1968 were instigated by Jewish subversives from Israel and the United States. The anti-Zionist campaign of 1968 accelerated the exodus of Polish Jews to Israel, Western Europe, and the United States.[75]

The pilgrimage to Auschwitz made by the Polish-born Pope John Paul II in 1979 and his efforts to expunge anti-Semitic doctrines from Catholicism augured the dawning of a new era in Polish Jewish relations. So did the emergence of the Solidarity movement out of the shipyard strikes in Gdansk in 1980. As part of its aim of creating a democratic and pluralistic civil society among Poles, the liberal wing of Solidarity encouraged a revival of Jewish culture and research into Polish Jewish history.[76]

The promotion of Polish–Jewish reconciliation quickly became mired in the swamp of deeply rooted animosities. Claude Lanzmann's documentary *Shoah* (1985) consists of interviews of Jewish survivors, German perpetrators, and Polish bystanders. Although one segment of it is devoted to Jan Karski, who communicated to Allied leaders what he had witnessed in the Warsaw ghetto and Belzec, other Poles queried by Lanzmann reiterated traditional economic, sexual, and theological stereotypes of Jews, even when they condemned Germany's policy of extermination.[77] Poland lodged an official protest with the French government, charging that the film accused Poles of "complicity in

Nazi genocide." When the movie was broadcast on Polish television and screened in theaters, it sparked an even greater uproar for slandering the Polish people. Heated exchanges over the Polish response to the Holocaust ratcheted up the tensions. The founding of a Carmelite Convent at Auschwitz in 1984 led to a fight between American Jewish protestors and local Polish workers at the site five years later. The primate of Poland, Cardinal Josef Glemp, retorted with an anti-Semitic homily that poured new salt into the old wounds of Jewish Polish antagonism.[78]

Amid these recriminations between Jews and Poles and the election of Poland's first postwar democratic government, Andrzej Wajda filmed *Korczak* (1990) and won a seat in the Polish senate. Since the 1950s, Wajda had earned the reputation of being Poland's "national director," whose movies often chronicled the resistance and repression of Poles during World War II. Three of Wajda's previous films had featured Jews as leading characters, but some film historians accused him of confirming traditional Polish stereotypes of Jews as passive victims or greedy capitalists in movies like *Samson* (1961), *Landscape after Liberation* (1970), and *Promised Land* (1975). Ewa Mazierska asserts, "On the whole, his films distort historical truth and convey, albeit in a subtle way, a conviction in the superiority of Polish culture over the Jewish way of life. Wajda is not an anti-Semite, but his attitude toward Jews is patronizing."[79] Conversely, Edward Rogerson commends Wajda for presenting "more well-rounded Jewish characters" than most other Polish directors.[80] According to Michael Stevenson, Wajda uses his films as a tool to promote mutual understanding between Jews and Poles since both were victims of Nazism.[81]

By choosing Korczak as a protagonist, Wajda "sought to reconcile Poles and Jews by demonstrating their compatibility in one character."[82] Moreover, Wajda intended *Korczak* to be a goodwill gesture toward Polish Jewry.[83] Korczak, whose real name was Henryk Goldszmit, remains one of the few wartime figures revered by Polish Gentiles and Jews alike.[84] In the eyes of the former, he spoke and wrote in Polish, achieved international recognition as an educator, and enjoyed a national following for his prewar radio show, *The Old Doctor*. In the eyes of the latter, he had contemplated immigrating to Palestine, sheltered two hundred Jewish orphans in the Warsaw ghetto, and sacrificed his life by remaining with them instead of accepting offers of hiding places or fake passports to save himself.[85]

When *Korczak* premiered at the Cannes Film Festival in 1990, it received a standing ovation from the audience but a cold shoulder from several French reviewers. The latter castigated Wajda for minimizing Korczak's Jewishness, exculpating the Poles of anti-Semitism, perpetuating Polish stereotypes of Jews, and detracting from the horrible fate of Korczak's orphans by ending the movie with their train car decoupling, allowing them to disembark into a heavenly mist. Writing in the pages of *Le Monde,* reviewer Daniele Heymann berated Wajda for showing wealthy Jewish black marketers and concealing Polish anti-Semitism.[86] Anne de Gaspieri similarly accused Wajda of "profound indifference" by shielding the audience from the "suffering and despair" Korczak's children experienced.[87] Never one to stifle his opinion about Polish anti-Semitism, Lanzmann created a "scandal" at the screening of *Korczak* by walking out after its presentation and declaring, "You do not know how evil this is!"[88]

Watching *Korczak* a decade latter, with his diary and biographies about him fresh in my mind, I find the movie remarkably realistic in its black-and-white documentary-like look that seamlessly segues several times into newsreel footage originally shot by German camera crews. When Korczak leaves the orphanage, he walks through overcrowded streets into dilapidated buildings populated by the dying, the dead, and the starving. Wajda probes Korczak's bifurcated Polish Jewish identity, his incessant efforts to provide a normal existence for his orphans, the extremes of privilege and poverty in the ghetto, and the stoic march of Korczak and his wards to the deportation transport.

The prologue reveals that Korczak possessed multiple allegiances. In his role as the Old Doctor, he advises his radio audience about compassionate childrearing. Korczak humbly confesses, "Me, I love children. This is not a sacrifice; the need is mine." In the hierarchy of his loyalties, averting the physical or psychological abuse of youngsters ranked highest. Upon completion of his broadcast, Korczak learns that his program has been cancelled because it has become too controversial to permit a Jew to have his own show. Korczak wonders if he misled people by calling himself the Old Doctor rather than using his Jewish name. In a subsequent scene, two orphans debate whether Korczak is the world's greatest Jew or the world's greatest Pole.[89]

Rather than denying the extent of Polish anti-Semitism, Wajda portrays it in several scenes. Korczak's firing by the radio station establishes that anti-Jewish discrimination existed among Poles before the German invasion. Although some Polish critics wondered why Wajda included this incident in the film, others perceived it as a protest against anti-Semitic elements within the Solidarity movement.[90] Before the outbreak of the war, Korczak escorts his orphans to the river for a swim. Former students rebuke him for promoting harmonious relations between Jews and Poles. They tell him that Poles have beaten them and smashed their windows. An irate Polish laundress rudely tells Korczak, "I don't wash Jewish shit!" Korczak hoped resistance to German rule would unite Poles and Jews but despaired that this would never happen.[91]

Although Wajda shows instances of Polish sympathy for the Jews, he offsets these with vignettes about Polish abandonment or hatred of Jews. Korczak's Polish colleague Maryna Falska shelters a Jewish girl of "suitable appearance" in her home and urges her long-time associate to go into hiding.[92] A Polish tram conductor who tosses bread to starving Jews is summarily executed. Yet, the budding romance between Joseph, one of Korczak's orphans, and his Gentile girlfriend, Ewa, is forbidden by her employer because Joseph is Jewish. Korczak recalls the death of his pet canary. When he wanted to bury the bird and mark its grave with a tiny wooden cross, his family's maid warned him that such an interment would constitute a sacrilege because the creature lacked a soul. Then, the janitor's son added that the canary, like its owner, was Jewish and therefore destined to spend eternity in hell.[93] While Wajda does not cite all the anti-Semitic incidents recorded in Korczak's diary,[94] those that he does include are more damning than Steven Spielberg's sparse references to Polish anti-Semitism in *Schindler's List*.[95]

Wajda's portrayal of the ghetto's Jewish Council and black marketers incensed some critics who charged that such characterizations confirmed Polish stereotypes of Jews collaborating with Germany or profiting from the suffering of their coreligionists. Philip Strick reviled how the film "contemptuously reveals the ghetto's less familiar obscenities of duplicity and ruthlessness."[96] If directors should be more concerned about political correctness than historical accuracy, these criticisms might have merit, but anyone familiar with the history of the ghettos will not be shocked to see Jewish councils following German orders and Jewish gangsters amassing wealth through smuggling.[97]

Wajda exhibits a genuine understanding of the terrible alternatives faced by Jewish leaders. Korczak approaches Adam Czerniakow, the chairman of Warsaw's Jewish Council, to procure rations for his orphans. Czerniakow summarizes the predicament the Jewish Council faced:

> I know our position is morally untenable, but believe me, I adopted it aware of my responsibilities. Without me, without us, the others [i.e., the Germans] would be worse. The choice is not between good and evil, but of the lesser evil. . . . I am fully aware of the fact that the majority, at least half, have little chance of seeing the end of the war. I know the poor and the deported will die first. We will try to save as many as we can. Save the elite, save the young, the children.

Korczak denounces this strategy as a betrayal of Jewish solidarity, but accepts the food the council donates. He later witnesses the Germans beating Czerniakow when he refuses to sign the first deportation order. For increased impact, Wajda times Czerniakow's suicide to coincide with the evacuation of Korczak's orphanage. The real Korczak eulogized Czerniakow at his funeral for fulfilling "his task of protecting the dignity of the Jews."[98]

Korczak has no compunction about consorting with disreputable elements in the ghetto if he could raise money from them. By chance, he meets a former student named Itzek Szulc, whose elegant clothes manifest his prosperity as a smuggler. Szulc brings Korczak to a nightclub where other Jewish racketeers gather to escape the despair of the ghetto by drinking, eating, gambling, and listening to music. He implores his cohorts to donate money to Korczak. Suddenly, a group of teenagers barge into the room and try to assassinate Abraham Gancwajch, the kingpin of the ghetto underworld. A boy from the orphanage participates in this attack and censures Korczak later that evening for mingling with the "dregs" of Jewish society. Korczak obstinately replies, "I will see the devil himself to save my children. I have no dignity. I have 200 children."

The rogues gallery of shady Jewish characters carousing at the nightclub outraged some reviewers who felt Wajda had stoked the embers of Polish anti-Semitism. Yet, in a diary entry about his meeting with Szulc, Korczak wondered what passersby must have thought about his conversing "in broad daylight on the church doorstep with a smuggler. The children must need money badly." He adds, "He [Szulc] was too honest for a crook."[99] Wajda has Szulc reappear on the train platform desperately trying to furnish Korczak with a forged American passport.[100] Korczak did solicit donations from the Jewish felons who congregated at the Esplanade Restaurant, which was notorious for being "one of the worst nests of drunkenness and vice" in the ghetto. Wajda's image of ghetto nightlife is not a malicious fabrication.[101] Korczak sought help for his children from Gancwajch, who previously had ransomed him out of prison in 1940 when he was arrested for refusing to wear a Jewish armband.[102] Contrary to Abraham Brumberg's claim that Wajda portrays Gancwajch "in stereotypical fashion—smarmy with beard and black kaftan," the actor cast as Gancwajch sports a suit, v-neck sweater, and a tie. To be sure, he is a corrupt man, but he is not the Jewish caricature Brumberg recalls seeing.[103]

The closing scene of *Korczak* is problematic, but not because Wajda imposes a Christian meaning on the deaths of the orphans or "wants to spare us pain," as his detractors have charged.[104] Betty Jean Lifton has suggested that Wajda may have revived a Polish legend that the Old Doctor and his children were spared when "the carriage with the transport became miraculously unlinked from the train."[105] Perhaps Wajda tried to honor Korczak's fervent wish that his children be granted a dignified death.[106] Yet, Wajda preceded the closing scene with an unforgettable shot of Korczak and his orphans waving a banner with a Star of David on one side and the emblem of his fictional hero, King Matt, on the other as they proceed to the *Umschlagplatz*. The ponderous beat of a dirge intensifies the impact of what has been perceived as a "mute protest" against Nazi genocide. Indeed, it is one of the few scenes in the movie that has any background music.[107] By following this scene with an uplifting ending, Wajda pulled "back from the brink over which the facts require his story to plunge."[108] Yet, it is difficult to believe that Korczak's half-Jewish scriptwriter,

Agnieszka Holland, Christianized the closing scene to please Polish Catholics.[109] Indeed, the closing caption informing viewers that Korczak and his children were gassed at Treblinka undercuts the illusion of a happy ending, as does the return of the dirge as background music for the closing credits.

Korczak deserved more acclaim and exposure than it initially received. It became the casualty of Jewish Polish polemics, Lanzmann's vendetta against it, and the timing of its Cannes premier, which coincided with a rash of Jewish grave desecrations in Carpentras, France. Interestingly, the movie received positive receptions in both Germany and Israel, prompting the latter to mandate that it be shown as part of the country's school curriculum.[110] The controversies surrounding the movie subsided by the late 1990s, when the American and French Academies of Motion Pictures recognized Wajda's cinematic career. In his letter nominating Wajda for the Lifetime Achievement Award, Spielberg called *Korczak* "one of the most important European pictures about the Holocaust."[111] John Hoberman has remarked that "in the face of annihilation, Janusz Korcak's tenderness is a terrifying reproach."[112]

THE JEW AS FUGITIVE: *EUROPA, EUROPA*
Directed by Agnieszka Holland
(France, Germany: Les Films du Lasange/CCC Filmkunst, 1991)

> Being half Polish and half Jewish makes you very confused and schizophrenic, also emigration opens up questions about who you really are. . . . The main question interesting to me is how much we are created by expectations of people, how people want to see us or to push us. In our decisions, opinions, are we ourselves and how much are we influenced by circumstances?[113]
>
> —Agnieszka Holland

Filmmakers have a long record of mining the comic or tragic potential of Jewish characters' being mistaken for Aryans or vice verse in pictures like *The Great Dictator* (1940), *To Be or Not to Be* (1942), *Bad Luck* (1960), *The Two of Us* (1966), and *Mr. Klein* (1976).[114] The irony inherent in the contradiction between the immutable traits ascribed to Jews by Hitler and the diverse appearances of Jews and Aryans renders the axioms of Nazi racial science ridiculous. If a Jewish barber looks identical to Chaplin's Adenoid Hynkel as happens in *The Great Dictator*, then the claim of Aryan superiority must be as fractured as Hynkel's German is.[115] If a Gentile art dealer who profits from the sale of paintings confiscated from Jewish homes can be detained and deported as a Jew, as occurs in *Mr. Klein,* then equality before the law is not a Jewish deception to deracinate society but a necessary guarantee against arbitrary arrest.[116]

Films based on true stories of Jews passing as Aryans usually have been dramas about attempts to hide Jews by furnishing them with false papers or spy movies about Jews infiltrating Nazi agencies or hate groups. Louis Malle's *Goodbye, Children* (1987) exemplifies the first kind of movie. The head priest of a Catholic school for boys provides refuge for a Jewish youngster, who all the other students think is Christian. One student discovers his real identity and befriends him, but the school's former kitchen assistant exacts his revenge for being fired by betraying the Jewish boy.[117] *A Woman at War* (1991) casts the Aryan imposter in the role of a resister. Helene Moszkiewiez relies on her Aryan looks and fluent German to get hired as a secretary at Gestapo headquarters in occupied Belgium. She copies lists with the names and addresses of Jews slated for arrest and gives them advance warnings.[118] *The Infiltrator* (1995) tells the true story of an Israeli journalist who poses as an agent for a wealthy American neo-Nazi to expose the racist activities of German skinhead gangs.[119]

Europa, Europa mixes the comedic and tragic modes of mistaken Jewish identity during the Holocaust. Based on Solomon Perel's memoir, it tells the implausible but true story of how a Jewish teenager parlayed his handsome face, linguistic abilities, and quick thinking into convincing imitations of a doctrinaire young communist in the Soviet Union and a Nazi zealot in the Hitler Youth. Solly's plasticity emerges as a survival reflex to a series of life-threatening situations. Perel and Holland perceived him as the "Candide of the Twentieth Century," who has "been cast among the cannibals" of war-torn Europe. He evades detection by mimicking the groups that adopt him.[120]

While outwitting the enemy through imitation is a humorous premise, the movie repeatedly reminds the audience that any lapse in Solly's masquerade can have fatal consequences. The beginning of the movie flashes forward to a scene where Solly is drowning while wearing his Hitler Youth uniform. His narration informs us that his birthday fell on the same day as Hitler's.[121] Two childhood memories foreshadow his future quandary, his circumcision, which marks him as a Jew, and a narrow escape from a Nazi mob that he eludes by jumping naked out of a bathtub, hiding in a barrel, and returning home clad only in a borrowed leather coat and sporting a swastika armband. When he enters the dining room, the bloodied body of his sister lays on a table as his grief stricken father pounds his head upon it.[122] The jacket Solly wears might have belonged to the person who killed his sister. His family moves to Lódz in Poland, but when Germany invades that country, his brother Isaac and he flee to the Soviet Union. Their escape route brings them to the Bug River, which they must cross to safety. Their ferry capsizes, plunging Solly into the water, from which he is saved by a Russian soldier.

Before he had embarked on his journey, Solly expressed his ambition to be an actor. Now he has the opportunity to play the roles assigned to him.

Placed in a Soviet orphanage, he parrots the communist opinions that his guardians inculcate in him. Although his Jewish ancestry is a matter of indifference to them, they expect him to renounce God and his bourgeois origins. He does both. Two years later, the Germans attack the Soviet Union and capture Solly. As they execute the Jews among their captives, Solly claims he is an ethnic German named Josef Peters whose parents were slain by Bolsheviks. His Nordic features and fluent German lend credibility to his alibi. Although Solly witnesses the shooting of Jews and the hanging of Russians, he deceives himself into believing that the Third Reich only intends to expel the Jews. Josef befriends a German homosexual named Robert, who learns Josef is circumcised when he tries to fondle him. By keeping Josef's secret, Robert belies Josef's notion of the German stereotype. This prompts Josef to ponder the vagaries of national and religious differences: "Who was my friend, who my enemy? How could they be so kind to me and at the same time kill others horribly. What set us apart? A simple foreskin?"

When the Red Army bombards his bivouac, Solly prepares to surrender and pretend to be a communist. Coincidentally, this places him in front of a German unit, which wins the battle, making it appear that he led the assault. To reward his valor, he is enrolled in a Hitler Youth academy. In the movie's funniest scene, Josef, now renamed Jupp, is selected by his racial science teacher to model what an "authentic Aryan" looks like.[123] Leni, a fanatical Nazi girl, tries to seduce Jupp because she wants to bear a baby for the führer. Jupp rejects her advances because he literally cannot risk having his penis fall into hostile hands. In a nightmare, he dons his Nazi leather jacket to attend a seder, but his family no longer recognizes him. When the Nazis raid the apartment, Jupp's sister shoves him into a closet, where Hitler is covering his allegedly circumcised penis.

Losing his sense of self in his disguise, Jupp searches for his roots by visiting the Lodz ghetto, where he last saw his parents alive. He boards a trolley that runs through the ghetto but from which he cannot disembark. He scratches a slit in a whitewashed streetcar window. Through this aperture, Jupp catches ghastly glimpses of gaunt figures milling about or stacking corpses onto overflowing carts. He briefly thinks that he recognizes his mother among these haggard apparitions. As Paul Coates has commented, "The boy straining to see through the hole also represents the film-maker and ourselves peering into the past, appalled by our inability to change it and the illusion of presence that feeds the impossible hope that a time-traveler might yet do so."[124]

Jupp fortunately finds a substitute mother in Leni's mother, who promises not to betray him, then seduces him. Just as it appears that his lack of identity papers might unravel his elaborate ruse, the Red Army defeats Jupp's detachment. A Soviet officer dismisses Solly's claim that he is Jewish because the Russian soldiers have seen how the Jewish population was decimated in the death camps they liberated in Poland. He hands Solly over to a group of Jewish survivors for execution, but his brother Isaac steps out from the group and embraces Solly. The two celebrate their reunion by urinating in the rain, exposing their penises without fear that their circumcisions will stigmatize them.[125]

Solly's voice-over records that from then on he "decided to be only a Jew" and immigrated to Israel. He adds that he "barely hesitated" to have his sons circumcised when they were born. The closing scene shows the real Solomon Perel standing by a river and singing the Hebrew song, "Hee Nay Ma Tov," whose lyrics proclaim, "How sweet it is to sit surrounded by your brothers." This ending alludes to a scene from *Shoah* in which a survivor returns to his Polish hometown, where he sings as he once had done to entertain the SS. Holland may be trying to prove that "fictional means can serve a Holocaust story just as well as Lanzmann's painstaking and long-winded devotion to documented 'real time.'"[126] Omer Bartov criticized the film for insinuating that Solly managed to survive because he possessed "qualities which seem to distinguish this resourceful youth from his less gifted six million brethren."[127] Other scholars felt the ending exploited the Holocaust to justify the need for a Jewish state. Yet, Solly evinces no awareness of Zionism until the real Solly relates what has happened to him since the defeat of Germany.[128]

Europa, Europa transgresses the ideological, national, socioeconomic, and theological borders that separate political parties, countries, classes, and religions. Solly "decided to be only a Jew" and "barely hesitated" to circumcise his sons. These words indicate that one's religion is voluntary and not genetic. One may choose to circumcise one's sons, but this ritual should not confer a death sentence on those who undergo it.[129] Judith Doneson's interpretation of the movie as affirming Nazi stereotypes of Aryan beauty and Jewish deformity with its emphasis on Solly's pretty face and telltale penis overlook how Holland satirizes the misuse of physical traits as markers of character.[130]

Holland mocks both the biological determinism of the Nazis and the material determinism of the Soviets. She draws an analogy between the ideological fanaticism of both in a dream sequence of Hitler dancing with Stalin when Germany and the Soviet Union partitioned Poland in 1939. Although equating the two totalitarian ideologies is a legacy of cold war America, the concept was resurrected in the 1990s by filmmakers from countries previously ruled by communist regimes. The continuity of oppression under Nazism and communism has appeared as a theme in other recent Eastern European movies like *All That Really Matters* (1992), *Underground* (1995), *Sunshine* (1999), *Divided We Fall* (2000), and *Zelary* (2003).[131]

Europa, Europa's multicultural message, multinational origins, and discomforting synthesis of comic, sensual, and violent elements hurt its reception in

Solomon Perel, posing as Hitler Youth Josef Peters (Marco Hofschneider), embraces the pro-Nazi Leni (Julie Delpy). Europa, Europa. Press kit, *courtesy of the Nostalgia Factory.*

the newly reunified Germany. The German title, *HitlerYouth Solomon,* may have repelled Germans wary of dredging up the Nazi past. The German Film Commission justified its refusal to nominate it as Germany's entry for the Oscar in the Best Foreign Film category by arguing that it was not solely a German production and that the "trashy" tale did not merit the award. German critics labeled the movie "voyeuristic" and "unbelievable."[132] This reaction may have reflected the rising resentment against the influx of asylum seekers into united Germany.[133] The movie failed dismally at the box office in Germany.[134]

In the United States, *Europa, Europa* attracted a larger following and won the Golden Globe Award for Best Foreign Language Film.[135] The trailer described it as "an unbelievable epic of survival" and "incredible adventure" combining "realistic drama and ironic humor."[136] Ads highlighted this mix of genres to broaden its appeal.[137] Some feminist critics hailed Holland's portrayal of the penis as a symbol of vulnerability rather than virility.[138] The website "Teach with Movies" recommended the movie as "an excellent platform for a discussion of the similarities and differences between Hitler and Stalin."[139] Hal Hinson concluded, "There are a great many movies about the tragic experiences of the Jews during the Second World War, but only a handful as passionate, as subtly intelligent, as universal as this one."[140]

THE JEW AS INMATE: *TRIUMPH OF THE SPIRIT*
Directed by Robert M. Young
(United States: Nova International Films, 1989)[141]

> The pretence that from the wreckage of mass murder we can salvage a tribute to the victory of the human spirit is a version of Holocaust reality more necessary than true.[142]
>
> —Lawrence Langer

The genre of the prison movie has served as the prototype for films about the incarceration of Jews in concentration and death camps. The Holocaust version of the prison film focuses on inmates whose actions have not warranted the degradation, deprivation, and death that awaits them in the camps. In this inverted universe of injustice, the drama arises from the struggle of the inmate to stay alive and retain his or her sanity and solidarity with other prisoners.[143]

In movies about convicts and prisoners of war, innocent or repentant inmates cultivate a special skill that provides meaning and structure for coping with the tedium and torment of imprisonment, like accounting in *The Shawshank Redemption* (1994), ornithology in *The Bird Man of Alcatraz* (1962), and faith healing in *The Green Mile* (1999). The memory of a loved one or a friendship with another prisoner might sustain the protagonist, as in *Midnight Express* (1978). The hope of reversing an unjust sentence or organizing an escape from what is patently an inhumane institution motivates other cinematic prisoners to endure their incarceration, as illustrated in films like *Gideon's Trumpet* (1980), *The Hurricane* (1999), *The Bridge over the River Kwai* (1957), and *The Great Escape* (1963).[144]

Biopics, docudramas, and fictional films about death camps feature characters who rely on the same repertoire of survival strategies. The SS spared the lives of some Jews who had talents they wanted to exploit. In *The Last Stop* (1948), the heroine Marta acts as a translator for the Germans and temporarily escapes with the aid of the Resistance to bring evidence to the Allies about the mass murder committed at the camp.[145] In *Playing for Time* (1980), Fania Fénelon rises above the assault on her dignity by performing in the women's orchestra at Auschwitz. She prevents members of her ensemble from becoming demoralized and divided by exemplifying decency and stressing their common plight over their national and political differences.[146] In *Kornblumenblau* (1988), a Polish Jew evades selection because the German guards enjoy his accordion rendition of the title melody.[147] Similarly, a French mime in *The Last Butterfly* (1990) is promised his release for staging a play for doomed children.[148]

Prison and concentration camp movies often have used athletic competition between inmates or against guards as a metaphor for the Darwinian struggle for existence within such institutions. Track in *The Loneliness of the Long Distance Runner* (1962), football in *The Longest Yard* (1974, 2005), boxing in *The Boxer and Death* (1962), and soccer in *The Last Goal* (1961) and *Victory* (1981)[149] allegorize the conflict between prison officials and prisoners or within the psyches of the inmates. Such contests can humiliate prisoners by reducing them to gladiators who entertain guards gambling on the results. The games between guards and prisoners are usually rigged in favor of the latter to dispirit the captives, but sports also can afford prisoners an opportunity to beat their superiors, sublimate their anger, or divert attention from an escape being mounted by other inmates.[150]

The ad campaign and title for Robert M. Young's *Triumph of the Spirit* (1989) misled viewers into believing the film was primarily about how the Jewish boxer Salamo Arouch "triumphed" over the system designed to degrade and destroy him by winning the boxing matches he fought to entertain and enrich the SS officers who attended and bet on them. The cover of the video box shows Salamo, played by Willem Dafoe, standing in the ring, gazing down at an opponent he has knocked out. On the back cover, stills of two scenes from boxing matches are situated beneath a larger picture of a transport train arriving at Auschwitz with SS guards forming a cordon in front of it. The film's trailer consists mostly of shots from Salamo's bouts. The narrator claims that "this is the true story of one man's fight for survival and victory in the face of death." One frame evokes the signature scene from *Rocky* (1976) with a close-up of Salamo raising his gloved fists above his head.[151]

Yet, the cumulative impression left by Young's movie undermines whatever uplifting impact its title and publicity imply. Filmed at Auschwitz, the film authentically re-creates each phase of the Jewish ordeal: ghettoization, deportation selection, head shaving, tattooing of identification numbers, lengthy role calls, exhausting drills, overcrowded wooden bunks, arduous labor, starvation, and the gassing and cremation of those unfit for work. Salamo boxes to win extra bread to share with his father and, reluctantly, other bunkmates begging for a morsel. Although he remains alive by knocking out his opponents, his brother is killed for refusing to carry corpses to the ovens; his father is gassed; his former best friend is transformed into a vicious *kapo*, and his lover's sister feigns pregnancy to obtain extra food from her starving sibling.

Although Young shows much of the physical violence and torture inflicted on individual characters, he leaves it to the imagination of the audience to visualize what mass gassings or cremations would look like. The camera documents the disrobing and anxiety of those shoved into the gas chambers, but pulls away at the last instant to reveal what happens to the fortunate few who have been selected to toil until they are no longer deemed productive. When Salamo gets reassigned to the *Sonderkommando*, whose members carry bodies from the gas chambers to the crematoria, the camera records the horrified expression on his face rather than the burning corpses.

A closer scrutiny of the movie reveals that it is not about the triumph of the spirit but rather about "choiceless choices," to use Lawrence Langer's term for the dilemma faced by death camp inmates, who were never offered any moral alternatives to prolong their survival.[152] The synopsis on the back of the video box succinctly describes this quandary: "For every time Salamo wins, his opponent dies in the gas showers."[153] Although this message initially is overshadowed by Salamo's pugilistic prowess, it becomes evident when he is summoned to fight his best friend, Jacko, by the SS major. Since Jacko is bleeding and staggering from a savage beating, Salamo balks at the order and tells the SS major, "This is not boxing!" The major agrees, shoots Jacko, and turns the gun on himself. Implicated in the dynamiting of a crematorium, Salamo is tortured, dragged up a flight of stairs, and left naked in a cold damp cell. The movie opens with Salamo recounting the events that led to this moment of utter abandonment and misery.

Following the liberation of the camp, Salamo wraps a blanket around his shoulders and hobbles down an empty road while pondering his fate: "All those I love are gone. Their faces and what happened here are forever burned in my mind. How can we do this to our brothers?" The only relief from his despair is the hope that he will find his fiancée, Allegra. The closing caption informs the audience that the two married after the war and immigrated to Israel, but their belated wedding cannot fill the loss to their families.

Triumph of the Spirit features Jewish and other ethnic characters rarely seen in Holocaust films. Its director, Robert Young, established his reputation as an independent filmmaker of movies that depicted Latino life in the United States. The best known of these is *The Ballad of Gregorio Cortez* (1982) about a Mexican fugitive eluding an American posse.[154] Salamo and his father are muscular stevedores dressed for dock work until they are stripped of their clothes at Auschwitz. Allegra and her sister have Mediterranean complexions and facial features. The Sephardic looks of the leading characters do not resemble those of actors usually typecast as Askenazi Jews in movies about the Holocaust. For example, many of the Jewish men in *Schindler's List* are bearded males wearing traditional religious garb or merchants initially attired in suits. The women are either pious wives wearing long dresses and babushkas to cover their heads or stylishly dressed daughters, mothers, or grandmothers from affluent families.[155]

The musical score of *Triumph of the Spirit* expresses this cultural difference by using traditional Sephardic instrumentation and melodies. The ominous choral odes accompanying the scenes of Jews being separated, slaughtered, and incinerated are sung in Ladino, the Sephardic language that evolved from medieval Spanish.[156] As the credits roll at the end of the film, images of Salamo, his brother, and father performing Greek folk dances emphasize their Sephardic heritage and the destruction of their culture.

The *kapo* in charge of Salamo's barracks is a gypsy played by Edward James Olmos, a veteran of many of Young's films.[157] He is a stern taskmaster when disciplining his fellow inmates. His privileged position enables him to obtain victuals, costumes for entertaining the Germans before boxing matches, and a doll for his daughter from the confiscated items the Germans have stockpiled. His efficacy as a *kapo* dispels suspicions that he could be an accomplice in the plot to bomb the crematorium. Compared to previous depictions of exotic gypsies in World War II movies like *The Golden Earrings* (1947), the gypsy in *Triumph of the Spirit* is a tough but ultimately decent figure who yields unemotionally to the power the Germans exert over him while preparing for the time when he can dynamite the crematoria and welcome the Russians when they liberate Auschwitz.[158] Young's inclusion of the gypsy reflects a growing awareness of the non-Jewish victims of the Third Reich[159] (see table 3.4).

Many of the criticisms leveled at *Triumph of the Spirit* faulted the movie for its unflinching depiction of the relentless degradation of the inmates through backbreaking labor, intolerable living conditions, and the omnipresent threat of death. Its main characters betray, harm, or discipline other prisoners to survive.[160] Roger Ebert gave the film a rating of one star and deemed Salamo's triumphs Pyrrhic because they "cost the lives of his opponents, who were fellow Jews." Ebert resented how the boxing matches manipulate the audience "to cheer for Salamo against his enemies" and "feel relieved" when he wins.[161] A reviewer for a religious website wrote that the film has no "Christian [or Jewish] moral content and is not particularly uplifting even at the end."[162]

Yet, Young's depiction of the ethical vacuum that the Nazis devised at Auschwitz makes the movie disturbing and effective. Dafoe's prior starring roles as the moral conscience of his army unit in *Platoon* (1986) and Jesus in

Table 3.4. Number of Holocaust Films Featuring Non-Jewish Victims of the Third Reich

Years	Gypsy	Homosexual	Disabled	Christian
1945–1949	1	0	1	3
1950–1959	1	0	1	2
1960–1969	2	1	5	3
1970–1979	1	7 (5 porn)	4	2
1980–1989	3	5	3	9
1990–1999	7	10	3	8

The Last Temptation of Christ (1988) evoke associations with characters who suffer for the choices they make. His lack of affect models how inmates suppressed their despair, fears, and rage. Only Salamo's intense love for Allegra prevents him from becoming demoralized as a gladiator who boxes in order to live. The movie's depressing content contributed to its poor box-office showing.[163] Some viewers found its somber message enlightening, as this Internet blog indicates: *"Triumph of the Spirit* made me squirm because it showed me just how complex the Holocaust experience was for individuals who had to make life and death decisions. This is what lifts *Triumph of the Spirit* way above most other Holocaust films."[164] While spurned as an incongruous blend of a sports movie with a Holocaust film, the movie paved the way for more graphic cinematic portrayals of Jewish suffering during World War II. In 2002, MGM released it on DVD.[165]

NOTES

1. Robert Rosenstone, *Visions of the Past: The Challenge of Film to Our Idea of History* (Cambridge, MA: Harvard University Press, 1995), 59.

2. George F. Custen, *Bio/Pics: How Hollywood Constructed Public History* (New Brunswick, NJ: Rutgers University Press, 1992), 6–7.

3. Steve Neale, *Genre and Hollywood* (New York: Routledge, 2000), 60–65.

4. Custen, *Bio/Pics*, 34–80.

5. Custen, *Bio/Pics*, 7.

6. *Playing for Time*, directed by Daniel Mann (United States, 1980); Fania Fénelon, *Playing for Time,* trans. Judith Landry (New York: Atheneum, 1976); Jeffrey Shandler, *While America Watches: Televising the Holocaust* (New York: Oxford University Press, 1999), 215–19.

7. *Wallenberg: A Hero's Story*, directed by Lamont Johnson (United States, 1985), based on Frederick E. Werbell and Thurston Clarke, *Lost Hero: The Mystery of Raoul Wallenberg* (New York: McGraw-Hill, 1982).

8. *The Attic: The Hiding of Anne Frank*, directed by John Erman (United States and United Kingdom, 1988), based on Miep Gies with Alison Leslie Gold, *Anne Frank Remembered: The Story of the Woman Who Helped to Hide the Frank Family* (New York: Simon and Schuster, 1987).

9. See Tino Balio, "Introduction to Part II," Michelle Himes, "Pay Television: Breaking the Broadcast Bottleneck," Bruce A. Austin, "Home Video: The Second-Run 'Theatre' of the 1990s," and Laurie Schulze, "The Made for TV Movie: Industrial Practice, Cultural Form, Popular Reception," in *Hollywood in the Age of Television*, ed. Tino Balio (Boston: Unwin Hyman, 1990), 259–96, 297–318, 319–49, 351–76; Mark Jancovich and Lucy Faire with Sarah Stubbins, *The Place of the Audience* (London: British Film Institute, 2003), 155–96.

10. Megan Mullen, *The Rise of Cable Programming in the United States: Revolution or Evolution* (Austin: University of Texas Press, 2003), 146–61.

11. *A Friendship in Vienna,* directed by Arthur Alan Seidelman (United States, 1988), based on Doris Orgel, *The Devil in Vienna* (New York: Dial Books, 1978).

12. *Rescuers: Stories of Courage—Two Women,* directed by Peter Bogdanovich (United States, 1997); *Rescuers: Stories of Courage—Two Couples,* directed by Tim Hunter and Lynn Litton (United States, 1998); *Rescuers: Stories of Courage—Two Families,* directed by Tim Hunter (United States, 1998).

13. Tino Balio, introduction to Part II in *Hollywood in the Age of Television,* 259–96; Neale, *Genre and Hollywood,* 60–65n10, 144.

14. Peter Novick, *The Holocaust in American Life* (Boston: Houghton Mifflin, 1999), 272–81; Oren Baruch Stier, *Committed to Memory: Cultural Mediations of the Holocaust* (Amherst: University of Massachusetts Press, 2003), 67–109.

15. *Reunion,* directed by Jerry Schatzberg (France and West Germany, 1989); *For Those I Loved,* directed by Robert Enrico (France and Canada, 1983); *Fragments of Isabella,* directed by Ronan O'Leary (Ireland, 1989).

16. Novick, *The Holocaust,* 189–203.

17. *The Last Five Days,* directed by Percy Adlon (West Germany, 1972); *The White Rose,* directed by Michael Verhoeven (West Germany, 1982); *Georg Elser,* directed by Klaus Maria Brandauer (West Germany, 1989).

18. *Charlotte,* directed by Franz Weisz (Netherlands, 1981).

19. *Pétain,* directed by Jean Marboeuf (France, 1993); *Hamsun,* directed by Jan Troell (Norway, 1996); Caroline Joan Picart, *The Holocaust Film Sourcebook,* Vol. 1 (Westport, CT: Praeger, 2004), 167–68.

20. *Red Cherry,* directed by Ye Ying (China, 1995).

21. *The Visas That Saved Lives,* directed by Katsumi Ohyama (Japan, 1992).

22. *Hanna's War,* directed by Menachem Golan (Israel, 1988); Lawrence Baron, "Women as Resistance Fighters in Recent Popular Films: The Case of Hanna Senesh and Helene Moszkiewiez," in *Women and the Holocaust: Narrative and Representation,* ed. Esther Fuchs (Lanham, MD: University Press of America, 1999), 89–96.

23. Rosenfeld, *Imagining Hitler* (Bloomington: Indiana University Press, 1985), xx.

24. See Ian Kershaw, *Hitler: 1889–1936 Hubris* (New York: W. W. Norton, 1999); Ian Kershaw, *Hitler: 1936–1945 Nemesis* (New York: W. W. Norton, 2000); John Lukacs, *The Hitler of History* (New York: Alfred A. Knopf, 1998); Ron Rosenbaum, *Explaining Hitler: The Search for the Origins of His Evil* (New York: Random House, Perennial, 1998).

25. *The Last Ten Days,* directed by Georg Wilhelm Papst (West Germany, 1955); *It Happened on the 20th of July,* directed by Georg Wilhelm Papst (West Germany, 1955); Marc Silberman, *German Cinema: Texts in Context* (Detroit, MI: Wayne State University Press, 1995), 128–42. Also see Charles P. Mitchell, *The Hitler Filmography: Worldwide Feature Film and Television Miniseries Portrayals, 1940 through 2000* (Jefferson, NC: McFarland and Co., 2002), 136–40.

26. Shandler, *While America Watches,* 83–124; *Engineer of Death: The Eichmann Story,* directed by Paul Bogard (United States, 1960); *Operation Eichmann,* directed by R. G. Springsteen (United States, 1961).

27. *Hitler,* directed by Stuart Heisler (United States, 1962); Mitchell, *The Hitler Filmography,* 92–96.

28. *The Death of Adolf Hitler,* directed by Rex Firkin (United Kingdom, 1972); Mitchell, *The Hitler Filmography,* 35–39; *Le Bunker,* directed by Roger Iglesis (France, 1972).

29. *Hitler: The Last Ten Days,* directed by Ennio de Concini (United Kingdom and Italy, 1972); Gerhard Boldt, *Hitler: The Last Ten Days,* trans. Sandra Bance (New York: Coward, McCann and Geoghegan, 1973); Lukacs, *The Hitler of History,* 8–9; Rosenbaum, *Explaining Hitler,* 63–77.

30. *The Bunker,* directed by George Schaeffer (United States, 1981); Mitchell, *The Hitler Filmography,* 25–29; *The Downfall,* directed by Oliver Hirschbiegel (Austria, Germany, Italy, 2004).

31. Uwe Dietrich Adam, *Judenpolitik im Dritten Reich* (Duesseldorf: Droste Verlag, 1972); Martin Broszat, *Der Staat Hitlers* (Munich: Deutscher Taschenbuch Verlag, 1969); Christopher Browning, *The Final Solution and the German Foreign Office* (New York: Holmes and Meier, 1978); Raul Hilberg, *The Destruction of the European Jews* (New York: Quadrangle Books, 1961); Karl Schleunes, *The Twisted Road to Auschwitz: Nazi Policy toward German Jews, 1933–1939* (Urbana: University of Illinois, 1970).

32. *Death Is My Trade,* directed by Theodor Kotulla (West Germany, 1977); Christine Haase, "Theodor Kotulla's *Excerpts from a German Life* (Aus einem deutschen Leben, 1977), or the Inability to Speak: Cinematic Holocaust Representation in Germany," *Film and History* 32, no. 2 (2002): 48–61.

33. *Reinhard Heydrich—Manager of Terror,* directed by Heinz Schirk (West Germany, 1977).

34. *The Wannsee Conference,* directed by Heinz Schirk (Austria and West Germany, 1984).

35. *Inside the Third Reich,* directed by Marvin Chomsky (United States, 1982).

36. *Our Hitler: A Film from Germany,* directed by Hans-Jürgen Syberberg (West Germany, 1978); Anton Kaes, *From Hitler to Heimat: The Return of History as Film* (Cambridge, MA: Harvard University Press, 1989), 39–72; Eric L. Santner, *Stranded Objects: Mourning, Memory, and Film in Postwar Germany* (Ithaca, NY: Cornell University Press, 1990), 130–48.

37. *Bob Roberts,* directed by Tim Robbins (United States, 1992); *Wag the Dog,* directed by Barry Levinson (United States, 1997); *Weapons of Mass Distraction,* directed by Stephen Surjik (United States, 1997).

38. See the script notes on the movie's official website, at www.emptymirror.com (accessed October 18, 2001); Gavriel Rosenfeld, *The World Hitler Never Made: Alternate History and the Memory of Nazism* (New York: Cambridge University Press, 2005), 254–56. Rosenfeld interprets the ending as "showing him (Hitler) capable of a kind of repentance."

39. Kevin Thomas, "Movie Review: *The Empty Mirror,*" *Los Angeles Times,* May 7, 1999; John Patterson, "Our Hitler: Barry J. Hershey's *The Empty Mirror,*" *LA Weekly* (May 7–13, 1999).

40. Rosenbaum, *Explaining Hitler,* 90.

41. "Awards," "Box office," *The Empty Mirror,* at www.imdb.com (accessed October 18, 2001); Mitchell, *The Hitler Filmography,* 49–53; David Rosen with Peter Hamilton, *Off-Hollywood: The Making and Marketing of Independent Films* (New York: Grove Weidenfeld, 1990), 296–303.

42. *Conversation with the Beast,* directed by Armin Mueller-Stahl (Germany, 1996). Armin Mueller-Stahl, quoted by Annette Insdorf, *Indelible Shadows: Film and the Holocaust,* 3rd ed. (New York: Cambridge University Press, 2003), 282–83. A similar theme of confronting an elderly Mengele is the plotline for *After the Truth,* directed by Roland Suso Richter (Germany and the United States, 1999).

43. *Molokh,* directed by Alexsandr Sokurov (France, Italy, Germany, Japan, Russia, 1999).

44. Martin Luther King Jr., quoted in *Bonhoeffer: Agent of Grace,* at www.pbs.org/ opbbonhoeffer/man/index.html (accessed February 28, 2002).

45. Bill Niven, *Facing the Nazi Past: United Germany and the Legacy of the Third Reich* (New York: Routledge, 2002), 62–69; Caroline W. Wiedmer, *The Claims of Memory: Representation of the Holocaust in Contemporary Germany and France* (Ithaca, NY: Cornell University Press, 1999), 164–89.

46. *The Murderers Are among Us,* directed by Wolfgang Staudte (East Germany, 1946); *Marriage in the Shadows,* directed by Kurt Maetzig (East Germany, 1947); *Lissy,* directed by Konrad Wolf (East Germany, 1957); *Professor Mamlock,* directed by Konrad Wolf (East Germany, 1960/1961); *I Was Nineteen,* directed by Konrad Wolf; *Mama, I Am Alive,* directed by Konrad Wolf (East Germany, 1976); *Sansibar,* directed by Bernhard Wicki (East Germany, 1987); Silberman, *Texts in Context,* 145–61; Sean Allan and John Sandford, *DEFA: East German Cinema, 1946–1992* (New York: Berghahn Books, 1999); Wiedmer, *The Claims,* 164–89.

47. Niven, *The Nazi Past,* 69–74.

48. *Canaris: Master Spy,* directed by Alfred Weidenmann (West Germany, 1954); *The Devil's General,* directed by Helmut Kaeutner (West Germany, 1955); *Winterspelt,* directed by Eberhard Fechner (West Germany, 1977); Reimer and Reimer, *Nazi-Retro Film,* 98–104.

49. Niven, *The Nazi Past,* 73–93; *Georg Elser: An Individual from Germany,* directed by Klaus Maria Brandauer (West Germany, 1989).

50. Niven, *The Nazi Past,* 77–84.

51. Niven, *The Nazi Past,* 16–19.

52. *The Hiding Place,* directed by James Collier (United States, 1975). Corrie ten Boom with John and Elizabeth Sherrill, *The Hiding Place* (Washington Depot, CT: Chosen Books, 1971).

53. Lawrence Baron, "Supersessionism without Contempt: The Holocaust Evangelism of Corrie ten Boom," in *Christian Responses to Nazi Germany,* ed. Donald J. Dietrich (Syracuse, NY: Syracuse University Press, 2003), 119–31.

54. *From a Far Country,* directed by Krzysztof Zanussi (Italy, 1981); *The Scarlet and the Black,* directed by Jerry London (United States, 1983); *Pope John Paul II,* directed by Herbert Wise (United States, 1984); *Life for Life,* directed by Krzystof Zanussi (Poland and Germany, 1991); *The Hill of a Thousand Children,* directed by Jean-Louis Lorenzi (France, 1996); *Witness against Hitler,* directed by Betsan Morris Evans (United Kingdom, 1996).

55. Dietrich Bonhoeffer, *The Cost of Discipleship,* trans. R. H. Fuller (New York: Macmillan, 1959); Dietrich Bonhoeffer, *Life Together: A Discussion of Christian Fellowship* (San Francisco: Harper and Row, 1979); Dietrich Bonhoeffer, *Letters and Papers from*

Prison, ed. Eberhard Bethge (New York: Scribner, 1997); Dietrich Bonhoeffer, *Ethics,* ed. Eberhard Bethge (New York: Simon and Schuster, 1995).

56. Eberhard Bethge, *Dietrich Bonhoeffer: A Biography*, ed. Victoria Barnett, rev. ed. (Minneapolis: Fortress Press, 2000); *Hanged on a Twisted Cross,* directed by T. N. Mohan (United States, 1996). *Bonhoeffer and Canaris: Enemies of the State,* directed by Uli Edel (Germany and United Kingdom: 2000); *Bonhoeffer*, directed by Martin Doblmeier (United States, 2003); Stephen R. Haynes, *The Bonhoeffer Phenomenon: Portraits of a Protestant Saint* (Minneapolis, MN: Fortress Press, 2004).

57. Niven, *The Nazi Past,* 89.

58. Peter, "Agrees with Ginsburg," June 17, 2000, at www.hollywoodjesus.com/bonhoeffer2.html (accessed February 28, 2002).

59. U. Mies, "*Bonhoeffer: Agent of Grace,*" at www.cityguide/de/event/kino/filme/bonhoeffer.html (accessed March 7, 2002).

60. See www1.aal.org/Bonhoeffer/aalsrole.html (accessed February 28, 2002).

61. "Videos," Gateway Films Vision Video catalog.

62. Mike McGranaghan, "Christian Cinema," at www.geocities.com/gamut_mag/christn.htm (accessed February 28, 2002).

63. *Mary and Joseph: A Story of Faith,* directed by Eric Till (Canada, West Germany, and Israel, 1979); *Clarence*, directed by Eric Till (Canada, New Zealand, and United States, 1990); *Luther*, directed by Eric Till (Germany and United States, 2003).

64. *Joseph of Nazareth,* directed by Raffaeli Mertes (Italy, 1999); *Mary Magdalene,* directed by Raffaeli Mertes (Germany and Italy, 2000); *St. Paul*, directed by Roger Young (Czech Republic and Italy, 2000).

65. Guenter Jekubzik, "Bonhoeffer die letzte Stufe," at www.arena.de (accessed February 2, 2002); Mies, "*Bonhoeffer: Agent of Grace.*"

66. Charles W. Colson, "*Dietrich Bonhoeffer: Agent of Grace,*" *Worthy News,* June 14, 2000. For a positive but more qualified review, see Elesha Coffman, "Christian History Corner: Agent of Grace," *Christianity Today,* June 5–12, 2000.

67. Kenneth C. Barnes, "Dietrich Bonhoeffer and Hitler's Persecution of the Jews," in *Betrayal: German Churches and the Holocaust,* ed. Robert P. Ericksen and Susannah Heschel (Minneapolis: Fortress Press, 1999), 110–28; Haynes, *The Bonhoeffer Phenomenon*, 175–76.

68. Jwm [psued.], "Bonhoeffer Caution," July 6, 2000, at www.hollywoodjesus .com/bonhoeffer2.html (accessed February 28, 2002).

69. John Mathews, "*Bonhoeffer: Agent of Grace,*" *Association of Contemporary Church Historians Newsletter* (July–August 2000): 6–7; Haynes, *The Bonhoeffer Phenomenon*, 160–62.

70. Michael C. Steinlauf, *Bondage to the Dead: Poland and the Memory of the Holocaust* (Syracuse, NY: Syracuse University Press, 1997), 144.

71. Kazimierz Iranek-Osmecki, *He Who Saves One Life: A Documented Story of the Poles Who Struggled to Save the Jews during World War II* (New York: Crown, 1971); Richard C. Lukas, *The Forgotten Holocaust: The Poles under German Occupation, 1939–1944* (Lexington: University Press of Kentucky, 1986).

72. Celia S. Heller, *On the Edge of Destruction: The Jews of Poland between the Two World Wars* (New York: Columbia University Press, 1977).

73. Emanuel Ringelblum, *Polish–Jewish Relations during the Second World War*, ed. Joseph Kermish and Shmuel Krakowski, trans. Dafna Allon, Danuta Dabrowska, and Dana Keren (New York: Howard Fertig, 1976); Israel Gutman and Shmuel Krakowski, *Unequal Victims: Poles and Jews during World War Two* (New York: Holocaust Library, 1986); Jan T. Gross, *Neighbors: The Destruction of the Jewish Community in Jedwabne, Poland* (Princeton, NJ: Princeton University Press, 2001); Leo Cooper, *In the Shadow of the Polish Eagle: The Poles, the Holocaust, and Beyond* (New York: Palgrave Macmillan, 2001).

74. Jeff Shatz, *The Generation: The Rise and Fall of the Jewish Communists in Poland* (Berkeley: University of California Press, 1991).

75. Josef Banas, *The Scapegoats: The Exodus of the Remnants of Polish Jewry*, trans. Tadeusz Szafar (New York: Holmes and Meier, 1979); Paul Lendvai, *Anti-Semitism without Jews: Communist Eastern Europe* (Garden City, NY: Doubleday, 1971).

76. Iwona Irwin-Zarecka, *Neutralizing Memory: The Jew in Contemporary Poland* (New Brunswick, NJ: Transaction Publishers, 1989), 75–123; Steinlauf, *Bondage*, 89–110.

77. *Shoah*, directed by Claude Lanzmann (France, 1985); Claude Lanzmann, *Shoah: An Oral History of the Holocaust* (New York: Pantheon Books, 1985).

78. Irwin-Zarecka, *Neutralizing Memory*, 125–60; Steinlauf, *Bondage*, 110–21; Carol Rittner and John K. Roth, eds., *Memory Offended: The Auschwitz Convent Controversy* (New York: Praeger, 1991); Władysław Bartoszewski, *The Convent at Auschwitz* (New York: George Braziller, 1991); Antony Polonsky, ed., *My Brother's Keeper? Recent Polish Debates on the Holocaust* (London: Routledge, 1990).

79. Ewa Mazierska, "Non-Jewish Jews, Good Poles and Historical Truth in the Films of Andrzej Wajda," *Historical Journal of Film, Radio, and Television* (June 2000): 5; Omer Bartov, *The "Jew" in Cinema: From the Golem to Don't Touch My Holocaust* (Bloomington: Indiana University Press, 2005), 23–27, 148–53; Paul Coates, "Walls and Frontiers: Polish Cinema's Portrayal of Polish–Jewish Relations," *Studies in Polish Jewry* 10 (1997); *Samson*, directed by Andrzej Wajda (Poland, 1961); *Landscape after Battle*, directed by Andrzej Wajda (Poland, 1970); *Promised Land*, directed by Andrzej Wajda (Poland, 1975).

80. Edward Rogerson, "Images of Jewish Poland in the Post-War Polish Cinema," *Polin* 2 (1987): 360–63.

81. Michael Stevenson, "Wajda's Filmic Representation of Polish–Jewish Relations," in *The Cinema of Andrzej Wajda: The Art of Irony and Defiance*, ed. John Orr and Elzbieta Ostrowska (London: Wallflower Press, 2003), 76–92.

82. Coates, "Walls and Frontiers," 243.

83. Andrzej Wajda, "Korczak," at www.wajda.pl.

84. Betty Jean Lifton, *The King of Children* (London: Pan Books, 1989), 350.

85. Joseph Hyams, *A Field of Buttercups* (Englewood Cliffs, NJ: Prentice Hall, 1968); Adir Cohen, *The Gate of Light: Janusz Korczak, the Educator and Writer Who Overcame the Holocaust* (Rutherford, NJ: Farleigh Dickinson University Press, 1994).

86. Daniele Heymann, "*Korczak*," *Le Monde*, May 13, 1990.

87. Anne de Gaspieri, "*Korczak*," *Le Quotidieu*, May 12, 1990.

88. Lanzmann quoted in Stevenson, "Wajda's Filmic Representation," 88.

89. Lifton, *King of Children*, 20–24, 67–76, 206–15.

90. Stevenson, "Wajda's Filmic Representation," 89–90.

91. Aaron Zeitlin, "The Last Walk of Janusz Korczak," in Januz Korczak, *Ghetto Diary* (New York: Holocaust Library, 1978), 30.

92. Lifton, *King of Children*, 292, 323. Actually, Falska hid three Jewish children in her home.

93. Korczak, *Ghetto Diary*, 85.

94. John Hoberman, "Korczak," *Village Voice*, April 16, 1991, 55.

95. Judith Doneson, *The Holocaust in American Film*, 2nd ed. (Syracuse, NY: Syracuse University Press, 2001), 207.

96. Phillip Strick, "*Korczak*," *Monthly Film Bulletin* (November 1990): 324; Mazierska, "Non-Jewish Jews," 3.

97. Isaiah Trunk, *Judenrat: The Jewish Councils in Eastern Europe* (New York: Macmillan, 1972); Aharon Weiss, "The Historiographical Controversy Concerning the Character and Function of Judenrats," in *The Historiography of the Holocaust Period*, ed. Yisrael Gutman and Gideon Grief (Jerusalem: Yad Vashem, 1988), 679–96.

98. Lifton, *King of Children*, 283–84, 311–12, 326–29.

99. Korczak, *Ghetto Diary*, 138–39.

100. Lifton, *King of Children*, 343–45.

101. Hyams, *A Field*, 28–33.

102. Lifton, *King of Children*, 261–67; Raul Hilberg, Stanislaw Staron, and Josef Kermisz, eds., *The Warsaw Diary of Adam Czerniakow: Prelude to Doom* (New York: Stein and Day, 1979), 231–32; Yisrael Gutman, *The Jews of Warsaw, 1939–1943: Ghetto, Underground, Revolt* (Brighton, UK: Harvester Press, 1982), 90–94.

103. Abraham Brumberg, "Poland, the Polish Intelligentsia, and Anti-Semitism," *Soviet Jewish Affairs* 20, nos. 2–3 (1990): 19.

104. Brumberg, "Poland," 19; Bartov, *The "Jew" in Cinema*, 157–58. Bartov argues that Wajda confers sainthood on a Jewish orphan by placing a subliminal halo around the head of one of the orphans.

105. Lifton, *King of Children*, 351.

106. Aaron Zeitlin, "The Last Walk of Janusz Korczak," in Korczak, *Ghetto Diary*, 51–63; Cohen, *The Gate*, 63–66.

107. Lifton, *King of Children*, 338–45; Hyams, *The Field*, 243–51.

108. Strick, *Korczak*, 324.

109. Coates, "Walls," 241.

110. Gordana P. Crnkovic, "Agnieszka Holland Interview," *Film Quarterly* (Winter 1998): 6; Tzvetan Todorov, "The Wajda Problem," *Salmagundi* 92 (Fall 1991): 29–35.

111. "Steven Spielberg's Letter to the American Academy of Motion Picture Art and Sciences," November 22, 1999, at www.wayda.pl/en.list.html (accessed March 7, 2002). The academy awarded a career Oscar to Wajda in 2000.

112. Hoberman, "Korczak," 55.

113. Agnieszka Holland, quoted in Crnkovic, "Agnieszka Holland Interview," 11.

114. *The Great Dictator*, directed by Charles Chaplin (United States, 1940); *To Be or Not to Be*, directed by Ernst Lubitsch (United States, 1942); *Bad Luck*, directed by Andrzej Munk (Poland, 1959); *The Two of Us*, directed by Claude Berri (France, 1966); *Mr. Klein*, directed by Joseph Losey (France and Italy, 1976).

115. Ilan Avisar, *Screening the Holocaust* (Bloomington: Indiana University Press, 1988), 134–48; Bartov, *The "Jew" in Cinema*, 127–42; Doneson, *The Holocaust in American Film*, 39–42; Insdorf, *Indelible* Shadows, 63–67.

116. Andre Pierre Colombat, *The Holocaust in French Film* (Metuchen, NJ: Scarecrow Press, 1993), 288–97.

117. *Goodbye Children*, directed by Louis Malle (France, 1987); Colombat, *The Holocaust in French Film*, 261–87.

118. *A Woman at War*, directed by Edward Bennett (Belgium, 1991); Baron, "Women as Resistance Fighters," 93–95; Helene Moszkiewiez, *Inside the Gestapo: A Jewish Woman's Secret War* (Toronto: Macmillan of Canada, 1985).

119. *The Infiltrator*, directed by John Mackenzie (United States, 1995); Yaron Svoray and Nick Taylor, *In Hitler's Shadow: An Israeli's Amazing Journey inside Germany's Neo-Nazi Movement* (New York: Doubleday, 1994).

120. Solomon Perel, *Europa, Europa* (New York: John Wiley and Sons, 1997), xii.

121. Perel, *Europa*, 1. Perel's birthday actually was one day after Hitler's.

122. Perel, *Europa*, 12–13, 206. Bertha was shot by a guard during a death march in late 1944.

123. Susan E. Linville, "Agnieszka Holland's *Europa, Europa*: Deconstructionist Humor in a Holocaust Film," *Film Criticism* 19, no. 3 (1995): 46.

124. Coates, "Walls," 236.

125. Perel, *Europa*, 185–206.

126. Perel, *Europa*, 233; Lanzmann, *Shoah*, 3–7.

127. Omer Bartov, "Spielberg's Oskar: Hollywood Tries Evil," in *Spielberg's Holocaust: Critical Perspectives on Schindler's List*, ed. Yosefa Loshitzky (Bloomington: Indiana University Press, 1997), 51–52.

128. Ingeborg Majer O'Sickey and Annette Van, "*Europa, Europa:* On the Borders of *Vergangen-heitsverdrängung* and *Vergangenheitsbewältigung*," in *Perspectives on German Cinema*, ed. Terri Ginsberg and Kirsten Mona Thompson (New York: G. K. Hall and Co., 1996), 231–50.

129. Linville, "Agnieszka," 43–47.

130. Judith E. Doneson, "Why Film?" in *Lessons and Legacies*, Vol. 2, *Teaching the Holocaust in a Changing World*, ed. Donald G. Schilling (Evanston, IL: Northwestern University Press, 1998), 144–56; Sander L. Gilman, "Decircumcision: The First Aesthetic Surgery," *Modern Judaism* 17, no. 3 (1997): 205.

131. *All That Really Matters*, directed by Robert Glinski (Poland, 1992); *Underground*, directed by Emir Kusterica (France, Germany, Hungary, 1995); *Sunshine*, directed by István Szabó (Hungary, 1999); *Divided We Fall*, directed by Han Hrebejk (Czech Republic, 2000); *Zelary*, directed by Ondrej Trojan (Austria, Czech Republic, and Slovakia, 2003).

132. Reimer and Reimer, *Nazi-Retro Film*, 146–47.

133. Susan Linville, "*Europa, Europa*: A Test Case for German National Cinema," *Wide Angle* 16, no. 2 (1995): 40–41.

134. "Box Office and Business," *Europa, Europa*, at www.imdb.com (accessed April 14, 2002).

135. "Awards and Nominations," *Europa, Europa*, at www.imdb.com (accessed April 14, 2002).

136. "Trailers," *Europa, Europa*, directed by Agnieszka Holland (United States: Orion, 1992), at www.imdb.com (accessed April 14, 2002).

137. Rick Altman, *Film/Genre* (London: British Film Institute, 1999), 123–43.

138. Linda Lopez McAlister, "*Europa, Europa*," *The Women's Show*, WMNF-FM, Tampa, FL, www.mith2.umd.edu/women'sstudies/filmreviews/europa-europa-mcalister (accessed April 14, 2002).

139. "*Europa, Europa*," Parent's Guide, *Teach with Movies*, at www.teachwithmovies .org (accessed April 14, 2002).

140. Hal Hinson, "*Europa, Europa*," *Washington Post*, August 9, 1991.

141. It premiered in New York and Los Angeles in 1989 but went into general release in 1990.

142. Lawrence L. Langer, *Holocaust Testimonies: The Ruins of Memory* (New Haven, CT: Yale University Press, 1991), 165.

143. Bruce Crowther, *Captured on Film: The Prison Movie* (London, UK: B. T. Batsford, Ltd., 1989), 99–111.

144. Crowther, *Captured*, 41–70, 113–40.

145. Avisar, *Screening the Holocaust*, 35–38.

146. *Playing for Time*, directed by Daniel Mann (United States, 1980); Shandler, *While America Watches*, 215–19.

147. *Kornblumenblau*, directed by Lexzek Wosiewicz (Poland, 1988).

148. *The Last Butterfly*, directed by Karel Kachyna (Czechoslovakia, France, United Kingdom, 1990).

149. *The Last Goal*, directed by Zoltan Fabri (Hungary, 1961); *The Boxer and Death*, directed by Peter Solan (Czechoslovakia, 1962); *Victory*, directed by John Huston (United States, 1981).

150. Crowther, *Captured*, 34–36.

151. *Triumph of the Spirit* (United States: RCA/Columbia, 1990). "Trailers," *Triumph of the Spirit*, at www.imdb.com (accessed April 23, 2002).

152. Lawrence L. Langer, *Versions of Survival: The Holocaust and the Human Spirit* (Albany: State University Press of New York, 1982).

153. *Triumph of the Spirit* (Epic Home Video/RCA/Columbia Pictures Home Video, 1990).

154. "A Tribute to Robert M. Young," *Cinequest* (2000), at www.cinequest.org/ 2000/guide/young.html (accessed April 23, 2002); Rosen, *Off Hollywood*, 2–21.

155. Judith E. Doneson, "The Image Lingers: The Feminization of the Jew in *Schindler's List*," in Loshitzky, *Spielberg's Holocaust*, 140–52.

156. "*Triumph of the Spirit*," *Filmtracks: Modern Soundtrack Reviews*, at www .filmtracks.com/titles/triumph_spirit.html (accessed April 29, 2002).

157. See Young's *The Ballad of Gregorio Cortez, Caught* (United States, 1996); *Saving Grace* (United States, 1986); *Talent for the Game* (United States, 1991); *Roosters* (United States, 1995).

158. *Golden Earrings*, directed by Mitchell Leisen (United States, 1947). See Ian F. Hancock, *The Pariah Syndrome: An Account of Gypsy Slavery and Persecution* (Ann Arbor, MI: Karoma, 1987); Donald Kendrick and Grattan Puxon, *The Destiny of Europe's*

Gypsies (New York: Basic Books, 1972); Gunter Lewy, *The Nazi Persecution of the Gypsies* (New York: Oxford University Press, 2000).

159. *And the Violins Stopped Playing*, directed by Alexander Ramati (Poland, United States, 1988). It was followed by the television movie *Sidonie,* directed by Karin Brandauer (Austria, 1990).

160. Insdorf, *Indelible Shadows,* 348–49.

161. Roger Ebert, "*Triumph of the Spirit*," *Chicago Sun-Times,* February 2, 1990.

162. Brett Willis, "*Triumph of the Spirit*," *Christian Spotlight on the Movies* (2000, at www.christiananswers.net/spotlight/movies/pre2000/triumph-of-the-spirit.html (accessed April 23, 2002).

163. The Internet Movie Database lists its box-office earnings as $400,000 in the United States.

164. Tony Rocchi, "Confronting the Hard Choices," "User Comments," *Triumph of the Spirit,* at www.imdb.com (accessed April 23, 2002).

165. *Triumph of the Spirit,* DVD (United States: MGM, 2002).

Condemned Couples:
Lovers and Liquidation

Only in a society in which their position in a social hierarchy assigns individuals their human worth would a couple be deemed inappropriate simply because it violated such principles of social ordering. By criticizing restrictive romantic norms, the unlikely couple film questions the divisions of society into groups of differing social value.[1]

—Thomas E. Wartenberg

The scenario of a loving couple torn asunder by the competing loyalties of each partner's family, nation, race, religion, or social class has provided compelling drama since the advent of mythology and literature. In his study of movies about "unlikely couples" who have transgressed the barriers erected by their primary groups to prevent defilement by the "forbidden Other," Thomas Wartenberg observes that these stories can be endowed with either a conventional or a subversive meaning.[2] Some reinforce the status quo by confirming the dangers of consorting with the stranger as in the infamous Nazi feature film *Jew Suss* (1940) in which the allure of the powerful Jewish parvenu culminates in the rape and suicide of the beautiful Aryan virgin.[3] Others privilege romance over repression. In *The Last Metro* (1980), for example, the Jewish director of a theater ensemble emerges after three years from his hiding place to take a bow with his Gentile wife, who had duped the authorities into believing her husband had immigrated.[4]

. Since the end of World War II, filmmakers have been fascinated with how the relationships between Jewish and Gentile lovers broke under or withstood peer pressure and state law against what was forbidden as miscegenation. To be sure, some directors have depicted how the forced separation and mutual suffering of Jewish couples strengthens their relationship, as in *Max and Helen*

(1990), or weakens it, as exemplified by the philandering survivor in *Enemies: A Love Story* (1989).[5] Yet, as table 4.1 indicates, the stark options faced by couples from mixed backgrounds have inspired more feature films than the impact of discrimination, incarceration, and imminent death on Jewish couples.

Like the biopic, the Holocaust version of the *Romeo and Juliet* story probes the personal ramifications of legally sanctioned prejudice. The responses of such condemned couples run the gamut from martyrdom to betrayal. In Kurt Maetzig's *Marriage in the Shadows* (1947), an Aryan actor married to a Jewish woman kills his family and himself rather than consent to a divorce, which would lead to the deportation of his wife and son.[6] Other Gentile partners sacrifice their Jewish families to protect themselves and advance their own careers. The Czech husband in *The Cremator* (1968) murders his wife and son to prove his Nazi loyalties. His is rewarded with an appointment as manager of the local crematorium, foreshadowing the fate of Jews in German death camps.[7] The focus of such films also can shift to how Jewish wives, deserted by their husbands, cope with their abandonment as evidenced in *The Jewish Wife* (1971) and *Temporary Paradise* (1981).[8]

A more common resolution to the dilemma of the condemned couple is the decision of the Gentile partner to hide his or her beloved from harm. The earliest example of a romantic rescue film was the Italian motion picture *Monastero di Santa Chiara* (1949), in which a Nazi officer shelters a Jewish singer who is being relentlessly pursued by her spurned lover.[9] In Jiri Weiss's *Sweet Light in a Dark Room*, whose original title tellingly was *Romeo, Juliet, and Darkness* (1959), adolescent infatuation collides with the fear Germany instilled in local populations. A Czech youth falls in love with a Jewish girl he is sheltering in the attic of his house. When his mother discovers his secret, she evicts the girl to avert punishment by the Germans.[10]

Judith Doneson argued in many of her writings that the recurring plot of a Christian male saving a Jewish woman in particular, and Jews in general, implicitly "feminized" Jewish characters by making them the passive recipients of masculine mercy.[11] In the 1980s, this rigid gender stereotyping started to break down. Films like *Forbidden* (1984), *'38: Vienna before the Fall* (1986), and *The Attic: The Hiding of Anne Frank* (1988) portrayed brave women who valiantly risked their lives to save their defenseless Jewish mates.[12] Esther Fuchs still

Table 4.1. Love Stories about Mixed or Jewish Couples

Couples	1945–1949	1950–1959	1960–1969	1970–1979	1980–1989	1990–1999
Mixed/ Unlikely	4	7	8	8	19	21
Jewish	1	2	2	5	7	8

maintains that despite the reversal of gender roles in these films, they affirm a Christian theological hierarchy that idealizes Gentile women as more proactive and virtuous than the Jewish characters they protect.[13]

While Doneson and Fuchs correctly identify the gendered and theological dynamics of pre-1990s Holocaust films, they have not discerned the changes in the depictions of Jewish and Gentile couples in some recent films.[14] Not all Christians who rescue Jews do so for righteous reasons, and not all Jews accept their fate as victims. In Agnieszka Holland's *Angry Harvest* (1985), for example, a Polish peasant saves a Jewish woman from deportation, but then rapes her. When his guilt prompts him to find another hiding place, she commits suicide rather than make herself vulnerable again. A woman rescuer's seducing the husband of a Jewish couple she is hiding leads to the love triangle featured in *Warszawa: Year 5307* (1992).[15] A few moviemakers have recently switched the dynamics of the relationships between Gentile and Jewish partners, featuring the Jew as the initiator of the challenge to social mores and the Gentile as the beneficiary of this assertiveness, as in *Martha and I* (1990) and *Aimée and Jaguar* (1999). The Jewish leads in *Aimée and Jaguar* and *The Harmonists* (1997) are more politically astute than their Gentile counterparts. Jewish heroines like Lilly (a.k.a. Aimée) and as brave as the courageous Gentile women in films like *Julia* (1977) are *Forbidden*.[16]

Until the 1980s, positive portrayals of homosexual couples from mixed religious backgrounds never appeared as the subject of serious Holocaust cinema. Directors either associated homosexuality with the decadence of Weimar Germany as epitomized by the bisexual Count and clientele who frequent the Kit Kat Klub in *Cabaret* (1972) or with the Nazi sadomasochism that pervades the sexual practices of the members of the Von Essenbeck family and the SA in Luchino Visconti's *The Damned* (1969).[17]

The production of movies with gay leading characters reflects the progress made by the gay rights movement, the opportunities it has created for gay directors, and the development of a viewing public open to watching pictures with overtly homosexual content.[18] Alexandra von Grote's *November Moon* (1985) paved the way for films like *Bent* (1996) and *Aimée and Jaguar* (1999), which add homophobia to the animosities encountered by couples who violate the Nazi ban on Jewish–Aryan relationships. November Messing, a German Jewish woman who fled to France to escape persecution in her homeland, finds herself the target of anti-Semitic taunts from French fascists while standing in a Paris breadline. A French woman named Ferial whisks her away from the hostile crowd and becomes her paramour and protector. After Germany defeats France, Ferial joins the staff of the Nazi Information Department to deflect suspicions that she is concealing a Jew. When France is liberated, an irate mob drags Ferial out of her apartment, shaves her head, and taunts her for being a "German whore." Cringing in her striped robe, she looks like a concentration camp survivor. Although ignored in studies of Holocaust cinema, *November Moon* won several awards for gay films and remains a popular picture with gay audiences.[19]

Since the reunification of Germany, several directors have dramatized love stories between Jewish and German characters as a way to reconstitute public memory of the Jewish contribution to German culture and society.[20] The best examples of these kinds of films are *My Heart Is Mine Alone* (1997) about the tragic love affair between the poets Else Lasker-Schüler and Gottfried Benn and *The Harmonists*, which revived the music of the Weimar Republic's most popular male singing group. Since the former is extremely difficult to obtain, I will not discuss it further in this chapter and instead will analyze the much more accessible *Harmonists*.[21] Another example of a German heritage film is *Jew Boy Levi,* which places a Jewish cattle dealer in a rural German village, whose peasant lifestyle epitomizes the premodern Aryan utopia envisioned by Nazi ideologues.

Some German film scholars accuse the heritage films of divorcing ordinary Germans from Nazism's public assault "on cooperation, friendship, and romances between Aryans and Jews." According to this interpretation, conventional melodramas about how the Third Reich's racism stigmatized personal relations between Gentiles and Jews "produce nostalgia for successful moments of German Jewish symbiosis" and idealize pluralism without confronting the Holocaust.[22] I contend that since the directors of these films assume the audience already knows that anti-Semitic discrimination led to genocide, they show how positive instances of German Jewish relationships were destined to end in the expulsion or obliteration of the Jewish partner. When genocide is part of a nation's historical legacy, nostalgia, as the joke goes, is not what it used to be. Instead, it serves as a painful reminder of a shameful past.

Most of the love stories analyzed in this chapter blend different genres. The majority are biopics about the romances between historical figures. Others easily could be categorized as musicals, prison films, period pieces, or buddy movies. The depictions of these embattled couples reflect several trends: the popularization of the Holocaust with greater attention paid to its Jewish victims, the raised awareness of the misogynist and homophobic aspects of Nazi policies, and the attempt of a new generation of German directors to incorporate Jews back into the narrative of their nation's history. In these films, Jewish characters either tend to be more active, principled, or trustworthy than their Gentile partners or to subordinate their religious descent to their sexual orientation. With the exception of *Bent*, the plots of these movies do not occur in the concentration and death camps. Audiences can empathize more easily with relationships strained or severed by bigotry than with the nihilistic extremes of the camps, which rendered love a luxury that might enhance someone's will to live but could not guarantee survival.

PYGMALION AND PERSECUTION: *MARTHA AND I*
Directed by Jiri Weiss
(Austria, France, Germany, Italy: Iduna Film, Le Studio Canal, RAI, Oesterreichisches Rundfunk, Progefi, TFI Films, Zweites Deutsches Fernsehen, 1990)

> A great love is played out in this film, and a great tragedy is born in the tide of the holocaust. But Weiss never plays this remarkable story for cheap sentiment or even for polemic. He is sharing a story that is alive with human ordinariness, and hardly a single moment of this lovely, sad movie, seems false.[23]
>
> —Peter Stack

The remarkable career of Czechoslovakian-born director Jiri Weiss dates back to the 1930s. After witnessing German troops overrunning Prague in 1939, he sought asylum in England and proceeded to combat fascism by making films like *John Smith Wakes Up* (1940) and semidocumentaries cast with amateur actors reenacting the exploits of the Resistance in Norway and the contributions of Czech volunteers to the Allied cause. During his exile, both his parents perished in German death camps. He returned to his native land in 1945 determined to use his craft to fight for social justice. His commitment to purge pro-Nazi collaborators and build an egalitarian society initially ingratiated him with the communist regime. He eventually chafed under the control the government exercised over the content of his films. When he exposed continuing discrimination against Czech gypsies in *My Friend Fabian* (1954), the country's film board demanded that he edit the film to portray the issue in a more positive light. Weiss fell further out of official grace with the release of *Sweet Light in a Dark Room*, which the authorities deemed Zionistic in its indictment of Czech indifference toward the plight of the Jews. In *The Coward* (1961), Weiss showed how a timorous Slovakian teacher realizes he must resist the fascist regime, thereby justifying dissidence against the postwar communist government.[24]

After the Soviet Union crushed reform efforts in Czechoslovakia in the summer of 1968, Weiss emigrated to the United States and stopped making films two years later. He had one final project, however, that he kept in abeyance and finally brought to fruition in *Martha and I* (1990). At the age of seventy-seven, he drew on his adolescent memories of being banished to his Uncle Ernst's home in the Sudetenland to prevent him from having an affair with his parent's maid. Uncle Ernst had a considerably younger Hungarian wife, whom he divorced when he caught her in bed with another man. Preferring fidelity to promiscuity, Ernst proposed to his housekeeper Martha, a rotund ethnic German who had waited upon him loyally for years. Ernst's sisters suspected that Martha married their brother for his money, whereas most of Martha's family appreciated her new affluence, except for her pro-Nazi brother Werner, who denounced her marriage to a "dirty, filthy Jew." The genuine affection that develops between the two lead characters from opposite religious and social backgrounds drives the plot of *Martha and I*.[25]

Weiss shot the first half of the movie through rich yellow filters that mirror the nostalgia of the nephew recounting how his uncle navigated him through the shoals of puberty. Emil, Weiss's teenage counterpart in the film, witnesses both his uncle's humiliation by his adulterous first wife and his unexpected offer of matrimony to the stalwart Martha. When Ernst's sisters hurl insults at Martha, Emil recognizes that she is a diamond in the rough. He chaperons Aunt Martha around Prague as Ernst transforms her from "a cook into a doctor's wife" by getting her teeth straightened and buying her a new wardrobe, including lingerie. Martha gradually emanates an inner radiance since this is the first time in her life she has been treated as Ernst's equal rather than as his employee.

The first omen of the fate of the Jews in a Sudetenland annexed by Germany comes at the wedding dinner, whose guests consist primarily of Martha's relatives with the exception of Emil and one of Ernst's Jewish friends. Ernst extols the Czech beer and cuisine and chides the Germans "for following Hitler like a Pied Piper." Werner responds by telling the gathering that the Czechs learned everything from the Germans. Emil reminds Werner that the Bohemian king Wenzel originally imported Germans into his domain to work in the mines. Werner gets into an argument with Ernst's friend over whether Germany deserved the harsh terms imposed on it by the Treaty of Versailles. Werner takes umbrage at what he considers "Jewish impertinence." Ernst declares himself an agnostic and a Czech and wittily remarks, "The fact that I'm circumcised concerns only one person here, and I hope she doesn't mind."

The second half of the film is shaded in darker yellows and browns to foreshadow the invasion of Czechoslovakia and the anti-Semitic noose slowly tightened around the necks of the Jews residing there. Several shots of locomotives belching gray smoke and emitting piercing whistles portend the deportations by tapping into the audience's familiarity with the Final Solution and the ubiquitous scenes of trains in Claude Lanzmann's *Shoah*. One night when Ernst is away delivering a baby, Martha senses there is a prowler outside the house. She and Emil find a Jewish star and the word "Jude" painted on the front gate. They scrub off all traces of it. Martha insists that Emil not tell Ernst what happened. A visit from Werner ignites a heated exchange with Martha in which he curses her for dishonoring the family by becoming a "whore" for a Jew. Then, Ernst and Martha move to Prague and sell the organ that he had always played to relax.

As the situation of Ernst worsens, Martha assumes the role of his benefactor. In a touching scene when Ernst mourns the death of a patient, she tenderly washes and kisses his feet, like Mary who anointed Jesus's feet with oil at Bethany. Indeed, a woman named Martha served Christ his dinner in that passage from the Gospel of John.[26] Martha drives a hard bargain to get a better price for the organ and sells her wedding ring to purchase Ernst a piano. She waits in a long line in front of the American embassy to procure a visa for Ernst. It is raining, and the row of black umbrellas resembles a funeral procession. The ambassador informs her that an American citizen must sponsor Ernst's immigration to the United States. Leafing through a New York telephone book, Martha copies the addresses of persons bearing Ernst's last name and writes to them seeking a relative who might act as his sponsor. On her wedding anniversary, Martha invites Ernst's sisters to celebrate by offering them strudel she has baked. One of them belatedly acknowledges Martha's good heartedness, but another accuses Martha of persuading Ernst to flee abroad. Ernst implores Martha to divorce him to avert her own ostracism or arrest for being married to a Jew, but she refuses. A fleeting shot of a caged canary hints at his future. Ernst arranges for Martha's brothers to abduct her. In an emotionally wrenching scene, Martha sobs inconsolably as they carry her away. Then, Ernst finalizes the divorce.

Before he separates from Martha, Ernst has two significant conversations. In the first, he advises Emil to leave Czechoslovakia as soon as possible. Paraphrasing Martin Niemoeller's quotation about the widening circle of Nazi persecution and evoking Weiss's own experience under communist rule, Ernst warns Emil, "Soon it will be your turn. Today it is the doctors, the lawyers, and the film directors. Next time, it will be the university students."[27] Thereafter, Ernst brings Martha to the old Jewish cemetery in Prague and shows her Rabbi Loew's tombstone. He tells her about the legend of the golem. The symbolism in this scene works on several levels. Ernst wanders among the Jewish dead, whose fate he will shortly share. Like Rabbi Loew giving life to the golem, Ernst has animated a once moribund Martha, who has evolved into a defender of the Jews. Martha leaves a note on Loew's grave that presumably asks God to save her husband.

Emil hides himself under a truckload of cucumbers to get across the Czech border. Ernst is not so fortunate. Emil returns after the war as a soldier in the Allied liberation army and learns that Ernst had been deported and never came back. Indeed, all of Emil's relatives are dead. He wonders what became of Martha and discovers that for several years she had made a daily pilgrimage to the trestle above the railroad tracks longing for Ernst to return for her. Finally, her despair overwhelmed her, and she jumped in front of an oncoming train. The final image shows dense smoke billowing from a locomotive and eclipsing the overpass where she had regularly stood. Perhaps Martha was reunited with her beloved Ernst in a plume that ascended to heaven, but visually, it is the couple's absence and not its presence that concludes the movie.

Although Ernst and Martha ultimately are victims of the Holocaust, they save each other while they are alive. After being cuckolded, Ernst desperately needs the companionship of a woman he can trust. Under Ernst's tutelage, Martha sheds her servility and blossoms into an assertive woman. Each makes Emil promise not to tell the other whenever he is privy to potentially upsetting information. Martha does everything in her power to nurture her husband spiritually and materially when the two move to Prague. Esther Fuchs has criticized Weiss for anchoring Martha's virtues in her "primordial maternal instincts: earthiness, simplicity, naturalness, and irrationality."[28] Martha undoubtedly possesses an abundance of the first three qualities, but her protectiveness of Ernst is hardly irrational. Indeed, both Martha and Ernst offer to sacrifice themselves to ensure each other's survival. This kind of deep devotion of the lover to the beloved is not only feminine. As one critic acutely observed, "What begins as a marriage of convenience slowly evolves into a soulful love between unlikely mates, and like all great loves, it is complex, painful and under assault from the outside world."[29]

Despite its appealing story, moving performances, and striking cinematography, *Martha and I* never attained the recognition it deserves. As a multinational production, it lacked a specific national market.[30] Weiss marketed the script for years until a consortium of Austrian, French, German, and Italian studios funded the film. The German dialog was spoken by a cast comprising mostly Czech actors with the exceptions of the French actor Michel Piccoli as Ernst and the German actress Marianne Sägebrecht as Martha. The latter had developed a popular following by making her girth glamorous in Percy Adlon's *Bagdad Café* (1988).[31] *Martha and I* was well received at American film festivals in 1991. Its German distributor, however, withdrew it from circulation, fearing it might offend German audiences. Soon thereafter, its American distributor went bankrupt. The film was rereleased in 1995 when Cinema Four of San Francisco purchased the distribution rights. In that year, *Martha and I* appeared in a few American cities but grossed less than $50,000 in ticket sales.[32] Jiri Weiss died in 2004.[33] Retrospectives of his films may secure *Martha and I* the place it merits in the annals of Holocaust cinema.

MUFFLED MUSIC: *THE HARMONISTS*
Directed by Joseph Vilsmaier
(Germany, Austria: Bavaria Film, Beta Film, Senator Film, Dor Film, 1997)

> If we hadn't been forced to split up, we would be more famous
> today than The Beatles. . . . The Comedian Harmonists were a
> bright light in a dark time.[34]
>
> —Roman Cycowski

Movies about the Holocaust are not immune to the genre hybridization that
typifies commercial film production in general. Genre mixing increases marketability by fitting a movie's plot into several narrative formulas that appeal to
different segments of the viewing public.[35] *The Harmonists* amalgamates many
genres. It has been categorized as a comedy, a "show biz biopic," a musical, a
buddy movie, and a love triangle.[36]

Publicity for *The Harmonists* varied from country to country according to
what its distributors thought would have the greatest audience appeal. In Germany, the poster for the movie catered to the nostalgia of older Germans and
the historical curiosity of younger Germans by advertising the film with the
tagline, "A legend returns."[37] The publicity logo in the United States evoked
comparisons with *Cabaret* by revealing the face of a woman tipping a fedora
over her eyes and looking very much like Lisa Minnelli in her role as Sally
Bowles. The tagline sold it as a buddy movie about friendship. The connection
with *Cabaret* was not publicity hype since production designer Rolf Zehet-
bauer created the sets for both films to capture the ambience of Berlin during
the Weimar Republic. The French poster superimposed swastikas cascading
down onto bars of music. At the bottom of the poster, the lead actress walks
between her two lovers as they rush with the other members of the group to
stay one step ahead of the Nazi avalanche. In visual terms, Nazism buries both
love and music.[38]

The striking parallels between *The Harmonists* and *Cabaret* invite a broader
consideration of the usage of music as an element in Holocaust feature films.
The Producers (1968) relied on the incongruity of a Broadway musical about
Hitler as a humorous paradox intended to guarantee the box-office failure of
the show.[39] *Cabaret*'s nightclub songs "are consistently crosscut with the reality
outside." For example, Nazi thugs beat a political opponent as women mud-
wrestle to the cheers of an audience. The angelic-looking and -sounding Hitler
Youth who sings "Tomorrow Belongs to Us" at a rustic beer garden epitomizes
Aryan purity and solidarity in sharp contrast to Berlin's squalor and the sexual
kinkiness of the Kit-Kat Club patrons.[40] Assuring one's fame by catering to the
musical tastes of the leaders of the Third Reich provides the motivation for

Martha (Marianne Sagebrecht) washes her husband Ernst's feet (Michel Piccoli). Martha and I. Press kit, courtesy of the Nostalgia Factory.

The Harmonists perform, from front to back: Max Tidof, Ulrich Noeten, Heino Ferch, Ben Becker, and Heinrich Schafmeister. The Harmonists. *Press kit, courtesy of the Nostalgia Factory.*

collaboration in *Lili Marlene* (1981).[41] Music emerges as a key to survival in *Playing for Time* (1980) and a sublimated form of resistance in *Swing Kids* (1993).[42]

As in *Swing Kids,* the German crooners in *The Harmonists* simply like the instrumentation and rhythms of American jazz. They do not create their fusion of vocal harmonization and syncopation as a political statement. Nazi ideologues, however, perceived jazz as a seductive Black and Jewish import that contaminated traditional Aryan culture.[43] Donning tuxedos to entertain an elegantly dressed audience, the five singers and pianist who comprise the Comedian Harmonists sing the ditty *Veronica, Spring Has Sprung,* which abounds in witty double entendres. The movie flashes back to 1927, when Harry Frommermann was unemployed. Harry is infatuated with Erna, who works at a music shop. Together they listen to the latest American recording by the Revellers, whose catchy arrangements of "Negro music" inspire Harry to form a German version of the group. Harry puts on a yarmulke to visit his parent's graves and confess to them that he loves a "shiksa."

As Harry conducts rehearsals for the group, he recruits a bass opera singer, Robert Biberti, who introduces him to the pianist Erwin Bootz, two tenors, Erich Colin and the Bulgarian Ari Leschnikoff, and the Polish Jewish baritone Roman Cycowski. Sticking to the clichés of the rags-to-riches show-business saga, Joseph Vilsmaier endows each character with a distinctive trait, like Ari's womanizing or Bootz's oversleeping, and follows the success story of the group. The rhythm of the tune they perform at their first audition is so slow that Harry's agent dismisses it as "funeral parlor music." Their artistic breakthrough comes when the bickering members of the group are on the verge of splitting up. In a stroke of genius, Bootz quickens the tempo of a Duke Ellington composition and the singers improvise the sounds of a big band orchestra. The next audition assures them a booking, which catapults them to fame. The impresario who hires them articulates the movie's theme: "The darker the times, the brighter the theatre lights."

As the group revels in its success, the first omen of Nazi anti-Semitism disrupts their celebration. Hans, a former boyfriend of Erna's, shames her for hanging out with a Jew. Roman retorts, "I'm a Jew and proud of it." Erna defiantly kisses Harry. Two years pass. It is now May 1930. On the radio, Hitler denounces the chaos caused by the Weimar Republic's political factionalism. The Comedian Harmonists' latest hit advises the young to enjoy themselves because "the happy days will soon be gone." The Nazis vandalize the music shop. Its Jewish owners shake their heads in disbelief and erase the swastikas and slogans painted on their windows. They believe Germany is a land of "law and order and will stay that way." Harry quips, "The teacher asks Moshe, 'What race do the Jews belong to?' 'The Semites,' Moshe answers. 'And what race do the Germans belong to? 'The anti-Semites,' Moshe replies."

Personal rifts in the group mirror the polarization of Germany. Robert courts Erna and invites her to one of the group's concerts. Afterwards, Robert accuses Harry of being an egomaniac who hams it up too much on stage. Taking umbrage at this insult, Harry disputes it until Robert reveals that Erna had confided to him that Harry only talked about his musical career and never inquired about her university studies. The overall tone of the film, however, remains light. When Roman proposes to his Gentile girlfriend, she agrees to convert to Judaism. The ensuing Jewish wedding scene with festive klezmer music diverts attention from the looming threat of Nazism. Indeed, when German focus groups previewed the movie, this scene proved to be the film's most popular one, particularly among viewers under twenty.[44]

The movie abruptly shifts to October 1933. Hitler now holds the reins of power. Nazi strong-arm tactics are symbolized by a boxing match that Robert attends with Erna. He professes his love to her and suggests she move into his apartment, where she will be safer. The Reich Music Association summons Harry and Robert to order the group to dismiss its three Jewish members and stop singing songs composed by Jews. The two are amazed to learn that according to Nazi racial criteria, even Erich is Jewish despite his conversion to Christianity. Yet, the Nazi official also wants them to autograph an album for his nephew, who is a big fan of their music. For the first time, the trappings of the Nazi dictatorship are omnipresent. Swastika flags are hung in the halls where civil servants greet each other with the Hitler salute. Storm Troopers ransack the music store, and the police advise its Jewish owners to "disappear." Robert fights back, while Harry stands helplessly by because a Storm Troopers holds a knife under his neck. Erna exits with the bloodied but undaunted Robert.

Esther Fuchs has claimed that this scene reinforces traditional male stereotypes of Gentiles as virile and Jews as cerebral.[45] Lutz Koepnick charges that Vilsmaier "encodes the male Jew's sexuality as muted, mediated, and decidedly non-aggressive."[46] While this contrast between Bob and Harry exists, a more plausible reason for Harry's passivity is that the Nazis consider his Jewish ancestry a mortal threat to Aryan supremacy and point the knife at him rather than a racial comrade who is merely defending his girlfriend. At his parents' graveside, Harry describes his quandary: "Maybe if I had let them stab me, she'd be with me now."

Still, the members of the group believe that their status as international stars will shield them from further harassment. This assessment of their situation seems to be validated when Julius Streicher, the notorious anti-Semitic propagandist, summons them for a command performance. The sextet sings the ideologically innocuous lyrics, "I have an uncle in Kalumba where politics have been forgotten." Streicher invites the group to his home and requests that they sing a German folk song popular among Nazi supporters. They comply, but Harry becomes nauseous and refuses to resume singing the politically tainted tune.

Just as the group's future appears bleak, they receive an offer to perform in New York. Vilsmaier depicts the United States as a utopia of racial tolerance. The antics of the group there replicate scenes of the Beatles frolicking on their American tour in a *Hard Day's Night* (1964). With American flags rippling in the wind and the Statue of Liberty in the background, the group performs on a U.S. Navy battleship. Despite the segregation of black sailors in this period, the camera captures the faces of African Americans listening intently among the crew. On the ferry ride back to the city, the group debates whether they should remain in America. Harry argues they should stay: "It is not about me; it is about us! Us Jews!" Robert thinks Harry has a "persecution complex" and envies the relationship between Erna and him. Nevertheless, Robert confesses that he is actually worried whether his elderly mother could adjust to the move. When five of the six decide to return, Harry overcomes his qualms and joins them.

Streicher grants the group permission to perform one concert before disbanding. Swastika banners dwarf the stage, and a few members of the audience walk out when informed that three of the Comedian Harmonists are Jews. Harry insists that the concert is for their fans. Their last song expresses their realization that fame provides them no refuge from fanaticism. "Our fairy tale is over. Give me one last kiss goodbye." Erna sobs throughout the number, distraught by the prospect of never seeing Harry again. The group receives a standing ovation. The camera alternates between views of the gargantuan swastika banners and the enthralled audience. Harry dutifully visits the graves of his parents to the accompaniment of a clarinet playing a mournful klezmer melody. He departs carrying his parrot's cage and resembles Alan Bates seeking asylum from the carnage of World War I in the final scene of *King of Hearts* (1966).

As the group's Jewish members ready themselves to leave, Erna runs to the train station platform and melodramatically declares, "I belong with Harry." The closing shot of a train carrying the exiles to Switzerland evokes associations with the transports that will soon shuttle Jews to death camps. The last shot of the train assumes the perspective of the Germans who stay behind. In my opinion, this vantage point heightens the sense that Germany was impoverished by the banishment of talented Jewish artists. Koepnick contends that the ending implies that Jews and Germans suffered equally under Nazism: "What makes audiences weep is not that Hitler's Germany exterminated the Jews of Europe in the name of the German nation, but rather that the Nazis betrayed the nation by prohibiting Germans to love their Jewish compatriots."[47]

The postscript informs the audience of what became of the members of the group. The Aryan and Jewish members formed separate singing groups, both of which broke up in 1941. Bootz divorced his Jewish wife and married the daughter of a Nazi sculptor. Robert became one of the designers of the V-2 rocket. Ari returned to Bulgaria. Erich became an eyeglass-frame manufacturer. Harry and Erna got married, but divorced in 1952. Harry obtained American citizenship and entertained Allied troops during World War II. Roman became a cantor and settled in San Francisco with his wife. The audience learns that the group's music has remained popular.

Vilsmaier avoided being too controversial in his portrayal of the rise and fall of the Comedian Harmonists. A renewed interest in their music began two decades earlier with the broadcast of Eberhard Fechner's television documentary about the group. In 1988, Fechner authored a book on the subject.[48] *Autumn Milk* (1988) and *Stalingrad* (1996), Vilsmaier's previous movies about the Nazi period, respectively depict Nazism as a movement with little support among German peasants and the plight of German soldiers as cannon fodder for Hitler's grandiose military ambitions. Films like *Stalingrad*, *Sleeper's Brother* (1995), and *The Harmonists* earned Vilsmaier the record for being the most commercially successful German director of the 1990s.[49] *The Harmonists* won many of the major Bavarian and German film awards for 1998.[50] In interviews about the picture, Vilsmaier admitted that he subordinated the Nazi theme to focus on the musical legacy of the sextet. He marveled that the members of the group were so "totally apolitical" that they themselves were unaware of who among them was Jewish.[51] Ultimately, the movie is about how Hitler's policies hurt German culture. As Jürgen Büscher, who scripted *The Harmonists* and *Stalingrad,* commented, "The film wants to express the sorrow of what it meant—and what it still means—for Germany that the country's best creative talents were persecuted, suppressed, driven away, and finally murdered."[52]

OSTRACIZING THE OUTSIDER: *JEW BOY LEVI*
Directed by Didi Danquart
(Austria, Germany, Switzerland: Dschoint Ventschr, Lotus, Schweizer Fernsehen, Suedwestdeutscher Rundfunk, Zero Film, arte, 1999)

> Closely connected to Nazi fantasies about *Volk* and *Heimat*, the *Heimatfilm* [homeland film] emerged as the most convenient narrative form for offering a romanticized, but completely depoliticized, view of country and nation.[53]

> —Sabine Hake

There is a genre of German films that criticizes industrialization, secularization, and urbanization by idealizing the lifestyle of rural villages, where agriculture and handicrafts remained the basis of the local economy, face-to-face relationships still predominated, and traditional family and religious values stayed intact. *Heimat* movies provided a diversion from the hectic pace of the cultural, economic, political, and social changes that modernized Germany. Since the Third Reich's capacity to wage total war depended on conscription, the monopolization of political power, science, and technology, and the suppression of political and racial opponents, the "homeland" film presented a nostalgic vision of the idyllic society Hitler aspired to restore. After the defeat by the Allies, the devastation of German cities, the division of the country, and the economic hardships of the immediate postwar decade, Heimat films revived the memory of happier times when communal solidarity, ethical norms, and vocational skills still flourished in small German towns. As Anton Kaes has noted, the concept of Heimat "promised order, permanence, and national pride."[54] Edgar Reitz's television series *Heimat* (1984) constituted the most elaborate "escape from the discourse of collective guilt to that of the other Germany identified with idyllic villages and beautiful landscapes."[55]

Didi Danquart's *Jew Boy Levi* draws a more discomforting picture of how an ostensibly congenial village turns against an amiable Jewish cattle dealer whose family has done business there for three generations. The beauty and serenity of the Black Forest belie the ugly mob mentality that infects the townspeople when a Nazi engineer and his team of workers come to the hamlet to clear the debris from a collapsed railroad tunnel. For the time being, the blockage of the tunnel stops Nazi ideology from spreading to the town. At first, the kindly and religiously observant Levi traverses the winding highways singing Yiddish songs to his pet rabbit, Jankel, and receives a warm welcome when he purchases livestock and sells domestic items at fair prices. The only thing he lacks is human companionship, but he hopes that Lisbeth, the waitress at the inn, will marry him.

Fabian Kohler, the head of the railroad crew, shatters this fragile harmony. His arrival is mocked by Lisbeth's unemployed boyfriend, Paul, who crudely remarks that it has "started smelling like brown shit here," alluding to the brown uniforms worn by Nazi Storm Troopers. Levi tries to defuse the confrontation by explaining that "shit" merely refers to manure that gets stuck on people's shoes. A peasant who cracks jokes about Hitler is beaten and advised to "figure out which way the wind is blowing." Fabian donates a radio to the local innkeeper to force his customers to listen to the news from Berlin. After unfurling a Nazi flag, Fabian stages a magic show, where he attempts to pull a rabbit out of a hat. Paul puts manure in the hat, and the humiliated Fabian orders his laborers to rough Paul up and dump his motorcycle in the river. Levi offers to help push the motorcycle back to town, but Paul snaps back, "Keep your Jewish hands off it."

Levi's livelihood and life are suddenly in jeopardy. Holger, Lisbeth's father, refuses Levi's bid to buy one of his cows, then sells it for a cheaper price to the government railroad company. Fabian tells Levi that he is a "nothing" in the Third Reich. Lisbeth's mother warns her daughter to spurn Levi's romantic overtures because she's a Catholic and he's a Jew. Someone slits the tires on Levi's truck. Then, he finds the limp body of his decapitated pet rabbit. When Levi asks Holger to sell him another rabbit, Holger calls Levi a "Christ killer." At the inn, the drunken workers sing a Nazi marching song and command Levi to sing something. They hold him up by both ears to make him look like his beheaded rabbit. To prove his Nazi sympathies, Holger denounces Levi as a "dirty Jew." Lisbeth grabs the innkeeper's pistol and urges Levi to leave. The closing scene shows the headlights of his truck slowly disappearing into the darkness that has descended upon the once tranquil valley. Danquart has explained why he left the meaning of this scene open to speculation: "Everyone knows that Levi finally ended up in Auschwitz. But why should he not have a chance to come to Palestine or New York? This poetic image, when the red backlights drive away and burn out, gives us time to go away with him, no matter where."[56]

Omer Bartov considers *Jew Boy Levi* an exercise in "redemptive nostalgia" since the German peasants remain immune to Nazi anti-Semitism until Fabian turns them against Levi. He also questions whether the presentation of Levi as a passive victim is offset by Levi's stereotypical appearance, occupation, and romantic interest in a Gentile maiden.[57] Public opinion reports, however, indicated that the Nazis initially had trouble persuading rural Bavarians to boycott trusted Jewish cattle dealers.[58] Furthermore, the abandonment of Levi by his former clients reveals how ordinary Germans found it politically expedient to sever their ties to Jews. Some, like Holger, invoke traditional Christian stereotypes of Jews to justify their stance. Despite his prior scorn for Nazism, Paul uses anti-Semitism to eliminate a rival for Lisbeth's affection. Responding to peer pressure or fear of reprisals, others do not intervene in Levi's behalf. Lisbeth orders him to leave because she realizes how marginalized he has become.

Danquart based his movie on a short play by Thomas Strittmatter, who remembered a story passed down from his father and neighbors about a cattle dealer named Levi who had plied his trade in Upper Bavaria until shunned by his former customers. He died in the late 1930s under suspicious circumstances. The dialog in Strittmatter's drama is written in dialect situating the story in prewar Bavaria. In the play, the railroad pays farmers more than Levi for their livestock, making it in their economic self-interest to boycott him. At the end of the play, Strittmatter speculates whether Levi committed suicide or was murdered by either the Nazis or Holger and his wife. The play contains no love story or rivalry with another suitor as possible explanations for Levi's ostracism or death. Strittmatter summarizes the plot this way: "The railroad workers brought the ideology of National Socialism. They destroyed Levi's source of income by purchasing the farmers' cows for meat at a higher price than Levi could afford to pay."[59]

Danquart transforms the play into an allegory about prejudice. The initial euphoria over the reunification of Germany in 1989 had faded when riots erupted against foreign workers and asylum seekers blamed for the high unemployment rate in East Germany. "Ethnic cleansing" in Bosnia marred Yugoslavia's transition to democracy. Danquart eliminated regional colloquialisms in the dialog to give Levi's story a more timeless and universal significance. Although Lisbeth rejects anti-Semitism, she fails to stop it. Emphasizing that it is Lisbeth who asks Levi to leave, Johannes von Moltke praises the movie as "a sober account of the exclusionary logic of fascist community, which leads from the precarious integration (not to say symbiosis) of the Jew within the non-Jewish 'Heimat' into an unnamed exile."[60]

Danquart furnished the following reasons for altering Strittmatter's play:

> If I tell a story set in 1935 in 1997, it has to be modern. It has to be up to the expectations of a cinema audience which is mostly between 20 and 30 years old. I am, therefore, not interested in reconstructing former victims and perpetrators authentically, but interpreting the past once again with new images, language, and attitudes. A film today should leave old patterns of thought behind, the easy division into good and bad, innocence and guilt. Levi is a microcosm in which one can discover fascism just as much as in contemporary ethnic conflicts.[61]

Danquart's cautionary tale impressed German and Israeli film critics. The movie not only won the Caligari Film Award at the Berlin International Film Festival but also the Mayor's Award at the Jerusalem Film Festival.[62]

For those seeking more devastating depictions of the antipathy and apathy civilians exhibited toward the victims of Nazi persecution, I strongly recommend *Three Days in April* (1994) or *Rabbit Hunt* (1994), both of which are based on historical incidents. The first surveys the spectrum of individual responses to the suffering of Jews, gypsies, and Poles huddled in railway cars stalled in a small Swabian town, where they plead for food and water. The second recounts how the Austrians living near Mauthausen assisted the SS in hunting and killing escaped Soviet prisoners of war.[63]

A DOUBLY DOOMED LOVE: *AIMÉE AND JAGUAR*
Directed by Max Färberböck
(Germany: Senator Films, 1999)

You shall read this diary when you are no longer the "Jewess Schragenheim," but a person among other persons. Dear God, let us live together or die. Do not allow for only one of us to survive.[64]

—Lilly Wust

Unlike gay males whom the Third Reich persecuted, German lesbians lived in a political purgatory. The state tolerated them if they maintained the pretence that they were heterosexuals and punished them only if they flaunted their homosexuality, because this lifestyle allegedly emasculated men and inhibited its proponents from bearing children. The police interned some lesbians and classified them as "asocials." Berlin had been a haven for gay men and women during the Weimar Republic. The Nazi Party attributed the increased visibility of homosexuals there to Jews and socialists who promoted deviant lifestyles to sap the vitality of the Aryan race. Since Ernst Röhm, the leader of the paramilitary SA, was gay, Hitler did not prosecute male homosexuals until he ordered the assassination of Röhm in 1934 to mollify military leaders who suspected Röhm was plotting to replace the regular army with the SA.[65]

Lesbian activities went underground during the Third Reich too. Some gay women led a double life, marrying and having children while discretely socializing with lesbian lovers. Since the number of married and single men in Germany decreased with the advent of the war, close friendships between women did not necessarily raise suspicions of lesbianism. The labor shortage created by the conscription of German men created opportunities for women to work, even though the government encouraged them to be prolific mothers and preferred enslaving foreign workers to fill job vacancies.[66]

Cinematic and scholarly interest in the precarious position of lesbians in Nazi Germany has paralleled the development of the feminist and gay rights movements. The latter previously campaigned for the repeal of Paragraph 175, which criminalized male homosexual activities. Under Hitler's rule, the law was amended to broaden the definition of what constituted a homosexual act and to increase the prison sentences for such transgressions. West Germany did not rescind these harsher provisions until 1969 and continued to prosecute male homosexual acts until it abolished Paragraph 175 in 1994.[67] The German directors Rainer Fassbinder and Rosa von Praunheim introduced gay and bisexual characters into their movies in the 1970s.[68] During the 1980s, the Berlin Museum mounted an exhibit on the city's gay subculture, and several pioneering histories of German homosexuals were published.[69] In the early 1990s, two documentary films and Claudia Schoppmann's book about the lesbian experience under Nazism appeared.[70]

By the time the movie *Aimée and Jaguar* premiered, the story of how Lilly Wust, a pro-Nazi housewife with four children, had divorced her husband to live with her Jewish lover, Felice Schragenheim, had received much publicity. Erica Fischer's dual biography of the couple became a bestseller in Germany in 1994. An American edition appeared the next year.[71] It inspired the documentary film *Love Story: Berlin 1942*, which featured interviews with the elderly Wust, her family members, and wartime friends. The film won a major award from the International Documentary Association in 1997.[72]

Director Max Färberböck tells the story of Lilly and Felice through the recollections of Ilse, who coincidentally meets Lilly in the present. Ilse had served as Lilly's maid and introduced her to Felice. Ilse had been Felice's lover until then and envies the relationship that developed between Lilly and Felice. She warns Felice that Lilly is a happily married woman who parrots Nazi slogans and claims she can identify Jews by their smell. Felice audaciously asks Lilly to sniff her perfume to test her olfactory radar and sends anonymous passionate love letters to her.

Felice leads a double life. Passing as an Aryan, she joins her fellow Berliners in underground shelters when the Allies bomb the city. These scenes present the Germans as victims in the eyes of the audience. As a Jew, however, Felice conceals her real identity and provides the British with photos of buildings to target and the schedules of trains carrying Jews from Hungary to Auschwitz. She gathers this intelligence by working as a stenographer for a Nazi newspaper. The precariousness of her situation pervades several key scenes. As she huddles in the bomb shelter during an air raid, a former patient of her deceased father recognizes her and advises her to be more discreet. When it is safe to come out, she witnesses the arrest and loading of Jews onto a truck by the Gestapo. She assists a little Jewish girl in finding her lost hat, but then looks wistfully as the child boards the lorry, perhaps envisioning herself in the same predicament. When Lilly is shown walking around the city, the camera creates the impression she is being stalked.

Overwhelmed by parenting four boys on her own, Lilly yearns to be loved. When her husband is fighting on the eastern front, she lounges on the sofa eagerly awaiting the arrival of an SS officer with whom she is having an affair. It is apparent she derives no pleasure from intercourse with him or her husband, Günther, when he returns home. This is why she is so smitten by the flattery showered upon her in the letters from her secret admirer. Lilly finds refuge from her loneliness in the companionship of Felice and her clique of girlfriends. When they celebrate New Year's Eve together, Guenther arrives home unexpectedly and pairs off with Ilse. Felice takes advantage of this moment to kiss Lilly, who rebuffs her advances with a slap in the face. Felice leaves, but Lilly pursues her and asks to see her again. This leads to a highly erotic love scene whose tender sensuality contrasts sharply with the image of Günther mechanically thrusting on top of a limp and expressionless Lilly until he climaxes and abruptly stops. Assured of her real sexual orientation, Lilly demands a divorce from Günther, who calls her a "queer" and hits her. As the love between Lilly (a.k.a. Aimée) and Felice (a.k.a. Jaguar) blossoms, the police dragnet to catch Felice is tightened. The authorities know that she is somewhere in Berlin because a picture of her had been found in the possession of a friend who was killed while trying to evade arrest. The police raid Felice's apartment and take her grandmother into custody. Felice moves in with Lilly. When Felice has the chance to escape to Switzerland, she turns it down, ostensibly because she thinks the war will be over soon, but actually because she refuses to abandon Lilly. Since Felice goes away on resistance missions, Lilly wonders what Felice does when she is absent and who she really is. Felice finally confesses to Lilly that she is Jewish. Suddenly understanding the motive for Felice's secretiveness, Lilly begs her for forgiveness.

Von Moltke asserts that her vulnerability at this moment "positions Lilly, not Felice, as the victim in need of consolation and reassurance that the Jew will not leave."[73] Yet, the emotional impact of watching the Gestapo dragging the resisting Felice out of the apartment building shifts the audience's sympathy back to her. Lilly musters enough courage to try to visit Felice at Theresienstadt. Back in the present, Ilse insinuates that this brash move caused the Germans to deport Felice. As Lilly fondly recalls a conversation with an effervescent Felice praising the joy of living for the moment, the postscript reports that she presumably died on a death march toward the end of the war. Lilly grieves her loss, but she survives while her lover perishes.

Färberböck adapted *Aimée and Jaguar* from Fischer's dual biography and emphasized the relationship between the two lovers more than its historical context. The tagline for the film was, "A love greater than death!"[74] According to Färberböck, the challenge for him as a director was "to avoid making a sentimental love story and yet evoke the power of emotions" with "no aesthetic embellishment or avoidance of things which were hard and painful in real life."[75] He admirably succeeds in elevating this storyline into an engrossing and poignant film that easily could have degenerated into a trite tale of a repressed wife awakened to her lesbian desires by a sexually alluring stranger who is her polar opposite.[76] In his review of *Aimée and Jaguar*, Kenneth Turan comments that the sacrifice lovers will make for each other "is the most familiar story in the lexicon of cinema, but watching it in this emotionally powerful film makes you feel like you've never quite seen it before."[77] The film's commercial success, nomination for the Golden Globe for Best Foreign Language Film, and multiple prizes from major German film festivals and organizations reflected the growing acceptance of lesbian portrayals in mainstream movies, especially when compared to *November Moon*'s recognition only by gay audiences and organizations fifteen years earlier.[78]

Yet, some of the changes Färberböck introduced diminish an appreciation of the circumstances that accounted for Felice's daredevil attitude. When Felice first encounters Lilly on screen, it is November 1943. She had actually met Lilly a year earlier. Keenly aware of the danger Hitler posed to the Jews, Felice had already submitted applications for visas to immigrate to Palestine, the United States, or Australia as early as 1938. In October 1941, an employment agency for Jews conscripted her to work in a factory for a paltry salary. The next August, her grandmother was deported to Theresienstadt, where she died within a month. In October 1942, Felice received orders to report for "resettlement." Left with no other options, she faked a suicide note and went into hiding, boarding with friends and eking out an existence by selling family heirlooms. She joined a resistance group that furnished housing and forged papers for dissidents and Jews evading arrest. Felice moved into Lilly's apartment in April 1943, a month after Goering staged raids to make Berlin *Judenrein*. In Fischer's opinion, "Under Lilly's care Felice was able to forget for a while that she was not even supposed to be alive."[79]

Färberböck's depiction of Lilly also downplays her Nazism and the courage she displays after learning Felice is Jewish. In the movie, Felice's revelation happens shortly before her arrest in 1944. It actually occurred over a year earlier and only a month after Felice had moved in with Lilly. Lilly quickly filed for divorce, wrote a "marriage contract" to formalize her relationship with Felice, and enrolled in courses to acquire vocational skills. She contemplated leaving her children and going to Switzerland with Felice. Lilly devised ingenious ways for Felice to get medical treatment and drugs when she became ill. When the Gestapo captured Felice and confined her in a Berlin detention center in August 1944, Lilly visited her daily, bringing baskets of food until the Nazi warden forbade her to do so. These meetings served as the precedent for her vain attempt to visit Felice at Theresienstadt. She corresponded with Felice until November, even though Felice had been transferred to Auschwitz and then to Gross-Rosen. Despite being interrogated and put under surveillance by the Gestapo, Lilly hid three Jewish women from February 1945 until the defeat of Germany in May. After the war, she celebrated Jewish holidays with her sons, strongly supported Israel, and compelled her youngest son, Eberhard, to learn Hebrew. He converted to Judaism and made aliyah to Israel.[80]

Färberböck exercises questionable directorial judgment in several scenes. Felice hands over photographs of Berlin's most beautiful buildings to a courier immediately after Berlin has been bombed. Felice never trafficked in this kind of intelligence, and the sequencing of events inadvertently lends credence to the Nazi canard articulated several times in the film that the Jews bore responsibility for the Allied bombardment of the city. In the same espionage drop, Felice provides lists of Jewish transports from Hungary to the death camps. This discredits the historical authenticity of the movie since the exchange happens a year before the deportations of Hungarian Jews began.[81] Finally, Ilse instills guilt in Lilly by intimating that her visit to Theresienstadt precipitated Felice's deportation to Auschwitz. By late 1944, the Germans sent most of the Jewish women at the Czech camp to Auschwitz, Gross-Rosen, and finally on death marches.[82]

The average moviegoer probably will concur with critic Charles Taylor's assessment that *Aimée and Jaguar* is a moving film because of what Fäberböck does right rather than what he does wrong.[83] The movie's appeal arises from the opposites-attract plotline and the tragic separation of the couple once Lilly overcomes her own prejudices. The motion picture also restores the memory of Berlin's vibrant lesbian subculture.[84] In an interview, Lilly Wust remarked that she had given her consent to the publication of the book and the production of the film because she "wanted to create a memorial to Felice."[85] As John Davidson has remarked, *Aimée and Jaguar*'s plot and close-ups of love scenes illustrate that "under the Nazis the space of intimacy becomes also the space of danger."[86]

PINK TRIANGLES AND YELLOW STARS: *BENT*
Directed by Sean Mathias
(United Kingdom: Channel 4 Films, Arts Council
of England, Ask Kodansha Co., NDF Inc., 1997)

> The prisoners, however, only ostracized those whom the SS
> marked with the pink triangle. The fate of the homosexuals in the
> concentration camps can only be described as ghastly.[87]
>
> —Eugen Kogon

Unlike *Aimée and Jaguar*, which never equates the social prejudices against lesbians with the policy of extermination reserved for the Jews, the movie *Bent* suggests that it was more dangerous to be a gay man in a Nazi concentration camp than to be a Jew. In the wake of the purge of Ernst Röhm and his cohorts, the Third Reich changed the definition of criminal homosexuality from the commission of such an act to a victim's perception that someone desired to engage in homosexual activity with him. The numbers of homosexual men convicted in 1935 doubled over the previous year to 2,106 and quadrupled to more than 8,000 by 1938. There never was a plan to kill all gay men because Nazi officials disagreed over whether homosexuality arose from genetic or social factors. Thus, detainees could gain release by proving they were heterosexuals who were attracted sexually to women and had engaged in intercourse with men only to earn money or as a result of living in all-male environments like boarding schools or prisons. Of the twenty thousand homosexuals interned in concentration camps, 60 percent died. Scholars neglected the history of their ordeal until the 1970s.[88]

Adapted from Martin Sherman's play *Bent*, which premiered in London in 1979, the film version directed by Sean Mathias maintains the premise that Jews were treated better than homosexuals in Dachau during the 1930s.[89] The movie opens with a scene that looks more like a bacchanalia than a cabaret. Sitting on a Romanesque swing, Greta, a transvestite played by Mick Jagger, hangs above the stage and sings a chanson about how lonely it is on the streets of Berlin. Brown-shirted SA men are seated in the audience in a reference to the mirror-ball reflections in the closing scene of *Cabaret*. The main character, Max, has the bad fortune to pick up a blond Storm Trooper shortly before the latter's throat is slit on the Night of the Long Knives. The garishness of the nightclub scene contrasts with the austere surroundings throughout the remainder of the movie. Black shirts replace brown ones as the SS now conducts the search for gay men.

Max (Clive Owen) and Horst (Lothaire Bluteau) become lovers in Dachau. Bent. *Press kit, courtesy of the Nostalgia Factory.*

Greta reappears dressed as a dapper gentleman because it is too risky to be a "fluff" anymore. Max and his roommate, Rudi, obtain false papers from Max's gay uncle but get arrested before they reach the border.

Aboard the train taking them to Dachau, the SS guards savagely beat Rudi with a truncheon. Hearing the agonized screams from the next car, Max keeps repeating that he cannot believe this is really happening. To prove he is a heterosexual, the guards order him to bludgeon Rudi to death and have sexual intercourse with the corpse of a teenage girl. Max does as commanded to convince his captors that he is a heterosexual Jew. He assumes that by posing as a Jew, he will be treated more leniently in the camp than those who are stigmatized as "bent," the slang term for homosexuals.

After arriving at Dachau, Max initially works alone but requests that a gay man he befriended on the train assist him. Eschewing realism, Mathias distills the essence of the Nazi policy of "destruction through labor" into highly stylized scenes of Max, and then Horst, moving rocks from one pile to another. As Nick Kimberly observes, "Prisons are usually represented as claustrophobic, but here we feel, almost in a physical way, the sheer belittling pointlessness of Max's solitary labor as the camera finds his tiny figure in the distance, trudging endlessly back and forth in a vast monochrome chamber."[90] The repetitive score by Phillip Glass heightens the sense of tedium.[91]

The movie's emphasis on dialog rather than action makes it more theatrical than cinematic. The central scenes of Max and Horst transcending their physical confinement through conversations describing imaginary sexual acts with each other rely on their verbal explicitness rather than graphic representation. Mathias admits this was a deliberate decision on his part: "The whole relationship of the two men falling in love whilst moving rocks, means that *Bent* is not about action or variety, but more about interior landscape. This isn't exactly the stuff from which great cinema is made."[92]

The closing scene, however, provides a visually striking metaphor for Max to assert his individuality and sexual identity and demonstrate that he is not just an emotionless robot performing Sisyphean drudgery. A guard notices that Horst has developed a serious cough that slows down his pace of work. For this reason, the guard shoots Horst in the head and orders Max to dispose of the body. In an image reminiscent of the pieta, Max holds Horst in his arms and confesses that he truly loved him. Max briefly lays Horst's cadaver in a shallow ditch and resumes his work. Then, he descends into the makeshift grave and emerges wearing Horst's prison jacket bearing the pink triangle. Having come out of his barbed wire closet, Max throws himself on the electrified fence and assumes the identity and fate of his lover in a gesture of gay solidarity. According to Eric Sterling, "Although his suicide might appear to some audiences as a futile gesture, this is not the case; instead of allowing the Nazis to control him, as he does throughout the play, in the conclusion, Max finally assumes control over his own life and becomes proud of his homosexual identity."[93]

Some scholars resent the movie's "suggestion that the Nazis' persecution of gays was even more vicious than their anti-Semitism."[94] In terms of the priorities of Nazi racial policies, their consternation is justified. Hitler clearly perceived international Jewry as posing a mortal threat to Germany's existence. Thus, the ultimate goal of the Final Solution was to exterminate Jews throughout Europe. The Third Reich never pursued its campaign against homosexuals with the same urgency and thoroughness. Determining who was gay was not a precise process. Since the Nazis feared that homosexuality would lower Aryan birthrates and undermine the military prowess of German soldiers, they did not prosecute homosexual relations among non-Aryans. Finally, the distinction between acquired and innate homosexuality opened a loophole for "situational" homosexuals to prove they were heterosexuals and qualify for release.[95] Rüdiger Lautmann, a leading scholar on the Nazi persecution of gay men, has concluded that in the hierarchy of concentration camp prisoners, "the lowest rank was always occupied by those who wore the yellow triangles, the Jews."[96]

This, however, does not invalidate *Bent*'s depiction of the torment homosexuals endured in the camps and the constant possibility that they would be killed by an SS officer or *kapo* supervising them. Although gay men fared better than Jews in that they were not slated for extermination, homophobia on the part of guards and prisoners made gay men a convenient target for the wrath of the former and the displaced anger of the latter. Furthermore, the time frame of *Bent* should be considered. Since Max and Horst are swept up in the antigay raids following the Night of the Long Knives and the stringent revisions of Paragraph 175 in 1935, they are interned in Dachau before the first major influx of Jewish prisoners arrived there as part of the mass arrests of Jewish men following *Kristallnacht* in November of 1938. One hundred fifty homosexuals were listed as prisoners in Dachau in March 1938, when the camp housed only several thousand inmates.[97] One heterosexual survivor of Dachau described the fate of homosexuals in these stark terms: "The inmates with the pink triangle never lived long: they were exterminated by the SS with systematic swiftness."[98] A memorial plaque for the homosexuals who died at Dachau was belatedly added to the camp museum's permanent collection in 1994.[99]

Bent deserves to be judged on its considerable merits and not castigated merely as an attempt to obscure the victimization of the Jews. It presents a stylized and dialogical alternative to the realistic brutality of concentration camp movies like *Triumph of the Sprit*. As one critic put it, "It is not just the violence of the Third Reich that is shocking, but the awful precision of the mental terror."[100] Rather than substituting homosexuals for Jews as the most endangered species in the Darwinian struggle created by Nazi racism, the play and movie reference "the history of the Jewish persecution as a thematic and stylistic 'horizon' that serves as the epistemological framework in which the events of the homosexual persecution can be conceptualized or imagined."[101] In other words, the assumed familiarity of the audience with the Jewish Holocaust provides the cognitive bridge that enables straight viewers to empathize with the plight of the homosexuals.

Moreover, the movie has become the definitive cinematic representation of the Nazi persecution of homosexuals. Not only was it the first full-length feature film to deal with this topic,[102] but both the author of the play and the director of the movie felt their involvement in it raised their own historical awareness as gay men.[103] Although the film received mixed reviews from critics and did not fare well at the box office, it was a hit with gay audiences and earned a spot among the top ten lesbian and gay films of 1997. The same year, it also garnered the Award of the Youth in the Foreign Film category at the Cannes Film Festival.[104] Kevin Thomas notes that the movie privileges the relationship between Max and Horst over their deaths: "The love that develops between Max and Horst gives them dignity, a way in which to give their long days of pointless, exhausting labor meaning."[105]

Since the movies discussed in this chapter conclude with departures or deaths, they disappoint the audience's expectation that lovers should live happily ever after. Prejudice displaces or destroys couples because one or both partners belong to a proscribed political, racial, or religious group. It is the emotional reaction to suppressed romances that serves as an emphatic bridge between the documentary images of the dehumanized victims of the Holocaust and the vibrant individuals and couples they once were.

NOTES

1. Thomas E. Wartenberg, *Unlikely Couples: Movie Romance as Social Criticism* (Boulder, CO: Westview Press, 1999), 7.

2. Wartenberg, *Unlikely Couples*, 8–9.

3. *Jew Suss,* directed by Veidt Harlan (Germany, 1940); Eric Rentschler, *Ministry of Illusions: Nazi Cinema and Its Afterlife* (Cambridge, MA: Harvard University Press, 1996), 149–69, 355–63; Linda Schulte-Sasse, *Entertaining the Third Reich: Illusions of Wholeness in Nazi Cinema* (Durham, NC: Duke University Press, 1996), 47–91.

4. *The Last Metro,* directed by Francois Truffaut (France, 1980).

5. *Max and Helen,* directed by Philip Saville (United States, 1990); *Enemies: A Love Story,* directed by Paul Mazursky (United States, 1989).

6. *Marriage in the Shadows,* directed by Kurt Maetzig (East Germany, 1947); Martin Bundy, "Discussion with Kurt Maetzig," in *DEFA East German Cinema, 1946–1992,* ed. Sean Allan and John Sandford (New York: Berghahn, 1999), 79–83.

7. *The Cremator,* directed by Spalovac Mrtvol (Czechoslovakia, 1968).

8. *The Jewish Wife,* directed by Jeff Young (United States, 1971); *Temporary Paradise,* directed by Andras Kovacs (Hungary, 1981).

9. *Monastero di Santa Chiara,* directed by Mario Sequi (Italy, 1949).

10. *Sweet Light in a Dark Room,* directed by Jiri Weiss (Czechoslovakia, 1959).

11. Judith Doneson, *The Holocaust in American Film* (Syracuse, NY: Syracuse University Press, 2002), 199–215; Esther Fuchs, "Gender and Representation: Love Stories in Holocaust Films," in *The Representation of the Holocaust in Literature and Film,* ed. Marc Lee Raphael (Williamsburg, VA: Department of Religion, College of William and Mary, 2003), 29–45.

12. *Forbidden,* directed by Anthony Page (United States, United Kingdom, West Germany, 1984); *'38: Vienna before the Fall,* directed by Wolfgang Gluck (Austria, 1986).

13. Esther Fuchs, "Gender and Holocaust Docudramas: Gentile Heroines in Rescue Films," *Shofar: An Interdisciplinary Journal of Jewish Studies* 22, no. 1 (Fall 2003): 80–94; Esther Fuchs, "Gender and Representation," 29–45.

14. Lawrence Baron, "The Moral Minority: Psycho-Social Research on the Righteous Gentiles," in *What Have We Learned? Telling the Story and Teaching the Lessons of the Holocaust,* ed. Franklin H. Littell, Alan L. Berger, and Hubert G. Locke (Lewiston, ME: Edwin Mellen Press, 1993), 119–40; David Gushee, "Many Paths to Righteousness: An Assessment of Research on Why Righteous Gentiles Helped Jews," *Holocaust and Genocide Studies* 7, no. 3 (Summer 1993): 372–401.

15. *Angry Harvest,* directed by Agnieszka Holland (Germany, 1985); *Warszawa: Year 5703,* directed by Janusz Kijowski (Germany, Poland, 1992).

16. *Julia,* directed by Fred Zinnemann (United States, 1977).

17. *Cabaret,* directed by Bob Fosse (United States, 1972); *The Damned,* directed by Luchino Visconti (Italy, 1969); Kriss Ravetto, *The Unmaking of Fascist Aesthetics* (Minneapolis: University of Minnesota Press, 2001), 87–96.

18. Anneke Smelik, "Gay and Lesbian Criticism," in *Film Studies: Critical Approaches,* ed. John Hill and Pamela Church (New York: Oxford University Press, 2000), 133–45, Alexander Doty, "Queer Theory," *Film Studies: Critical Approaches,* 146–50.

19. *November Moon,* directed by Alexandra von Grote (West Germany, 1985); "November Moon," at www.lesbianworlds.com; "November Moon," at www.gay.com .kleptomaniac.com; "November Moon," at www.Planetout.com; Julia Knight, *Women and the New German Cinema* (New York: Verso, 1992), 155–56; see also *The Red Skirt,* directed by Geneviève Lefebre (France, 1987).

20. Sabine Hake, *German National Cinema* (New York: Routledge, 2002), 188.

21. *My Heart Is Mine Alone,* directed by Helma Sanders-Brahms (Germany, 1997). Else Lasker-Schüler, "Friendship and Love," in *C·O·N·C·E·R·T,* trans. Jean M. Snook (Lincoln: University of Nebraska Press, 1994); Hans W. Cohn, *Else Lasker-Schüler: The Broken World* (New York: Cambridge University Press, 1974), Betty Falkenberg, *Else Lasker-Schüler* (Jefferson, NC: McFarland and Co., 2003).

22. Lutz Koepnick, "Reframing the Past: Heritage Cinema and Holocaust in the 1990s," *New German Critique* 87 (Fall 2002): 47–70.

23. Peter Stack, "Czech Gem Makes It Through," *San Francisco Chronicle,* June 9, 1995.

24. Antonín J. Liehm, *Closely Watched Films: The Czechoslovak Experience* (White Plaines, NY: International Arts and Science Press, 1974), 57–74.

25. Mira Liehm and Antonín J. Liehm, *The Most Important Art: Eastern European Film after 1945* (Berkeley: University of California Press, 1977), 302–3; Gary Kamiya, "Moving Czech Love Story Has Heart," *San Francisco Examiner*, June 9, 1995.

26. John 12:2–3.

27. Franklin H. Littell, "First They Came for the Jews," *Christian Ethics Today: Journal of Christian Ethics* 3, no. 1 (February 1997).

28. Fuchs, "Gender and Representation," 35–36.

29. Kamiya, "Moving Czech Story."

30. Tina Balio, "A Major Presence in All of the World's Important Markets: The Globalization of Hollywood in the 1990s," in *Contemporary Hollywood Cinema*, ed. Steve Neale and Murray Smith (New York: Routledge, 1998), 58–74.

31. *Bagdad Café*, directed by Percy Adlon (West Germany, 1988).

32. Stack, "Czech Gem"; Kevin Thomas, "Love Finds New Depth in *Martha and I*," *Los Angeles Times*, April 21, 1995; *Martha and I*, "Box Office and Business," at www.imdb.com (accessed June 9, 2005).

33. Ronald Bergan, "Jiri Weiss," *Guardian*, May 27, 2004.

34. Roman Cycowski, quoted in Carol Traxler, "Comedian Harmonists," *Quarter Notes: Newsletter of the Washington Sängerbund* (February 1998).

35. Rick Altman, *Film/Genre* (London: British Film Institute, 1999), 123–43.

36. Elias Savada, "*The Harmonists*," March 26, 1999, at www.nitrateonline.com/1999/rharmonists.html (accessed June 12, 2002); Roger Ebert, "*The Harmonists*," *Chicago Sun-Times*, March 19, 1999.

37 See the movie's website at www.comedian-harmonists.de (accessed June 14, 2002).

38. Vilsmaier's film *Comedian Harmonists*, the posters, at www.anum.tuwien.ac.at/~dirk/harmonists/ch.htm#cinema (accessed February 22, 2003).

39. *The Producers,* directed by Mel Brooks (United States, 1966).

40. Annette Insdorf, *Indelible Shadows: Film and the Holocaust,* 3rd ed. (New York: Cambridge University Press, 2003), 47–49.

41. *Lili Marleen,* directed by Werner Fassbinder (West Germany, 1981).

42. *Playing for Time,* directed by Daniel Mann (United States, 1980); Jeffrey Shandler, *While America Watches: Televising the Holocaust* (New York: Oxford University Press, 1999), 214–19; *Swing Kids*, directed by Thomas Carter (United States, 1993).

43. Michael Zwerin, *La Tristesse de St. Louis: Swing under the Nazis* (New York: W. Morrow, 1985); Michael H. Kater, *Different Drummers: Jazz in the Culture of Nazi Germany* (New York: Oxford University Press, 1992); Michael Meyer, *The Politics of Music in the Third Reich* (New York: Peter Lang, 1993).

44. Dieter Osswald, "Die Altererste Boy-Group: Interview with Joseph Vilsmaier zu *Comedian Harmonists*," January 1998, at www.subway-net.de/magazin/1998/oljoseph.shtml (accessed June 12, 2002). On the klezmer revival in Germany, see Jeremy Eichler, "Klezmer's Final Frontier," *New York Times*, August 29, 2004.

45. Fuchs, "Gender and Representation," 39–41.

46. Koepnick, "Reframing the Past," 62.

47. Koepnick, "Reframing the Past," 72.

48. *Die Comedian Harmonists*, directed by Eberhard Fechner (West Germany, 1976); Eberhard Fechner, *Die Comedian Harmonists: Sechs Lebenslaeufe* (Berlin: Quadriga, 1988).

49. *Autumn Milk*, directed by Joseph Vilsmaier (West Germany, 1988); *Stalingrad*, directed by Joseph Vilsmaier (Germany, Sweden, 1993); Hake, *German National, Cinema*, 187–88.

50. "Awards," *Comedian Harmonists*, at www.imdb.com (accessed June 9, 2005).

51. "Der Regisseur," at www.comedian-harmonists.de/interview/html (accessed June 14, 2002); "Die Altererste Boy-Group," 2.

52. Quoted in Arthur Lazare, *The Harmonists*, at www.culturevulture.net/movies/harmonists.htm (accessed June 14, 2002).

53. Hake, *German National Cinema*, 76.

54. Anton Kaes, *From Heimat to Hitler* (Cambridge, MA: Harvard University Press, 1989), 163–92; Eric Rentsler, *The Ministry of Illusion: Nazi Cinema and Its Afterlife* (Cambridge, MA: Harvard University Press), 188–92; Marc Silberman, *German Cinema: Texts in Context* (Detroit: Wayne State University Press, 1995), 114–27.

55. Reinhold Rauh, *Edgar Reitz: Film Als Heimat* (Munich: Heyne Filmbibliothek, 1993); Robert C. Reimer and Carol J. Reimer, *Nazi-Retro Film: How German Narrative Cinema Remembers the Past* (New York: Twayne, 1992), 188–92; Eric Santner, *Stranded Objects: Mourning, Memory, and Film in Postwar Germany* (Ithaca, NY: Cornell University Press, 1990), 57–102.

56. Cited in "'Im Kern feige': Parabel vs. Authenzität, quälende Langsamkeit als Programm: Didi Danquart über seinen preisgekekrönten Film, *Viehjud Levi*," *Tageszeitung*, September 30, 1999.

57. Omer Bartov, *The "Jew" in Cinema: From the Golem to Don't Touch My Holocaust* (Bloomington: Indiana University Press, 2005), 100–105.

58. Ian Kershaw, *Popular Opinion and Political Dissent in the Third Reich: Bavarian 1933–1945* (New York: Oxford University Press, 1983), 127–28, 233, 240–44.

59. Thomas Strittmatter, *Viehhud Levi und andere Stücke* (Zürich: Diogenes Verlag, 1992), 7–33.

60. Johannes von Moltke, "*Heimat* and History: *Viehjud Levi*," *New German Critique* 87 (Fall 2002), 103.

61. Didi Danquart, quoted in "*Viehjud Levi*," at www.fdk-berlin.de/forum 99/viehjud.html (accessed June 18, 2002).

62. "Awards," *Viehjud Levi*, at www.imdb.com (accessed June 18, 2002).

63. *Three Days in April*, directed by Oliver Storz (Germany, 1994); *Rabbit Hunt*, directed by Andreas Gruber (Austria, Germany, 1994).

64. Erica Fischer, *Aimée und Jaguar* (Cologne: Kiepenheuer und Witsch, 1994). Footnotes refer to Erica Fischer, *Aimée and Jaguar: A Love Story, Berlin 1943*, trans. Edna McCown (New York: Harper Collins, 1995), 181.

65. Claudia Schoppmann, *Days of Masquerade: Life Stories of Lesbians during the Third Reich*, trans. Allison Brown (New York: Columbia University Press, 1996), 1–30.

66. Schoppmann, *Days of Masquerade*, 41–54, 92–101, 116–22.

67. Bill Niven, *Facing the Nazi Past: United Germany and the Legacy of the Third Reich* (New York: Routledge, 2002), 222.

68. Alice A. Kuzniar, *The Queer German Cinema* (Palo Alto, CA: Stanford University Press, 2000), 69–112.

69. *Eldorado: Homsexuelle Frauen und Männer in Berlin, 1850–1950* (Berlin: Berlin Museum, 1984).

70. *Nitrate Kisses*, directed by Barbara Hammer (United States, 1992); *Verzaubert*, directed by Joerg Foeckele et al. (Germany, 1993).

71. See footnote 64.

72. *Love Story: Berlin 1942,* directed by Catrine Clay (United Kingdom, 1997); "Awards," *Love Story: Berlin 1942,* at www.imdb.com (accessed June 19, 2002).

73. Von Moltke, "*Heimat* and History," 100–102.

74. "Taglines," *Aimée and Jaguar*, at www.imdb.com (accessed June 19, 2002).

75. "An Interview with Max Färberböck," *Aimée and Jaguar*, at www.zeitgeist films.com/current/aimeejaguar/ajintmf.html (accessed June 19, 2005).

76. *Lianna,* directed by John Sayles (United States, 1983); *Desert Hearts,* directed by Donna Deitch (United States, 1986); Wartenberg, *Unlikely Couples,* 193–207.

77. Kenneth Turan, "*Aimée and Jaguar* Reinvigorates Story of Love," *Los Angeles Times*, August 11, 2000.

78. "Awards," "Box-Office," *Aimée and Jaguar*, at www.imdb.com (accessed June 19, 2002).

79. Fischer, *Aimée and Jaguar,* 22–107; John E. Davidson, "A Story of Faces and Intimate Spaces: Form and History in Max Färberböck's *Aimée and Jaguar*," *Quarterly Review of Film and Video* 19 (October–December 2002): 323–41; Muriel Cormican, "*Aimée and Jaguar* and the Banality of Evil, *German Studies Review* 26, no. 1 (February 2003): 105–19.

80. Fischer, *Aimée and Jaguar,* 112–267. Charles Taylor also felt that Lilly's Nazism seems too innocuous. See Charles Taylor, "*Aimée and Jaguar*," August 11, 2000, at www .salon.com/ent/movies/review/2000/08/11/aimee_jaguar.html (accessed June 21, 2002).

81. Felice copied lists of Jewish transports from Hungary but never had the opportunity to give them to an Allied agent. Fischer, *Aimée and Jaguar,* 167–73. See Randolph L. Braham, *The Politics of Genocide: The Holocaust in Hungary* (New York: Columbia University Press, 1981).

82. Fischer, *Aimée and Jaguar,* 211–18, Ruth Elias, *From Theresienstadt and Auschwitz to Israel* (New York: John Wiley and Sons, 1998); Ruth Klüger, *Still Alive: A Holocaust Girlhood Remembered* (New York: Feminist Press of the City University of New York, 2001).

83. Taylor, "*Aimée and Jaguar*," 2. For a similar appreciation of the film, see Gerda Wurzenberger, "Eine Liebe im Ausnahmezustand," *Neue Zürcher Zeitung,* June 11, 1999.

84. Jennifer Bendery, "*Aimée and Jaguar*," ca. 2000, at www.popmatters.com/film/ reviews/a/aimee-and-jaguar.html (accessed June 21, 2002).

85. "An Interview with the Real Lilly Wust," *Aimée and Jaguar*, at www.zeitgeist films.com/current/aimeejaguar/ajaimee.html (accessed June 19, 2002). Compare the entire interview with the flippant quote cited in Bartov, *The "Jew" in Cinema*, 73.

86. Davidson, "A Story of Faces and Intimate Spaces," 324. Like Davidson, Katrin Sieg worries that the emphasis on sexual preference obscures the political resistance of Felice and Lilly after Felice's arrest. See Katrin Sieg, "Sexual Desire and Social

Transformation in *Aimée and Jaguar,*" *Signs: Journal of Women in Culture and Society* 28, no. 1 (2002), 303–31.

87. Eugen Kogon, *The Theory and Practice of Hell* (New York: Berkley, 1968), 44.

88. Michael Burleigh and Wolfgang Wippermann, *The Racial State: Germany, 1933–1945* (New York: Cambridge University Press, 1991), 182–97; Richard Plant, *The Pink Triangle: The Nazi War against Homosexuals* (New York: Henry Holt, 1986).

89. Martin Sherman, *Bent* (New York: Avon, 1979).

90. Nick Kimberly, "*Bent,*" *Sight and Sound* (March 1998): 39.

91. Sean Mathias, quoted in James Kleinmann, "*Bent* but Not Broken," *London Student* 13, at www.londonstudent.org.uk/13issue/film/bent.htm (accessed June 30, 2002).

92. Mathias in Kleinmann, "*Bent* but Not Broken"; James Berardinelli, "*Bent,*" 1997, at www.movie-reviews.colossus.net/movies/b/bent.htm (accessed June 29, 2002).

93. Eric Sterling, "Bent Straight: The Destruction of Self in Martin Sherman's *Bent,*" *European Studies* 32, no. 4 (December 2002): 373–74.

94. Kimberly, "*Bent,*" 39; Robert Skloot, *The Darkness We Carry: The Drama of the Holocaust* (Madison: University of Wisconsin Press, 1988), 120.

95. Plant, *The Pink Triangle,* 117–25, 148–49, 235.

96. Rüdiger Lautmann, "The Pink Triangle: Homosexuals as 'Enemies of the State,'" in *The Holocaust and History: The Known, the Unknown, the Disputed, and the Reexamined,* ed. Michael Berenbaum and Abraham J. Peck (Bloomington: Indiana University Press, 1998), 352.

97. Harold Marcuse, *Legacies of Dachau: The Uses and Abuses of a Concentration Camp 1933–2001* (New York: Cambridge University Press, 2001), 21–38; Sterling, "Bent Straight," 379–82.

98. Raimund Schnabel, *Die Frommer in der Hölle* (Frankfurt: Roederberg, 1966), 19.

99. Marcuse, *Legacies of Dachau,* 354–55.

100. Kimberly, "*Bent,*" at www.queer-view.com/00600er/655bent/english655.htm (accessed June 29, 2002).

101. Dorthe Seifert, "Between Silence and License: The Representation of the National Socialist Persecution of Homosexuality in Anglo-American Fiction and Film," *History and Memory* 15, no. 2 (Fall/Winter 2003): 122.

102. *Desire,* directed by Stuart Marshall (United Kingdom, 1989); *Paragraph 175,* directed by Robert Epstein and Jeffrey Friedman (Germany, United Kingdom, United States, 1999); Robin Wood, "Gays and the Holocaust: Two Documentaries," in *Image and Remembrance: Representation and the Holocaust,* ed. Shelley Hornstein and Florence Jacobowitz (Bloomington: Indiana University Press, 2003), 114–36.

103. Frank Noack, "Interview with Martin Sherman, Writer of *Bent,*" at www.queer-view.com/00600er/655bent/interviews655df_Sherman.htm (accessed June 29, 2002).

104. Roger Ebert, "*Bent,*" *Chicago Sun-Times,* November 11, 1997; James Berardinelli, "*Bent,*" December 5, 1997, at www.movie-reviews.colossus.net; Thelma Adams, "*Bent,*" *New York Post,* November 26, 1997; Albert Williams, "The Hidden Holocaust," *Chicago Reader,* November 11, 1997; Mary Dickson, "*Bent,*" *Salt Lake City Weekly* (May 11, 1998). "Awards" and "Box-Office and Business," *Bent,* at www.imdb.com (accessed June 9, 2002).

105. Kevin Thomas, "*Bent,*" *Los Angeles Times Calendar* (November 26, 1997): 8.

• 5 •

Serious Humor: Laughter as Lamentation

> Whereas tragedy and lamentation affirm *what is* and proceed largely in a mimetic mode that elevates, the comic spirit proceeds in an anti-mimetic mode that often mocks *what is*, that patiently deflates, demotes, or even denies the authority of its subject matter.[1]
>
> —Terrence Des Pres

The phrase "Holocaust humor" seems like an oxymoron. It violates three cardinal rules that Terrence Des Pres felt unofficially governed Holocaust discourse: (1) that the Holocaust be portrayed as a unique event, (2) that representations of the Holocaust be accurate, and (3) that the Holocaust be approached solemnly.[2] Yet, even the Jews languishing in the ghettoes or anticipating their deaths in the camps exchanged jokes to ridicule their executioners, extract hope out of despair, or cope with the absurdity of their dilemma. Their resort to humor provided a defense mechanism to sublimate their rage against their oppressors and transform their misery into something bearable.[3]

Before the Holocaust had reached its awful apex, filmmakers armed with their cameras took humorous potshots at Hitler and his henchmen. Charlie Chaplin's *The Great Dictator* (1940) satirized Hitler as an egotistical demagogue whose guttural anti-Semitic tirades wilted microphones and who juggled the globe like a child playing with a ball. Chaplin demolished the myth of Aryan purity by playing both the Jewish barber and the Phooey (Chaplin's epithet for the führer). He concluded the movie by having the barber drop his charade as Hynkel and deliver a serious speech condemning fascism and racism. In retrospect, Chaplin regretted his comic treatment of Nazi oppression: "Had I known of the actual horrors of the German concentration camps, I could not have made fun of the homicidal insanity of the Nazis."[4]

135

Ernst Lubitsch's *To Be or Not to Be* (1942) elicits laughter by having a troupe of actors outwit their oppressors. The movie opens with footage of battle-ravaged Warsaw and features an excerpt from one of Hitler's radio addresses. These actualities serve as a framework for Lubitsch to satirize "the Nazis and their ridiculous ideology." Lubitsch draws attention to the plight of the Jews by putting Shylock's famous speech from *The Merchant of Venice* (i.e., "Hath not a Jew eyes?") into the mouth of a Jewish extra, who rehearses these lines backstage, on a debris covered street, and in front of an audience of German soldiers and an actor masquerading as Hitler. Lubitsch does not trivialize the severity of the German occupation, but rather, as Annette Insdorf maintains, fights "horror with the ammunition of sharp humor." Mel Brook's remake of *To Be or Not to Be* (1983) lacks the political pungency of the original.[5]

By the late 1950s, a few films were produced that employed humor to mock Nazi racism and sympathize with its victims, as table 5.1 indicates. The first postwar comedy about the German persecution of Jews did not appear until 1958. Adapted from Franz Werfel's play *Jacobowsky and the Colonel*, *Me and the Colonel* replicates *To Be or Not to Be's* formula of fugitives evading the Germans through a series of clever deceptions. It features humorous banter between a Polish Jew and an anti-Semitic Polish aristocrat, who grow to respect each other as they stay one step ahead of their common enemy.[6] Sander Gilman's criticism of the film's omission of direct references to the Shoah exhibits an extremely narrow concept of what constitutes a Holocaust movie and ignores how Jewish refugees like Werfel derived vicarious revenge from outsmarting the Nazis on screen.[7]

Made in the same year, Kurt Hoffmann's *Aren't We Wonderful* satirizes the historical amnesia of many West Germans who conveniently forgot the Third Reich as they switched allegiances to the democracy that replaced it. Staged as a series of cabaret skits linked by the experiences of recurring characters from the 1930s until the 1950s, the movie depicts Nazism as a lower-class phenomenon that middle-class Germans tolerated more out of conformity than conviction. Its hero, Hans Böckel, never loses his liberal moorings and does the right things, like saving a Jewish friend, refusing to support Hitler to advance his career, and fighting neo-Nazism in the postwar period. Although Hoffmann assumes that the audience would identify with Böckel's disdain for

Table 5.1. Holocaust Comedies as Percentage of Holocaust Films

	1945–1959	1960–1969	1970–1979	1980–1989	1990-1999
Comedies	4	6	8	10	26
Percentage of Films	3.6	4.4	6.4	4.4	11.7

Hitler, he insinuates that many decent Germans had retreated inward and re-linquished control of their country to fanatics. To awaken them from their complacent slumber, Hoffmann tickled their funny bones rather than rattling the skeletons in their closets.[8]

Comedies remained rare, even as the output of Holocaust feature films doubled in the 1960s and 1970s. The odd-couple scenario provided the most common vehicle for pairing victims with those who might betray or befriend them. As already noted in chapter 2, *The Shop on Main Street* mines the incongruous relationship between Tono and Rosalie to keep the film's tone light until its tragic ending. Claude Berri's *The Two of Us* (1966) and *Harold and Maude* (1971) elicit laughs by mismatching the lead characters. In the former, an anti-Semitic French peasant unwittingly shelters a Jewish boy who has been taken to the countryside to escape the Germans. Every canard the old man utters about Jews is discredited by his affection for the child.[9] *Harold and Maude* pairs a morbid teenage boy with a free-spirited eighty-year-old woman. Maude's unbridled libertinism reflects her aversion to any authority as a Holocaust survivor. Her past is discreetly hinted at through a glimpse of the numbers tattooed on her arm and her fond memories of prewar Vienna. Appreciative of the second chance afforded by her survival, she teaches Harold, who regularly stages phony suicide attempts to attract his mother's attention, to relish life.[10]

Mel Brooks premised *The Producers* (1968) on the assumption that any comic portrayal of Hitler would offend Americans. Upon the advice of his new accountant, impresario Max Bialystock scours scripts for a play so terrible that it will fold the first night, entitling him to keep the money raised to produce it. The musical *Springtime for Hitler* seems destined to flop, but audiences find its tastelessness campy. Brooks does not simply let kitsch prevail. He lampoons the composer of the romp, Franz Liebkind, who alternates between being an American patriot and regressing into a loyal Nazi. Liebkind hopes to prove that Hitler was a better dancer than Winston Churchill.[11]

Making comedies about concentration camps remained taboo until the 1970s. The checkered fate of Jerry Lewis's *The Day the Clown Cried* (1972) is a case in point. Lewis plays a clown imprisoned in a transit camp for cracking derogatory jokes about Hitler. There he regains his passion for performing by entertaining Jewish children before they are deported. The movie was never released, but a dramatic version of a similar story provided the plotline for *The Last Butterfly* (1990).[12]

Lina Wertmueller's *Seven Beauties* (1975) became the first film to extract laughter from the plight of an inmate at Auschwitz. Wertmueller sandwiches the pathetic attempts of her sleazy protagonist to survive between footage of the devastation caused by World War II and the imminence of death in the camp where he is interned. The antihero, Pasqualino, murders a pimp who had "corrupted" his sister. Sentenced to serve as an orderly in a hospital, he rapes a comatose patient. At Auschwitz, he is ordered to select seven men for execution and kill his best friend. To get an extra ration of food, he seduces the repulsively obese female commandant who has made his existence miserable. In the process, the victimizer becomes the victim.[13] The film sparked a controversy between Terrence Des Pres and Bruno Bettelheim over whether it glorified survival at any cost. In retrospect, its portrayal of Pasqualino's dilemma accords closely with Lawrence Langer's theory that camp inmates were forced to make "choiceless choices" designed to demoralize them either way.[14]

Jewish desperation provided the sardonic theme of the other notable Holocaust comedy produced in the 1970s. Frank Beyer adapted *Jacob the Liar* (1974) from Jurek Becker's novel of the same name. Becker and his family had been confined in the Lodz ghetto before they were deported to various concentration camps.[15] Jacob hears a radio broadcast about the Soviets' advancing on the eastern front. The Jews of the ghetto cling to this bit of hopeful news. Jacob sustains their optimism by monitoring the progress of the war as broadcast on a radio he purportedly owns. The expectation of liberation soon deters Jews from committing suicide or organizing resistance. When Jacob confides to a friend that he has no radio, his friend hangs himself. The closing scene shows Jacob trying to buoy the spirits of a girl by vouching for the truth of a fairy tale he once had told her about clouds consisting of cotton balls. The film ends as Jacob, the girl, and other deported Jews gaze at clouds through a slit in the side of a railroad car.[16] This strategy of concocting a lie to conceal the dispiriting truth serves as the premise of subsequent comedies, like *Life Is Beautiful* (1997) and *Train of Life* (1998).

Although the number of Holocaust feature films released in the 1980s increased over the prior decade, the percentage constituted by comedies decreased. In the wake of the success of the television miniseries *Holocaust*, the decision to build an American Holocaust museum, and the increased prominence of the Holocaust in public education and the mass media, the unwritten rules mandating tragic depictions of the Holocaust were rigorously adhered to by the movie industry. The rise in the proportion of Holocaust films adapted from memoirs and nonfiction sources militated against the production of comedies with Holocaust themes. Gilman has observed that the irreverent satire of *The Producers* worked with audiences in the 1960s because the movie appeared "at a moment in time when the name Hitler was not solely identified with the *Shoah*."[17] By the 1980s, the use of comedy to depict the worst genocide of the twentieth century seemed too offensive.

Woody Allen's *Crimes and Misdemeanors* (1989) was one of the few movies from the 1980s to mix comedy into a film with a subplot about a Holocaust survivor and Jewish faith after Auschwitz. Unlike *Deconstructing Harry* (1997), in which Harry tastelessly quips that six million Jewish dead is "a record made

Table 5.2. Backgrounds of Filmmakers of Holocaust Comedies Made in the 1990s

Jewish child survivors	2
Gentile minors in Europe during the war	6
Children of survivors	7
Born 1945–1960 in war-zone states	5
Born after 1960 or in neutral states	3
Insufficient background information	3

to be broken," Allen reserved his one-liners in the former film for his failed love life and career as a filmmaker and dealt with the crimes of murder and the Holocaust in a more serious vein. His nemesis, Lester, a successful television director, pontificates that "comedy is tragedy plus time" and cites jokes about Lincoln's assassination as proof of this axiom. In the documentary Allen's character makes about Lester, he likens Lester, in his arrogance, to Mussolini not Hitler. Within the core stories in which two antagonists prevail, Allen cites the Holocaust as a metaphor for a world in which God and moral justice do not exist.[18]

Time may not have healed the wounds of the Shoah, but it has altered the modes of representing the event in feature films. Almost 12 percent of the Holocaust films made in the 1990s were comedies. Three factors fostered this sharp increase: the search for original approaches to subject matter, the presumed familiarity of the public with the basic facts of the Holocaust, and the passing of a generation of filmmakers who experienced World War II as adults and rise of those who were minors during the war or who were born after it.[19] Alan Berger surmises that children of Holocaust survivors (and, I would argue, of children raised in nations in the 1940s and 1950s where the memory of the war remained vivid) have found that humor "permits them both to accept their helplessness to undo the past and also to explore their relationship to their parents' past."[20] Table 5.2 reveals the high proportion of directors and writers of Holocaust comedies who share this background.

THE NASTY GHOUL: *GENGHIS COHN*
Directed by Elijah Moshinsky
(United Kingdom, United States:
British Broadcasting Corporation/A&E Network, 1993)

I do not wish to sound bitter, but I do believe that six million Jews left without any help at all by the civilized world could not address the latter a more heartfelt and befitting message than, "Kiss my ass."[21]

—Romain Gary

Ghost stories run the gamut from horror to humor. Ghosts materialize to frighten those who have desecrated their resting places as in Tobe Hooper's *Poltergeist* (1982), to manifest their abiding affection to a bereaved lover as in Jerry Zucker's *Ghost* (1990), or to serve as a bad conscience for someone who has wronged them in the past or continues to harm others in the present like the ghosts who haunt Scrooge in Charles Dickens's *A Christmas Carol* (1951).[22] The Yiddish equivalent of such a ghost is called a *dybbuk*. According to Romain Gary, author of the novel on which the film *Genghis Cohn* is based, a dybbuk is an "evil spirit, a demon who grabs you, gets within you, and starts to reign and lord it over you, as master."[23] The dybbuk created by Gary differs from previous spirits of murdered Jews in Holocaust films in that he exacts his revenge by telling jokes to his former tormentor instead of terrifying him.[24]

Born in Russia in 1914 to a Jewish mother, Roman Kacew, spent much of his childhood in Poland, where he absorbed Yiddish culture even though he was never an observant Jew. He moved to France in 1927 and obtained French citizenship in 1935. During World War II, Roman refused to accept France's defeat in 1940 and served with distinction in the French Resistance under his nom de guerre Romain Gary. His first novel, *Forest of Anger* (1944), portrayed the noble, but ineffectual, struggles of Polish partisans against the Germans. During Charles de Gaulle's presidency, Gary served as a French diplomat. He was inducted into the French Legion of Honor for Cultural Affairs in 1971.

Having already created a gallery of fictional characters who delight in skewering contemporary politics and society, he penned *The Dance of Genghis Cohn* in 1967. It follows the escapades of the ghost of a Yiddish comedian out to avenge the Holocaust by inhabiting the mind of an ostensibly respectable police chief of a Bavarian village, Otto Schatz. Schatz had ordered the killing of Cohn in a mass execution of Jews during the war. Under the pseudonym Émile Ajar, Gary also authored *Madame Rosa*, the novel that inspired the acclaimed film about an elderly prostitute who survived Auschwitz.[25]

Gary's wisecracking wraith orchestrates a series of homicides that implicate Schatz to teach him how it feels to be unjustly accused of a crime. The witty repartee between Cohn and Schatz and the comic premise of reforming Schatz by transforming him from an anti-Semite into a Jew attracted the British Broadcasting Corporation and the Arts and Entertainment Network to produce a television movie adapted from Gary's novel in the early 1990s. Elijah Moshinsky, an accomplished Australian director of operas and Shakespearean plays, directed the film. Staging gallows humor marked an artistic departure for Moshinsky. Perhaps the subject appealed to him because his parents were Polish Jews who found refuge in Shanghai during World War II.[26]

The mere name Genghis Cohn conjures up incongruent images of the fearsome Mongol warlord and a Jewish schlemiel from the shtetl. Ruth Wisse has noted that much of Yiddish humor derives from the discrepancy between the skepticism and the idealism of Jews living in the Diaspora. She contends that Jews developed an ironic sensibility to explain why the Chosen People suffered so much in their exile. While the Holocaust prompted many Jews to question the existence of God, some found it more ironic that Christian perpetrators killed rather than loved their Jewish neighbors.[27]

Cohn belongs in the second category. After the credits roll to the Andrews Sisters' rendition of "Bei Mir Bist Du Schön," Cohn performs as a ventriloquist interviewing a Hitler dummy in a Berlin nightclub in 1933. The Hitler puppet seems cordial until Cohn asks whether he would let his daughter date a Jew. This provokes a torrent of anti-Semitic invectives followed by involuntary shouts of *Sieg Heil*. As Cohn leaves the theater, Nazi thugs beat him. The place and time shift to Vienna in 1936. Dressed as a Hasidic Jew, Cohn describes the traits of Jews as being dark and short, speaking too loudly, and gesticulating too much. He quickly sheds his beard and caftan to mimic Hitler as a dark short man who gesticulates wildly and shouts how much he hates the Jews. Once again, a gang of Nazis pounce on him after the show. Finally, a subdued Cohn performs in Warsaw in 1939 and asks, "How do you kill a Jewish comedian? The same way you kill any comedian. You don't laugh at his jokes." Then, he observes that when a comedian flops, people say, "He died." Cohn foresees his future: "Finally, I died in. . . . "

The action flashes to Cohn climbing off a truck and lining up with other Jews in front of the ditch where they will be buried after their execution. As Schatz orders his unit to fire, Cohn yells out, *Kush mir in tokhes!* which means "Kiss my ass" in Yiddish. This brash gesture leaves an impression on Schatz, who checks into the identity of his insolent victim and the meaning of the words he uttered. In a later scene, Schatz interrogates Cohn's ghost about why he didn't die quietly like other Jews. Cohn replies, "I didn't have a machine gun, only my chutzpa." In Judith Kaufmann's opinion, Cohn's defiant posterior and kibitzing serve as forms of "unarmed aggression."[28]

When Germany lost the war, Schatz destroyed any record of his affiliation with the SS and rose to the rank of police chief. Yearning for the good old days, he meets a decadent baroness who shares his sentiments because her deceased husband had fallen on the eastern front. Before she consents to sexual intercourse, she insists that Schatz don her husband's SS uniform, which is enshrined in her bedroom closet. Titillated by the SS regalia, she eagerly begins to take Schatz's clothes off. Just then Cohn, dressed in his striped concentration camp outfit, enters the room and catches Schatz with his SS pants down. Schatz, resembling an embarrassed and disheveled Hitler, sneaks back to his apartment where Cohn reappears. Cohn explains that he nipped Schatz's romantic ardor in the bud to protest his Nazi fashion statement.

The association of sex and death is central to the story. A wave of sexually motivated murders sweeps Schatz's idyllic village. All the victims are men who are stabbed in the back when they reach orgasm with their lovers. This is a difficult crime to solve, as Cohn drolly observes, because the female witnesses had their eyes closed when the victims were killed. Schatz puzzles over why someone would murder his or her partner in the midst of coitus, but Cohn quips, "If you can kill someone for being Jewish, communist, or homosexual, you can kill them for *shtupping.*" The next time the baroness and Schatz are in bed, their foreplay is disrupted by the screams of a woman whose naked lover has died as he climaxed. Now the police need a scapegoat to blame because, as Cohn sarcastically remarks, crimes of passion interest the public more than the murder of six million Jews.

Cohn manipulates Schatz into acting like a Jew. He begins by getting Schatz to eat Jewish foods like chopped liver. He replicates his ventriloquism routines using Schatz as the dummy, who jests with Yiddish phrases at inappropriate times like a police meeting about the murder investigation or during a session with a psychoanalyst trying to diagnose Schatz's erratic behavior. Cohn even coaxes Schatz to join him in reciting the kaddish, the Jewish mourning prayer, at the local synagogue. Since Cohn is invisible to everyone else, a detective walks into the sanctuary and sees Schatz alone wearing a *tallit* and yarmulke and chanting in Hebrew. Conniving to replace Schatz, he accuses his boss of being the culprit behind the chain of murders. Eventually exonerated but deeply humbled, Schatz resigns from the police, returns to his apartment whose walls are covered with anti-Semitic graffiti, and accepts his new status by opening a kosher food stand. When he closes it at night, a bunch of neo-Nazis beat him up, just as their precursors did to Cohn when Hitler was in power. And like Cohn, the only response he can think of is the tried but never trite putdown, "Kiss my ass!" Mission accomplished, Cohn sets out to haunt the new police chief, who fired the rifle that killed Cohn.

Some critics complained that *Genghis Cohn* simplifies the plot of the novel.[29] In adapting written sources for the screen, directors typically combine or eliminate characters and omit extraneous subplots. The focus on Cohn's conversion of Schatz results in a coherent and funnier narrative. Conversely, Gary's book bogs down in part II, which features Cohn and Schatz discussing the relationship between eros and thanatos, the significance of Christ's crucifixion, discrimination against American blacks, and the war in Vietnam.[30]

Gilman contends that "since the murder of Cohn did not result in his obliteration but in his continued existence, laughter can result."[31] In the final scene, however, Cohn does not get the last laugh. Instead, he meanders in his concentration camp garb through well-dressed passersby walking to work or shopping in downtown Munich and comments, "And so it goes on. Believe me, you want fun, a few cuts and bruises, a bullet or two, go join a minority, any minority." He wonders whether punishing the guilty for committing genocide has taught humanity anything: "When it comes to mass murder, you don't ask who did it; you ask why? It couldn't happen again, could it?"

Cohn's striped outfit, scraggly beard, pale face, and shaved head are a post-Holocaust incarnation of the Wandering Jew. He seems condemned to roam eternally because there is no credible answer to the troubling questions he has posed. Insdorf praised the film for presenting "a new take on the Holocaust, with a psychological revenge that is both sweet and bitter." Her recognition of the serious intent behind the movie's levity does more justice to the film than Gilman's blanket dismissal of it as an evasion of the death of Cohn and the millions of other European Jews who shared his fate.[32]

LIES HIS FATHER TOLD HIM: *LIFE IS BEAUTIFUL*
Directed by Roberto Benigni
(Italy: Cecchi Gori Group and Milampo Cinematografica, 1997)

> As the father carries his sleeping son back to their barracks in the night and fog, what appears to be a mass grave full of twisted corpses opens behind him. . . . The mortal stake of Guido's game emerges here, for Giosué's survival is contingent upon his father's ability to skirt that pit, to keep the child from falling into the despair that would mean surrender to Nazi attempts at dehumanization.[33]
>
> —Millicent Marcus

> In *Life Is Beautiful*, writer-director Benigni does to his audience exactly what the father played by the actor Benigni does to his screen son: he shows the audience just a small part, a very particular, doctored, cute little "frame" out of the whole picture. . . . And he thus creates in them the impression that this fake reality . . . is in fact what took place in the death camps and, by implication, what happened to the Jews in the Holocaust.[34]
>
> —Kobi Niv

Detractors and fans of Roberto Benigni associate his comedic style with bawdiness, pratfalls, sight gags, and a rapid-fire stream of jokes.[35] His film persona has made it difficult for critics to accept his films as highbrow entertainment. Benigni sought to prove that his brand of humor could accommodate serious subjects. He chose to place his buffoonish character in an extermination camp, which he regarded as "the symbol of our century, the negative one, the worst thing imaginable." The theme was personal to him as well because his father had been confined in a German labor camp for siding with the Italian monarchy's shift of allegiance to the Allies in the autumn of 1943. Benigni recalled how his father spoke about this ordeal: "Night and day fellow prisoners were dying all around him. He told us about it, as if to protect me and my sisters, he told it in an almost funny way—saying tragic, painful things, but finally his way of telling them was really very particular. Sometimes we laughed at the stories he told."[36]

Benigni cast himself as a lovable jokester who protects his young son from the horrors of a death camp by pretending it is part of a game to win a tank. This narrative device struck many critics as an exploitative gimmick to elicit laughs by desecrating the memory of those who died in the extermination centers. Charles Taylor's scathing review of *Life Is Beautiful* typifies the resistance the film encountered: "The point, I think, is the sheer callous inappropriateness of comedy existing within the physical reality of the camps—even the imagined reality of a movie."[37]

Anticipating such criticism, Benigni took a number of precautions to insure that his "fable" of a child surviving in a concentration camp did not deviate too far from the truth. He recruited Marcello Pezzetti of the Contemporary Jewish Documentation Center of Milan to serve as the historical consultant for *Life Is Beautiful*. Pezzetti had extensive experience in interviewing Italian survivors of Auschwitz and put Benigni in contact with some of them, particularly those who had been adolescents when they were inmates. A survivor designed the uniforms worn by the prisoners in the film. Schlomo Venezia, the sole surviving Italian member of the *Sonderkommando*, which collected the clothes of those about to die and disposed of their corpses afterward, advised Benigni on staging the scene where Guido's uncle and other Jews undress before being gassed.[38] Most of the children who survived Auschwitz were the twins whom Dr. Mengele kept alive as guinea pigs for medical experiments.[39] Some however, survived in concentration and labor camps because adult prisoners hid and nurtured them. Benigni knew the story of a four-year-old child who was smuggled into Buchenwald in a suitcase and protected by the camp's underground.[40] This incident became the basis for a novel by Bruno Apitz and Frank Beyer's adaptation of it into the East German film *Naked among Wolves* (1962).[41]

One of the most common charges leveled at *Life Is Beautiful* is that it consists of two discordant halves. The first part is a light comedy about coincidences that lead to the marriage of Guido the waiter and his beautiful wife Dora. The second is a tragedy about the family's deportation and internment. To shield his son from the reality of camp life, Guido fabricates far-fetched rationales to convince his son, Giosué, that the cruelties he witnesses and hears about in the death camp have been fabricated by the other prisoners to scare him into quitting the game and losing the tank.[42] Maurizio Viano's insightful analysis of *Life Is Beautiful*, to which I am indebted, sees this dualism as an artistic device: "Spatially, the two opposites are kept separate and yet overdetermine one another, a bit like the Yin-Yang symbol, where the black and the white are well defined and symmetrically juxtaposed but each contains a speck of the other as a memento of their interdependence."[43]

The title of the movie seemingly implies an unqualified optimism contradicted by the fact that Guido is executed the night before the camp is liberated. The film's original working title was *Buongiorno Principessa* (Good Morning, Princess) since this was how Guido first greeted Dora when she fell out of a barn loft into his arms. After the film was completed, Benigni read a letter written by Leon Trotsky shortly before his assassination. Therein, the exiled revolutionary expressed his gratitude toward his wife and for his Mexican asylum: "Life is beautiful. Let the future generations cleanse it of all evil, oppression, and violence, and enjoy it to the full." By referring to this passage, Benigni celebrates life and acknowledges how ephemeral it is.[44]

Many scenes in the first half of *Life Is Beautiful* foreshadow the dangers lurking behind Mussolini's dictatorship. The opening scene shows Guido carrying his son through a thick fog in a howling wind. Toward the end of the movie, this scene is presented in its entirety. It comes right before the moment when Guido stumbles upon a pile of corpses in the concentration camp. The fog may be smoke from the crematoria. The voice-over, we learn at the end of the film, is Giosué speaking as an adult. He informs the audience, "This is a simple story, yet it's not easy to tell. As in a fable, there is pain, and as in a fable, it is full of marvels and happiness." Millicent Marcus notes that this technique of having the narrator recall his childhood during World War II has its origins in a genre of Italian movies about how the era of Mussolini's rule appeared to youngsters who grew up during it. She adds that this preview of the film's only glimpse at the casualties of Nazi mass murder looms larger in the audience's imagination than the impression that would have been left by a graphic depiction of the carnage.[45]

The opening shot audiences usually remember provides a metaphor for the precariousness of the Jewish condition under fascist and Nazi dictatorships. Speeding down a hill in Tuscany, Guido and his friend Ferruccio suddenly realize that the brakes of their car no longer work. Guido, whose name means to steer or direct in Italian, believes that he wills the comic coincidences that bring Dora and him together. The limits of the powers of his volition become painfully evident when he cannot protect himself or his family from the anti-Semitic provisions of the race laws that Italy enacted in 1938.

Although Guido's Jewish identity is not revealed until later, his uncle's warehouse is vandalized by three young hooligans whom his uncle calls "barbarians." At the shop of the upholsterer where Ferruccio gets a job, two mischievous children named Benito and Adolf are admonished to behave. Guido's initial encounter with the fascist prefect also exemplifies the abuse of power. Since Dr. Rodolfo is anxious to go to lunch, he refuses to sign Guido's application to open a bookstore, even though Guido has arrived at his office before it is scheduled to close. The hapless Guido accidentally drops a flowerpot on Rodolfo's head and rubs smashed eggs on his jacket in an effort to clean it off. Rodolfo utters what eventually turns out not to be an idle threat: "I'll kill you."[46]

As the film progresses, the jeopardy facing Guido becomes more explicit. At first, he ridicules the notion of Italian Aryan purity in a scene that is reminiscent of Chaplin's *The Great Dictator.* Posing as an inspector dispatched by Rome to lecture about the race laws to the students and faculty of the school where Dora teaches, Guido jumps onto a table, claiming that his ears represent Aryan perfection, then strips down to the waist to display his tightly knotted "Italian belly button."[47] Next, his uncle's horse is painted green. A black thunderbolt and skull next to the words "Attention, Jewish Horse" cover its flanks.[48] Oblivious to what this portends for him, Guido jokes that he didn't know the horse was Jewish, a hint that Guido might be Jewish.

The horse becomes Guido's steed to rescue Dora from her impending marriage to Dr. Rodolfo. As the movie flashes forward five years, Guido and Dora have a son, but their town is occupied by German troops. Seeing a sign in a pastry shop window that reads "No Jews or Dogs Allowed," Giosué asks his father what this means. Protecting his son from prejudice, Guido responds that everyone is entitled to hate certain creatures and groups of people. Since Giosué fears spiders and Guido Visigoths, they decide to bar both from entering their bookstore. When Guido reports to the police station, Giosué remains at the shop and meets his maternal grandmother for the first time. It is obvious that until now, she has never visited her daughter because she married a Jew. Guido returns to pull the shutters down over the windows of his store, which are covered with big capital letters identifying the shop as a "JEWISH STORE." Soon a truck and then a cattle car carry the father and son away. Dora demands to join them on their journey, and a German officer grants her request.[49]

Benigni uses a bluish-gray filter to film the concentration camp scenes. He plants many clues about the dreadful fate that awaits the captives there but leaves the horrid details to the viewer's imagination. For example, the German guard tells the new inmates that their only purpose is to work. Anyone engaged in sabotage will be executed. The SS will weed out the weak and sick from the labor brigades. A woman in Dora's barracks whispers to her that the Germans kill old women and children in a gas chamber. Guido's uncle undresses in the anteroom before entering the chamber. A doctor perfunctorily performs a medical examination among the male prisoners to spare those still strong enough to work and condemn those who cannot to their deaths. Finally, Guido sees the mounds of cadavers and knows his worst fears have been realized. When he is taken into a cul-de-sac by a guard, the audience hears two gunshots ring out in the night.[50] Benigni defended his oblique approach to portraying genocide with this paradox: "Anything you can see directly will never have the same impact as something you cannot see"[51] (see figure 5.1).

Benigni brightens the darkness of the last half of the film with Guido's efforts to deceive his son into believing the hardships they endure are part of a game. Guido mistranslates the orders newcomers receive in German. The guard yells, "You are here for one reason, and one reason only!" Guido changes this to, "The first one to get a thousand points wins a real tank!" The guard demands blind obedience and threatens to hang anyone who resists. Guido relays this as, "You can lose all your points for any of three things. One: If you cry. Two: If you ask to see your mother. Three: If you're hungry and ask for a snack!" Guido minimizes sinister signs of the camp's real purpose as ruses to scare players into quitting.[52] After the Germans retreat, an American tank rumbles into the camp and gives Giosué a ride. He finds his mother and exclaims, "We won!" In the voice-over, Giosué recognizes the sacrifice his father made to save him.[53]

Benigni realizes that culture serves contradictory purposes. It either embodies humanity's noblest virtues or provides a patina for its vilest vices. Guido plays an opera record to express his love for Dora. He broadcasts it on the camp intercom to remind her of the evening they fell in love. The soothing tones of an Offenbach aria contrast sharply with the bellicose passages from Wagnerian operas that often serve as musical leitmotifs for Nazism in feature films.[54] As a waiter, Guido impresses his German customer, Doctor Lessing, with his talent for solving riddles. This character's namesake is Gotthold Lessing, the prominent German advocate of religious toleration in the eighteenth century, whose parable of the three rings likened Christianity, Islam, and Judaism to children of the same father who loves them equally. When Guido pleads with Dr. Lessing to protect his family and him in the camp, the doctor preoccupies himself with a silly riddle.[55] The film's references to Arthur Schopenhauer follow the same pattern. To Guido, Schopenhauer's theory of the will is a benign exercise of mind over matter. To the Nazis, it justifies the primacy of Hitler's will. Benigni's movie and Guido's sacrifice illustrate the other side of Schopenhauer's conception of will: its sublimation into art or compassion for others.[56]

Many critics faulted Benigni for minimizing Guido's Jewish identity. It is not until his uncle's painted horse gallops onto the screen that Guido's religious background is disclosed. As one reviewer put it, "[Guido's] innocent in a generic way."[57] Benigni left clues for more knowledgeable viewers. Guido's last name is Orefice, which is a common Italian Jewish name literally meaning "goldsmith." His son's name is the Italian equivalent of Joshua.[58] If one looks for biblical analogies, Joshua leads the Israelites into the Promise Land because Moses died before he could reach it. There are two other reasons, however, for concealing Guido's origins until the middle of the picture. The first is historical. Many Italian Jews were highly acculturated and supportive of Mussolini's regime until 1938.[59] The second stems from Benigni's intent to have Italians empathize with his clownish persona and then ask themselves, Why did they go after Benigni? The next logical question is why persecute the Jews at all.[60]

In what strikes me as an egregious case of intellectual casuistry, Kobi Niv argues that the name Giosué is actually "synonymous with Jesus." Accordingly, Guido's name sounds like the Italian for Judas. Thus, Niv maintains that Guido deceived Giosué like Judas deceived Jesus by concealing the truth from him, but eventually redeemed himself by dying so that Giosué could be reborn when the camp was liberated by the Allies. As if this reasoning were not sufficiently convoluted, Niv cites an insignificant piece of dialog spoken by Guido at the beginning of the movie. Upon repairing his car, Guido casually says, "I'm going to wash my hands." Niv claims this line replicates how Pontius Pilate washed his hands of the responsibility for ordering the crucifixion of Jesus. Since Niv accuses Benigni of minimizing the Jewish genocide to highlight the redemptive power of marital and parental love, he postulates that Guido's words announce "the purpose of the film we are about to see: it seeks to wash Europe's hands, the hands of Christian civilization, clean of the Jewish blood it spilled during World War II."[61]

Life Is Beautiful has a cinematic lineage in the *Comedia del'italiano*, which parodies serious themes of national identity and the collective memory of fascism. Films like Luigi Comencini's *Everybody's Home* (1960), Frederico Fellini's *Amarcord* (1974), Giuseppe Tornatore's *Cinema Paradiso* (1988), and Gabriele Salvatores's *Mediterraneo* (1991) have spun humorous tales from the combustible mixture of Italian customs, everyday concerns, government repression, and war.[62] Marcus observes that Benigni was also influenced by the Italian dramatist Luigi Pirandello, who distinguished between the comic, which arises from an awareness of disparate perspectives, and humor, which results from philosophical reflection on the meaning of this disparity. Benigni accomplishes this by doubling the perspective of the audience. It experiences the story from the viewpoint of Giosué recounting his father's game; unlike the boy, it also recognizes from its prior awareness of the Holocaust how implausible Guido's explanations of the daily routines in the death camp really are.[63]

Although the Italian movie market is saturated with Hollywood and multinational productions, *Life Is Beautiful* outsold the imports at the box office at home and became both the most financially successful film in Italian cinematic history and the most successful foreign film in American cinematic history. It not only won the Grand Jury Prize at Cannes and the Oscar for Best Foreign Language Film but also captured the Jerusalem Film Festival Award for the Best Jewish Experience.[64] One hears the echo of Bettelheim's cynical critique of the popularity of *The Diary of Anne Frank* in Niv's attribution of *Life Is Beautiful*'s international acclaim to a "profound, and still growing, need to blot this horrific event out of history, to erase it from the collective memory of Western, Judeo-Christian, European-American civilization, thus enabling this civilization to free itself of the guilt of having committed the Holocaust."[65]

While Bettelheim's analysis possessed some validity in the 1950s, when public awareness of the Holocaust was still limited, Niv's lacks credibility because it fails to take into account the popularization of the Holocaust that has occurred in the interim. The surfeit rather than paucity of images about the Holocaust by the 1990s motivated some directors to experiment with genres like comedy to represent the event. I find Hilene Flanzbaum's explanation for the positive reception of *Life Is Beautiful* more convincing because she acknowledges the innovative impulse among filmmakers:

> Benigni plays to a sophisticated audience—one that has seen plenty of graphic and horrific cinematic scenes—some about the Holocaust and some not. His job then is to defamiliarize this violence: he does this by focusing on only one aspect of psychological suffering experienced in the Holocaust. For the parents in the audience who have lost sleep over what they might do to protect their own child, the film proved overwhelming. Benigni accomplishes a great deal when he defamiliarizes the Holocaust enough to make viewers feel it all over again.[66]

FIDDLER ON THE CATTLE-CAR ROOF: *TRAIN OF LIFE*
Directed by Radu Mihaileanu
(Belgium, France, Israel, Italy, Netherlands: Belfilms, Centre du Cinema et de la Communaute Francaise de Belgique, Centre national de la Cinematographie, Eurimages, Hungry Eye Lowland Pictures, La Sofica Sonfinergie 4, Le Studio Canal+, Noe Productions, PolyGram Audiovisuel, RTL-Tvi, Raphael Films, 1998)

> Stories of Chelm, showing up the folly of its inhabitants, usually follow a single pattern—when a problem must be solved, the Chelmites come up with a formula that is theoretically correct, but practically absurd.[67]

> —Ruth Wisse

> *Train of Life* is not the first comic take on the Holocaust—one
> which is not about to be unanimously accepted as kosher by
> those who feel that the Shoah must be treated with utter solem-
> nity. But if the Yiddish proverb is valid," Laughter is heard further
> than weeping," *Train of Life* is all the more likely to help keep the
> memory of the Holocaust alive.[68]
>
> —Harvey S. Karten

In his autobiographical novel *Night*, Elie Wiesel recalls that Moché, the beadle
of his synagogue, returned after being deported and frantically reported to the
remaining Jewish residents of Sighet that the Germans had killed everyone else
on his transport. He implored his neighbors to heed his warning. They dismissed him as a madman. Two years later, the Germans deported the Jews of
Sighet to Auschwitz.[69]

What if the Jews of Sighet had believed the beadle and taken his advice?
What if the beadle had devised a daring escape plan so implausible that it was
bound to confound the Nazis? Rumanian director Radu Milhaileanu explores
this premise in *Train of Life*. In an opening headshot, the village fool, Shlomo,
recalls what happened to his shtetl during World War II. Next, he rushes
through the forest to the front of his synagogue. Frenzied music, rhythmic
screams, and the sound of breaking glass reflect his panic. As he approaches the
little synagogue, he falls on the ground, rolls onto his back, and beats his chest
and forehead with his fists. The rabbi summons the town's sages to listen to
Shlomo's eyewitness report about the Germans slaughtering the Jews in a
nearby town. Like many of Wiesel's characters, Shlomo blames God for allowing the Germans to do this and questions whether heaven can ever reside in
Jewish hearts again. While many of the village elders doubt the incredible tale
told by Shlomo, the rabbi believes him and wonders how they can save the
Jews in the shtetl. Shlomo proposes that they buy an old train, refurbish it to
look like a German transport, and deport themselves to Palestine. To complete
the deception, some of the Jews will learn German, wear Nazi uniforms, and
pretend to be guards. Like the inane inhabitants of Chelm, the wise men of the
town approve of Shlomo's scheme. After all, is Shlomo's plan anymore prepos-
terous than the notion that a civilized country like Germany would liquidate
European Jewry?[70]

Notwithstanding the gravity of their dilemma, the townspeople act like
the stock Jewish characters from *Fiddler on the Roof*, which, in turn, was based
on the Tevye stories of Sholom Aleichem. Aleichem's clever colloquial Yiddish
delighted readers by revealing the eccentricities, pettiness, and spiritual resilience
of Russian Jews embroiled in internal squabbles and perpetual struggles with
external persecution, endemic poverty, and secular alternatives to Judaism.[71]

Upon hearing of Shlomo's suggestion, for example, one man vetoes the idea because he thinks the Jews should not do the Germans any favors: "If they deport us, they should sweat!" A second objects because his wife prefers to travel by boat; a third worries that God will punish them for dressing like Nazis.

As the Jews commence cooking food, making uniforms, and repairing the dilapidated train purchased for their escape, joyful klezmer music and dancing accompany their activities. The communal effort of the villagers transforms the rickety railroad cars and locomotive hulk into an authentic-looking German transport. They affix swastikas on each wagon to conceal the mezuzahs nailed onto the sliding doors. The festive mood resembles the opening scene of *Fiddler on the Roof*, where the lyrics of the song "Tradition" mirror the rituals and collective solidarity that permeate the lives of the Jews of Anatevka. Even Jewish–Gentile relations in the town seem cordial until the Third Reich, like the tsarist government in *Fiddler on the Roof*, initiates a policy of persecuting the Jews. The poster for *Train of Life* visually links the two films with a still of Shlomo clambering over the roof of the train and carrying a violin. In the movie, he is only holding his hat when he leans into the wind atop the speeding train. To affirm the movie's Yiddish lineage, its press kit included a newspaper called the *Shtetl Times*, which mixed articles about the film with Borscht Belt humor like a personal ad reading, "Paranoid Jew looking for a disaster."[72]

Ideological and religious disputes beset the Jewish passengers on what the Germans eventually dub the "ghost train." Mordecai, the Jewish woodworker selected to serve as the Nazi commander, becomes intoxicated by his power and irritated when his fellow Jews disobey him. Practicing his German, Mordecai learns from his tutor that German is Yiddish spoken "without the fun." Mordecai eventually outwits a Nazi officer who has arrested a Jew from the train who had lost his glasses and strayed into a group of German soldiers. Mordecai insinuates that the officer's refusal to relinquish the hostage might create the impression that he might be a "Jew lover" or even a homosexual. A communist faction of the passengers follows Yossi, who shaves his beard, sheds his Jewish garments, and dons a Red Army uniform. They mutiny and scurry into the forest away from the Jewish "reactionaries," the phony Nazis, and those deluded by religion. Yossi's mother prays that his loyalty to his fellow Jews will override his dogmatism. The rabbi realizes he must be flexible in interpreting Jewish law in this unprecedented situation. In the end, the survival of the community prevails over all other considerations.

Since the train is ostensibly German, partisans plant a bomb under the tracks to blow it up. Spying on the target through binoculars, their leader notices that the German soldiers are bowing and davening like Jews, even though they are wearing helmets instead of yarmulkes. He aborts the planned act of sabotage.

Then, a German detachment halts the train. As Mordecai protests this obstruction of his orders, his German counterpart detects his accent and realizes he is dealing with a Jew. Shlomo recognizes that one of the German soldiers is his gypsy brother. By coincidence, a band of gypsies has devised a plan similar to Shlomo's and decided to hijack a train to India rather than buy and repair one. That night the two groups dance, feast, and perform klezmer songs and Romany melodies in a musical virtuosity contest that evokes the dueling banjos scene from the movie *Deliverance* (1972).[73] Two mixed couples sexually consummate this alliance of outcasts. Mihaileanu's inclusion of gypsies as fellow victims not only reflects a growing awareness of the Third Reich's attempt to eradicate the Sinti and Roma but also protests their persecution in postcommunist Rumania.[74]

The movie's comic premise and subplots do not overshadow what the Nazis will do to the passengers of the train if they capture them. When the Germans realize that the Jews have vacated their shtetl, they burn the empty buildings down. Flames engulf the synagogue's Star of David in a shot resembling the famous picture of the stained glass window of a German temple being consumed by fire on *Kristallnacht*. The fire spreads to family photos scattered on the ground, reducing them to ash and smoke.

When the two groups despair that their train is heading the wrong way, it comes under an artillery attack from opposite directions. They speed up the engine, believing they have crossed the battle line between the German and Russian armies. The facial close-up of Shlomo that opened the movie ends it as well, but now Shlomo's narration starts sounding improbable. He reports that most of the Jews settled in India, and most of the gypsies went to Palestine. The camera then reveals that Shlomo is wearing a concentration camp uniform and is standing behind a barbed wire fence. Grinning sheepishly, he confesses, "Well that's the true story of my shtetl . . . well almost true." He softly sings about his shtetl. His is a tale told by a fool, full of fanciful thinking, eulogizing a community and culture that no longer exists. The credits roll over a black background with a violin sustaining mournful chords.

Train of Life went into production before *Life Is Beautiful* was released. Mihaileanu had mailed the script to Benigni and offered him the part of Shlomo, but Benigni declined since he was busy making his own comedy about the Holocaust. Mihaileanu submitted his movie to the Cannes Film Festival, where it was rejected because of its irreverent mix of humor and the Holocaust. Yet, the more renowned Benigni got his picture screened at Cannes after adopting a recommendation made by the festival's director to pitch his story as a fable rather than as reality. Mihaileanu subsequently accused Benigni of plagiarizing the bracketing structure of Shlomo's recollections in *Train of Life* by sandwiching his story between voice-overs of Giosué recounting how his father had sacrificed himself.[75]

Actually, the two movies represent different perspectives on the Holocaust. *Life Is Beautiful* reflects the comedic persona of Benigni in particular and Italian comedies about everyday life under fascism in general. Although the audience eventually learns that Guido is Jewish, his slapstick antics and satirical jibes possess little that is distinctively Jewish. Mihaileanu, on the other hand, once belonged to Bucharest's Yiddish theater ensemble. His movie is steeped in Eastern European Jewish folklore, literature, politics, and religiosity. His parents survived the camps while other members of his family perished. Whereas the survival of Giosué and Dora leaves the audience with hope, Shlomo's final soliloquy and internment shatter the alternate reality he has imagined and conjure up the obliteration of the community he fondly recalls. To Mihaileanu, "Jewish humor has always been a shield against madness. Comedy is tragedy's balm. We don't laugh at a tragic event. But we continue to laugh in order to persevere."[76]

Like many Eastern European directors after the collapse of the Soviet Union, Mihaileanu required financing from Western European studios to produce his picture.[77] Although the use of French as the film's language initially interferes with the credibility of its characters as Jews from the shtetl, they break into Yiddish expressions and Hebrew prayers frequently enough to imbue the movie with a Jewish sensibility.[78] On this point, Mihaileanu might have emulated Yolande Zauberman's decision in *Ivan and Abraham* (1993) to retain the dialects spoken by ethnic groups who comprised the populations in Eastern Europe since this reflects the cultural and linguistic barriers that divided them.[79]

Mihaileanu fled Romania in 1980 when it was under communist rule. His caricature of the doctrinaire Yossi mirrors his own disillusionment with Marxism. This had been the theme of his first feature film, *Betrayal* (1993).[80] The scene of the train being bombarded draws freely from Emir Kusterica's *Underground* (1995), a zany satire about the Yugoslavian communist partisans, Titoism, and the recent ethnic wars in Bosnia and Serbia. Mihaileanu depicts the incoming shells in cartoon style. They whiz randomly, exploding on impact, except for a dud that skids along the ground upon landing. The frenetic musical score sounds like a Spike Jones composition.[81]

Although *Train of Life* stood in the box-office shadows of *Life Is Beautiful*, it received many prestigious prizes, including the Audience Award from the Sundance Film Festival and the Italian Academy Award for Best Foreign Language in a year when its main competitor was *Shakespeare in Love*.[82] Mihaileanu clearly felt an obligation as a child of survivors to preserve the memory of the murdered European Jews. Interviewed by his father, he described his film as "an allegory nourished by our blood, our culture, and our memory, a deep desire to re-create the world of the shtetl I never knew, but which our family experienced in the flesh."[83] He also hoped that his film would serve as a warning to halt the rise of neo-Nazism in Germany and Austria and "ethnic cleansing" in the former Yugoslavia.[84] Although driven from their homes, the Jews in *Fiddler on the Roof* eventually find refuge in Palestine, Poland, or the United States. Mihaileanu's colorful characters board a train bound for a death camp.

FALSE HOPE IS BETTER THAN NO HOPE: *JAKOB THE LIAR*
Directed by Peter Kassovitz
(France, Hungary, United States: Blue Wolf, Kasso, Columbia Pictures, 1999)

> The first lie, which may not even have been one, such a little lie, and Kowalski is satisfied. It's worth it; hope must not be allowed to fade away, otherwise they won't survive.[85]
>
> —Jurek Becker

> This tendency to take comfort from nothing irritates me. It's better not to say anything.[86]
>
> —David Sierakowiak

For the Jews confined in the ghettoes of Eastern Europe, knowledge of how the war was going for Germany after its defeat at Stalingrad provided some solace. Hope and preparations for resistance might be sparked by rumors that liberation by Soviet troops from the East or by American and British soldiers from the West was at hand. The Germans confiscated radios from Jews and limited their access to news to censored reports issued by the Jewish councils that acted as intermediaries between the occupiers and the Jewish community. The Germans executed Jews who possessed illegal radios.

Born in Poland in 1937, Becker grew up in the Lodz ghetto and spent the last two years of the war with his mother, first in Ravensbrück and then in Sachsenhausen. His mother died in the latter, but his father managed to survive Auschwitz. After the war, his father feared that Polish Gentiles would attack Jews to vent their anger over the Soviet occupation of their country. Since his father could legitimately claim German citizenship, he fled with his son to the Soviet sector of Germany, where he expected the Russians would suppress anti-Semitism. Becker initially toed the Communist Party line, idealizing World War II as a struggle between capitalism and communism.[87]

He recalled his father's telling him a story of how the Gestapo shot a Jewish man in the Lodz ghetto for concealing a radio. To Becker's father, this act of bravery earned the man a place in the pantheon of the antifascist resistance. To Becker, it highlighted the limited options Jews had during the war. He decided to retell the story in a humorous manner in which a Jew inadvertently hears a radio broadcast about Russian advances in the East while detained at Gestapo offices for a curfew violation. When he shares this news with his demoralized friends in the ghetto, it lifts their spirits so much that he starts fabricating new reports he supposedly receives on a radio set he has in his possession. Eventually, Jacob must admit that he has invented the stories to boost the morale of the ghetto. The East German censors rejected Becker's screenplay in 1965 for being too focused on Jewish suffering and too flippant about the Soviet contribution to the liberation of Germany. Becker redrafted the script into the novel *Jacob the Liar,* a book that sold well in both Germanys.[88] In 1974, Becker teamed up with director Frank Beyer, whom the state-owned DEFA movie studio in East Germany had barred from making films since 1960, to produce a movie version of *Jacob the Liar* (1974). Although the Moscow Film Festival refused to screen it, it became the first and only East German movie nominated for the Oscar for Best Foreign Language Film.[89]

Directors and producers of Holocaust films have not been immune to the trend of remaking successful films to improve the box office potential of their pictures.[90] During the 1990s, *The Diary of Anne Frank* (1995 and 1999) was remade twice as a feature length cartoon.[91] Rod Serling's teleplay *In the Presence of Mine Enemies* (1917) was adapted as a television movie by director Joan Micklin Silver,[92] and *The Music Box's* (1989) storyline about a Nazi war criminal who had concealed his past from his own family was recycled in several films.[93]

The critical acclaim *Jacob the Liar* received in the 1970s had probably not filtered down to the public sufficiently to guarantee an American audience for a remake of the movie. French director Peter Kassovitz undertook the project for more personal reasons. His family history paralleled that of Becker. Born in Hungary in 1938, Kassovitz's parents hid him with a Catholic family before their deportation to death camps. They both survived and were united with their son after the war. Kassovitz sought asylum in France following the Soviet Union's suppression of the Hungarian uprising in 1956.[94] He optioned the film rights for Becker's novel at the beginning of the 1990s. The success of *Schindler's List* and Kassovitz's signing of Robin Williams to play Jakob made this look like a profitable venture to Sony Pictures, Columbia Pictures, and William's Blue Wolf Company.[95] Although the filming of *Jakob the Liar* did not begin until 1997, it derived some advantages and disadvantages from being released after *Life is Beautiful* and *Train of Life*, depending on how critics and audiences responded to the idea of Holocaust comedies in general or to Williams's cinematic persona in particular.[96]

Unlike Becker's novel or Beyer's film, Kassovitz's film depicts Jakob more heroically. The first shot of Jakob shows him seated on a bench, then curiously chasing a sheet of newspaper swirling in the wind like the white feather in the opening scene of *Forrest Gump* (1994).[97] This reference to *Forrest Gump* conveys the original sense of Jakob as a simple man in the right place at the right time. Jakob's pursuit of the news leads him to the police station, where he is apprehended for violating curfew. While waiting to be interrogated, he overhears a radio broadcast that Soviet troops are only four hundred kilometers away from his ghetto. Since the officer in charge of his case notices that there is still time before the curfew begins, he releases Jakob.

In the novel and earlier film, the audience is told that the story they are about to hear may or may not be true. Unaware of the time because he no longer owns a wristwatch, Jakob is arrested by a guard who thinks it is past curfew. Not knowing where he should report, Jakob wanders through a hall until he hears music coming from a room and the bulletin about the Russian advance. The officer finds Jakob loitering behind an office door on which his sleeve has become snagged and sends him home.[98]

Kassovitz fails to present this tale with any subtlety. In the Becker and Beyer renditions, Jacob reveals what he knows about the Russian troop movements to stop his fellow worker Mischa from risking his life to steal a few potatoes. Jacob insists that Mischa keep the news secret, but the news spreads by word of mouth until Jacob's old friend Kowalski asks Jacob if he knows anything about the location of the Red Army. Jacob reluctantly starts to embellish the truth to satiate the need for hope among his compatriots.[99] In the Kassovitz movie, Jakob walks into Kowalski's apartment and finds his friend standing on a chair with a noose around his neck ready to commit suicide. Jakob invents good news to give Kowalski a reason to live.

Yet, many of the jokes in the Kassovitz film seem to be Williams's one-liners and don't arise intrinsically from Jakob's character as they do for Genghis Cohn or the shtetl Jews in *Train of Life*. In Becker's and Beyer's versions, Jacob is a timid man who tries to avoid drawing attention to himself. Kassovitz's Jakob has a punch line for every occasion. The opening sequence features him telling an anti-Hitler joke. A fortune-teller predicts a man will die on a Jewish holiday. He interprets this to mean that this man will die on the same day as Hitler because any day Hitler dies will be a Jewish holiday. When Kowalski is about to commit suicide, Jakob blurts out, "If you hang yourself, I'll kill you." Although Jakob is a secular Jew who does not observe the Sabbath, he paraphrases Tevye's remark in *Fiddler on the Roof* when the future of the ghetto looks bleak: "I believe we're the Chosen People, but I wish the Almighty had chosen someone else."

The incongruence of Jakob's demeanor and dialog is nowhere more glaring than in his exchanges with Lina, the young girl he shelters in his apartment, who bears an uncanny resemblance to Anne Frank. If this association was not apparent when the movie premiered, it is now since Hannah Taylor-Gordon, the young actress playing Lina, starred in the television miniseries

Anne Frank (2001). To cheer Lina up in the Becker novel and Beyer movie, Jacob goes behind a curtain and mimics Churchill confirming the story about the Russian victories. Then, he imitates instruments playing music, but Lina peeks behind the curtain and sees that Jacob doesn't have a radio. Jacob completes his fake broadcast with a fairy tale about a young princess who is dying. She believes she will recover if someone brings her a cloud. Since she thinks clouds are pillows made of cotton balls, a young man fulfills her wish. When Lina dreams that she is the princess, she is still wearing a yellow star on her dress. At the end of the movie Jacob and Lina are huddled inside a railroad car that is transporting them to a camp. Lina sees clouds and asks Jakob to reassure her that they are made of cotton. In the book, Jacob refers her to another passenger, knowing that she no longer believes him.[100] In the Beyer movie, Jakob insists the clouds are cotton, and Lina humors him by nodding affirmatively. But the clouds they see in the distance are as wispy as their prospects for survival.

In the Kassovitz film, Jakob stages a convincing radio program that verges on becoming the Holocaust equivalent of *Good Morning, Vietnam* (1987).[101] His Churchill imitation is what we would expect from the talented comedian Williams, but not from Jakob. Lina accepts the authenticity of the broadcast,

Guido [Roberto Benigni] pretends that surviving a concentration camp is a game to shield his son, Giosué [Giorgio Cantarini], from the camp's harshness. Life Is Beautiful. *Press kit, courtesy of the Nostalgia Factory.*

Jakob [Robin Williams] feeds food and hope to Lina [Hannah Taylor-Gordon]. Jakob the Liar. Press kit, courtesy of the Nostalgia Factory.

Alan [Lukas Haas] helps Naomi [Vanessa Zaoui] recover her childhood. Alan and Naomi. Press kit, courtesy of the Nostalgia Factory

Hannah [Kirsten Dunst] travels back to wartime Poland to share the fate of Rivka [Brittany Murphy], the girl she was named after. The Devil's Arithmetic. Press kit, courtesy of the Nostalgia Factory.

despite a number of obvious slips Jakob makes. Jakob's Churchill seems to be conversant in Yiddish and concludes his speech by declaring, "The whole megillah will soon be over and that *shmendrick* Hitler will be gone!" He defies the laws of geography by replying directly to a question posed by Lina. Jakob plays a record on an old phonograph enabling him to come out from behind the curtain and dance with Lina. She believes the illusion rather than seeing through it. Kassovitz omits the fairy tale that symbolized how the Jews in the ghetto were grasping at straws. Like Anne Frank, Lina still believes in human goodness.

Becker and Beyer use the hope Jacob engenders to stifle resistance. Why do anything to provoke the Germans into launching reprisals when the Russians will arrive soon? In the Kassovitz film, Jakob foments a rebellion. Those who trust Jakob organize, procure guns, and elect him their leader. When Jakob confides to Kowalski that he never owned a radio, Kowalski hangs himself. The rumor of the radio and the stirrings of revolt result in the roundup of the remnant of Jews in the ghetto. It is here that Kassovitz puts a heroic spin on the story. Gilman argues that the transformation of Jakob from an improviser of morale-boosting news to a defiant martyr enables the audience to admire Jakob and perceive his humor as a form of resistance. Thereafter, the Germans arrest and torture Jakob. They march him in front of his peers and order him to confess that there never was a radio. Jakob refuses and is executed. Sunlight briefly pierces through the clouds, vibrantly coloring the faces and facades of the ghetto that had previously looked dingy.[102] Jakob's voice initially reports that the ghetto will be liquidated, but then snatches victory from the jaws of defeat by imagining that it might not end that way at all. Instead, perhaps the Russian Army would liberate the ghetto. The closing scene consists of a surreal vision of the advancing Soviet troops and a cattle car in a pasture surrounded by well-dressed musicians accompanying the Andrew Sisters, who sing the "Beer Barrel Polka," the tune to which Jakob and Lina had danced in the attic.

The contrast with the resolution of the story in the original novel and movie could not be starker. Becker provided two endings: an "invented" one and a "pallid and depressing" true one. In the first, Jacob crawls under a barbed wire fence and is shot while escaping. Beyer used the second in his film: the ghetto is deported, and Lina stares at the clouds and realizes that they are not made of cotton.[103] A freeze-frame superimposes stills of the faces of the deported to preserve their visual memory.[104]

Leo Braudy has commented that "to remake is to want to reread—to believe in an explicit (and thematized) way that the past reading was wrong or outdated and that a new one must be done."[105] Kassovitz tried to rescue Becker's novel and Beyer's movie from obscurity by tailoring the part of Jakob to Williams's comedic talents.[106] Bigger budgets, more sophisticated cinematography, and a popular star don't guarantee a better film unless the director possesses a coherent vision for the remake. Kassovitz never provides this vision. Is Jakob an ordinary man in the right place at the right time, like Forrest Gump, or a brilliant stand-up comedian? Is false hope better than no hope? Kowalski despairs when he learns the truth; Jakob steps out of character and embraces martyrdom. And perhaps the Russian Army was close enough to save the day. Anthony Leong has remarked that *Jakob the Liar* epitomizes what can go wrong when Hollywood produces a movie whose subject requires restraint: "With a big name star, unremarkable characters doing predictable things, and a force-fed feel-good ending, *Jakob the Liar* seems optimistic in the way it recounts one of the darkest periods of recent history."[107] The best thing about the Kassovitz film is that it renewed interest in Beyer's movie.[108]

A GEFILTE FISH OUT OF WATER: *MENDEL*
Directed by Alexander Røsler
(Denmark, Germany, Norway:
Zentropa, Lichtblick, Norsk, Northern Lights, 1997)

The films of second-generation witnesses focus on psychosocial issues that played a prominent role in the filmmakers' lives as children and adolescents. These films are significant in visualizing an important transition in the lives of second-generation witnesses. As young adults they are now prepared to confront the anxiety, pain, and uncertainty of growing up in survivor households.[109]

—Alan L. Berger

Since they mark the passing of one generation and the maturation of the next, films by and about children of survivors or perpetrators did not appear in significant numbers until the 1980s. In that decade, movies about survivors outnumbered those about the challenges of being raised by people who bore the psychological scars of their complicity or suffering in the Shoah. By the 1990s, however, motion pictures about the transmission of the trauma of genocide to the succeeding generation emerged as the fourth most common theme of Holocaust feature films. The first wave of second-generation films consisted of psychodramas about searches for the identity of a deceased parent, as in Jeanine Meerapfel's *Malou* (1982).[110] While this genre remained popular, humor emerged in the 1990s as a means for children of survivors and perpetrators to trace the historical origins of their parents' idiosyncrasies and regard them with more sympathy than bitterness. This is exemplified in the poignant comedy skits performed by Deb Filler in her concert film *Punch Me in the Stomach* (1996).[111]

Director Alexander Røsler's parents were German Jews who survived the Nazi camps. Having lost their home during the war, in 1945 they moved to the displaced persons camp located at Dachau, where Røsler was born. In 1954, his parents accepted a Norwegian offer of citizenship to Jews from Germany and Poland who felt compelled to leave countries they regarded as anti-Semitic. Røsler mines the comic elements of the unusual circumstances of his youth as the subject matter for his film *Mendel* (1997). In addition to the awkwardness preteens feel as they individuate from their parents, Mendel has to confront the secrecy surrounding their past, avenge their persecution once he learns about it, and adjust to a society where Jews stand out like bagels in a basket of *lefse*, Norwegian flat bread.[112]

The movie begins with an image that symbolizes the Jewish condition in the Diaspora after World War II. Trees teeter on roots that are not anchored deeply in the soil. Mendel recalls a nice German neighbor taking his family for a scenic car ride in the Bavarian countryside. Although he has no bad memories of Germany, his family does and immigrates to Norway because Jews should not stay in a country that has treated them so terribly. To capture glimpses of the land of his birth, Mendel blinks his eyes as if he were a camera taking snapshots. Mendel worries about the polar bears in Norway, especially after his brother David informs him that they eat little children. His consumptive father continually cracks ironic jokes about Jewish life under Nazism. For example, an SS officer inquires if Reboines lives in an overcrowded flat in the ghetto. Reboines says no. The German then asks with whom he is speaking. Reboines tells him. The German yells at Reboines for not identifying himself. Reboines retorts, "You call this living?"

Everything in Norway strikes Mendel as odd: the sanctimonious Protestant relief workers who proselytize to his family, the tasteless fish balls, the nauseating cod-liver oil he is supposed to take to restore his health, and the dour cleaning lady who resents the newcomers because she considers them Germans. What is more difficult for Mendel to fathom is why his father and brother wake up from nightmares and hide photos of dead relatives from him. His parents keep telling Mendel that he is too young to know about such horrible things. After seeing the numbers on the wrist of Mr. Freund, who lives with his family, he paints numbers on his arm and on that of Freund's son, much to the consternation of their parents. He draws crosses in the empty spaces where photographs of deceased relatives once were hinged in the family album.

Mendel is perplexed about his religious identity. His father has lost faith in God but repeatedly addresses the Almighty to complain about being abandoned during World War II. His Jewish neighbors are Orthodox. Bela, Mendel's mother, observes Jewish rituals and sings Yiddish lullabies to comfort her sons. Since Christians persist in trying to convert Mendel's family, Mendel fears both Jesus and Santa Claus. Worried that his family could be expelled from Norway or that he might be punished for stealing an apple, Mendel appeals to "God, Allah, Buddha, and Jesus" for divine intervention.[113]

Whenever the family gathers with its Jewish friends, he overhears stories about how Gentile neighbors betrayed them and how someone stole his father's clogs when he was stricken with typhus.[114] Yet, Mendel's relations with the Norwegians he meets are friendly, even when they parrot the anti-Semitic slurs they have learned. An old man named Ole lives in the attic of Mendel's apartment building and whittles him a wooden horse. His Norwegian playmate proudly recounts how his father fought in the resistance against the Germans. His friends harass the menacing Mitten Man, who whips his horse too hard and wears a mitten in place of the hand that he purportedly lost for molesting little girls.

When Mendel dreams, the good memories he has blur into the bad things he knows happened to his parents. The cleaning woman and Ole appear as uncaring neighbors who fail to intervene on behalf of his parents when they are arrested. A screen in the attic located next to the fuse box metamorphoses into an electrified barbed wire fence.[115] After furtively skimming a book of pictures from the Holocaust that his parents had hidden in a grandfather clock, these images are chiseled into Mendel's brain, particularly the iconic photo of a young boy from the Warsaw ghetto holding his hands above his head while German soldiers point rifles at him. One evening, a fire breaks out in the apartment. Mendel's parents gather their possessions and dress themselves and their children. When a firefighter wearing a ventilating mask knocks down the door with an axe, Mendel wonders whether the war is reoccurring. He perceives the firefighter as an SS guard sent to arrest them. Suitcase in hand and cap on head, Mendel assumes the pose of the surrendering boy from the Warsaw ghetto. This visualization of the defilement of childhood innocence obscures the life-saving mission that is transpiring on the screen.

From this point on, Mendel is determined never to be a passive victim like his parents. He asks his friend's father to teach him how to shoot his gun. Mendel plans to kill the Mitten Man, whom he suspects of being an "anti-Simon." Although Mendel cannot pronounce the word anti-Semite, he is certain that someone as evil as the Mitten Man must be one. Mendel gets knocked down standing in the path of the Mitten Man's wagon. When the Mitten Man circles back to check if Mendel is hurt, Mendel aims a rifle at him. What could have been a deadly encounter turns into a lesson about stereotyping people. The Mitten Man has never met a Jew before and wears the glove to cover eczema on his hand. He cracks his whip loudly because the noise makes his mare run faster.

Obsessed with the notion that his relatives went like lambs to the slaughter, Mendel gets into an argument with his brother David. David tests Mendel's bravery by grabbing his legs and dangling him out of the window until he begs for mercy. Mendel defies him by baaing like a sheep. Finally, David shows Mendel the photograph that Mendel's parents have not allowed him to see. The man in the picture is David's real father who died participating in the Warsaw Ghetto Uprising. David judges his father's heroism harshly by remarking, "He made us alone." It never occurred to Mendel that resistance against such overwhelming odds was tantamount to suicide.

Mendel still feels compelled to prove his courage. As his alarmed friends and parents watch, he climbs a ladder to the roof of his house and perches on the top rung holding an umbrella to cushion his impending fall. Mendel jumps and lands with a thud. The onlookers rush to his still body, fearing the worst. Although Mendel is bruised, his spirit is unbroken. His relieved parents and friends cheer his bravery.[116]

The issues of distrust of Gentiles, lost faith in God, and compensating for shame over Jewish passivity by acting heroically plague many children of survivors.[117] Although these are serious concerns, Mendel's perceptions of Norway, religion, and the Shoah are generally portrayed as funny. Since the themes of individuation and adaptation to a new culture are so sensitively handled, *Mendel* became one of the few Norwegian movies that did well outside of

Scandinavia. It won the Jury Award at the Shanghai Film Festival and became a favorite on the Jewish film festival circuit.[118] It also reflected an important new trend in Scandinavian films, namely the promotion of multiculturalism in previously homogenous countries that have become havens for foreign workers. The Jew as "Other" and the Holocaust serve as a warning against xenophobic agitation against the ethnic, racial, and religious minority groups that have immigrated to Denmark, Finland, Norway, and Sweden from former communist countries, southern Europe, and Third World nations.[119]

Like Mendel transplanted to Norway, the Holocaust in movie comedies seems out of place. Yet, it is precisely the dissonance of the genre with the content that makes us smile and laugh. Reversing the order of things has the potential to be funny. The ghost of Genghis Cohn converts an unrepentant Nazi into a Jew by engineering circumstances that make him the lead suspect in a series of sex murders. Guido pretends that remaining inconspicuous in a concentration camp is an elaborate game of hide and seek but never hints to his son that the punishment for getting caught is death. *Train of Life* deceives the audience into believing Shlomo's harebrained scheme might succeed, then exposes it as a fantasy. Jakob invents a comforting lie because the Jews in his ghetto cannot live with the discomforting truth. Mendel does not understand the trauma that haunts his parents. He is unable to distinguish between firemen and cremators. He believes that if only the Jews had resisted, the Holocaust would never have happened. When he leaps from the roof with an umbrella as his parachute, gravity brings him down to earth.[120]

NOTES

1. Terrence Des Pres, "Holocaust Laughter," *Writing in the World: Essays 1973–1987* (New York: Viking, 1987), 279; also see Geoff King, *Film Comedy* (London: Wallflower Press, 2002), 191.

2. Des Pres, "Holocaust Laughter," 277–78.

3. Steve Lipman, *Laughter in Hell: The Use of Humor during the Holocaust* (Northvale, NJ: Jason Aronson, 1991); Chaya Ostrower, *Humor as a Defense Mechanism in the Holocaust* (PhD diss., Tel Aviv University, 2000); Lynn Rapaport, "Laughter and Heartache: The Functions of Humor in Holocaust Tragedy," in *Gray Zones: Ambiguity and Compromise in the Holocaust and Its Aftermath*, ed. John Roth and Jonathan Petropolus (New York: Berghahn, 2005).

4. *The Great Dictator*, directed by Charles Chaplin (United States, 1940); Jodi Sherman, "Humor, Resistance, and the Abject: Roberto Benigni's *Life Is Beautiful* and Charlie Chaplin's *The Great Dictator*," *Film and History* 32, no. 2 (2002): 74–76.

5. *To Be or Not to Be*, directed by Ernst Lubitsch (United States, 1942); *To Be or Not to Be*, directed by Mel Brooks (United States, 1983).

6. *Me and the Colonel,* directed by Peter Glenville (United States, 1958).

7. Sander L. Gilman, "Is Life Beautiful? Can the Shoah Be Funny? On the Frontier between Acceptable and Unacceptable Representations of the Holocaust in Some Newer and Older Films," in *Jewish Frontiers: Essays on Bodies, Histories, and Identities* (New York: Palgrave Macmillan, 2003), 75.

8. *Aren't We Wonderful,* directed by Kurt Hoffmann (West Germany, 1958); Max Frisch's satirical play about German complacency in failing to recognize the danger Hitler posed to Weimar democracy was adapted several times for television productions. *Biedermann und die Brandstifter,* directed by Fritz Schröder-Jahn (W. Germany, 1958); *Biedermann en de Brandstifters,* directed by Willy van Hemert (Belgium, 1961); *Biedermann und die Brandstifter,* directed by Rainer Wolffhardt (W. Germany, 1967); *Biedermann och pyromanerna,* directed by Tom Segerberg (Finland, 1984).

9. *The Two of Us,* directed by Claude Berri (France, 1966).

10. *Harold and Maude,* directed by Hal Ashby (United States, 1971); Aneta Champman, "Let Life Begin—*Harold and Maude,*" in *The Film Comedy Reader,* ed. Gregg Rickman (New York: Limelight Editions, 2001), 303–8.

11. *The Producers,* directed by Mel Brooks (United States, 1968); Gregg Rickman, "*The Producers,*" in *The Film Comedy Reader,* 298–302.

12. *The Day the Clown Cried,* directed by Jerry Lewis (United States, 1972); *The Last Butterfly,* directed by Karel Kachyna (Czechoslovakia, France, United Kingdom, 1990); Omer Bartov, *The "Jew" in Cinema: From the Golem to Don't Touch My Holocaust* (Bloomington: Indiana University Press, 2005), 162–65; David Gussak, "Survival as a Work of Art: Representing Theresienstadt," in Caroline Joan Picart, *The Holocaust Film Sourcebook* (Westport, CT: Praeger, 2004), 2:180–82.

13. *Seven Beauties,* directed by Lina Wertmueller (Italy, 1975); Ernest Ferlita and John R. May, *The Parables of Line Wertmueller* (New York: Paulist Press, 1977); Kriss Ravetto, *The Unmaking of Fascist Aesthetics* (Minneapolis: University of Minnesota Press, 2001), 187–225.

14. Bruno Bettelheim, *Surviving and Other Essays* (New York: Alfred A. Knopf, 1979); Terrence Des Pres, "The Bettelheim Problem," in *Writing in the World,* 63–87; John Michalczyk, "In the Eye of the Storm: Controversies Surrounding Holocaust Films" (paper presented at the Popular Culture Association Conference, San Diego, California, March 24, 2005).

15. Sander L. Gilman, *Jurek Becker: How I Became a German: Jurek Becker's Life in Five Worlds* (Washington, DC: German Historical Institute, 1999); David Rock, *Jurek Becker: A Jew Who Became a German?* (New York: Berghahn, 2000).

16. *Jacob the Liar,* directed by Frank Beyer (East Germany, 1974); Annette Insdorf, *Indelible Shadows: Film and the Holocaust,* 3rd ed. (New York: Cambridge University Press, 2003), 142–44.

17. Gilman, "Is Life Beautiful?" 74.

18. Woody Allen, *Woody Allen on Woody Allen: In Conversation with Stig Bjorkman* (New York: Grove, 1994), 209–26; Peter J. Bailey, *The Reluctant Film Art of Woody Allen* (Lexington: University of Kentucky Press, 2003), 131–44; David Desser and Lester D. Friedman, *American-Jewish Filmmakers* (Urbana: University of Illinois Press, 1993), 92–101; Sander Lee, *Eighteen Woody Allen Films Analyzed: Anguish, God, and Existentialism* (Jefferson, NC: McFarland and Co., 2002), 139–63.

19. Rick Altman, *Film/Genre* (London: British Film Institute, 1999), 179–94; Sabine Hake, *German National Cinema* (New York: Routledge, 2002), 186–92.

20. Alan Berger, *Children of Job: American Second-Generation Witnesses to the Holocaust* (Albany: State University of Press of New York, 1997), 150–52.

21. Romain Gary, *The Dance of Genghis Cohn* (New York: World Publishing Co., 1968), 23.

22. Katherine A. Fowkes, *Giving Up the Ghost: Spirits, Ghosts, and Angels in Mainstream Comedy Films* (Detroit, MI: Wayne State University Press, 1998); Tom Ruffles, *Ghost Images: Cinema of the Afterlife* (Jefferson, NC: McFarland and Co., 2004).

23. Gary, *The Dance of Genghis Cohn,* 81; Joachim Neugroschel, ed., *The Dybbuk and the Yiddish Imagination: A Haunted Reader* (Syracuse, NY: Syracuse University Press, 2000).

24. *Remu Cemetery,* directed by Edward Etler (Poland, 1961); "Death's Head Revisited," *The Twilight Zone,* directed by Rod Serling (United States, 1962); *The Keep,* directed by Michael Mann (United States, 1983).

25. Ralph Schoolcraft, *Romain Gary: The Man Who Sold His Shadow* (Philadelphia: University of Pennsylvania, 2002); *Madame Rosa,* directed by Moshe Mizrahi (France, 1977); Bartov, *The "Jew" in Cinema,* 226–28; Jeffrey Mehlman, "On the Holocaust Comedies of 'Emile Ajar, '" in *Auschwitz and After: Race, Culture, and the Jewish Question in France,* ed. Lawrence D. Kritzman (New York: Routledge, 1994), 219–34.

26. "Elijah Moshinsky: Filmography," at www.imdb.com (accessed July 2, 2002).

27. Ruth R. Wisse, *The Schlemiel as Modern Hero* (Chicago: University of Chicago Press, 1971), 40–61.

28. Judith Kaufman, "Gallows Humor and Jewish Humor: A Reading of *The Dance of Genghis Cohn* by Romain Gary," in *Jewish Humor,* ed. Avner Ziv (New Brunswick, NJ: Transaction Press, 1998), 99–106.

29. Rbadac [pseud.], "Romain Gary's *The Dance of Genghis Cohn,*" *The Weird Review,* 2000, at www.violetbooks.com/reviews/rhadac-gary.html (accessed July 2, 2002); Eli Pfefferkorn, "The Art of Survival: Romain Gary's *The Dance of Genghis Cohn,*" *Modern Language Studies* 10, no. 3 (Fall 1980): 76–87.

30. Gary, *The Dance,* 105–244.

31. Gilman, "Is Life Beautiful?" 75–76.

32. Insdorf, *Indelible Shadows,* 285.

33. Millicent Marcus, "The Seriousness of Humor in Roberto Benigni's *Life Is Beautiful,*" in *After Fellini: National Cinema in the Postmodern Age* (Baltimore: Johns Hopkins University Press, 2002), 271.

34. Kobi Niv, *Life Is Beautiful, but Not for Jews,* trans. Jonathan Beyrak Lev (Lanham, MD: Scarecrow Press, 2003), xxii.

35. Carlo Celli, *The Divine Comic: The Cinema of Roberto Benigni* (Lanham, MD: Scarecrow Press, 2001), 1–41.

36. Benigni quoted in Alexandra Stanley, "The Funniest Italian You've Probably Never Heard Of," *New York Times Magazine* (October 11, 1988): 44.

37. Charles Taylor, "The Unbearable Lightness of Benigni," *Salon* (October 30, 1998): 4.

38. Celli, *Divine Comic,* 111–16, 153–54.

39. Lucette Matalon Lagnado, *Children of the Flames: Dr. Josef Mengele and the Untold Story of the Twins of Auschwitz* (New York: Morrow, 1991); Deborah Dwork, *Children with a Star: Jewish Youth in Nazi Europe* (New Haven, CT: Yale University Press, 1991), 209–49, 309n99.

40. Celli, *The Divine Comic,* 152; Insdorf, *Indelible Shadows,* 289–90.

41. Bruno Apitz, *Nackt unter Wöelfen: Roman* (Halle, East Germany: Mitteldeutscher Verlag, 1958); *Naked among Wolves,* directed by Frank Beyer (East Germany, 1962); Bill Niven, "Der Not gehorchend, nicht dem eigenen Triebe, ich tüs der Werbung nur zuliebe! The Genesis of Bruno Apitz's Nackt unfer Wölfen," *German Studies Review* 28, no. 2 (May 2005), 265–83.

42. Peter Bondanella, *Italian Cinema from Neorealism to the Present,* 3rd ed. (New York: Continuum, 2001), 449–50.

43. Maurizio Viano, *"Life Is Beautiful:* Reception, Allegory, and Holocaust Laughter," *Jewish Social Studies: The New Series* 5, no. 3 (Spring/Summer 1999): 53–56.

44. Viano, *"Life Is Beautiful,"* 52.

45. Marcus, "The Seriousness of Humor," 269–72.

46. Roberto Benigni and Vincenzo Cerami, *Life Is Beautiful (La vita e bella): A Screenplay,* trans. Lisa Taruschio (New York: Hyperion, 1998), 1–19.

47. Benigni and Cerami, *Life Is Beautiful,* 38–43.

48. Benigni and Cerami, *Life Is Beautiful,* 63–65.

49. Benigni and Cerami, *Life Is Beautiful,* 82–101.

50. Benigni and Cerami, *Life Is Beautiful,* 108–59.

51. Celli, *The Divine Comic,* 151–52.

52. Benigni and Cerami, *Life Is Beautiful,* 109–10.

53. Benigni and Cerami, *Life Is Beautiful,* 158–62.

54. Celli, *The Divine Comic,* 108–11; Viano, *"Life Is Beautiful,"* 59–61.

55. Jacqueline Eckardt, *Lessing's Nathan the Wise and the Critics, 1779–1991* (Columbia, SC: Camden House, 1993).

56. John E. Atwell, *Schopenhauer and the Character of the World: The Metaphysics of Will* (Berkeley: University of California Press, 1995); Christopher Janaway, *Self and World in Schopenhauer's Philosophy* (New York: Oxford University Press, 1989).

57. Michael Fox, "Beautiful Italian Fable Dumbs Down Holocaust Horrors," *Jewish Bulletin of Northern California* (October 30, 1998): 2.

58. Viano, *Life Is Beautiful,* 61–62.

59. Susan Zuccotti, *The Italians and the Holocaust: Persecution, Rescue, and Survival* (New York: Basic Books, 1987); Alexander Stille, "Jews in Fascist Italy," *Life Is Beautiful* Tribute Page, at www.geocities.com/Broadway/Wing/6027.index.html (accessed July 25, 2002).

60. Celli, *The Divine Comic,* 51.

61. Niv, *Life Is Beautiful,* 85–101.

62. Marcia Landy, *Italian Film* (New York: Cambridge University Press, 2000), 98–120, 253–57, 363–65; Bondanella, *Italian Cinema,* 142–95, 347–83, 435–61.

63. Marcus, "The Seriousness of Humor," 277–81; Caroline Joan Picart and Jennifer Perrine, "Laughter, Terror, and Revolt in Three Recent Holocaust Films," in Picart, *Holocaust Film Sourcebook,* 1:402–7.

64. "Awards," and "Business Data," *La vita e bella*, at www.imdb.com; Carlo Testo, *Italian Cinema and Modern European Literatures: 1945–2000* (Westport, CT: Praeger, 2002), 139–48.

65. Niv, *Life Is Beautiful*, 103.

66. Hilene Flanzbaum, "But Wasn't It Terrific? A Defense of Liking *Life Is Beautiful*," *Yale Journal of Criticism* 14, no. 1 (Spring 2001): 273–86.

67. Wisse, *The Schlemiel*, 10–14.

68. Harvey S. Karten, "*Train de vie*," 1999, at www.imdb.com/Reviews/208/20818 (accessed April 13, 2001).

69. Elie Wiesel, *Night*, trans. Stella Rodway (New York: Avon, 1969), 12–32.

70. See Solomon Simon, *The Wise Men of Helm and Their Merry Tales* (New York: Behrman House, 1945); Isaac Bashevis Singer, *The Fools of Chelm and Their History*, trans. Elizabeth Shub (New York: Farrar, Straus, and Giroux, 1973).

71. Joseph Butwin and Francis Butwin, *Sholom Aleichem* (Boston: Twayne, 1977); Dan Miron, *The Image of the Shtetl and Other Studies of Modern Jewish Literary Imagination* (Syracuse, NY: Syracuse University Press, 2000), 128–56, 179–334; Maurice Samuel, *The World of Sholom Aleichem* (New York: Knopf, 1945).

72. "Production Notes" and *The Shtetl Times, Train of Life* Press Kit (Los Angeles: Paramount Classics, 1999); Picart and Perrine, "Laughter," 1:407–8.

73. Henry Sapoznik and Pete Sokolow, *The Complete Klezmer* (New York: Tara, 1998); Mark Slobin, *Fiddler on the Move: Exploring the Klezmer World* (New York: Oxford University Press, 2000); Yale Strom, *The Book of Klezmer: The History, the Music and the Folklore* (Chicago: Acapella, 2002).

74. Donald Kenrick and Grattan Puxon, *The Destiny of Europe's Gypsies* (New York: Basic Books, 1972); Ian F. Hancock, *The Pariah Syndrome: An Account of Gypsy Slavery and Persecution* (Ann Arbor, MI: Karoma Publishers, 1988); David Crown and John Kolsti, eds., *The Gypsies of Eastern Europe* (Armonk, NY: M. E. Sharpe, 1991); Guenter Lewy, *The Nazi Persecution of the Gypsies* (New York: Oxford University Press, 2000); Radu Ionid, *The Holocaust in Romania: The Destruction of Jews and Gypsies under the Antonescu Regime, 1940–1944* (Chicago: Ivan Dee, 2000); Zoltan D. Barany, *The East European Gypsies: Regime Change, Marginality, and Ethnopolitics* (New York: Cambridge University Press, 2002); Tony Sonneman, "Old Hatreds in the New Europe," *Tikkun* 7, no. 1 (January/February 1992): 49–52, 93–94.

75. Anne Thompson, "The Evolution of 'Life,'" *Premiere Magazine* (April 1999): 1–2.

76. "Production Notes," and "An Interview between Father and Son," *The Shtetl Times, Train of Life* Press Kit. Stefan Steinberg, "An Interview with Radu Mihaileanu: The Director of *Train of Life*: 'We have to learn to articulate these deep emotions,'" March 31, 2000, at www.wsws.org/articles/2000/mar2000/radu-m31.shtml (accessed July 12, 2002).

77. Anne Jäckel, "Too Late? Recent Developments in Romanian Cinema," in *The Seeing Century: Film, Vision, and Identity*, ed. Wendy Everett (Amsterdam: Rodopi, 2000), 106–7.

78. *The BFI Companion to Eastern European and Russian Cinema*, ed. Richard Taylor, Nancy Wood, Julian Graffy, and Dina Iordanova (London: British Film Institute, 2000), 701.

79. *Ivan and Abraham*, directed by Yolande Zauberman (France and Belarus: 1993).

80. *Betrayal*, directed by Radu Mihaileanu (France, Romania, Spain, Switzerland, 1993).

81. Wade Major, "*Train of Life*," at www.boxoffice.com/scrpts/fiw.dll?getreview &whare=names&terms=train-of-lif (accessed July 31, 2002); Stefan Steinberg, "'Not to Banalize, not to Rewrite, but to Keep the Discussion Going': Radu Mihaileanu's *Train of Life*," November 26, 1998, at www.wsws.org/arts/1998/nov1998/tra-n26.shtml (accessed July 31, 2002); *Underground*, directed by Emir Kusterica (France, Germany, Hungary, 1995). See Goran Goric, *Notes from the Underground: The Cinema of Emir Kusterica* (London: Wallflower Press, 2001).

82. "Awards," *Train of Life*, at www.imdb.com.

83. "An Interview between Father and Son," *The Shtetl Times, Train of Life* Press Kit, 3.

84. Steinberg, "Not to Banalise," 2.

85. Jurek Becker, *Jacob the Liar*, trans. Leila Vennewitz (New York: Plume, 1997), 60.

86. *The Diary of Dawid Sierakowiak: Five Notebooks from the Lodz Ghetto,* ed. Alan Adelson, trans. Kamil Torowski (New York: Oxford University Press, 1996), 69.

87. David Rock, *Jurek Becker: A Jew Who Became a German?* (New York: Berg, 2000), 9–14; Fox, *Stated Memory,* 1–38.

88. Sander L. Gilman, "How I Became a German: Jurek Becker's Life in Five Worlds," 8th Alois Mertes Memorial Lecture: Occasional Paper #23, Washington, D.C.: German Historical Institute, 1999, 10–20; Rock, *Jurek Becker,* 35–68.

89. *Jacob the Liar*, directed by Frank Beyer (East Germany, Czechoslovakia, 1974); Sean Allan, "DEFA: An Historical Overview," in *DEFA*, 13–15.

90. Andrew Horton and Stuart Y. McDougal, eds., *Play It Again, Sam: Retakes on Remakes* (Berkeley: University of California Press, 1998).

91. *Anne no nikki*, directed by Akinori Nagaoka (Japan, 1995); *Anne Frank's Diary*, directed by Julian Wolff (France, Ireland, Netherlands, United Kingdom, 1999); Hemamalini Ramachandran, "The Animation of Anne: Japanese Anime Encounters the Diary of Holocaust Icon" (paper presented at the Film and History Conference, Dallas, Texas, November 12, 2004).

92. *In the Presence of Mine Enemies*, directed by Joan Micklin Silver (United States, 1996).

93. *Father,* directed by John Power (Australia, 1990); *Descending Angel,* directed by Jeremy Paul Kagan (United States, 1990); *Prague,* directed by Ian Stellar (France, United Kingdom, 1992); *Prague Duet,* directed by Roger L. Simon (Czech Republic, Germany, United States, 1997).

94. "Peter Kassovitz," at www.filmbug.com/db/37044 (accessed August 2, 2002).

95. "Behind the Scenes and Cast Bios," "*Jakob the Liar*," at www.sonypictures.com/ movies/jakobtheliar/castmain.html (accessed August 2, 2002).

96. Rick Groen, "Casting of Williams Merely First Mistake," September 24, 1999, at www.globeandmail.com/servlet/articlenews/movieprint/tvconnect/00010101/ 1024 (accessed August 2, 2002); Harry Haun, "*Jakob the Liar*," at www.filmjournal .com/article.cfm/page10/28526652 (accessed August 2, 2002); Anthony Leong, "*Jacob the Liar* Movie Review," 1999, at www.mediacircus.net/jacobtheliar.html (accessed August 2, 2002).

97. Roger Ebert, "*Jakob the Liar,*" *Chicago Sun-Times*, September 24, 1999.

98. Becker, *Jakob the Liar,* 3–12.

99. Becker, *Jakob the Liar,* 17–60.

100. Becker, *Jakob the Liar,* 139–47, 240–44.

101. Groen, "Casting of Williams," 1.

102. Gilman, "Is Life Beautiful?" 86–92.

103. Becker, *Jakob the Liar,* 222–44.

104. Insdorf, *Indelible Shadows,* 142–44. Beyer's original movie contained this freeze frame. The video version released by Ice Storm International (1999) ends with a view of the clouds in the sky.

105. Leo Braudy, "Afterword: Rethinking Remakes," in *Play It Again Sam*, 332.

106. "*Jakob the Liar:* Behind the Scenes and Cast Bios," at www.sonypictures.com.

107. Leong, "Jakob the Liar"; Picart and Perrine, "Laughter," 1:408–12.

108. *Jacob the Liar,* directed by Frank Beyer (Reissued by the University of Massachusetts and Icestorm Video, 1999); Peter Stack, "East German 'Liar' is Truly Devastating: Original Version Simply Told, Heartbreaking," *San Francisco Chronicle*, November 5, 1999.

109. Alan L. Berger, *Children of Job: American Second Generation Witnesses to the Holocaust* (Albany: State University of New York Press, 1997), 129.

110. *Malou,* directed by Jeanine Meerapfel (West Germany, 1982).

111. *Punch Me in the Stomach,* directed by Deb Filler (Canada, 1996); Deb Filler, "Kicking and Weeping," in *Daughters of Absence: Transforming a Legacy of Loss*, ed. Mindy Weisel (Sterling, VA: Capital Books, 2000), 71–99; Berger, *Children of Job,* 150–52.

112. *Mendel,* Australian Festival of Jewish Cinema, at www.afc.gov.au (accessed August 5, 2002); Brenda Sokolowski, "*Mendel,*" *Anchorage Press* 8, no. 30 (July 29–August 4, 1999); Samuel Abrahamsen, *Norway's Response to the Holocaust* (New York: Holocaust Library, 1991), 151–53.

113. Aaron Hass, *In the Shadow of the Holocaust: The Second Generation* (Ithaca, NY: Cornell University Press, 1990), 144–53.

114. Hass, *In the Shadow,* 106–26.

115. Stephen Holden, "*Mendel:* Overcoming the Horrors of the Past in a Strange Land," *New York Times*, March 20, 1998.

116. Hass, *In the Shadow,* 127–43.

117. For more on the "intergenerational transmission of trauma," see Hass, *In the Shadow,* 25–50.

118. "Awards and Nominations," *Mendel,* at www.imdb.com (accessed August 5, 2002).

119. Rochelle Wright, *The Visible Wall: Jews and Other Ethnic Outsiders in Swedish Film* (Carbondale: Southern Illinois University Press, 1998), 248–387.

120. Steve Neale and Frank Krutnik, *Popular Film and Television Comedy* (New York: Routledge, 1990); Wes D. Gehring, *Parody as Film Genre: "Never Give a Saga an Even Break,"* (Westport, CT: Greenwood Press, 1999); Don Harries, *Film Parody* (London: British Film Institute, 2000).

· 6 ·

The Children Are Watching:
Holocaust Films for Youngsters

> If we persist in thinking that children need hope and happy end-
> ings, then the stories we give them about the Holocaust will be
> shaped by those expectations, and we will need to consider nar-
> rative strategies that give child readers a double narrative, one that
> simultaneously respects our need for hope and happy endings
> even as it teaches a different lesson about history.[1]
>
> —Adrienne Kertzer

*I*n 1977, Eric Kimmel, the renowned author of Jewish children's books, pon-
dered the dearth of juvenile fiction about the mass murder of European Jewry
and predicted that it was only a matter of time before such novels would be
written.[2] The incorporation of the Holocaust into the public school curriculum, starting at the local and state levels in the 1970s and snowballing into a
national phenomenon since then, has generated a demand and supply for age-
appropriate books and audiovisual materials on the topic.[3] Parents and teachers naturally want to avoid traumatizing children and adolescents with overly
graphic depictions of violence or instilling in them a sense of despair over human nature. Karen Shawn advises that readings about the Holocaust assigned
to elementary school students be "hopeful and life affirming, and include acts
of religious, spiritual, and armed resistance" to illustrate the will to survive and
the resiliency of the human spirit.[4] Some scholars doubt whether anything
positive should be salvaged from the Holocaust.[5]

One might legitimately question whether children's films constitute a
separate genre. Such movies can be plotted as adventures, animal fiction,
biopics, buddy movies, cartoons, comedies, dramas, fairy tales, musicals, mys-
teries, sports stories, and other common cinematic genres. Cary Bazalgette and
Terry Staples define children's films as productions appealing to a general

audience consisting of both adults and children or targeted at viewers who are twelve years old or younger.[6] The Motion Picture Association of America introduced its rating system in 1968 and added the PG-13 rating in 1984. This intermediate rating reserved the G and PG ratings for films for children twelve and under by allowing the new category of films to include more mature themes, violence, and profanity within limits that parents would find tolerable for their children.[7] The movie industry has lowered the bar of propriety for PG-13 films by casting them with actors and actresses popular with preteens and loading these movies with dazzling special effects, gross humor, or nonstop action that replicates the pace of video games.[8]

As Holocaust units were incorporated into the middle and high school curricula from the 1970s on, teachers sought audiovisual materials suitable for pupils as young as ten years old.[9] Books with records as bestsellers among this target audience often serve as sources for film adaptations to bolster their chances of commercial success and minimize the risks of offending the sensibilities of either children or their parents.

The steady stream of remakes of *The Diary of Anne Frank* epitomizes this process. Shortly after the publication of the American edition of the book in 1952, the Sunday morning religious series *Frontiers of Faith* broadcast a thirty-minute teleplay entitled *Anne Frank: The Diary of a Young Girl*. Like the famous feature film, which premiered seven years later, the television show emphasized the trust of the Frank family in their Christian rescuers and Anne's maturation as a young woman and aspiring writer. Its appeal to preteen and teenage girls arose from their identification with Anne's adolescent rebellion against her mother, menarche, and awkward romance with Peter. The slaughter of European Jewry was mentioned but never shown.[10] Movies and even several cartoons based on the diary and biographies of Anne or featuring her as a character account for almost a fifth of the Holocaust films produced for children between 1952 and 1999.[11] With the publication of passages deleted by her father, depictions of Anne have become less idealized. The last hour of the miniseries *Anne Frank: The Whole Story* (2001) shows Anne's deportation to Auschwitz and her physical deterioration and excruciating death in Bergen-Belsen.[12]

Most early children's films about the Holocaust originally appeared as religious programs or television movies. Eight of the fifteen Holocaust television dramatizations for family viewing produced in the 1950s and 1960s debuted in the so-called Sunday Ghetto in series like *Directions* (1960–1984), *The Eternal Light* (1952), *Frontiers of Faith* (1951–1970), and *Insight* (1960–1984).[13] By the late 1970s, a few films like *Nightmare: The Immigration of Joachim and Rachel* (1978) were designed specifically for schoolroom usage.[14] Both kinds of movies adhered to the Federal Communications Commission or public education reg-

Table 6.1.   Children and Family Films about the Holocaust

Years	Number of Films	TV/School	Theatrical Releases
1950–1959	10	7	3
1960–1969	11	7	4
1970–1979	9	6	3
1980–1989	13	9	4
1990–1999	22	12	10

ulations governing acceptable subject material and language for the airwaves or schools. Only two of the early Holocaust movies for children aired in prime-time slots.[15] During the 1950s, *Me and the Colonel* (1958) and *The Diary of Anne Frank* were the sole American family films with Holocaust themes released directly to theaters.[16] This pattern of restricting children's films on the Holocaust to television and school persisted until the 1980s (see table 6.1).

The broadcast and popular impact of NBC's miniseries *Holocaust* revitalized the lobbying campaigns for state and local laws recommending or mandating the teaching of the Holocaust as part of the high school curriculum. Since the 1980s, Holocaust-based plotlines appeared more frequently in prime-time slots and cable television movies. The introduction of the PG-13 rating and its subsequent liberalization facilitated the making of more explicit Holocaust feature films targeted at teen and preteen audiences (see table 6.2).

The entry of Disney Studios into the production of Holocaust films is symptomatic of how the Nazi persecution of the Jews and other groups has become an acceptable topic for family programming. In 1988, the Disney Channel broadcast *A Friendship in Vienna*. Starring actor Ed Asner and actress Jane Alexander, both familiar faces on network television at the time, this made-for-cable movie is based on Doris Orgel's novel *The Devil in Vienna*, which enjoyed a large readership among junior high school students. The story focuses on how the German annexation of Austria strained but failed to sever the friendship between a Jewish thirteen-year-old girl and her best friend, who is a Christian. When released on video, it was marketed by Disney's Buena

Table 6.2.   Ratings or Timeslots for Children's Holocaust Films

Years	Prime or Cable	Ed/Daytime/G	PG	PG-13	NR
1950–1959	1	6	NA	NA	
1960–1969	3	4	NA	NA	
1970–1979	3	3	3	0	
1980–1989	7	2	2	2	
1990–1999	9	3	3	6	1

Vista subsidiary.[17] In 1993, Walt Disney Pictures produced its first feature film dealing with subject matter from the Nazi era, *Swing Kids*, which earned a PG-13 rating and featured an ensemble of rising teenage stars.[18] In 1998, ABC's *Wonderful World of Disney* aired *Miracle at Midnight*, a heartwarming tale of how a Gentile family rescued Jewish friends in Denmark.[19]

Like other realistic Hollywood movies, children's movies about the Holocaust have followed a "classic disruption-resolution narrative structure."[20] The disruption takes various forms: the impact of Nazi anti-Semitic policies on relationships between Jews and Gentiles; the testing of individuals' religious faith under trying circumstances; separation from family and friends while hiding from the Germans and their accomplices; the lingering, traumatic memories of the persecuted, which inhibit their integration into their families or adopted homelands after the war; and time travel back to the Shoah by descendents of survivors or contemporary neo-Nazis.

Since children's movies teach moral lessons and end happily, the resolutions to these disruptions normally are that Gentile friends and strangers protect the Jews, the victim's faith withstands the ordeal, fugitives from the authorities fend for themselves or with the help of new friends and usually find their loved ones, someone helps traumatized survivors to overcome their past, and the lessons learned from the Holocaust enable those who experienced it to empathize with other survivors and reject racist doctrines.

The main themes of children's films about the Holocaust are tailored to fit this disruption-resolution pattern. Nearly half have been about the rescue of Jews. Next to remakes of *The Diary of Anne Frank*, the most frequently recurring topic in such movies has been Denmark's exceptional feat of ferrying its Jews to Sweden.[21] The third most common theme in children's Holocaust films deals with how the faith and morality of practicing Christians and Jews prevail despite persecution.[22] Resisting German rule or hiding takes on a gamelike quality in children's movies like *Snow Treasure* (1968), *Lucky Star* (1980), and *Sarah and the Squirrel* (1983).[23] The genres blend in a movie like *Alan and Naomi*, which is simultaneously about the psychologically induced catatonia of a young, traumatized refugee and a new American friend trying to facilitate her healing process. Most buddy movies, however, depict Jewish–Gentile friendships that are not broken by peer pressure and intimidation. Time travel that figuratively or literally transports contemporaries back to the horrific events haunting relatives or inspiring neo-Nazis has emerged as a plot device in several children's Holocaust films produced in the 1990s (see table 6.3)

To be realistic and yet uplifting, children's movies usually employ the double-narrative plotline of which Adrienne Kertzer speaks. The main story

Table 6.3.   Themes in Children's Holocaust Movies, 1945–1999

	Rescue	Test of Faith	Trauma	Resistance/ Escape	Buddy	Survival/ Martyrdom	Neo-Nazism	Time Travel
N = 65	29	6	7	8	5	4	3	3

follows the lead characters as they manage to elude arrest, deportation, and death. Hope remains for their future. Most other characters disappear in roundups (i.e., understood to have been shot on the spot) or perish in concentration camps. The fate of these secondary figures reveals what happened to most Jews whom the Germans and their allies captured. The tension between this unsettling subtext and the primary happy ending enables filmmakers to convey the disturbing nature of the Shoah without frightening younger audiences.

Recent children's films about the Holocaust have increasingly capitalized on the success of plays and books that possess a loyal following among youngsters.[24] Studios avoid risks by counting on the appeal of stories that have proven themselves with preteens and teenagers. Other movies based on original screenplays employ plotlines that intentionally resemble those of children's bestsellers (see table 6.4).

Peter Novick and Norman Finkelstein have criticized how the memory of the Holocaust has been exploited in the United States to heighten Jewish identity with and public sympathy for Israel.[25] The messages conveyed by most children's movies about the Holocaust universalize the meaning of the Holocaust since they are targeted at general audiences. Even though such pictures no longer minimize the Jewish descent of their protagonists, they aim at cultivating, as Alan Mintz has observed, "a deeper tolerance for cultural, religious, and ethnic differences."[26] Children's movies that cite the Holocaust to promote Jewish identity or support for Israel are the exceptions to this rule.

Table 6.4.   Sources for Children's Movies about the Holocaust

Years	Adaptations	Original Screenplays
1950–1959	4	6
1960–1969	5	6
1970–1979	3	6
1980–1989	9	4
1990–1999	12	10

GIVE US YOUR TRAUMATIZED, YEARNING
TO BREATHE FREE: *ALAN AND NAOMI*
Directed by Sterling Van Wagenen
(United States: Leucadia Film Corporation, 1991)

> The violent resurgence in the present of images from the past that
> a peacetime existence has necessarily sought to repress is the im-
> age of memory offered by Holocaust films.[27]

—Maureen Turim

How can a Jewish boy growing up in the United States understand what it was like for a French Jewish girl to watch helplessly while the Gestapo beat her father to death? That is the premise of Myron Levoy's award-winning children's book *Alan and Naomi* (1991) and the faithful film adaptation of it directed by Sterling Van Wagenen.[28] Lukas Haas, best remembered for his role as the sweet Amish youngster who saw a murder committed in the movie *Witness* (1985), plays Alan Silverman, a gawky adolescent whose Jewish background, squeaky voice, lanky body, and success in school mark him as a target for bullies in his tough immigrant neighborhood.

The opening scene appears to show a playground blacktop with a child jumping through the squares of a hopscotch frame. Then, the camera narrows its focus to reveal that the playground is a street covered with chalk graffiti. Drawings of a Jewish star, a five-pointed star, an American flag, and a combat plane set the stage for a story about a Jewish boy who befriends a psychological casualty of Nazi oppression. A brawny Italian kid named Joe Condello cancels a stickball game after Alan hits a ball that shatters a window. When Alan's teammate Shaun complains that they never finished the inning, Joe retorts to Alan, "Eat that with your pickled herring!" and labels Shaun a "Jew lover." Although Alan lives far from Europe, he has experienced anti-Semitism.

Returning home from the game, Alan sees Naomi Kirschenbaum huddled on a staircase landing in the apartment building where he lives. She stares vacantly into space and tears paper. Since Alan is carrying a stick, she panics and starts screaming in French for her mother to rescue her. When Alan's parents ask him to help Naomi overcome the grip her father's murder has on her mind, he declines. Becoming a companion to a crazy girl would validate his reputation as a sissy. Alan's father appeals to his son's conscience. Alan knows that the Germans are killing Jews in Europe. Alan's father suggests that God chose his son to perform this mission because Alan is "one of the lucky ones." In the book, he says this opportunity has arisen because Alan is "lucky."[29] This subtle alteration may make no difference to younger viewers, but for adults it transforms an individual act of kindness into a collective responsibility of American Jews.

Van Wagenen includes musical, visual, and verbal cues that remind the audience that this is a Jewish story. Alan must defend himself against anti-Semitic slurs. The Jewish characters interject Yiddish colloquialisms when they are talking. Alan kisses the mezuzah as he enters Naomi's apartment and describes a Passover seder to his Irish American friend Shaun. Clarinet riffs in the score sound like klezmer melodies. When Alan first tries to talk to Naomi by speaking through a ventriloquist's dummy, Naomi shreds the pages of the Yiddish newspaper *The Forward*.

Nevertheless, Van Wagenen broadens the appeal of the narrative. Alan goes to the movies and sees newsreels of the advance of the American troops on the western front. The footage ends with an image of German children standing in the rubble of their destroyed house. The camera focuses on the anguished, dirty face of a girl around Naomi's age. That night, Alan has a nightmare that prompts him to resume trying to pierce the wall of silence Naomi has built around herself. He tells his father, "I thought that if anything that terrible had happened to me, I sure would hope someone would give me another chance." This recapitulates a chapter in the book with one crucial difference. There Alan's conscience is jarred by a newsreel image of a Jewish girl resembling Naomi being herded onto a truck with other Jews.[30]

Compare the universal meaning of the above scene with a similar one from the movie based on Chaim Potok's *The Chosen*.[31] This too is a buddy film, but the tension between Danny and Reuven arises from the Hasidic shunning of the modern world and Conservative Judaism's accommodation to it. Reuven takes his new friend to see a movie for the first time. The newsreel they watch contains graphic scenes of the rotting corpses and emaciated survivors the Allied soldiers found in the camps they liberated. This revelation divides the two because Danny's father, a revered Lubavitcher zaddik, denounces the establishment of a secular Jewish state in Israel as a heresy, whereas Reuven and his father campaign for the creation of Israel as the only way to avert future Holocausts.[32] In *The Chosen*, the Holocaust legitimates support for Israel; in *Alan and Naomi*, it symbolizes the victimization of children by war.

Although it is a tedious process, Alan eventually wins Naomi's trust. Initially, her doll Yvette converses with his dummy and informs him that Naomi has disappeared. Naomi's doctor then advises Alan to talk directly to Naomi and wean her from using the doll as a proxy. Alan's persistence pays off. As their friendship blossoms, he learns that Naomi blames herself for her father's death because she failed to destroy the maps he had drawn for the French Resistance. She has several flashbacks to that bloody scene. Alan assures Naomi that the Gestapo alone is guilty of her father's murder.[33]

Once Naomi comes out of her shell, Alan takes her to an abandoned airfield where Shaun and he have flown model planes. By sharing this activity with Naomi, Alan initiates Naomi into the world of childhood play. Alan's yellow plane soars above an overgrown field of grass with a semicircular Quonset hangar on the horizon. When Alan and Naomi sit down together to relax on the grass, the image recalls the woman reclining in the pasture in Andrew Wyeth's famous painting *Christina's World*.[34] The scene conveys a spatial sense of boundless opportunities, but the vision of the two youngsters enjoying each other's company replaces the solitary figure of the woman.

Most children's movies would conclude at this point. The slaying of Naomi's father had shattered her faith in humankind, and Alan's patient cultivation of her friendship had restored it. Neither the novel nor the movie ends so optimistically. As Alan escorts Naomi to school, Joe Condello taunts them as "Yids" whose conspiracies justify Hitler's desire to exterminate them. Alan pounces on Joe, who handily overpowers him and punches him in the nose. When Naomi sees that Alan is bleeding profusely, she associates the image with the killing of her father and runs away. Shaun intervenes on Alan's behalf and beats Joe into submission. That evening Shaun finds Naomi tunneled under a pile of coal next to the furnace in the basement of Alan's tenement. The allusion to the crematoria is obvious to adults but probably lost on children. Naomi's sooty face resembles that of the German girl Alan saw in the newsreel. Naomi must be institutionalized. Alan cannot console her when he visits her at the sanatorium, and his father's assurances that someday she will recover ring hollow. The movie closes with a black-and-white shot of the sad expressions on Alan's and Naomi's faces. Friendship alone cannot exorcise Naomi's inner demons.

Alan and Naomi won both the Heartland Film Festival's Crystal Heart Award for an independent film that "expressed hope and respect for the positive values of life" and the German Youth Video Prize for Best Children's Video of 1994.[35] While one critic praised its "old-fashioned values,"[36] another speculated that it might be "too sophisticated for children" and too boring for adults.[37] Its troubling ending appears to have doomed it at the box office.[38] Its "avoidance of pat solutions" is considered a virtue by educators because it can stimulate discussions about "either mental illness or the events of World War Two."[39] Moreover, it illustrates how Nazi brutality has robbed Naomi of her childhood and forced Alan to grow up by assuming the role of the father she lost.[40]

DANCING TO A DIFFERENT DRUMMER: *SWING KIDS*
Directed by Thomas Carter
(United States: Hollywood Pictures, 1993)

Taking dramatic advantage of the rock 'n' roll controversy that *Rock around the Clock* had helped foment, subsequent teenpics used it as a narrative frame for their musical presentations, addressing the intergenerational squabble with explicit dialogue and transparent sympathies.[41]

—Thomas Doherty

Since the 1950s, generational conflict between adults and teenagers has often been depicted as clashes over the latest music and dance fads. Bill Haley's recording of "Rock around the Clock" became the anthem of this adolescent rebellion when it served as the opening and closing background music for *Blackboard Jungle* (1955), one of the earliest films to deal with juvenile delinquency. While the movie *Rock around the Clock* (1956) is a success saga about Bill Haley and the Comets, other pictures like *Shake, Rattle, and Rock* (1956) and *Don't Knock the Rock* (1956) portray parents and civic groups trying to ban rock music for corrupting the morals of teenagers, then eventually accepting it as a harmless outlet for youthful exuberance. Since these movies cater to adolescent tastes in fashion, music, and stars, they draw an audience consisting primarily of preteens and teens.[42] The basic plotline of such pictures has been resuscitated to depict the tension between community standards and liberating new dance styles, as transpires in *Footloose* (1984), and parent-child disputes over dating a partner who differs socially, as portrayed in *Dirty Dancing* (1987), or racially, as in *Save the Last Dance* (2001). Incidentally, Thomas Carter, the director of *Swing Kids*, directed *Save the Last Dance*.

There are several reasons why Hollywood Pictures, a Disney subsidiary, chose the Third Reich's suppression of jazz and swing dancing by German teenagers as the subject matter of its first theatrical release about the Nazi period. First, it provided a more mature variation on the cartoon musical, which has been the mainstay of Disney family films.[43] Second, it followed on the heels of the swing dancing revival that originated in the late 1980s.[44] Third, it placed perennial teenage concerns about appearance, friendship, nonconformity, and peer pressure in a historical context that had been the setting for past box-office successes like *The Diary of Anne Frank* and more recent ones like *Europa, Europa* (1991).[45] Finally, by chance, the screenwriter Jonathan Feldman stumbled upon a reference to the first scholarly research published in English on the Swing Youth, who, as the movie's prologue tells us, "refused to join the Hitler Youth, wore long hair, and were obsessed by American movies, British fashions, and Swing music."[46]

The film's first two scenes visually illustrate the struggle that is about to ensue. As the doors open to the Club Bismarck, the viewer is drawn into a microcosm of acrobatic dancing and pulsating music. The stylishly dressed couples perform spectacular jumps, spins, steps, and tosses amid a backdrop of vivid yellow walls adorned with art deco designs. When Arvid, Peter, and Thomas, the triad of swing enthusiasts, leave this haven of free expression, they are shrouded by the darkness of night. Still intoxicated by the energetic rhythms of swing melodies, they defiantly urinate on several Nazi propaganda posters. Suddenly, they are knocked over by a terrified man fleeing the Gestapo. He runs onto a bridge and plunges into the river. His pursuers fire their pistols at him. The next day, Peter notices the police fishing the man's body out of the water.

The specter of persecution reappears in the next two scenes. Willie, Peter's younger brother, alerts Peter and Thomas that Hitler Youth members are beating a swing kid. Peter and Thomas rush to defend one of their compatriots only to discover that he is a Jew and not a swing kid. One Hitler Youth sternly warns them, "You keep helping them and we'll deal with you the way we deal with all traitors!" Although they hate the Hitler Youth, the swing kids are not particularly alarmed by the plight of the Jews. Yet, Peter unwittingly aids Jews and other fugitives in his job as a delivery boy for a bookstore. He later discovers that the books contain counterfeit birth certificates. Peter's conversations with a woman who regularly receives these volumes reveal that Peter was selected for this task because his deceased father was a communist violinist who had been arrested for protesting the firing of a Jewish colleague at the university where he taught.

Peter and his friends are so fixated on swing music that they are oblivious to the plight of the Jews. Anti-Semitism only affects them insofar as the jackets of Benny Goodman and Artie Shaw albums carry pseudonyms to prevent their confiscation as "kike" and "nigger" music. The first real crime committed by Thomas and Peter involves stealing a radio and ends in Peter's arrest. He is pressured into joining the Hitler Youth by a Gestapo officer who is courting his mother. Thomas joins too, assuming that being a Hitler Youth is the perfect cover for indulging his passion for swing music.

This alternation between flashy dance numbers and racist indoctrination could easily trivialize the severity of Nazi oppression. A subplot about the third member of the cohort prevents this from happening. Arvid, a talented guitarist who aspires to be the next Django Reinhardt, is mugged by the Hitler Youth for being a "Jew lover" and a "cripple" with a clubfoot. The Hitler Youth smash Arvid's hand to stop him from playing "nigger-kike" music. As Arvid concentrates on learning how to play the guitar with only two fingers, just like Django, Thomas accepts the Nazi doctrines of Aryan superiority and anti-Semitism after watching newsreels about the "liberation" of the Sudetenland and propaganda films like *The Eternal Jew*. Roger Ebert faulted the movie for allowing the anti-Semitic claims in these clips to go "unanswered," but by introducing this material to a captive audience of Hitler Youth, the movie reenacts the indoctrination process.[47]

Arvid emerges as the first character to speak out against the bigotry and militarism that threaten pariahs like himself and the countries bordering Germany. After he plays a jazz set, German pilots ask Arvid to play a German song. Arvid gives a fiery speech that becomes a clarion call for Peter but not for Thomas:

> We are murdering Austrians. Next it will be the Czechs, then the Poles, not to mention the Gypsies and the Jews, who are unmentionable. You think that just because you're not doing it that you're not part of it.

Thomas taunts Arvid for not including the "cripples and the retards" in his speech because he obviously belongs among them. Arvid retorts, "I would rather belong to anyone but the Nazis because that's who you belong to."

It gradually dawns on Peter that he cannot reconcile his friendship with Arvid, his love of swing music, and the fate of his father with his membership in the Hitler Youth. The implications of his double life become disconcertingly apparent when Arvid commits suicide. The scene of Arvid sitting in a bathtub in a pool of blood recalls Louis David's famous painting of the assassination of Jean-Paul Marat, a victim of a past "terror." Peter now remembers how his father had been reduced to a frightened mute by his imprisonment in a concentration camp. He quarrels with Thomas when the latter dismisses Arvid's death as insignificant. Peter realizes that Arvid killed himself because he refused to become a killer. When ordered to deliver packages for the Gestapo, Peter opens one of the boxes and finds the cremated ashes of a person labeled a traitor on the container. He seeks out the woman who knew his father. She gives him a letter his father had left for his family. It reads, "We must all take responsibility for what is happening in our country. Outside the doors, all they hear is Hitler's cries of hate."

Peter dons his swing clothes and goes to the dance hall. The singer and band are performing a sluggish rendition of "Bei Mir Bist Du Schön," the most popular Yiddish tune in the swing repertoire.[48] The other dancers on the floor are moving listlessly. Their languid motions preview how stultifying the Nazi repression of modern culture is. Peter improvises a series of fancy steps that are dazzling compared to the drab footwork of those surrounding him. Peter's uninhibited style is infectious and soon the joint is jumping. The police van pulls up in front of the club, and Hitler Youth cadets and police officers file out in an orderly manner and launch a raid on the nightclub. Their mechanical obedience sharply contrasts with the spontaneity of the swing dancers.

Thomas assaults Peter with a truncheon and tries to choke him. With Peter gasping for breath, Thomas relents. The Gestapo officer shakes his head and laments that Peter's potential has been squandered on something so trivial. Emboldened by his act of cultural resistance, Peter chants, "It don't mean a thing, if it ain't got that swing" and punctuates the final verse by shouting, "Swing

Heil." Thomas echoes this salutation. Running behind the van as it disappears into the night, Willie, utters "Swing Heil" to affirm his solidarity with his brother. The epilogue tells us that hundreds of swing kids were put in labor camps and that thousands were drafted and died in the war.

There is much that is problematic in this film. The swing kids were a fringe movement whose fate pales in comparison with that of the Jews, gypsies, and physically and mentally handicapped. The point that they were conscripted and sent to fight is meaningless since that was the fate of every German male who was fit and old enough to serve in the military. The swing kids were martyrs by choice, not because of race, ethnicity, or disability. The movie modernizes the swing kids by having them speak in slang used by today's teens, like saying "man" at the end of sentences or advising friends to "loosen up."

Yet, *Swing Kids* touches on several crucial themes. The biological basis for the Nazi ban on jazz is explicitly linked to Nazi racism. After the first raid on the Café Bismarck, the infamous poster from the Degenerate Music Exhibition showing a Negro saxophonist wearing a Jewish star is posted on the door of the dancehall. The clip from *The Eternal Jew* graphically depicts how the Nazis considered the Jews vermin. Arvid's speech is prescient in listing the countries Germany would occupy and the groups the Nazis would persecute. The stigmatization of his physical deformity is something that rarely appears in Holocaust movies. Similarly, how often do we learn that many political prisoners in the concentration camps died in captivity? Above all, the seductiveness of privilege and the power of peer pressure that enticed German boys to join the Hitler Youth are presented effectively in the film.

The juxtaposition of the uninhibited swing Kids with the robotically obedient Hitler Youth symbolizes the Nazi regimentation of everyday life. The use of music need not trivialize the subject, as pictures like *Cabaret* and *The Harmonists* demonstrate. Otis Sallid had previously choreographed dance numbers that enhanced the depiction of serious themes in Spike Lee's films *School Daze, Do the Right Thing* (1989), and *Malcolm X* (1992).[49] The authentic look of the dance-hall scenes and the intimidating presence of the Nazis are captured in the cinematography of Jerzy Zielinski who filmed many of Agnieszka Holland's movies.[50] Despite my reservations about the colloquial dialog and the analogy of the fate of the swing kids with the victims of Nazi genocide, I concur with Frank Maloney's appreciation of the spectacular dance scenes:

> The young dancers display a kind of raw enthusiasm for jitterbug that is chaotic and as un-Nazi as anything one could imagine. Some reviewers have objected to making swing a metaphor for freedom, but to me it seems natural and earned. Anyone who experienced the first years of rock 'n' roll knows how rebellious and in the broadest sense political mere music and dance can be.[51]

Ultimately, *Swing Kids* serves as a warning to teenagers about the power of the state to inculcate a sense of national and racial superiority in members of an age group that is particularly vulnerable to peer pressure.

ALONE AMONG THE CANNIBALS:
THE ISLAND ON BIRD STREET
Directed by Søren Kragh-Jacobsen
(Denmark, Germany, United Kingdom: April Productions, Connexion Film,
Det Danske Filminstitute, M and M Productions, Moonstone, 1997)

> Alex, the hero of my story, hides in a ruined house that was bombed out at the beginning of the war. This house is not very different from a desert island. So he must survive by himself for many months, taking what he needs from other houses the way Robinson Crusoe took what he needed from the wrecks of other ships that were washed up on the beach.[52]
>
> —Uri Orlev

Children's books and movies often pit a youngster against a fiendish villain or hostile environment where he or she has been abandoned or transported. *Alice in Wonderland* (1951), *The Black Stallion* (1979), and *The Wizard of Oz* (1939) typify this genre, which teaches children that they can be resourceful enough to survive on their own or with the help of friends they meet in the course of their ordeals. The numerous remakes of *Robinson Crusoe* (1952) attest to the enduring appeal the theme of inventiveness in the face of adversity holds for juveniles, who constantly must prove their competency to adults and peers.[53]

Uri Orlev's *The Island on Bird Street* substitutes a concealed loft in the ruins of a bombed out apartment in a vacated Polish ghetto for Crusoe's deserted island. Waiting for his deported father to return, eleven-year-old Alex emulates his fictional hero, Robinson Crusoe, by erecting a hiding place from the German "cannibals." His companion Friday is a white mouse named Snow. Alex finds drinking water, gathers food, and steals building materials from vacant homes. He deftly constructs a rope ladder that he can lower quickly to enable him to climb up its rungs to safety. Published in 1984, Orlev's semiautobiographical novel earned its author several major awards for children's literature and has become a favorite among Holocaust educators.[54]

It was not purely coincidental that Orlev's novel was adapted into a feature film by Danish director Søren Kragh-Jacobsen. Since 1982, Danish law has mandated that one-quarter of all government film subsidies be allocated for the making of children's and youth movies.[55] Kragh-Jacobsen has specialized in the production of children's films. His *The Boys from St. Petri* (1991) followed the exploits of schoolmates who playfully put up anti-Nazi posters and steal the helmets of German soldiers in wartime Denmark as a prelude to engaging in armed resistance against the invaders.[56] Kragh-Jacobsen intended *The Island on Bird Street* to be "a film for everybody with a child in the lead." He counted on the broad appeal of a child's resiliency to "understand how to live in the present and squeeze a little optimism out of the most hopeless situations."[57]

The sense of being cut off from the outside world pervades *The Island on Bird Street*. The opening scene lasts more than two minutes. It features a darkly lit shot of a sign prohibiting people from entering the ghetto. The cadence of boots marching toward the gate is heard. A soldier walking a watchdog approaches the Jewish enclave. The camera pulls back to reveal the barbed wire atop the wall surrounding the ghetto. Alex's voice-over reinforces the feeling of confinement: "Imagine if someone built a high wall around your neighborhood so you couldn't get out. That's what the Nazis did to us."

The following scene imparts the constant fear of deportation. Before German soldiers and the Jewish police stage a roundup in the ghetto, Alex observes matter-of-factly, "Every week the Nazis take more people away. They call this selection. You never know when a selection is going to happen or who they are going to take away next." Alex plays hide-and-seek with friends amid the rubble at the bottom of a canyon of bricks and the craggy edges of destroyed tenement buildings. When the Germans and their accomplices march in, the game turns into a scramble to find a bunker beneath the debris. Later that night, Alex's father cautiously reconnoiters the empty street littered with the suitcases of those apprehended in the raid. He fetches Alex from the hole he has burrowed into below the pavement. The pattern for the movie is set. Although the hunt for Jews is relentless, Alex can elude the Germans if he can maintain hope that his father will return.

Alex's father and Uncle Boruch disagree over how to save Alex. The muscular father, played by Patrick Bergin, believes his son must learn how to defend himself. Boruch, played by Jack Warden, stresses that Alex should never lose his faith and must rely on his intelligence. He gives Alex *Robinson Crusoe* to read and a mezuzah to ward off evil. A passage from the book predicts Alex's future: "I was shipwrecked. There wasn't a house to live in or any food or clothing. At night I thought I'd get eaten by wild animals." Disobeying orders to stay in a cellar during the daytime, Alex goes to the rope factory where his father and uncle work. Boruch warns Alex that the bigger gray mice might eat Snow, an analogy for the plight of the Jews too. The ropes hanging loosely from hooks resemble nooses, but Boruch transforms them into connective tissue by teaching Alex how to tie knots. Alex cowers in a corner watching Boruch savagely beaten by an SS officer who has entered the factory. That evening, Alex's father instructs him on how to shoot a pistol in case he must defend himself. The uncle and father equip Alex with the survival skills he will need when the former is murdered, alluded to by a shot of his hat lying in the street after a round up, and the latter is deported after ordering his son to wait for him "no matter what happens."

Salvaging what he can from the ransacked apartments of the Jews, Alex builds a shelter in a second-story room, which can only be accessed by the rope ladder and pulley he assembles. The room is adjacent to the ruins of a kitchen. The only remnants of the kitchen are a functioning sink and a cupboard that serves as the entrance and exit for Alex's cubby. On one foraging expedition, Snow, whom Alex dubs his servant Friday, sniffs out food that has been stored under floorboards. The Jewish couple who stashed it there will not share it with Alex. The Germans burst in and kill the husband and wife. Meanwhile, Alex ducks under a washbasin and goes undetected. When he retreats to his "island," Alex tells Snow, "It is just you and me, and the cannibals."

Both the book and the movie avoid stereotyping all Germans as Nazis. The German commander is obsessed with ferreting out the Jewish stragglers. Alex watches as the officer forces a terrified Jewish man to reveal where a bunch of Jews are hiding. After their lair is discovered and they are herded away, the officer dynamites the bunker. Yet, another time when Alex is chased by Germans, one of them finds him, looks at his innocent face, and decides not to shoot or arrest him.

Alex receives mixed responses from the Poles on the other side of the wall too. Peeling the shading off a window in his room, he glimpses Polish boys roughhousing, patients being examined by a doctor, and a girl putting a vase of flowers on a windowsill. The normalcy of daily life in the Polish quarter is shot in vibrant colors in contrast to the drab browns, grays, and blues of the ghetto. Alex descends into a tunnel to cross over to the Polish side seeking medical help for a wounded Jewish partisan whom he nurses back to health after firing his pistol to kill the German who had trapped the man and his comrade. The Polish boys immediately suspect Alex of being a "Jewfish" and chase him whenever he goes. The doctor calls the police to report Alex but then agrees to treat the wounded man in the ghetto. The girl pretends she recognizes Alex when he is on the verge of being caught by the Polish boys. Declining her mother's invitation to go with them to a farm, Alex insists he must wait in the ghetto for his father.

As the German troops withdraw from the city, the sounds of Russian mortars can be heard in the distance. The Poles enter what is left of the Jewish quarter and occupy the abandoned Jewish apartments. The rope ladder breaks, dropping Alex back to the ground. He takes up residence in his old bunker. When Snow dies, Alex marks his grave with the mezuzah. Soon thereafter, someone kicks a hole in the wall of the bunker. Sunlight streams into the darkened cavern. Alex cannot believe that his father has returned. In a closing voice-over, Alex reads the section from *Robinson Crusoe* where Robinson sees the sails of the schooner that will whisk him off the island. Sheets hung on clotheslines flap in the wind like the sails described in the book.

The movie omits parts of the book that might make its message less universal and more objectionable to the parents of children who view it. One reviewer of Orlev's book criticized him for glorifying Jewish armed resistance and Zionism.[58] Since Alex's father is a former soldier and certain that Germany will liquidate European Jewry, he carries a gun with him and trains Alex to use a pistol. Alex recalls that his mother believed that Jews would never be accepted as citizens in Poland and urged them to settle in Palestine to establish a state of their own.[59] When Alex saves the two partisans, he considers them heroes of the Jewish resistance. He feels no remorse for killing the German soldier.[60]

Kragh-Jacobsen does not interject Zionism or any Jewish ethnocentrism to justify Alex's struggle to survive. His father and uncle have no idea what happens to the Jews when they are deported. Unlike his reaction in Oriev's book, Alex regrets that he shot the German and sobs shamefully. The partisans invite him to join them, but he refuses. Only a careful look at the video jacket reveals a tiny yellow Jewish star in one of Alex's eyes.

Reviewer Andrew Horton questioned why Orlev attached a fairy-tale ending to what happened to him during the war. In the preface to his book, Orlev admits that he imagined himself as Robinson Crusoe when he scavenged for provisions for his aunt, brother, and himself in the Warsaw ghetto. The Germans captured the Orlev brothers and interned them at Bergen-Belsen for two years.[61] Horton charges that the novel represents "Orlev's attempt to paint over the past rather than reconcile himself with it."[62]

On this point, Orlev and Kragh-Jacobsen may have heeded Shawn's admonition that Holocaust stories for children should present "the truth without unduly traumatizing young readers" and "personalize the statistics, fostering empathy, compassion, involvement, and identification with victims and survivors."[63] The publisher of the novel recommended that it was appropriate for readers between nine and twelve years old. Orlev wrote another semiautobiographical novel, *The Lead Soldiers,* which is specifically about what he and his brother endured in the ghetto and camp. It is aimed at older readers ranging from thirteen to eighteen years old.[64] *The Island of Bird Street* neither mitigates the implacable threat the Nazis posed to the Jews nor implies that self-defense is a virtue in itself. The double narrative shows that Alex's survival is the exception to the rule. Alex relies on his wits but needs the presence of Snow, the assistance of the Polish doctor and girl, and the hope that his father will return to persevere.[65]

The Island of Bird Street became the most internationally acclaimed Holocaust children's film of the 1990s. It received awards and nominations from major film festivals in Denmark, Germany, and the United States when it was released in 1997. After being broadcast on Showtime, it won three Daytime Emmy Awards in the categories for children's specials, as well as earning a Film Advisory Board Award. It even has been screened in Hong Kong, Tokyo, and Singapore.[66] *The Island on Bird Street* is a child's version of *The Pianist* (2002), in which close calls, quick thinking, and good luck spare the protagonist from ever being captured or killed by the Germans.

OZ-SCHWITZ: *THE DEVIL'S ARITHMETIC*
Directed by Donna Deitch
(United States: Millbrook Farm, Punch, Showtime, 1999)

"So let me tell you about *Wizard of Oz*," she said. She couldn't remember which was the movie and which was the book. Shrugging her shoulders, she began a strange mixture of the two, speeding along until the line "Gosh, Toto, this sure doesn't look like Kansas."[67]

—Jane Yolen

Directors of Holocaust films for youngsters not only gravitate toward scripts based on Holocaust books with a large juvenile readership, but these books, in turn, often borrow their storylines from earlier children's classics. Just as *The Island on Bird Street* compares Alex's ordeal in the ghetto to Robinson's Crusoe's arduous struggle to survive, *The Devil's Arithmetic* employs the transposition of place from *The Wizard of Oz* to enable an assimilated Jewish American teenager to empathize with the suffering her relatives experienced in Nazi-occupied Poland.

Dustin Hoffman coproduced the film with actress Mimi Rogers. In the prologue to the videotape, he recalls that when he brought the screenplay home to evaluate, his daughter pointed out that she was reading the book by Jane Yolen for school. He remarks that what attracted him to this script was how Yolen's story combined "harsh reality with the magic element of fable." Hoffman cautions the audience that the violence they will witness is disturbing but adds that its purpose is to educate rather than entertain.

The film starts out like a typical teenager movie with neon lights blinking behind the profile of the popular young actress Kirsten Dunst before she became associated with her role in the *Spider-Man* movies. Hannah Stern, the character she plays, is hanging out at a tattoo parlor with her best girlfriends trying to pick a design to have inscribed on her skin. After they mull over what they will do during the upcoming weekend, Hannah realizes it is the first night of Passover and that she must attend the family seder. She rushes to her car and drives home to the accompaniment of a folk-rock song. The prosperity of her parent's house is emphasized with long shots of spacious and tastefully furnished rooms. Despite Hannah's pleas to stay home, her parents insist she join the family for the seder. Nearing her aunt's apartment, Hannah stares at the archaic garments and unkempt side-locks of several ultra-Orthodox boys.

Although Hannah displays a warm affection for her Aunt Eva, she is noticeably bored with the rituals of the seder that are performed on-screen in considerable detail. Her aunt kindles the candles, her uncle recites the blessing over the first cup of wine, the youngest children chant the Four Questions, and various members of the family narrate the biblical saga of how God freed the Jews from bondage and parted the Red Sea to let them escape Pharaoh's army. During the service, glimpses of the numbers tattooed on the arms of the Holocaust survivors serve as a visual link between the bondage of the Jews in ancient Egypt and their status as nameless slaves under Hitler.

Toward the end of the meal, Hannah has become tipsy from drinking too much wine. Aunt Eva urges her to open the door for the prophet Elijah, whose arrival will herald the coming of the Messianic Age. Hannah complies and finds herself in a hallway where a flash of bright light and the roar of howling wind initiate her journey back to the Polish shtetl where Eva's family dwelled until the Nazis deported them. Unaware of when and where she has awoken, her cousin Rivka explains that she has been stricken with typhus, which has made her delirious for several weeks and killed her parents. Despite her new surroundings, Hannah insists that she is from New Rochelle, which prompts her relatives to ask where old Rochelle was. Rivka chooses a dress for Hannah to wear to a wedding, but Hannah finds her taste too "virginal." Rivka dismisses these odd remarks as side effects of Hannah's bout with typhus.

As Jews gather for the marriage, Hannah is struck by the resemblance of the yeshiva students to the boys she saw near her aunt's apartment. Director Donna Deitch pays the same attention to the marriage ceremony as she does to the seder. Rivka explains each custom to her confused cousin. German troops disrupt the wedding in a scene that parallels the pogrom at the end of the wedding in *Fiddler on the Roof*. It finally dawns on Hannah that this is the beginning of the Holocaust. She predicts that six million Jews will be systematically murdered by Germany, but none of her Polish relatives believes that something so barbarous will happen. As the town's Jews climb onto the trucks that will transport them to a death camp, the synagogue is set ablaze.

Hannah compares her memories of suburban life to the deprivations she faces daily in the camp. She realizes how shallow she had been, particularly when the Germans engrave her identification number on her arm, reminding her how she once had wanted to get a tattoo. She regrets that she ignored the unit on the Holocaust in her high school history class. In the nameless desolate camp where Hannah is incarcerated, the men and women converse with each other through the fence that separates their barracks. There she befriends a young man who looks like the Orthodox boys she formerly shunned. He asks her if they could go out on a date in the future, and she reverts to her old self, suggesting that they see a movie in Times Square.

Since Hannah knows the outcome of the war, she assures her bunkmates that some Jews will survive and immigrate to the United States. In Yolen's novel, Hannah foresees the establishment of Israel.[68] She gives hope to women in her barracks by telling them stories about the prosperity Jews will enjoy in America and recapitulating the plots of films she has seen, like *The Wizard of Oz*. The fearful vulnerability of the Cowardly Lion and the melting of the Wicked Witch serve as metaphors for the eventual defeat of Hitler.

Deitch does not spare her audience the horrors of daily existence in the camp. Hannah and all the other Jews are malnourished, overworked, and overcrowded. They live in constant dread of being selected for gassing. When a number of the yeshiva boys conspire to escape, they are hung. A woman who had wrapped a belt around her abdomen to hide her advanced state of pregnancy gives birth to a daughter. The commandant learns about the baby and sends the mother and newborn child to the gas chamber.

Yet, interspersed among these moments of despair are instances when their Judaism comforts the otherwise despondent inmates. Mourning the murder of his wife and daughters, a rabbi utters the kaddish, whose Hebrew words echo throughout the camp. Hannah asks her boyfriend to teach her how to pray. During Passover, the women in Hannah's barracks secretly bake *matza* and conduct a seder that compensates for its lack of a meal with spiritual sustenance. Hannah devotedly performs the rituals that she had previously found meaningless.

As they toil, breaking clumps of mud in a barren field, Rivka confides in Hannah that if she survives, she will change her name to Eva. Hannah recognizes that Rivka is her future aunt and that she herself is destined to die and be reborn as Eva's niece. Thus, she exchanges places with Rivka when the commandant selects her cousin to be gassed. In the novel, Yolen handles the gassing scene discreetly by writing that Hannah and the other women "walked in through the door into endless night."[69] In what strikes me as poor directorial judgment, Deitch brings the viewer inside the gas chamber as cyanide pellets rain down from a grate onto the panicked women. After their screams subside, their faces and nude torsos are positioned vertically next to each other like a collection of pretty dolls whose serene and symmetric appearance undercuts the visceral terror that the gassing, gasps, and tumult of the women had evoked up until that point.

Hannah awakes on her bed with her parents and relatives standing around her. The black-and-white shot of her regaining consciousness while still wearing a modest 1930s-style dress gradually becomes colorized. The scene refers the audience to Dorothy's miraculous return from Oz as she comes out of the coma induced by being hit on the head by debris during the tornado. Upon seeing her aunt, she calls her Rivka instead of Eva. Astounded that Hannah knows her childhood name, Eva shows her niece a photograph that was taken of the two girls shortly before the German troops occupied their shtetl. Hanna vows to her aunt that she will never forget the Holocaust.

The closing scene returns to the dinner table for the conclusion of the seder. Hannah joins the family in a rousing rendition of the Passover song "Chad Gad Yad." Whereas Dorothy discovers that there's no place like home, Hannah has expanded her concept of home and family to include all Jewish people, their traditions, and the Six Million, whose martyrdom she had witnessed.

The cultivation of Jewish identity distinguishes *The Devil's Arithmetic* from most children's movies about the Holocaust. Such films usually emphasize universal themes that appeal to a wider audience. *Alan and Naomi* is about friendship, *Swing Kids* about adolescent nonconformity, and *The Island on Bird Street* about resourcefulness. When being Jewish is a central issue, it is depicted as the source of unjust discrimination rather than the fulcrum of one's ethnic or religious identity. For example, in *I Love You, I Love You Not* (1996), Daisy eventually asserts her Jewish identity as a act of solidarity with her survivor grandmother rather than an expression of religious conviction.[70]

The Devil's Arithmetic differs from these other movies because many of the people involved in its production considered it a tribute to the lost world of European Jewry, as well as a warning against contemporary racism. Yolen recalls that she used to be like Hannah, oblivious to the significance of Passover and the traumatic impact the Holocaust had had on older members of her family.[71] Screenwriter Robert Avrech, a former rabbinical student, has authored several movies about neo-Nazis, as well as *A Stranger among Us* (1992), a murder mystery set in a Hasidic community.[72] Deitch established her reputation as a director by making films that portray minority groups like the lesbian couple in *Desert Hearts* (1985), the African American women in *The Women of Brewster Place* (1989), and homosexuals in an anthology of three short films called *Common Ground* (2000). She has credited the research she did for *The Devil's Arithmetic* with deepening her awareness of her own Jewish roots.[73] Mimi Rogers believed the movie would strengthen family ties, Jewish identity, and the memory of Jewish relatives who perished in the Holocaust.[74]

Honored with awards for children's literature and television, *The Devil's Arithmetic* has become a standard introductory work for teens learning about the Holocaust.[75] Both the book and the movie have benefited from new communications technologies and the increased emphasis on the Holocaust and cultural diversity in private and public education. The film has been made available to schools through Showtime's Cable in the Classroom system. Students can download a study guide to the movie from Showtime's website.[76] *The Devil's Arithmetic* has become a favorite assignment to stimulate discussions among high school students about religious minorities, prejudice, female role models, and tolerance. Although, as Dustin Hoffman asserts, it hardly treats the death camp scenes "with kid gloves," the film only received a parental-guidance warning when it was issued on video.[77]

The glib dialog and unbelievable plotline of the book and movie will undoubtedly offend many Holocaust scholars. They will shudder as Hannah chatters about contemporary American habits in response to the cruelty meted out to her concentration camp inmates. Hungering for an extra morsel of bread, she lifts the spirits of her friends by describing how delicious pizza and cheeseburgers are. Catching herself in a faux pas, she realizes that cheeseburgers are not kosher and her religiously devout peers might prefer veggie burgers. Yet, incongruous slips like this entertain teen viewers, just as they have in other time-travel movies like the *Back to the Future* (1985, 1989, 1990) trilogy.

Imagining oneself in such a terrifying situation has pedagogic value, despite the disparity between a student's idea of the Holocaust and the extremity of the event. The time-travel formula informs the recent play and novel *Anne Frank and Me*. The latter's suburban heroine returns from meeting Anne Frank in Auschwitz and earnestly warns her sister, "We could have been in the Holocaust. You and me. Anne Frank could have been a friend of ours."[78] Confident of how appealing this plot device is to its intended audience, Yolen has proclaimed, "The video is a Blockbuster staple. I expect Showtime will play it every Passover."[79] The novel and the movie based on it respect the double-narrative convention of exposing the audience to the inhumanity of the Holocaust while ending the story on a more positive note.

THE SILVER LINING: *MIRACLE AT MIDNIGHT*
Directed by Ken Cameron
(United States: Davis Entertainment, Disney Educational, 1998)

> In those dark days of the cruel war and the Nazi regime's overpowering deeds of horror, a ray of light appeared. The brotherhood of nations and the dignity of man were turned into rapid and courageous action by two Nordic peoples—conquered Denmark and neutral Sweden.[80]
>
> —Leni Yahil

In *Exodus* (1960), Otto Preminger's epic film about Israel's War of Independence, two teenagers embody the opposite experiences of Jews during the Holocaust. Dov, a darkly complexioned young man, angrily seeks revenge for his internment in Auschwitz. He joins the terrorist Irgun. Karen, nicknamed the "child of light" for her light blond hair, fair skin, and sunny disposition, hails from Denmark. She chides the embittered Dov for his nihilism and reminds him that in her country, the king donned the yellow star in sympathy with the Jews, and his subjects emulated him by helping their Jews flee to neutral Sweden. Although the legend of King Christian is apocryphal, Auschwitz and Denmark symbolize the most vicious and virtuous aspects of human nature.[81]

The exceptional response of the Danes in foiling the German attempt to arrest and deport the Jews in their country in one surprise raid inherently possesses the uplifting message that parents want their children to take away from the films they watch. An evil regime targets an innocent group of victims, and decent people do not waver in affording them protection and sanctuary. The drama of a tiny nation outsmarting a military giant had been dramatized in religious television programs as early as the 1960s and inspired two Danish American productions, *The Only Way* (1970) and *A Day in October* (1991).[82]

The enduring popularity of Lois Lowry's *Number the Stars* (1989) illustrates the appeal of the rescue of Danish Jewry to juvenile audiences. Its annual sales have placed it in the top thousand titles carried by Barnes and Noble since its publication.[83] A winner of the prestigious Newberry Award for Children's Literature, its commercial success has been sustained by the fact that it is probably the most assigned book about the Holocaust for pupils aged nine through twelve. Thus, there are numerous guides for teaching Lowry's novel to middle school students.[84]

When Disney Studios chose to produce a feature film about the rescue of Danish Jewry for broadcast on its prime-time network series *The Wonderful World of Disney*, it must have been aware of how this subject resonated with its target audience and promoted moral values that parents appreciated too. The screener sent to video stores touted the movie as "an inspiring true story that's perfect for the whole family" and promised them that it would "lift profits with an inspirational story."[85]

The casting of *Miracle at Midnight* contributed to the impression that it would be a wholesome movie. From his roles in *The Killing Fields* (1984) and the television series *I'll Fly Away* (1991–1993) and *Law and Order* (1994–2005), the male lead, Sam Waterston, has usually played compassionate and principled characters. Although Mia Farrow's private life, particularly her messy divorce from Woody Allen, had tarnished her reputation, she began to refurbish it in 1997 in an interview aired on ABC's *20/20* and in her memoir published the following year.[86] Justin Whalin, who plays Farrow and Waterston's teenage son who joins the Danish underground, also evokes viewer associations with innocence from his previous role as Jimmy Olsen on the television series *Lois and Clark* (1994–1997). As Graeme Turner has observed, "Often the power of the star to carry contributory meanings relieves the script of the burden of constructing a complex character."[87]

The film opens with a map of Denmark with swastikas drawn inside its borders to indicate that it is under German control. Black-and-white stills of everyday life in wartime Denmark segue into a live, colored scene of Else and Hendrik Koster walking to school and passing beneath a Nazi banner. A German guard stops Hendrik and searches his backpack for weapons and contraband literature. He explains that the security check has been prompted by an attack mounted by a young Danish saboteur the night before. For youngsters who have read *Number the Stars*, this incident resembles how the heroine, Annemarie, and her Jewish friend, Ellen, are frisked by a German soldier due to a recent bombing by the Resistance. Both scenes reveal how the Germans violated the boundaries between childhood and adulthood.[88]

Soon thereafter, Hendrik is brandishing a pistol and tossing a Molotov cocktail at the Germans. During the ensuing gun battle, a fellow resister is wounded and then brought to the hospital. The emergency room physician is Hendrik's father, Karl. He treats the boy but falsifies the medical report to allay German suspicions. Although not aware of his son's involvement in the underground, Dr. Koster becomes implicated in the conspiracy against German rule by harboring the wounded fugitive. It is only when the Koster family invites their Jewish neighbors to hide in their apartment that he discovers his son has been engaged in resistance activities. The parallel with the plot of *Number the Stars* is striking. After helping Ellen and her family to embark on the fishing boat that will carry them to Sweden, Annemarie learns that her deceased sister and the young man to whom she was betrothed were members of the Resistance.[89]

The action then shifts to German headquarters. The military presence is massive. The fireplace in the office of the SS plenipotentiary, Werner Best, is flanked by Nazi banners with a decorative German eagle perched on a swastika above the mantle. Best boasts to his businessman friend Georg Duckwitz that now that martial law has been imposed on Denmark, the time is ripe to deport the Jews. The movie creates the impression that this operation will go smoothly because Best is so decisive and has such a large army contingent at his disposal. This enhances the dramatic effect of the David-versus-Goliath theme but overlooks the special circumstances enabling the Danes to rescue almost all of the Jews in their country. Since Denmark surrendered in two hours and acceded to Germany's initial political and economic demands, only a token

German force was stationed there. Best never received the number of SS men he had requested to conduct the raid against the Jews and lacked full cooperation from the army. Duckwitz warned the Jews, and Sweden then offered them sanctuary.[90]

A Mercedes sedan ominously parks in front of the Jewish Community Center, and Gestapo men wearing long black-leather coats descend upon it, breaking down the door and confiscating the membership lists stored there. The Jewish friends of Dr. Koster worry about what this portends for them, and the Duckwitz leak emboldens the chief rabbi to cancel Rosh Hashanah services and to counsel his congregants to vacate their homes and find Danes willing to shelter them until they can be transported to nearby Sweden. The collective crisis is reduced to its individual dimensions in a discussion between Dr. Koster and his wife over whether they should hide their Jewish neighbors. Mrs. Koster objects because it will endanger her family, but Dr. Koster replies with an answer that cuts to the crux of the matter: "How do we live with ourselves if we don't? And what is the message we would give our children?" With this rhetorical question, the made-for-television movie fades for a commercial break.

In both Lowry's book and the Disney film, the dire consequence of not helping their Jewish friends is symbolized by the closing of Jewish shops where Annemarie's and Hendrik's mothers had been regular customers. Annemarie convinces her parents to offer refuge to Ellen after she goes to purchase a button for her little sister at a store and finds that the Germans have boarded its windows and its Jewish owner has vanished.[91] Mrs. Koster still has qualms about helping the Abrams until she goes to pick up clothing she had altered by a Jewish tailor and discovers he has hung himself.

Meanwhile, both her husband and son are organizing their respective forms of resistance, allowing Jews to stay in the hospital until their departure to Sweden, and distributing leaflets urging the Danes to resist German rule. When an SS commandant comes to the hospital to visit a wounded German soldier, the Jews disguised as patients attend a funeral ceremony in the chapel and pretend they are Christians. Lowry also has her characters stage a phony wake at the coastal home of Annemarie's uncle, which serves as a halfway house for Jews who will soon board boats to Sweden.[92]

When the Germans suspect Dr. Koster of assisting the Jews, they return to search his house. This time they discover the door to the attic where the Abrams family had slept before leaving for Sweden. Lying on the floor is the sole vestige of the Kosters's stay in the room, a necklace with a gold Jewish star that Anna Abrams had dropped during her hasty departure. Koster's daughter nonchalantly places her foot over the incriminating piece of jewelry and subsequently stuffs it into one of her dolls. Lowry's Annemarie grabs a similar necklace from Ellen when the Nazis are inspecting her house and keeps it in her possession to return to her after the war. Indeed, the cover illustration on Lowry's book is a photo of a girl's face beside a necklace with a Jewish star pendant.[93]

The climactic scenes of the book and movie allude to *Little Red Riding Hood*. Annemarie imagines herself as the fairy-tale heroine as she walks alone through the forest carrying a basket containing a handkerchief with a chemical mixture invented by the underground to numb the noses of German police dogs.[94] When Mrs. Koster and her daughter go to rendezvous with Dr. Koster, she wears a bright red coat. This probably reminds adults of the girl roaming through the massacre in *Schindler's List* and youngsters of Annemarie's identification with Red Riding Hood. Holding a suitcase rather than a basket, Mrs. Koster proceeds separately to allow her daughter to join her father while the Gestapo follows and arrests her instead. The German wolf fails to catch its prey as Dr. Koster and his daughter catch a boat to Sweden in the closing scene.

To make the story more exciting, *Miracle at Midnight* features several gun battles between those rescuing the Jews and the Germans. Not only do these scenes detract from the largely nonviolent nature of the Danish rescue operation,[95] but they also contradict the noble sentiments expressed by key characters. The following snippets of dialog may seem prosaic, but they reflect the motivations the movie attributes to its heroes: "A man must live with himself a long time. If he can do something to ease the terrible ache in this world, he must." "In every language and religion, to be humane is to love your neighbor. People have said, 'You Danes showed enormous courage in that time,' but I think we all felt we only did what was normal."

Miracle at Midnight provides a benign introduction to the Holocaust for younger viewers. It creates an inkling of the threat the Final Solution posed to the Jews without traumatizing its target audience. More importantly, it teaches students that moral options existed even under a brutal dictatorship. The director assumes that many of the children who see the film have read *Number the Stars* and will relate incidents from the book to the movie. Like Lowry's novel, the film has won its share of awards for children's entertainment and is available for classroom use with curricular materials that can be accessed via the Internet.[96] Chastened by the successful opposition to Disney's plans to build an American history theme park, CEO Michael Eisner claimed that his company remained committed to providing educationally enriching programming.[97] *Miracle at Midnight* constitutes a right step in that direction.

NOTES

1. Adrienne Kertzer, *My Mother's Voice: Children, Literature, and the Holocaust* (Peterborough, Canada: Broadview Press, 2002), 74–75. For Kertzer's most recent discussion of Holocaust children's literature, see Adrienne Kertzer, "The Problem of Childhood: Children's Literature and Holocaust Representation," in *Teaching the Representation of the Holocaust,* ed. Marianne Hirsch and Irene Kacandes (New York: Modern Language Association, 2004), 250–61.

2. Eric Kimmel, "Confronting the Ovens: The Holocaust and Juvenile Fiction," *Horn Book Magazine* 53, no. 1 (February 1977): 84–91.

3. Diane K. Roskies, *Teaching the Holocaust to Children: A Review and Bibliography* (New York: KTAV, 1975); Rona Sheramy, "Defining Lessons: Holocaust Education and American Jewish Youth from World War II to the Present," (PhD diss., Brandeis University, 2000).

4. Karen Shawn, "Choosing Holocaust Literature for Early Adolescents," in *Teaching and Studying the Holocaust,* ed. Samuel Totten and Stephen Feinberg (Boston: Allyn and Bacon, 2001), 149; Simone Schweber and Gloria Ladson-Billings, *Making Sense of the Holocaust: Lessons from Classroom Practice* (New York: Teachers College Press, 2004).

5. David L. Russell, "Reading the Shards and Fragments: Holocaust Literature for Young Readers, *The Lion and the Unicorn* 21, no. 2 (1997): 267–80; Edward T. Sullivan, *The Holocaust in Literature for Youth: A Guide and Resource Book* (Lanham, MD: Scarecrow Press, 1999), Elizabeth R. Baer, "A New Algorithm in Evil: Children's Literature in a Post-Holocaust World," *The Lion and the Unicorn* 24, no. 3 (September 2000): 379–401.

6. Cary Bazalgette and Terry Staples, "Unshrinking the Kids: Children's Cinema and the Family Film," in *In Front of the Children: Screen Entertainment and Young Audiences,* ed. Cary Bazalgette and David Buckingham (London: British Film Institute, 1995), 92.

7. Anthony Breznigan, "PG-13 Remade Hollywood Ratings System," *Associated Press,* August 23, 2004.

8. Sharon Waxman, "Study Finds Film Ratings Are Growing More Lenient," *New York Times,* July 14, 2004.

9. Shawn, "Choosing Holocaust Literature," 142–44.

10. Jeffrey Shandler, *While America Watches: Televising the Holocaust* (New York: Oxford University Press, 1999), 62–64.

11. Of the sixty-five children's films about the Holocaust made between 1952 and 1999, thirteen focus on Anne Frank's life or cite the diary.

12. Kertzer, *My Mother's Voice,* 109–41.

13. Shandler, *While America Watches,* 61–69; Jeffrey Shandler and Elihu Katz, "Broadcasting American Judaism: The Radio and Television Department of the Jewish Theological Seminary," in *Tradition Reviewed: A History of the Jewish Theological Seminary,* ed. Jack Wertheimer (New York: New York Theological Seminary, 1997), 363–481.

14. *Nightmare: The Immigration of Joachim and Rachel,* directed by Tim Roberson (United States, 1978). Lillian Polus Gerstner, *Films on the Holocaust for Students: An An-*

notated Videography of Suggested Viewing for Grade 4 through High School (Skokie, IL: Holocaust Memorial Foundation of Illinois, 2002), 17.

15. *Conspiracy of Hearts,* directed by Robert Mulligan (United States, 1956); *The Diary of Anne Frank,* directed by Alex Segal (United States, 1967).

16. *Me and the Colonel,* directed by Peter Glenville (United States, 1958).

17. *A Friendship in Vienna,* directed by Arthur Allan Seidelman (United States, 1988); Doris Orgel, *The Devil in Vienna* (New York: Dial Press, 1978); Lawrence Baron, "Not In Kansas Anymore: Holocaust Films for Children," *The Lion and the Unicorn* 27, no. 3 (September 2003): 396–98.

18. *Swing Kids,* directed by Thomas Carter (United States, 1993).

19. *Miracle at Midnight,* directed by Ken Cameron (United States, 1998).

20. See Ian Wojcik-Andrews, *Children's Films: History, Ideology, Pedagogy, Theory* (New York: Garland, 2000), 7–16.

21. *The Bookseller,* directed by Martin Hoade (United States, 1962); *The Only Way,* directed by Bent Christensen (Denmark, 1970); *A Day in October,* directed by Kenneth Madsen (Denmark, 1992).

22. *The Hiding Place,* directed by James F. Collier (United States, 1975).

23. *Snow Treasure,* directed by Irving Jacoby (United States, 1968); *The Lucky Star,* directed by Max Fischer (Canada, 1980); *Sarah and the Squirrel,* directed by Yoran Gross and Athol Henry (Australia and Israel, 1982).

24. Douglas Street, "Introduction," in *Children's Novels and the Movies,* ed. Douglas Street (New York: Frederick Ungar, 1983), xvii–xxiv.

25. Peter Novick, *The Holocaust in American Life* (Boston: Houghton Mifflin, 1999), 146–203.

26. Alan Mintz, *Popular Culture and the Shaping of Holocaust Memory in America* (Seattle: University of Washington Press, 2001), 157.

27. Maureen Turim, *Flashbacks in Film* (New York: Routledge, 1989), 231.

28. Myron Levoy, *Alan and Naomi* (New York: Harper and Row, 1977).

29. Levoy, *Alan and Naomi,* 21.

30. Levoy, *Alan and Naomi,* 149.

31. *The Chosen,* directed by Jeremy Paul Kagan (United States, 1981).

32. Lester Friedman, *Jewish Image in American Film: 70 Years of Hollywood's Vision of Jewish Characters and Themes* (Secaucus, NJ: Citadel Press, 1987), 243–45.

33. Levoy, *Alan and Naomi,* 150.

34. Andrew Wyeth, *Christina's World* (1948), Museum of Modern Art, New York.

35. "Awards," *Alan and Naomi,* at www.imdb.com; "*Alan and Naomi,*" at www.top-videos.de/archiv/daten/vd/v2/htm (accessed September 11, 2002).

36. Rita Kempley, "*Alan and Naomi,*" *Washington Post,* January 31, 1992.

37. Kathleen Maher, "*Alan and Naomi,*" *Austin Chronicle,* April 24, 1992.

38. "Business Data," *Alan and Naomi,* at www.imdb.com. It grossed only $257, 311.

39. "Alan and Naomi," "Carol Hurst's Children Literature Site," at www.carolhurst.com/titles/alanandnaomi.html (accessed September 20, 2002).

40. See Don Latham, "Childhood under Siege: Lois Lowry's *Number the Stars* and *The Giver,*" *The Lion and the Unicorn* 26, no. 1 (January 2002): 1–13.

41. Thomas Doherty, *Teenagers and Teenpics: The Juvenilization of American Movies in the 1950s* (Boston: Unwin Hyman, 1988), 87.

42. Doherty, *Teenagers and Teenpics*, 41–104.

43. Marc Miller, "Of Tunes and Toons: The Movie Musical in the 1990s," in *Film Genre 2000: New Critical Essays,* ed. Wheeler Winston Dixon (Albany: State University Press of New York, 2000), 45–62.

44. "A History of Swing," at www.unh.edu/hepcats/history.html (accessed September 28, 2002).

45. Frank Maloney, "Newsgroup Reviews," *Swing Kids,* 1993, at www.imdb.com (accessed September 28, 2002).

46. Detlev Peukert "Youth in the Third Reich," in *Life in the Third Reich,* ed. Richard Bessel (New York: Oxford University Press, 1987), 25–40; Michael Meyer, *The Politics of Music in the Third Reich* (New York: Peter Lang, 1991); Michael H. Kater, *Different Drummers: Jazz in the Culture of Nazi Germany* (New York: Oxford University Press, 1992).

47. Roger Ebert, *"Swing Kids,"* *Chicago Sun-Times*, March 5, 1993.

48. "Bei Mir Bist Du Schoen," at www.yiddishradioproject.org/exhibits/ymis/ymis.php3?pg=2 (accessed September 28, 2002).

49. "Otis Sallid," at www.imdb.com.

50. "Jerzy Zielinski," at www.imdb.com.

51. Frank Maloney, *"Swing Kids* (1993)," http://us.imdb.com/reviews/18/1805 (accessed September 28, 2002).

52. Uri Orlev, *The Island on Bird Street,* trans. Hillel Halkin (Boston: Houghton Mifflin, 1984), xi.

53. *Robinson Crusoe on Mars,* directed by Bryon Haskin (United States, 1964); *Robinson Crusoe,* directed by Rod K. Hardy (United States, 1998); Martin Green, *The Robinson Crusoe Story* (University Station: Pennsylvania State University Press, 1990). "Robinson Crusoe," title search, www.imdb.com (accessed June 14, 2005).

54. *The Island on Bird Street* won the Mildred L. Batchelder Award and the Association of Jewish Libraries Best Book Award. On the use of his book in Holocaust courses, see Marilyn Henry, "Sharing Life in the Shadow of Death," *Internet Jerusalem Post,* May 1, 2000.

55. Astrid Söderbergh Widding, "Denmark," in *Nordic National Cinemas,* ed. Tytti Soili, Astrid Söderberg Widding, and Gunnar Iverson (New York: Routledge, 1998), 28–29.

56. *Drengene Fra Sankt Petri,* directed by Søren Kragh-Jacobsen (Denmark, Finland, Norway, Sweden, 1991), at www.imdb.com.

57. Søren Kragh-Jacobsen, quoted in Jørn Rossing Jensen, "Øen i fuglegaden," at www.filmfestivals.com/berlin97/bfilmd21.htm (accessed October 10, 2002).

58. "From the Critics," *The Island on Bird Street,* at www.bn.com (accessed October 10, 2002).

59. Orlev, *The Island,* 1–14.

60. Orlev, *The Island,* 96–105.

61. Orlev, *The Island,* x–xi, 163.

62. Andrew J. Horton, "Hiding from Good and Evil," *Central Europe Review* 22 (February 22, 1998).

63. Karen Shawn, "Choosing Holocaust Literature," 41; Simone Schweber, "Teaching Your Children about the Holocaust" (paper presented at the Association for Jewish Studies Conference, Chicago, Illinois, December 2004).

64. Uri Orlev, *The Lead Soldiers*, trans. Hillel Halkin (New York: Taplinger, 1980).

65. Michael Fox, "Eloquent Film Depicts Boy's Survival in Polish Ghetto," *Jewish Bulletin of Northern California* (December 11, 1998).

66. "Awards," and "Release Dates," *The Island on Bird Street*, at www.imdb.com; "*The Island on Bird Street*," at www.filmadvisoryboard.org/aoe/detail.asp?titleID=51 (accessed October 9, 2002).

67. Jane Yolen, *The Devil's Arithmetic* (New York: Viking, 1988), 51.

68. Yolen, *The Devil's Arithmetic*, 156.

69. Yolen, *The Devil's Arithmetic*, 160.

70. *I Love You, I Love You Not,* directed by Billy Hopkins (France, Germany, United Kingdom, United States, 1996). See Kevin Thomas's review, *Los Angeles Times*, October 31, 1997.

71. Yolen, *The Devil's Arithmetic*, 167–70.

72. "Robert J. Avrech," at www.imdb.com.

73. Barbara Pepe, "Ten Years Gone," *The Advocate* (August 20, 1996); Gail Shister, "A Gay *Our Town*," *The Advocate* (February 1, 2000); Debra Wallace, "*The Devil's Arithmetic* Depicts a Surreal View of the Holocaust," *Jewish Bulletin of Northern California* (March 26, 1999).

74. Hillary Atkin, "A Teen's View of the Holocaust: A Project of Passion for Actress/Executive Producer Mimi Rogers," at www.generationj.com/archive/culture/holocaust2.html (accessed October 18, 2002); "*The Devil's Arithmetic*," Cable TCA Press Tour (Pasadena, CA: Showtime, 1999).

75. "Awards," "Jane Yolen Home Page," at www.janeyolen.com/janeawards2.html (accessed October 18, 2002); "Awards," *The Devil's Arithmetic*, at www.imdb.com (accessed October 18, 2002).

76. "Cable in the Classroom," at www.sho.com/cic/html (accessed October 26, 2002).

77. "The *Devil's Arithmetic* Unit," at www.homepages.wmich.edu (accessed October 26, 2002); "The Devil's Arithmetic: Cable TCA Press Tour" (Pasadena, CA: Showtime, 1999).

78. Cherie Bennett and Jeff Gottesfeld, *Anne Frank and Me* (New York: G. P. Putnam's Sons, 2001), 282. For a discussion of how alternate historical narratives, like time-travel stories, may distract from the real history of the Holocaust or trivialize it, see Gavriel Rosenfeld, *The World Hitler Never Made* (New York: Cambridge University Press, 2005), 385–95.

79. Jane Yolen, "Movies Made from My Books and Stories," at www.janeyolen.com/movies.html (accessed October 20, 2002).

80. Leni Yahil, *The Rescue of Danish Jewry: Test of a Democracy*, trans. Morris Gradel (Philadelphia: Jewish Publication Society, 1969), xi.

81. *Exodus,* directed by Otto Preminger (United States, 1960).

82. Carol Rittner, "Denmark 1943: A Documentary Discussion Guide to the Rescue of Denmark's Jews," *Dimensions: A Journal of Holocaust Studies* 7, no. 3 (1993).

83. Lois Lowry, *Number the Stars* (Boston: Houghton Mifflin, 1989).

84. Tara McCarthy, *Literature Circle Guide: Number the Stars* (Danbury, CT: Scholastic Professional Book Division, 2002); Q. L. Pearce, *Literature Notes for Number the Stars* (Torrance, CA: Frank Schaeffer Publications, 2001); Joel D. Chaston, *Lois Lowry* (New York: Twayne, 1997).

85. *Miracle at Midnight*, directed by Ken Cameron (United States, 1998), demo tape, back cover.

86. Mia Farrow, *What Falls Away: A Memoir* (New York: Bantam Books, 1998).

87. Graeme Turner, *Film as Social Practice,* 2nd ed. (New York: Routledge, 199), 105.

88. Lowry, *Number the Stars,* 2–9; Latham, "Childhood under Siege," 3–8.

89. Lowry, *Number the Stars,* 120–30.

90. Yahil, *The Rescue,* 31–83, 147–222; Jørgen Hæstrup, "The Danish Jews and the German Occupation," in *The Rescue of Danish Jewry: Moral Courage under Stress,* ed. Leo Goldberger (New York: New York University Press, 1987), 13–53.

91. Lowry, *Number the Stars,* 18–26.

92. Lowry, *Number the Stars,* 67–87.

93. Lowry, *Number the Stars,* 45–49, 131–32.

94. Lowry, *Number the Stars,* 106–27, 135–36.

95. Yahil, *The Rescue,* 280–82.

96. "Awards," *Miracle at Midnight,* at www.imdb.com; "*Miracle at Midnight*," EduStation/Video Corner, at www.disney.go.com/educational/video-jan.html (accessed October 26, 2002).

97. Mike Wallace, "Disney's America," in *Mickey Mouse History and Other Essays on American Memory* (Philadelphia: Temple University Press, 1996), 160–73.

· 7 ·

Relevant Remembrances:
Themes in Recent Holocaust Movies

NEO-NAZIS AS HOLOCAUST GHOSTS:
ROSENZWEIG'S FREEDOM
Directed by Liliane Targownik
(Germany: Südwestfunk, 1998)

Images taken from and inspired by the Third Reich saturate our culture functioning as concrete representations of that specific historical era, free-floating signifiers of universal evil, and for some, emblems of purity, power, and erotic fascination.[1]

—Lester D. Friedman

$\mathcal{D}$uring the 1990s, stories about neo-Nazis outnumbered all other themes in feature films dealing with the Holocaust. Although the Holocaust is not their primary focus, these films associate the event with white supremacists by depicting their admiration for Hitler, espousal of racist doctrines, and displays of Nazi symbols like the swastika. This linkage implies that neo-Nazis are potential perpetrators of genocide (see table 7.1).

In American and British movies produced in the postwar period, neo-Nazis appeared as die-hard supporters of Hitler, conspiring to overthrow the Allied occupation of Germany or seize world power by devising diabolical schemes from remote regions where they had fled after 1945.[2] Samuel Fuller's *Verboten* (1958) and Ronald Neame's *The ODESSA File* (1974) epitomize the first scenario. In Fuller's film, the German wife of an American soldier forces her neo-Nazi brother to attend the Nuremberg Trials and watch the atrocity footage filmed at the liberated concentration camps in which the American prosecutor accuses the defendants of "the premeditated destruction of an entire people."[3] *The ODESSA File* forges the connection to the Holocaust with

Table 7.1.   Relevant Remembrance: Common Themes of Holocaust Feature Films

Decade	1st	2nd	3rd	4th
1945–1949	DPs (10)	War criminals (8)	Resistance (6)	POW camps (3) KZ camps* (3)
1950s	Resistance (13)	Rescue (11)	Mixed couples (9)	Survivors (9)
1960s	Rescue (14)	Survivors (13)	KZ (12)	Trials (11)
1970s	Perpetrators (21)	Persecution** (17)	Resistance (15)	Survivors (13)
1980s	Rescue (30)	Neo-Nazism (26)	Survivors (24)	Persecution (23)
1990s	Neo-Nazism (38)	Rescue (27)	Survivors (24)	Second generation (23)

* KZ = concentration/death camps
** Persecution = anti-Semitic discrimination, ghettoization, deportation

a grisly black-and-white flashback of the gassings and shootings of Jews in Riga ordered by an officer who returned to West Germany under a false identity furnished by the SS network ODESSA.[4]

Since the Soviet Union replaced Germany as the archenemy of the United States, American directors initially marginalized the significance of neo-Nazism by relegating its proponents to escapist science fiction and horror movies. The fiendish villains of these pictures withdraw to distant islands or jungle compounds where they plotted to conquer the world.[5] Most of these films are potboilers, like *They Saved Hitler's Brain* (1963).[6]

The Boys from Brazil (1978) represents an exception to this rule.[7] Directed by Franklin Schaffner, it stars Gregory Peck as Dr. Josef Mengele and Laurence Olivier as Ezra Liebermann, a Nazi-hunter modeled after Simon Wiesenthal. Operating from his refuge in Paraguay, Mengele creates ninety-four clones of Hitler and places the boys in families with a doting mother and a domineering father like Hitler's. When they reach adolescence, the doctor dispatches assassins to murder their fathers, thereby replicating the paternal loss Hitler suffered when he was a teen. Liebermann discerns the pattern of the killings and tries to prevent the next one. He corners Mengele, who is mauled to death by guard dogs in the scuffle. Liebermann refuses to provide a list of names of the clones to a Jewish vigilante to avert the killing of innocent children.[8]

While British films treated neo-Nazism as a viable political threat in West Germany, few American films took the movement seriously until the 1980s. The only depiction of fascism triumphing in the United States occurred in the alternate-future TV movie *Shadow on the Land* (1968).[9] American films typified neo-Nazis as deeply disturbed individuals, like Bobby Darin's psychotic character in *Pressure Point* (1962) or the vicious motorcycle gang members in *The Tormentors* (1971).[10] As table 7.2 indicates, American movies usually situated neo-Nazi cabals in remote places or in the future.[11]

Table 7.2.   Feature Films about Neo-Nazis, 1945–1979

Countries	United States 21			United Kingdom 5		Austria 1
Settings	U.S.	Future	Europe	Remote	Europe	Remote	Austria
	8	2	3	8	5	0	1

In the 1980s, the activities of neo-Nazis became the second most recurrent theme in films referencing the Holocaust, and by the 1990s, they provided the most common plotline in such movies. This preoccupation with white supremacist movements can be traced to two developments. The first reflects the resurgence of right-wing extremism in Australia, Europe, and the United States. Militants from the radical right engaged in terrorist attacks against racially diverse societies. Their violent activities proved a popular topic for docudramas dealing with current social problems.

Symbolic confrontations like the attempt of members of the American National Socialist Party to march through the predominantly Jewish suburb of Skokie, Illinois, the lawsuit filed by Holocaust survivor Mel Mermelstein against the Institute for Historical Review for failing to honor its offer of a cash reward to anyone who could prove that Jews were gassed at Auschwitz, and the campaign to fire a Canadian high school teacher who denied the Holocaust ever happened attracted much media attention and served as the bases of made-for-TV movies.[12] The rise of racist skinhead groups in England spread to other countries where working-class whites blamed multinational corporations, Jewish financiers, and immigrant laborers from Third World countries for lower salaries and higher crime and unemployment rates. In the United States, the spate of foreclosures on small family farms in the early 1980s spawned rural cells training for armed struggle against a global conspiracy purportedly led by Jewish bankers, the mass media, and internationalists. Eventually, such beliefs motivated a wave of terrorist acts that culminated in the bombing of the Murrah Federal Building in Oklahoma City in 1995.[13]

In the same period, the major television networks, cable movie stations like HBO, and independent filmmakers produced more movies for broadcast or direct distribution to video stores. Employing the docudrama format, these films portrayed recent events or social issues that were presumably familiar to target audiences. When these films "ripped from the headlines" did well in the ratings, movie studios in other countries emulated the trend.[14] Table 7.3 demonstrates how this shift in cinematic formats paralleled the increase in the production of films about neo-Nazi activities.

Some of the movies produced in the 1990s still portrayed neo-Nazis as fantasy figures, like the Aryan sprites in *Elves* (1990) or the fascist skating gang that menaces an earthquake-ravaged Los Angeles in *Prayer of the Rollerboys*

Table 7.3.   Neo-Nazi Films: Countries of Origins, Venues, Factuality

Years	Country	Theatrical Releases	TV/Cable	Video	True Story	Social Problem	Fiction
1945–1979	US 19	20	5	N/A	2	7	16
N = 25	UK 5						
1980–1989	US 14	9	7	5	6	7	8
N = 21	UK 4						
1990–1999	US 21	18	12	8	10	16	12
N = 38	GER 6						

(1991).[15] The majority of recent films with this theme, however, treat neo-Nazis as dangerous militants perpetrating racially motivated assaults on minority groups or training for paramilitary operations against the United States or American allies. Films like *Midnight Murders* (1991), *The Best of the Best 3* (1995), and *Brotherhood of Murder* (1999) are action movies about heroic loners or law-enforcement officers infiltrating groups suspected of planning attacks on government agencies or minority groups. These films climax in fiercely fought showdowns with the extremists.[16]

The other genre for handling this subject matter is the social-problem movie, which explores the private and public roots of racist rage.[17] The best-known example is *American History X* (1998). Embittered by the murder of his father by a black and the deterioration of his neighborhood, Derek, a charismatic skinhead, galvanizes his white cohorts to engage in turf battles with the ethnic and racial minorities who have moved into the area. He blames the eroding status of working-class whites on affirmative action, the laxness of prosecuting illegal aliens, and the welfare system. Convicted of the brutal killing of two African American teens caught stealing his truck, Derek continues his fight inside the penitentiary by allying himself with white supremacist inmates. When he denounces them for trafficking in drugs, they retaliate by raping him in the shower stalls. A black prisoner befriends him and arranges for the black prisoners to protect Derek from further attacks. Upon his parole, Derek sheds his neo-Nazi identity by pulling down the Nazi banners and Hitler posters hung on his bedroom wall and warning his brother to sever his ties with the skinheads.[18] The references to the Holocaust in *American History X* taint skinhead racism by linking it to Nazi genocide.

German motion pictures about neo-Nazis mirror the upsurge in xenophobic violence against asylum seekers, immigrant workers, and Jews that erupted in the wake of German reunification in 1989 and peaked in 1993.[19] The asymmetrical economic development between West and East Germany led to higher taxes in the former and unemployment in the latter. Germany's liberal postwar immigration policies opened its borders to refugees from former Eastern Bloc countries and immigrants from Africa, Asia, and southern

Europe seeking work or asylum there. With the collapse of the Soviet Union, American cultural hegemony became unchallenged. The growing influence of multinational corporations in the global economy and the outsourcing of jobs to cheaper labor markets in the Third World worsened the economic opportunities for un- or underemployed Germans. Finally, external funding and computer networking fostered transnational cooperation among radical right-wing groups in Europe, North America, and Australia. Germany's belated crackdown on neo-Nazi agitators emboldened them to escalate their assaults on foreigners and Jews.[20]

Although advertised with the tagline "Germany Is out of Control," Christoph Schlingensief's *Terror 2000* (1992) quickly degenerates into gratuitous violence and crude sexuality, with the police and the foreign asylum seekers acting as depraved and racist as their neo-Nazi persecutors. The culprits guilty for a crime spree against immigrants and the social workers assigned to their cases consist of a sadomasochistic Catholic priest, a local sheriff dressed like the bigoted southern marshal from *In the Heat of the Night*, and a hooded member of the Ku Klux Klan (KKK). Armed with rifles, they scour the environs of the village of Rassau, a conflation of the German words for "race" and "pig," maiming and killing the Africans, Jews, Poles, and transvestites they encounter. Consistently mixing his metaphors, Schlingensief shows this motley bunch burning a wooden swastika KKK-style at the gates of the refugee shelter. Schlingensief makes it impossible to empathize with the victims, who appear lazy, promiscuous, superstitious, or ungrateful. The police officer pursuing the neo-Nazis dons a swastika armband to stalk a woman he raped while on a past case. His female partner naively asks, "Where does all this hate come from?" The movie identifies the source in human nature rather than German history.[21]

Fortunately, several German documentaries and feature films have related their nation's Nazi past to the outpouring of violence against asylum seekers, guest workers, and Jews. Thomas Heise's *Now It's Boiling Over* (1992) records the conversations and activities of a skinhead gang in Halle. Subsidized by several provincial governments, Winfried Bonengel's *Occupation Neo-Nazi* aims to undercut the appeal of neo-Nazism by interviewing its exponents, who spout implausible conspiracy theories and vehement racist opinions. Both films sparked charges that they inadvertently abetted neo-Nazi hate mongering.[22] Ralf Huettner's *The Parrot* (1992) satirizes how easily a respectable salesman succumbs to the simplistic campaign rhetoric of a neo-Nazi politician.[23] German television aired a collection of short films assembled under the title *New Germany* (1993). *Without Me*, the segment directed by Dani Levi, echoes the postwar rationale of Germans who claimed that they never actively supported Hitler, therefore bore no responsibility for the sins of the Third Reich. The title of the compilation raised the question whether the new Germany really differed from the old Germany.[24]

Liliane Targownik's *Rosenzweig's Freedom* (1998) employs a murder-mystery scenario to show the persistence of anti-Semitism in German society and how the Holocaust continues to exert an influence on the children of survivors. On the evening when a refugee shelter is set ablaze by neo-Nazis, Michael Rosenzweig, the outraged Jewish lover of a Vietnamese woman who is a resident of the facility, grabs a revolver and fires randomly into the crowd. Minutes later, someone assassinates a neo-Nazi leader in a home located within walking distance of the shelter. Since the bullets from Michael's gun match those lodged in the slain neo-Nazi, the prosecutor charges Michael with homicide.[25]

Michael has a brother named Jacob. Their parents are Holocaust survivors. Jacob's mother asks him to serve as his brother's attorney. Jacob hesitates because he considers it unprofessional but relents when he disagrees with the temporary-insanity plea lodged by Michael's court-appointed attorney Ahrendt. Michael distrusts Ahrendt, who once belonged to the Hitler Youth. Ahrendt makes several casual anti-Semitic remarks in the course of their conversations. The legacy of the Holocaust weighs heavily on the consciences of the Rosenzweig brothers. It has motivated Jacob to devote much of his practice to prosecuting neo-Nazi hate crimes and probably inclined Michael to fall in love with an asylum seeker who has been a victim of persecution.

Targownik perceives continuities and discontinuities with Nazi anti-Semitism in postwar German society. One scene vividly recalls the burning of a Munich synagogue in 1970 that killed several residents of a senior-citizen center located on its second floor. Documentary footage from a funeral procession honoring an assassinated neo-Nazi leader illustrates the sympathy that exists for neo-Nazi martyrs. The local skinheads play a computer game called "Concentration Camp Manager," which simulates how an SS commandant liquidates Jewish and Turkish inmates in a death camp.[26]

Ahrendt is not a Nazi. His anti-Semitism stems more from common stereotypes than from racist ideology. When Michael remembers that a homeless man witnessed his being beaten by skinheads who took his gun, Jacob enlists Ahrendt's help to track down the vagrant. Based on his testimony, the police drop the murder charges against Michael, who receives only a suspended sentence for reckless endangerment.

The ending of the movie is deliberately ambiguous. Michael and his Vietnamese bride have a joyful Jewish wedding during which skinheads break into the Rosenzweig family's apartment and set fire to it. The flames consume the only keepsake Michael and Jacob have of their siblings who perished in the

Holocaust, their shoes. Targownik explains the mixed message she wanted to convey in this closing scene:

> It won't be paradise for a Jewish-Vietnamese couple to live in Germany, raising a Vietnamese son. It is also necessary for Michael and Jacob that the shrine with those memory shoes is burnt. They'll remember history anyway, but they should not be kept from living their lives by those memories. There will be new children, with new shoes; there will also be new Nazis.[27]

Rosenzweig's Freedom received more exposure and honors than any other recent German film about neo-Nazis. Germany's largest television network broadcast it in 1999. It won the German Trade Union's Gold Prize for Best Television Movie and the Hollywood Film Festival Award for Best Original Feature Film. Targownik, who grew up in Germany but now resides in Israel, admits that she "looks at the events in Germany from a Jewish perspective."[28] The Rosenzweig family is a composite of several German Jewish families she knew personally. She based all of the incidents of right-wing violence on actual events. The mystery plotline enables Jacob to probe how the Holocaust permeates his identity as a child of survivors. When Jacob recalls the arson at the synagogue, he remarks, "I understood for the first time that history is not a story, but is really happening."[29] *Rosenzweig's Freedom* belongs to a new wave of multicultural films directed by asylum seekers, guest workers, and Jews in reunified Germany.[30]

RESCUERS—FROM SAINTS TO SINNERS: *SCHINDLER'S LIST*
Directed by Steven Spielberg
(United States: Amblin Entertainment, Universal Pictures, 1993)

> By representing the Holocaust as an immediate, visually resonant, and dramatic spectacle, *Schindler's List* invites viewers to feel closer to an event that otherwise feels too distant to be responded to with genuine horror.[31]
>
> —Gary Weissman

In his critique "Americanization of the Holocaust," Alvin Rosenfeld cites the increasing prominence of rescuers in popular representations and scholarly studies of the Shoah as "part of a larger cultural quest for religious meaning or what today is loosely called 'spirituality.'" He fears that the centrality of rescuers in recent Holocaust narratives will "obscure how truly horrendous the Holocaust actually was."[32]

Rosenfeld, however, overlooks that the public fascination with the European Gentiles who shielded Jews from the Nazis emerged neither as a recent nor distinctly American development. In the immediate postwar period, interest in altruism in general and the specific individuals who risked their own lives to save Jews already existed. Searching for the psychological and sociological antidotes to the violence that had stained the twentieth century with blood, Pitirim Sorokin wrote four pioneering studies on altruism between 1948 and 1954.[33] Many early accounts of the Holocaust focus on the rescue of the Jews, such as Eric Boehm's *We Survived* (1949), *The Diary of Anne Frank* (1952), Aage Bertelsen's *October '43* (1954), Kurt Grossmann's *Unsung Heroes* (1957), and Philip Friedman's *Their Brothers' Keepers* (1957).[34] These books served a variety of purposes: to establish that there were viable moral alternatives to indifference toward the persecution of the Jews, to restore Jewish trust in Gentiles, to redeem tarnished national identities, and as Bruno Bettelheim pointed out in his critique of *The Diary of Anne Frank*, to mitigate the terrible reality of the Holocaust.[35] The Israeli legislation creating the Holocaust museum Yad Vashem in 1953 mandated the honoring of "Righteous Gentiles" who risked their lives to rescue Jews without any ulterior motives. Systematic research on the individuals who received this recognition commenced in the 1980s.[36]

The drama inherent in Gentile individuals or groups defending Jewish victims against the Third Reich has made this an intriguing topic for feature films since 1945. Be it escaped Allied prisoners of war guiding refugees to neutral Switzerland in *The Last Chance* (1945), a German soldier protecting a Jewish woman with whom he had fallen in love in *Monastero di Santa Chiara* (1949), nuns spiriting Jewish children across the Italian border in *Conspiracy of Hearts* (1956, 1960), or associates of Jews hiding their Jewish friends as depicted in *The Diary of Anne Frank*, most movies about rescuers produced prior to the 1990s attributed admirable motives to their actions.[37] American directors found the rescue plotline upbeat and profitable, whereas filmmakers from Germany and countries allied with or occupied by it turned to this theme to dissociate ordinary citizens from the crimes of their leaders. For instance, the West German movie *I Know What I'm Living For* (1955) portrays a Red Cross nurse who shelters two Jewish boys and then wages a postwar fight to maintain custody of them.[38]

Before the 1990s, relatively few films exposed how some rescuers of Jews economically or sexually exploited those they sheltered or opportunistically saved Jews late in the war to curry favor with the Allied liberation authorities.[39] The films of the 1990s differ not in the sudden appearance of rescuers but rather in their less idealized depictions of them[40] (see table 7.4).

To get a perspective on this shift in emphasis, consider how Raoul Wallenberg, the organizer of the most successful rescue operation during World

Table 7.4.   Motives of Rescuers of Jews in Feature Films

Years	Political/Religious	Friendship/Love	Ulterior/Unlikely
1945–1959	5	6	0
1960–1969	7	5	2
1970–1979	3	2	2
1980–1989	14	12	4
1990–1999	9	9	9

War II, captured the American public imagination in the 1980s. Between 1981 and 1985, six biographies, two documentaries, and a television movie about him were released in the United States.[41] During this period, the U.S. Senate and House of Representatives approved a resolution granting Wallenberg honorary American citizenship, a status conferred only once before on a foreigner, Winston Churchill.[42] When President Reagan signed the Wallenberg Bill, he characteristically promoted his anticommunist agenda by stressing that Wallenberg had been arrested by the Soviet Union in 1945 and might still be languishing in a gulag camp.[43] In 1986, the street next to the future site of the U.S. Holocaust Memorial Museum was renamed Raoul Wallenberg Place.[44]

The television docudrama *Wallenberg: A Hero's Story* (1985) portrays Wallenberg as a virtuous hero battling the twin foes of Nazism and communism.[45] Richard Chamberlain, who previously had been cast as the debonair male lead in *Shogun* (1980) and *The Thornbirds* (1983), plays Wallenberg as a fearless aristocrat who brazenly outwits the German and Hungarian authorities. The viewers' guide to the movie glorifies Wallenberg's willingness "to leave everything behind and go to the storm of war-torn Europe on a dangerous and purely humanitarian mission to rescue Hungary's besieged Jews." The guide vilifies the Soviet arrest of Wallenberg and contests the official claim that he died in 1947.[46] The image of Wallenberg as a valiant loner paralleled the reemergence of the rugged individualist in the action movies of the 1980s, like the *Rambo* (1982, 1985, 1988) and *Missing in Action* (1984, 1985, 1988) franchises. Susan Jeffords interprets this trend as an attempt of "remasculinize" American culture after the U.S. withdrawal from Vietnam.[47]

Contrarily, the feature film *Good Evening, Mr. Wallenberg* (1990) deflates the epic saga surrounding the Swedish diplomat by depicting him as an exhausted figure whose frantic efforts to save Jews fail as often as they succeed. One reviewer commented that the "film drives home with pitiless force that noble acts such as his were stark exceptions in a landscape of evil."[48] One leaves the movie with the impression that Wallenberg had tried to bail out a sinking *Titanic* with a teaspoon. At the end of his harrowing descent into hell, Wallenberg's only reward is arrest by the Soviets. The epigraph at the end of the

Swedish version of the film is accusatory: "Raoul Wallenberg saved directly and indirectly a hundred thousand lives. We didn't save his."[49]

Although there are still many inspirational, often explicitly Christian, presentations of rescuers as faultless role models, like *Life for Life—Maximilian Kolbe* (1991), *The Hill of a Thousand Children* (1996), and the Showtime trilogy *Rescuers: Stories of Courage* (1987, 1988, 1988) produced by Barbra Streisand, the shift from idealized characterizations of rescuers to less flattering ones is a hallmark of Holocaust cinema in the 1990s.[50] In *Warszawa, Year 5703* (1993), a Polish woman seduces the Jewish man she is hiding in her apartment despite the presence of his pregnant wife.[51] A couple that shelters a Jewish man in Claude Lelouche's updating of Victor Hugo's *Les Misérables* (1995) never tells him that the war is over so that they can continue to receive his monthly support checks. The modern incarnation of Jean Valjean chauffeurs his Jewish employer's family to the Swiss border but also steals the property of Jews who have been deported.[52] The antihero of *The Ogre* (1996) kidnaps German boys to serve in the Wehrmacht, but when Germany is on the verge of defeat, he tries to redeem himself by rescuing a Jewish boy.[53]

Schindler's List belongs to this latter category of films. Until the publication of Thomas Keneally's *Schindler's List* in 1982, Oskar Schindler's rescue of eleven hundred Jews had received little public attention in the United States.[54] What intrigued readers and reviewers of Keneally's historical novel was the paradox between Schindler's character flaws and his altruism. One critic contrasted Schindler's vices with Wallenberg's virtues: "But what makes Schindler's story of compelling interest to novelist Keneally seems to be Schindler's moral stance, a more equivocal one than that of the brave heedless Nordic knight Wallenberg."[55]

Although Steven Spielberg purchased the rights to film *Schindler's List* in 1982, he waited ten years to make the picture. Spielberg explained the delay as necessary for him to reach a point in his career where he could tackle such a serious subject:

> It took me years before I was really ready to make *Schindler's List*. I had a lot of projects on my shelves that were of a political nature and had "social deed" written all over them—even had "politically correct" stamped on top of them. And I didn't make those films because I was censoring that part of me by saying to myself, "That's not what the public will accept from you. What they will accept from you is thrills, chills, spills, and awe and wonder and that sort of thing."[56]

When he finally adapted Keneally's novel into a movie, Spielberg deliberately avoided casting the movie with superstars, resorting to color cinematography, or letting the moral metamorphosis of Schindler eclipse Germany's guilt for the Final Solution.

Opening with the warm yellow glow of the candles kindled by a Jewish family on the Sabbath, the darkness of the German occupation quickly descends on the Jews of Krakow as the room is emptied of people and the smoke rising from the extinguished tapers is match cut with the exhaust from a locomotive smokestack, portending the deportation and cremation of the Jewish populace. German clerks set up tables and start registering a procession of Jews who utter their names, which are typed on lists that will comprise the database for ghettoizing them, confiscating their property, conscripting them as laborers, and eventually executing them on the spot or transporting them to death camps. While many scholars faulted Spielberg for incarnating Nazi evil in the monstrous villain Amon Goeth, they ignored or minimized the recurring scenes of the bureaucratic steps that preceded the Jews' liquidation.[57]

The rich black, gray, and white tones in which Spielberg films the movie and his frequent use of shadows to cover the faces of the actors imbue the motion picture with a newsreel look and a film noir atmosphere. The sense of foreboding, moral ambiguity, and mystery evoked by this style provides a fitting backdrop for the enigmatic Schindler, who hatches a plan to profit from the sweat of Jewish slave laborers in a time of war.[58] After procuring Jewish financing to purchase an abandoned factory to manufacture mess kits for the German Army, Schindler enlists Yitzhak Stern as his bookkeeper to conceal the graft necessary for securing military contracts. He confides in Stern that the only asset he brings to the enterprise is "pizzazz" in marketing the deal to the Wehrmacht. Schindler's character development follows the cinematic convention of scoundrels whose mercenary motives evolve into moral ones as they become emotionally involved with the people they are helping like the gunslingers in *The Magnificent Seven* (1960) or the drunken captain in *The African Queen* (1951). Spielberg imagined Schindler as cut from the same cloth as the cunning swindlers in *The Sting* (1973), who excel at conning people.[59]

Schindler's humane treatment of his Jewish workers assumes epic proportions because it occurs within an environment where murder and mayhem rule. Critics who accuse Spielberg of diminishing the horrors of the Holocaust by focusing on Schindler's moral metamorphosis ignore how the scenes of Jews being deported, shot, selected, or tormented place Schindler's actions in the broader panorama of the Holocaust. Omar Bartov adopts this viewpoint when he writes, "By concentrating on a particular, unique tale, whose power lies in its label of 'authenticity' and considering the ignorance of many viewers regarding the historical context in which this tale took place, the film distorts the 'reality' of the Holocaust, or at least leaves out too many other 'realities,' especially that most common and typical reality of all, namely, mass industrial killing."[60]

There are twenty-one scenes in *Schindler's List* of the atrocities inflicted on Jews by the Germans. Most show Goeth shooting Jews for recreation, as a reprisal for minor infractions, or to terrorize them. The massacre of the Jews interned in the Krakow ghetto lasts for over twenty minutes. Spielberg heightens the revulsion of the audience at this slaughter by turning his lens on the most vulnerable victims—children, women, and the elderly—who scurry to find a nook or cranny where they can hide. The girl in the red coat personifies the defenselessness and innocence of those being slaughtered around her. Although a few minutes of the *Aktion* are seen from Schindler's vantage point on a hill above the Krakow ghetto, most of the scene is shot by a shaky hand-held camera simulating how the perpetrators and victims perceived this homicidal rampage. Moshe Bejski, who was one Schindler's Jews, praised Spielberg for recreating scenes that "were so accurate that a participant like myself would not know that actual footage was not being used."[61] Comparing the graphic reenactments of the German war against Polish Jewry in *Schindler's List* to the verbal references to Nazi anti-Semitism in *The Diary of Anne Frank,* Stephen Whitfield remarks, "By 1993, the Holocaust had seeped so fully into consciousness that the context in which goodness could be shown had altered."[62]

Later, when Goeth exhumes and incinerates the corpses of all the Jews killed under his command, the number of bodies mentioned is ten thousand. Compared to the eleven hundred Schindler saved, this death toll hardly leaves the impression that most of Krakow's Jews were rescued during World War II. The ashes rising from the pyres darken the sky in what appears to be a blizzard. This image of swirling snow recurs when the women working for Schindler are sent to Auschwitz. After emerging unscathed from a real shower in a scene that prompts the audience to expect the worst, these women pass another line of Jews entering the gas chamber next to the crematorium smokestack out of which flames and cinders are pouring. The juxtaposition of falling snow with falling ash marks the progression from the attempt to dispose of the incriminating evidence of mass executions in Krakow to the routine "mass industrial killing" at Auschwitz. As Gary Weissman observes, "*Schindler's List* is composed of vertical 'scenes' that develop the Schindler story and 'horizontal' scenes that re-create the Holocaust in broader terms."[63]

By focusing on Germans killing Jews, Spielberg minimizes the role of the Poles as bystanders or informers. The scenes of a Polish girl sneering, "Goodbye Jews," as they walk to the ghetto and of a Polish boy pulling his finger across his throat to symbolize that Jews headed for Auschwitz will die reveal little about Polish–Jewish relations and more about reducing cinematic conflict to a struggle between Nazis and Jews.[64]

In case the magnitude of the Shoah has not permeated the consciousness of the audience, the closing moments of the movie drive home the point. Schindler's Jews and their descendents number over six thousand, but only four thousand Jews still live in Poland. The film memorializes the six million Jews who perished in the Holocaust. The last two scenes occur in cemeteries. The first is the procession of the actors and the survivors they played to Schindler's grave in Jerusalem, where they pay homage to the flawed man who saved them in the film or real life. This celebration of Schindler and Israel is heralded by the background music, "Jerusalem of Gold," a song composed to celebrate the reunification of Jerusalem in 1967. For Israeli audiences, the melody was changed to "Eli, Eli," a simple declaration of faith composed by the martyred poet Hanna Senesh, who conducted an ill-fated mission to wartime Hungary. The credits roll over an image of the street in Plaszòw that was paved over with tombstones from the Jewish cemetery in Krakow. Thus, the road to Israel runs over the bodies of the millions who died in the Holocaust.[65]

In spite of its affirmation of Zionism, the movie's relegation of Jews to the role of passive victims prompted a number of scholars to castigate Spielberg for omitting scenes of Jewish resistance or for feminizing Jewish characters by rendering them dependent on the mercy of a Christian male.[66] I do not dispute that Spielberg elevates Schindler into a father figure for the Jews and frequently elicits sympathy for the Jews by presenting them as frightened children and women. Yet, by casting Ben Kingsley as Stern and ascribing deeds solely to him that were performed by several Jewish characters in Keneally's book, Spielberg fashions a character whose patient goodness slowly converts Schindler from a boss driven only by profit motives to an unlikely hero devoted to saving as many Jews as he can. Before *Schindler's List*, Kingsley was best known for his performance as Gandhi. Here, he harnesses the same humble resolve to coax Schindler to enlarge the size of his labor pool. Stern forges the first false documents reclassifying Jews as essential skilled workers, narrates a flashback of Goeth's execution of twenty-five prisoners to show Schindler why it is imperative to hire more Jews whenever an opportunity arises, and types the list that serves as the passport to survival.[67]

While some critics chided Spielberg for not clarifying the reasons for Schindler's change of heart, others lauded him for not turning his story into a preachy morality tale.[68] Spielberg exhibited more concern with the choices ordinary individuals make when faced with ethical dilemmas than with the ideological, psychological, or sociological reasons for such behavior. This is why Spielberg portrays Schindler as Goeth's alter ego. Not only do the two men resemble each other physically, but both share a passion for beautiful women, fine liquor, gourmet food, partying, and profiting from the war. The film is filled with parallel images of the two men admiring themselves in the mirror, kissing lovers, shaving, or talking to Goeth's maid Helen. Similarly, they superficially appear to have the same ends in mind, even when they disagree about the means, like when they discuss how to exert power, raise false hope among doomed Jews, or spare Helen from being sent to Auschwitz. In each of these situations, Schindler decides to do good while Goeth chooses to do evil. Schindler's suggestion that real power means exercising restraint briefly changes Goeth's behavior, but he soon lapses back into his murderous ways. Schindler assures Helen that Goeth will not harm her, but Goeth's awkward advances culminate in physical abuse. Goeth wants to grant Helen a quick death by shooting her in the back of the head; Schindler wants to transfer her to his new munitions factory.

Art Spiegelman's charge that *Schindler's List* glorifies "the benign aspects of capitalism" does not accord with Spielberg's characterization of Schindler in the last half of the movie.[69] Schindler's acceptance of his role as a rescuer is marked by the reversal of his financial motivation for hiring Jews. After Goeth announces that Plaszòw will be closed and the inmates transferred to Auschwitz, Schindler approaches Julius Madritsch, a factory owner who also treats his Jewish workers humanely, to convince him to buy Jews from Goeth and open a new business where they can toil in safety. Madritsch declines. Schindler insists that his munitions factory be a "model of non-production" and goes bankrupt. His remorseful insight that he could have saved more Jews if he had relinquished more of his wealth is inconsistent with Schindler's persona but does jibe with the monetary sacrifices he made to keep his Jews alive.

That Schindler has replaced Wallenberg as the quintessential rescuer may reveal a change in public attitudes. Back in the 1980s, I became involved in psychosocial research into the traits and values of "Righteous Gentiles" because I felt that such an analysis would "reduce the rescuers to their human dimensions and thereby enable the average American to realize that they were plausible and relevant role models of moral activism."[70] Bejski once asked Schindler why he had gone to such lengths to ensure the survival of his Jews. Schindler replied, "I knew the people who worked for me. When you know people, you have to behave toward them like human beings."[71]

Although Western ethics teaches us that morality is about upholding abstract ideals, Schindler's unpretentious answer reminds us that morality is about how we treat other people.[72] Wallenberg's valor and martyrdom appealed more to Americans in the 1980s when Ronald Reagan rallied the world's democracies to topple communism. The discrepancy between Schindler's vices and virtues may have been better attuned to a decade when the "Evil Empire" no longer existed and when the president's reputation was repeatedly tainted by private indiscretions. As Alan Berger has put it, "If there is one lesson to be learned from the Holocaust, apart from the fact that one can get away with it, it is that even in a kingdom devoted to death, a single person's act can save a life."[73]

The popularity of *Schindler's List* worried Holocaust scholars that it would become the definitive Holocaust narrative. It grossed $95 million in the United

States and over $200 million abroad. When broadcast on NBC in 1997, sixty-five million people watched it. Spielberg offered free screenings and study guides to high school classes studying the Holocaust, which in turn increased the number of states where the Holocaust was taught in the public schools.[74] Concerned scholars feared that seeing *Schindler's List* might be the only exposure to the Holocaust many people would ever have.[75] Movie attendance statistics indicate that most Europeans and Americans see several films annually.[76] Public opinion polls on Holocaust awareness among Americans reveal that reading a book or article and watching a movie on this topic are not mutually exclusive activities.[77]

NEW LIVES, OLD ARGUMENTS: *THE QUARREL*
Directed by Eli Cohen
(Canada: Apple and Honey Productions; Atlantis Films Limited, 1991)

> It might have been expected that a certain number of survivors would be predisposed from the outset to see the hand of God through the darkness, sustaining and buttressing their already vigorously robust faith. . . . In most cases, the atheist survivor, when asked to justify his own disbelief, feels convinced in the face of the death camp experience, he has the right, more than any other man alive, to declare God non-existent and deny that the omnipotent God of Israel can ever again be affirmed.[78]
>
> —Reeve Robert Brenner

Since 1945, the cinematic image of Holocaust survivors gradually has evolved from that of traumatized victims dependent on assistance from others to paragons of endurance and moral integrity. In the immediate postwar era, survivors were depicted as displaced, disturbed, or orphaned. Their deeply scarred psyches required patient healing by finding lost family members, forging new friendships, remarrying and building new families, and leaving the sites of their ordeal behind through immigration to Israel or the United States. Their restoration to normality had relatively simple solutions, like a boy relocating his mother in *The Search* (1948), an embittered refugee mentoring a child in *The Juggler* (1953), or an amnesiac recovering his identity by returning to his musical calling as a cantor in *Singing in the Dark* (1956).[79]

The most memorable characterization of a Holocaust survivor as an unfeeling and unstable prisoner of the past is Rod Steiger's powerful performance as Sol Nazerman in *The Pawnbroker* (1965).[80] Nazerman exhibits contempt for the destitute people who frequent his store. He locks himself behind a cagelike enclosure and never reciprocates the love of his mistress, the admiration of his ambitious apprentice, or the emotional support proffered by a social worker. He seems indifferent to the muggings and poverty in Harlem and the use of his business as a front for laundering illicit profits for a local crime boss. Flashbacks of the deportation of his family, the death of his son in transit, and the sexual exploitation of his wife in the concentration camp increasingly enter his mind. Nazerman is both a victim of Nazism and a potential Nazi, as his name intimates. Alan Mintz has argued that *The Pawnbroker* played a key role in the 1960s in equating the survivor with "the moral disfigurement that results from oppression."[81]

During the 1970s, several new books challenged what had become the standard interpretations of Jewish responses to Nazi persecution. Countering the charges of Jewish accommodation and servility in Raul Hilberg's *The Destruction of the European Jews* (1961) and Hannah Arendt's *Eichmann in Jerusalem* (1963), Lucy Dawidowicz's *The War against the Jews* (1975) presents a much more sympathetic account of Jewish responses to the Shoah.[82] Terrence Des Pres's *The Survivor* (1976) challenges Bettelheim's contention that the remnants who stayed alive in the camps regressed to infantile dependency on their captors and saved themselves by enforcing SS orders in their capacity as *kapos*.[83] Dorothy Rabinowitz's *New Lives* (1976) portrays survivors as resilient individuals who prospered in the United States.[84]

The almost universal respect survivors have been accorded in the last twenty-five years has been the cumulative effect of increased public awareness of the Holocaust in this period. The broadcast of NBC's miniseries *Holocaust* in 1978 accelerated this process.[85] President Carter's appointment of a presidential commission the next year led to the decision to build the U.S. Holocaust Memorial Museum, which opened its doors in 1993.[86] Israel's convening of the first "World Gathering of Holocaust Survivors" in 1981 and the awarding of the Nobel Peace Prize to Elie Wiesel in 1986 further enhanced the image of survivors. The flood of survivors' memoirs, visits by survivors to public schools, the opening of Holocaust museums, and the recording of survivors' testimonies ensure that their memories will be preserved.[87]

Coinciding with the increased prominence of survivors, their representation on-screen has become more favorable, although stereotypes of them as neurotic or psychotic remain. In the 1970s, for example, the survivor could be the irrepressible Maud who instills a love of life into the morbid Harold in *Harold and Maud* (1971) or the masochistic Lucia obsessed with reenacting acts of sexual bondage with her former SS guard in *The Night Porter* (1974).[88] The Auschwitz survivor in *Madame Rosa* (1977) cares for the children of prostitutes despite her daily ritual of mourning her wartime incarceration. During the 1980s, survivors were depicted in diverse ways ranging from the guilt-ridden

Sophie, who ultimately commits suicide, in *Sophie's Choice* (1982) to Simon Wiesenthal, whose career as a hunter of Nazi war criminals is chronicled in *The Murderers among Us* (1989).[89]

In the latest edition of *Indelible Shadows*, Annette Insdorf has added a chapter on the distorted image of Holocaust survivors in recent feature films. Based on the movies *The Summer of Aviya* (1988), *Under the Donim Tree* (1995), *Shine* (1996), and *The Substance of Fire* (1997), she concludes that the cinematic depiction of Holocaust survivors continues to stereotype them as "tyrannical, suicidal, or mentally unhinged."[90] These films have in common their primary concern with the children of survivors. Since such stories focus on how the trauma of the parents has been transmitted to their children, they dwell on the compulsive, domineering, paranoid, or psychotic traits survivors may exhibit as a consequence of their persecution.[91] Insdorf's generalization, however, ignores the trend toward increasingly positive cinematic portrayals of Holocaust survivors as leading characters. Movies like *Never Forget* (1991) about Mel Mermelstein's lawsuit against Holocaust deniers and *The Truce* (1997) about Primo Levi's geographical and mental trek back to Italy hardly demean the image of survivors[92] (see table 7.5).

Insdorf strangely never mentions Eli Cohen's *The Quarrel* (1990), a thoughtful film about two survivors debating whether Jews should still believe in God after the Holocaust.[93] *The Quarrel* is one of those rare films based on a literary source that equals or surpasses the original in its impact. Compared to the movie, Chaim Grade's Yiddish story is less balanced, leaving the impression that the humanist Chaim triumphs intellectually over the fanatically pious Hersh.[94] The adaptation of the short story into a play by Rabbi Joseph Telushkin, who also coproduced the movie, softened the rough edges of Hersh's intolerance toward his boyhood friend's atheism.[95] In the film, Hersh remains just as adamant in his faith but clearly possesses a compassionate heart and never loses his fondness for Chaim despite the theological rift between them. The performance of Saul Rubinek, himself a child of survivors, also makes Hersh a sympathetic character.[96]

Table 7.5.   Movies about Survivors

Years	Number of Films	Positive Portrayal	Negative Portrayal
1945–1959	12	5	7
1960–1969	13	5	8
1970–1979	13	5	8
1980–1989	24	12	12
1900–1999	24	16	8

Having the chance reunion occur on the first day of Rosh Hashanah in Montreal provides a more conciliatory backdrop than does Chaim's meeting Hersh on the Paris Mètro in the short story. In the film, Chaim is awoken by the ringing of a telephone but admits his sleep had been disturbed that evening by nightmares of the war. Although Chaim knows it is Rosh Hashanah, he profanes the Holy Day by eating a breakfast of bacon and eggs and smoking a cigarette. Nevertheless, his Jewish appearance attracts the attention of a man who asks him to participate in a minyan for a hospitalized Jew.

When Chaim subsequently walks to Mount Royale to return a necklace to a woman he slept with two nights earlier, he is impressed by the inscription on a park statue: "We of different races must never war against each other." Across a wading pool, he stares at Orthodox Jewish men casting breadcrumbs symbolizing their sins into the water. He recognizes Hersh, his childhood friend who had excoriated him for leaving the yeshiva to become a writer.

In Grade's original story, the setting is France, a country whose wartime record of collaboration with the Nazis made it an antithetical setting for coming to terms with the past. Moreover, Hersh runs a yeshiva in Germany, where the memory of the Shoah haunts the present. Hersh warns Chaim, "It's time for you to start thinking about repentance." Whatever affection Chaim feels toward Hersh is diminished by his strident denunciations of Chaim's secularism. Grade describes Hersh's speech as "a dry flame, progressively taking fire from itself" as he unburdens "himself of much accumulated anger." Chaim patiently hears Hersh out, then has the final word. Whereas Hersh ends his tirade by questioning Chaim's values, Chaim calls for a truce: "Reb Hersh, let us embrace each other."[97]

The film alludes to the biblical story of Joseph and his brothers to reinforce the theme of forgiveness. When Chaim strolls along with Hersh, he thinks, "I remembered how Joseph, after years of separation in Egypt, revealed himself to his brothers, 'I am Joseph, your brother. Is our father still alive?'" The two recount what they know about the fate of family members and friends during the war. Believing the German lie that only men would be conscripted for labor, Chaim left his wife and sons to flee to the Soviet Union. Now he is racked with guilt over his decision, but Hersh advises him not to blame himself because there was no "right choice." When Hersh accuses Chaim of glorifying human failings by writing fiction, Chaim stomps away. Hersh halts him by saying, "If Joseph and his brothers can make peace, then, Chaim, so can we." As they part at sunset, Chaim's voice-over reiterates this theme: "Joseph had friends, disciples, wealth, and slaves—he had everything. But until his brothers came, Joseph was alone."[98]

Advertised as "a searing encounter in the tradition of *My Dinner with Andre* (1981)," *The Quarrel* revolves around a verbal duel between Chaim and

Hersh over faith in God after Auschwitz.[99] Chaim blames God for breaking his covenant with the Jewish people. Hersh replies that the Jews provoked the wrath of God because they wanted "to become like other nations." Chaim fires back, "Since when is punishment for assimilation death by gas?" Hersh contends that the same level of religious observance in the face of such a catastrophe would be an insult to God. His piety is fortified by his conviction that Nazism was the extrapolation of the moral relativism fostered by rationalism. Chaim remembers meeting an atheist who saved Jews because she loved humanity. He shares her faith in the potential goodness of other people. The two represent the poles of Jewish universalism and parochialism that Berger identifies as the primary dichotomy in postwar Jewish fiction and film about the meaning of the Holocaust.[100]

Hersh's need to be forgiven by Chaim stems from guilt over his own spiteful refusal to accept his father's Yom Kippur apology for snubbing Hersh's wife and her family because they lacked the religious and social status befitting his son. By the time Hersh had changed his mind, the Germans had killed his father. Chaim too admits that when he learned that women and children had been deported, he still could have returned to his family but did not do so. Thus, Hersh, who beseeches Chaim for forgiveness, could not grant it to his own father, and Chaim, who preaches human solidarity, did not exhibit it when the lives of his wife and son were in danger. Both must put their pasts behind them. As Chaim wisely declares, "We are a devastated people. This is precisely why we should start to treasure each other like you would a rare jewel. Be tolerant." Hersh also makes a strong case for respecting his Orthodox beliefs and practices. He relates the story of an elegantly dressed Jewish woman who felt embarrassed by his unkempt beard and black caftan. When he told her that he was Amish, she hypocritically reversed herself by professing how much she admired the Amish for maintaining their traditions.

Although the movie's strengths are its crisp dialog and superb acting, it contains audio and visual effects that heighten its impact. The verdant groves of trees, the rustle of the wind through their leaves, and the bright sunlight at the beginning of the movie create the impression that Hersh and Chaim are wandering through the Garden of Eden. When their argument becomes most intense, the sky darkens, and it rains. Chaim remarks, "The clouds are as heavy as our memories." During the storm, they share an apple, which at Rosh Hashanah is customarily dipped in honey to auger a sweet new year. In the movie, it may symbolize the partaking of the fruit from the tree of the knowledge of good and evil. Twice the sound of a train whistle blowing in the distance recalls the transports that carted away their friends and family. Fearing anyone in uniform, Hersh panics when startled by a gendarme on horseback. After their most heated exchange, Hersh and Chaim embark on different paths, but the trails converge in a clearing. Near the end of the film, they recall a religious melody that Chaim once felt "could coax the Messiah down to earth." As they dance to it, time and place seem suspended. A crowd gathers and applauds their graceful performance. For this brief moment, they move in harmony. They part as friends.

The Quarrel depicts how survivors rebuilt their lives and understood the losses they had suffered. Rabbi Irving Greenberg, a leading post-Holocaust theologian, praised the film as "the most powerful, cinematically effective, intellectually exciting, and personally moving portrayal on the screen of the conflict within the modern soul between tradition and change." The film earned numerous awards and nominations.[101] It eventually aired on PBS.[102] Mark Leeper noted that "few films have respected their audience sufficiently to give them this density of ideas and concepts."[103]

THE SECOND GENERATION—CARRYING THE PARENTS' BAGGAGE: *LEFT LUGGAGE*
Directed by Jeroen Krabbé
(Belgium, Netherlands, United States, United Kingdom: Favorite Films, Greystone Films, *Left Luggage,* Shooting Star Film Company, Flying Dutchman, 1998)

> Resilience was the most common psychological strength described by children of survivors. They had successfully transformed their inherited status as victim to one of survivor, and they took pride in their resourcefulness and tenacity.[104]
>
> —Aaron Hass

Since the late 1970s, there has been a steady increase of second-generation groups and research into how children of survivors coped growing up "in the shadow of the Holocaust," to borrow the title of Aaron Hass's book. Director Gina Blumenfeld's film *In Dark Places* (1978) combines interviews of survivors and children to promote the mutual understanding between the two groups.[105] Helen Epstein's book of interviews with the "children of the Holocaust" appeared the next year.[106] These two works ushered in a wave of documentaries in which children of survivors assessed the impact of their parents' traumas on their own development or returned to the places in Europe where their parents had endured persecution or found refuge from it.[107]

As might be expected given the time it takes for a new generation to become adults, there was a paucity of feature films about children of Holocaust survivors or victims until the 1980s. The few early pictures on this subject avoided the issue of how the psychological scars left by the Holocaust altered the relationship between survivor parents and their children. The Israeli movie *Out of Evil* (1950) typically idealizes how the son of parents who died in the Final Solution returned to Palestine to help build the fledgling Jewish state.[108] Luchino Visconti's *Sandra* (1965) concerns the unresolved guilt a daughter feels for remaining safely with her Gentile mother while her Jewish father perished in Auschwitz.[109] Alexander Kluge's *Yesterday Girl* (1966) portrays a Jewish girl growing up in postwar Germany but never explores the impact the murder of her parents by the Nazis might have had on her personality.[110] Lelouche's *And Now My Love* (1974) and Peter Kassovitz's *Make Room for Tomorrow* are generational sagas in which the memory of the Holocaust is but one of several factors influencing the interactions between family members.[111]

Plumbing the recesses of memory to comprehend how parents' wartime traumas impact their children became a more prominent theme in both German and Jewish movies in the 1980s. The narration of the daughter in *Germany, Pale Mother* (1980) surveys the damage Nazism inflicted on her family as she recalls the absence of her father serving in the army, the terror of aerial bombings, and the rape of her mother by Allied soldiers.[112] *Marianne and Juliane* (1981) traces how the political radicalism of two West German sisters grows out of their shame over the atrocities committed by their parents' generation.[113] In Jeanine Meerapfel's *Malou* (1982), a Jewish woman searches for clues about what happened to her mother during the Holocaust to establish her identity as a Jew in postwar Germany.[114] *Bastille* (1984) shows how a historian's research into the French Revolution turns into a quest to discover the wartime fate of his family.[115]

With the notable exception of *The Summer of Aviya* (1988), a majority of recent second-generation films are distinguished from their predecessors by their focus on the current relationships of children with their parents. Most of these films were either directed or written by children of survivors (see table 7.6). In her criticism of the negative portrayals of survivors, Insdorf asks and answers this rhetorical question: "But would we recognize our parents in the images presented by films as well as plays? Probably not, given that the protagonists consumed by insanity or destructiveness ring false or, at least reductive." Stereotypes like the domineering fathers in *Shine* (1996) and *The Substance of Fire* (1997) persist.[116] Yet, second-generation films increasingly treat survivor parents and relatives with more sympathy. One could point to the sagacious grandmother in *I Love You, I Love You Not* (1997) or the father who cares for his sons when their mother has a nervous breakdown in *A Call to Remember* (1997).[117]

Jeroen Krabbé's *Left Luggage* (1998) provides an example of how cinematic depictions of survivors have become more balanced. Although Insdorf

Table 7.6.   Second-Generation Movies

Years	Number of Films	Child Survivor or Second-Generation Director or Writer
1950–1959	1	0
1960–1969	3	1
1970–1979	3	3
1980–1989	12	9
1990–1999	23	16

acknowledges the film's moving plot and fine acting, she feels it perpetuates "simplistic stereotypes" of "dysfunctional survivors."[118] The story centers on the maturation of a rebellious college student named Chaya. Speaking to her when she was a girl, Chaya's father recalls how his family hurriedly stuffed its belongings into two suitcases before they went into hiding. As the sepia-toned images of the burial of the luggage appear on screen, the thud of the clods of dirt tossed on the suitcases gets louder. A scream is heard, segueing into Chaya's yelling at a student protest at her university. After she quits her job as a dish-washer, she visits her parents. Her mother ignores the past by compulsively baking and cooking, but her father hopes to retrieve it by finding the site of the heirlooms he interred. Chaya's mother resents his obsession more than her daughter. As she leaves, her father tenderly reminds her, "Never part without saying I love you."

Mr. Apfelschnitt lives upstairs from Chaya's parents and serves as her Jewish conscience. Played by Chaim Topol, whose acting style and homespun wisdom hearken back to his best-known role as Tevye in *Fiddler on the Roof,* Mr. Apfelschnitt calls out, "Always knock on an old man's door, lest there come a day when he is there no more." He suggests that Chaya apply for a position as a nanny for a Hasidic family. Since she is "fed up with this whole Jewish thing," Chaya balks at the idea of working for such observant Jews, but Mr. Apfelschnitt accompanies her to the Hasidic neighborhood and dismisses her revulsion over the traditional Jewish appearance of the Hasidim by remarking, "That's the price they are willing to pay to remain who they are."

Chaya's first impression of the Kalmans is that they are prisoners of their faith. Residing in an otherwise vacant apartment building, the Kalmans tolerate the anti-Semitic slurs of the concierge, who treats them more like a warden than a doorman. He is clearly a reactionary character who has named his dog Atilla. He lies to Chaya that the elevator is broken, forcing her to walk up the steep, winding staircase. Mrs. Kalman loans Chaya an apron to cover her jeans because Hasidic women are not allowed to wear trousers. As she orients Chaya to the flat, she warns her never to enter her husband's study. Mr. Kalman chastises his wife for hiring a "whore" as a nanny. His inflexibility has retarded the maturation of his four-year-old son, Simcha, who still wets his pants and cannot speak.

Chaya finds no refuge from the past at her parent's home either. When they sit down for dinner, there is an empty chair placed in front of a photograph of her father's deceased sister, who committed suicide after the war. Chaya's mother refuses to dwell on such bad memories, but her father chides her for trying "to bury the past under a pile of cakes." Admitting that he moved ahead with his life out of fear that looking back would turn him into a "pillar of salt," he chides his wife for now forgetting that she stacked corpses at Auschwitz and adds, "You never want to talk about it. Is that normal?"

As Chaya bonds with Simcha, he responds by talking. First, he imitates the quacking of the ducks he watches swim in a nearby pond. Then, he says "duck" when she buys him a toy duck whose wings flap as its wheels turn. Simcha starts naming objects in his parent's house. To surprise Simcha's father on Passover, Chaya learns how to chant the Four Questions in Hebrew from Mr. Apfelschnitt so that she can teach them to Simcha. At the seder, Simcha haltingly chants the questions. Despite Mr. Kalman's pride over his son's accomplishment, he corrects a mistake, which causes Simcha to urinate in his pants. Chaya chases Mr. Kalman into his study and bluntly asks him, "Are you afraid of loving your son?" Then she glimpses an aging photograph sitting on the mantle. It is a portrait of Mr. Kalman's father and his two sons. Mr. Kalman's younger brother looks exactly like Simcha. Chaya learns that the Germans hung him for refusing to spit on the Torah and curse God's name. Does Mr. Kalman emotionally distance himself from Simcha to protect himself from suffering this kind of loss again? Is his rigid observance of Jewish law motivated by guilt for having performed the sacrilege his brother refused to commit?

The impact of the Holocaust on Chaya's father and the persistence of anti-Semitism sensitize her to the significance the past holds for her as the daughter of survivors. Her father looks for the luggage to remember his family. He dislikes the Hasidim for ghettoizing themselves. As he puts it, "Do I wear my prison clothes from the camp?" Unlike the aloof Mr. Kalman, he constantly assures his daughter he loves her. When vandals daub park benches with anti-Jewish and pro-Nazi graffiti, Mr. Apfelschnitt derides their scribbles as "primitive paintings made by cave men who don't possess sufficient language to carry on the simplest conversation." Even Chaya's girlfriend blames Jews for causing hostility by refusing to blend into their surroundings. It dawns on Chaya that "adapt or not, they were killed anyway."

This insight emboldens her to confront the doorman. After he nearly shuts the elevator door on Simcha's hand, she rips his coat and urges Mrs. Kalman to fight the "crazy Nazi." He retaliates by blockading the stairway with furniture so Chaya cannot leave the apartment. Rather than stay trapped, Chaya climbs down the gutter pipes of the building while Mrs. Kalman and her children cheer her on. Mr. Apfelschnitt justifies her act of defiance in Jewish terms: "If you see a person being attacked by someone, it is your duty to put a stop to it, even by force if necessary." When Mrs. Kalman advises Chaya to stay away for a week to let tempers cool, Chaya assures Simcha that she loves him.

Chaya's capacity for loving Simcha improves her relationship with her mother and father. Her mother weaves a Navajo-style blanket whose warp and weft are tied so tightly it can repel water. Chaya wonders why this would be useful for a bed covering. Her mother replies that you never know when you will need to sleep outside. She then confides to her daughter that all survivors lost a part of themselves during the war and begins to weep. Having broken her taboo against speaking about the Holocaust, Chaya's mother is more at ease with her daughter. They laugh together upon seeing how their neighbor's wife wallpapers his apartment with stamps from a collection he had devoted more attention to than her. The compassionate side of Chaya's mother also surfaces when she comforts her distraught husband after his arrest for digging holes on public property to find the luggage. He muses that John F. Kennedy's speech in Berlin really meant, "I am a donut," an apt allusion for a man who feels he lost part of himself during the war.

The next day, Mr. Apfelschnitt informs Chaya that Simcha has drowned. He consoles her by telling her that she bore as little responsibility for Simcha's death as the water that embraced him, the trees that stood idly by, and the ducks that lured him into the pond. As he speaks, the camera scans the exterior walls of building where Chaya and the Kalmans reside to visualize the barriers that exist between them. The Hasidic men surround Mr. Kalman and blame Chaya for Simcha's death when she goes to mourn with the family. Mr. Kalman silences them by saying they must accept God's will. He clasps the toy duck Chaya had given to Simcha as if it were a holy relic. Mrs. Kalman cuts the collar of Chaya's dress as a sign of mourning and expresses her gratitude for bringing Simcha out of his shell and defying the concierge: "Many daughters of Israel have behaved courageously, but you—you surpassed them all!" At the funeral, the soil emptied on Simcha's casket resounds like the dirt striking the suitcases earlier in the film. Despite his anguish, Mr. Kalman nods in gratitude toward Chaya.

The pain of losing a loved one allows Chaya to empathize with her father. In the final scene, she joins him in digging for the buried luggage. A panoramic shot shows that the hole they have dug is near the bridge across the river that runs through Antwerp. This image connects Chaya with her parents rather than condemning "the characters to continue to let the past destroy their present and future," as Roger Ebert has contended.[119]

Left Luggage does not pigeonhole survivors. Mr. Kalman comes closest to the stereotype of the survivor who has shut down his emotions to avoid being hurt again. Director Krabbé, who plays Mr. Kalman, is the son of a mixed marriage between a Jewish mother and a Gentile father. Although most of his mother's relatives died in the Holocaust, she never spoke about the tragedy that decimated her family.[120] Chaya's mother initially shuts out the past but eventually lets it seep into her mind, enabling her to communicate better with her daughter. Chaya's father never repressed his memories (as the scene with Chaya as a child indicates) and had decided only recently to unearth the suitcases. His displays of affection for his daughter are genuine and premised on the unpredictability of the future. In the novel on which the movie is based, Mr. Apfelschnitt is a survivor of Auschwitz too. In the film, he voices the compassionate side of Judaism in contrast to the ritualism of Mr. Kalman.[121] The film commands the second generation to transmit the heritage and history of their ancestors to guarantee the survival of the Jewish people and Judaism

COLLECTIVE SILENCE IS NOT GOLDEN: *THE NASTY GIRL*
Directed by Michael Verhoeven
(Germany: Filmverlag der Autoren, Sentena Filmproduktion, Zweites Deutsches Fernsehen, 1990)

> I so much would like to live among a people that does not fear or suppress the truth, a nation that admits to its past mistakes. I would so much like to live in a nation where somebody who thinks "against the stream" can be an adversary but not necessarily the enemy. I would like to live among people who can take criticism, among people who will try to right their wrongs instead of trying to hide them.[122]
>
> —Anna Elisabeth Rosmus

Just as children of survivors cope with the psychological impact of the Holocaust on their parents, German children born after 1945 harbor suspicions that their parents have concealed secrets about supporting Hitler, committing wartime atrocities, or standing idly by as their Jewish neighbors faced discrimination and deportation.[123] When the United States rehabilitated West Germany as an ally in the cold war, Konrad Adenauer promoted a foreign policy of accepting national responsibility for the crimes of the Third Reich and a domestic policy of welcoming all but the most politically compromised Nazi functionaries back into civil service positions.[124] The educational system accentuated the Judeo-Christian tradition of the West but minimized study of the Nazi era as an aberrant chapter in German history. In the late 1960s, the student movement perceived its demands as a generational protest against an adult establishment besmirched by the Nazi past. The transfer of power to a coalition of liberals and socialists opened a window of opportunity for the government, media, and schools to raise public awareness of the Final Solution. The popular catharsis engendered by the miniseries *Holocaust* revealed that many younger Germans welcomed the end of public silence about this topic.[125]

Although the relevance of the Hitler era to West German society remained a divisive issue in the 1980s, increasing numbers of German filmmakers drew upon the Third Reich as a source for the plots of their movies.[126] Michael Verhoeven's trilogy—*The White Rose* (1982), *The Nasty Girl* (1990), and *My Mother's Courage* (1995)—represents the most conscientious attempt by a German director to come to terms with the meaning of Hitler's regime for his parent's generation and their children. Verhoeven ties these three pictures together with the theme of resistance to the Jewish genocide or to the repression of its memory, but he emphasizes the exceptionality of this stance to prevent the audience from developing a smug identification with the dissidents.

For example, *The White Rose* plays as a suspenseful docudrama that evokes audience sympathy for a group of idealistic university students who clandestinely print and disseminate leaflets calling for the overthrow of Hitler. Verhoeven contrasts the isolated indignation of the members of the cell with the obedience of most Germans, who followed orders by massacring Jews on the eastern front and celebrated the betrayal and execution of the White Rose conspirators. He concludes the film with a prologue noting that West German courts had never overturned the conviction of treason pronounced against the members of the White Rose. Consequently, the provincial boards that approve films for screening in German public schools denied *The White Rose* this certification. Two years later, the Federal Ministry of Justice rescinded the verdicts.[127]

In *The Nasty Girl*, Verhoeven employs Brechtian alienation techniques to counter the audience's natural sympathy for its courageous heroine. Brecht introduced choruses, humor, music, narrative interpolations, movie clips, and newspaper headlines into his plays to cultivate a critical understanding of the social forces that influence the behavior of the characters.[128] Based upon the experiences of Anna Rosmus of Passau, Sonya Wegmus incurs the wrath of the inhabitants of the imaginary city of Pfilzing as she doggedly pursues access to archives that contain evidence about local perpetrators of Nazi crimes. *The Nasty Girl* opens with a series of scenes that are seemingly unrelated but set the pattern for the collage of styles and themes that Verhoeven uses to encourage a thoughtful perspective on Sonya's inquiry into the past. Before the credits start, an inebriated man momentarily mumbles a song in a beer hall. The director's statement declares that even though Rosmus inspired the film and her story is pertinent for all of Germany, the characters and events of his movie are fictitious. A classic statue of a woman appears as verses from the Nordic *Niebelungen* are recited. Next Sonya, walks onto a stage to a round of applause. Recalling how she came to write her first essay, she stops speaking to let her projectionist center a slide she is showing. Finally, the credits roll over a shot of graffiti that asks the citizens of Passau/Pfilzing, "Where were you from '39 until '45? Where are you now?" Although workers are busy painting over the writing on the wall, one wonders if they are merely "whitewashing" it.

Sonya recounts her story from atop a statue in front of the town's cathedral. This gargantuan bronze figure and the statue of the woman stand as immobile sentinels of German historical memory. Sonya's recollections of events that transpired after her research into Pfilzing's first appear in color, but whenever Sonya recalls her childhood, the stock switches to black and white. Although Verhoeven claims the changes in color are random, they can be interpreted as meaning that good and evil were more clearly defined when Sonya was younger. Her father, an ethnic German barred from returning to his native Silesia, teaches social studies but cannot utter the terms *German Democratic Republic* or *Oder-Neisse border* without adding the adjective "so-called." Her mother instructs her pupils about Jesus' ejecting the moneychangers from the temple, a lesson that hardly presents Jews and Judaism in a positive light. The Catholic school fires her mother because she is pregnant and might set a bad example to her students, who would know she had engaged in sexual intercourse. Since the faculty members know Sonya's parents and uncle, they give her the answers to exams ahead of time. Sonya has a crush on her physics teacher and eventually marries him. When she wins an essay contest, she tours Paris, where she fixates on statues of nude women who exude sensuality instead of steadfastness like the German statues.

Another distancing device that Verhoeven uses is the projection of stills or exterior shots as artificial backdrops for the action. For example, when Sonya requests files at the city archives, she sits in front of a photograph of a library. Similarly, as she and her family listen to the vile threats left on her telephone answering machine, the sofa on which they are sitting glides past scenes of Pfilzing's shops and streets. This implies that the private harassment Sonya encounters emanates from common attitudes held by the townspeople. David Denby defends these deliberate disruptions of the film's storyline as illustrations of "German defensiveness and deceit."[129]

Sonya respects her college professor, whose record of resistance against the Nazis is allegedly unblemished. As she unravels the layers of deception that insulate Pfilzing from the truth about the town's Nazi past, she discovers that the professor endorsed the Third Reich's military and racial policies in columns he wrote for the city's newspaper. After he and a fellow priest denounced a Jewish merchant for swindling them, the police arrested and deported the Jew. Neo-Nazis crucify Sonya's cat, throw bricks at her car, heave bombs into her home, and wear masks to disguise their identities. The audience knows who they are because Verhoeven repeatedly returns to a scene of drunks singing Nazi songs in a pub that was shown in the opening sequence.

Verhoeven never reduces Sonya's persistence to an adolescent rebellion against an authoritarian family. Although her parents espouse reactionary ideas, they support their daughter's crusade. Her brother eventually tests his parent's tolerance by dating a black woman. Uncle Franz, a priest at the church, provides Sonya with the names of people who might remember something significant about the Nazi period. Sonya's grandmother defied the Nazi authorities when they tried to confiscate crucifixes and prohibited her from feeding emaciated inmates at the local concentration camp. When a court orders Pfilzing to open its archives to Sonya, journalists swamp her to ask if she has a political or religious agenda. One reporter wonders if Simon Wiesenthal is her role model. Sonya responds that her grandmother inspired her probe. Circumventing one official excuse after another for the delays in obtaining the files she has requested, Sonya finally procures and furtively copies them. Based upon these records, she authors a book about Pfilzing under Nazism. She initially withholds the names of the priests who accused the Jewish salesman of cheating them. During a heated exchange with a hostile audience attending her lecture at the city's university, Sonya divulges that the history professor is one of the guilty parties. He retaliates by filing a slander suit against her but drops the case when it becomes apparent that he will lose.

Sonya becomes an international celebrity. Many prestigious universities grant her honorary doctorates. To honor her pursuit of truth and justice, the leaders of Pfilzing commission a bronze sculpture of her. At the unveiling ceremony, Sonya realizes that the city merely wants to placate her. She rejects this attempt to co-opt her: "Oh, I won't let you turn me into a bust and stick me in the town hall. I'm a living human being! Just because you're scared shitless, because you're afraid of what I might still find out. I won't do you the favor." She retreats to the "tree of mercy" and hides in its gnarled branches like a wild animal fleeing hunters. The closing image of Sonya's eyes peering through branches hearkens back to two prior scenes where she seeks refuge in what appears to be either a tree house or an abandoned guard tower. All three shots resemble the famous photo of Jews looking out from the ventilation slits of a railroad car.

Many critics felt that the movie's depiction of Sonya as an unassuming teenager, its satiric humor, and its visual gimmickry detracted from its serious theme. Roger Ebert appreciated Verhoeven's intent but felt that the form of the film sabotaged its message: "The story is fascinating, but the style seems to add another tone, a level of irony that is somehow confusing. Does Verhoeven see this as quite the cheery romp he pretends, or is there a sly edge to his method?"[130] Roy Grundmann contends that the "film's neo-Brechtian style subverts its aims" and that Sonya comes off more like "a suave TV anchorperson than a true Brechtian character."[131]

Caroline Wiedmer finds the picture politically objectionable. Since the film is plotted as a mystery, the audience becomes more involved in whether Sonya's detective work and legal challenges will prevail against the Pfilzing establishment than in the crimes that she suspects the townspeople of abetting. To prove this point, Wiedmer faults the relatively small amount of screen time devoted to the persecution and genocide of the Jews. The only camp survivor Sonya interviews is a communist imprisoned by the Third Reich, then the Americans, for his political affiliation. Wiedmer interprets Sonya's disinterest in her parents' activities during the Third Reich and her idealization of her grandmother as an evasion of the generational chasm in postwar Germany. On these grounds, Wiedmer concludes, "*The Nasty Girl* participates to some extent in this conscious forgetting of the Nazi period."[132]

Wiedmer's criticisms reflect the political correctness Holocaust scholars often try to impose on German films. Verhoeven hews quite closely to Rosmus's experiences up until the 1983 publication of her first book, *Resistance and Persecution in Passau from 1933–1939*. In her autobiography, Rosmus confirms that Verhoeven's dramatization of her life is generally accurate: "Despite many deviations, the film remained, to my surprise, true to reality. I had not expected to actually recognize 'myself,' and to find 'my' family there on screen."[133] Although Wiedmer's book appeared in 1999, she neglects the fact that Rosmus's subsequent book, *Wintergreen—Suppressed Murders* (1993), reveals that Soviet POWs, children of foreign descent, and local Jews were slaughtered in the two auxiliary camps of Mauthausen located near Passau.[134] Nor does Wiedmer acknowledge that Verhoeven's next movie, *My Mother's Courage* (1995), adapted George Tabori's script about how his docile Hungarian Jewish mother persuaded an SS officer to release her even though he had no moral compunction about sending the rest of the Jews on her transport to Auschwitz.[135] However effective one finds Verhoeven's distancing effects, irreverent comedy, and selection of stories about resisters to Nazism and its legacy, it is difficult to deny his commitment to a cinema that raises consciousness about the Nazi era as a prophylactic against xenophobia and racism.[136]

Although *The Nasty Girl* amassed a trove of major film awards,[137] its American distributor marketed it as a sexual comedy. A more precise translation of its title would have been the "horrible" or "terrible" girl. "Nasty" carries pornographic connotations, as an Internet search with the keywords "nasty girl" reveals. Lena Stolze's alluring half face and bare shoulder adorn the video-tape cover. The tagline reads, "A provocative comedy about secrets and surprises." While the synopsis of the movie never specifically says that Sonya is researching the history of her hometown under Nazism, it does stress that *she* seduced her teacher.[138]

The most popular themes of recent Holocaust movies relate directly to the present. Neo-Nazis may be political fossils, but their ideologies remain as ferocious as their predecessors', even if they only can mount acts of terrorism rather than mobilize the masses. Rescuers, particularly morally ambiguous ones, serve as gadflies, compelling viewers to recognize that political passivity constitutes a form of complicity. Survivors bear witness to the Shoah and distill relevant meanings from it. Their children and those of the perpetrators inherit an obligation to ensure that genocide will never occur again.

NOTES

1. Lester Friedman, "Darkness Visible: Images of Nazis in American Film," in *Bad: Infamy, Darkness, Evil, and Slime on Screen,* ed. Murray Pomerance (Albany: State University of New York Press, 2004), 256.

2. See Lawrence Baron, "Holocaust Iconography in American Feature Films about Neo-Nazis," *Film and History* 32, no. 2 (2002): 38–42.

3. *Verboten*, directed by Samuel Fuller (United States, 1958).

4. *The ODESSA File,* directed by Ronald Neame (United Kingdom, 1974).

5. David J. Skal, *Screams of Reason: Mad Science and Modern Culture* (New York: W. W. Norton and Co., 1998), 234–41; Andrew Tudor, *Monsters and Mad Scientists* (Cambridge, MA: Basil Blackwell, 1989), 141–50.

6. *They Saved Hitler's Brain,* directed by David Bradley (United States, 1963); *The Frozen Dead,* directed by Herbert J. Leder (United Kingdom, 1966); *Flesh Feast,* directed by Brad F. Ginter (United States, 1970); *Shock Waves,* directed by Ken Wiederhorn (United States, 1976); Gavriel Rosenfeld, *The World Hitler Never Made* (New York: Cambridge University Press, 2005), 212–13.

7. *The Boys from Brazil,* directed by Franklin J. Schaffner (United Kingdom, 1978).

8. Lester Friedman, *Jewish Image in American Film: 70 Years of Hollywood's Vision of Jewish Characters and Themes* (Secaucus, NJ: Citadel Press, 1987), 213.

9. *Shadow on the Land,* directed by Richard C. Sarafian (United States, 1968).

10. *Pressure Point,* directed by Hubert Cornfield (United States, 1962). *The Tormentors,* directed by David L. Hewitt (United States, 1971); Andrea Slane, *A Not So Foreign Affair: Fascism, Sexuality, and the Cultural Rhetoric of American Democracy* (Durham, NC: Duke University Press, 2001), 138–75.

11. *Kassbach,* directed by Peter Patzak (Austria: 1979); Annette Insdorf, *Indelible Shadows: Film and the Holocaust,* 3rd ed. (New York: Cambridge University Press, 2003), 193.

12. *Skokie,* directed by Herbert Wise (United States, 1981); *Evil in Clear River,* directed by Karen Arthur (United States, 1988); *Never Forget,* directed by Joseph Sargent (United States, 1991).

13. James Ridgeway, *Blood in the Face: The Ku Klux Klan, Aryan Nation, Nazi Skinheads, and the Rise of a New White Culture* (New York: Thunder's Mouth Press, 1995); Kenneth S. Stern, *A Force upon the Plains: The American Militia Movement and the Politics of Hate* (New York: Simon and Schuster, 1996); Morris Dees, *Gathering Storm: America's Militia Threat* (New York: Harper-Collins, 1997); Betty A. Dobratz and Stephanie L. Shanks, *The White Separatist Movement in the United States* (Baltimore: Johns Hopkins University Press, 2000).

14. Alan Rosenthal, ed., *Why Docudrama? Fact-Fiction on Film and TV* (Carbondale: Southern Illinois University Press, 1999).

15. *Elves,* directed by Jeff Mandel (United States, 1990); *Prayer of the Rollerboys,* directed by Rick King (United States, 1991).

16. *Midnight Murders,* directed by Dick Lowry (United States, 1991); *Best of the Best 3,* directed by Philip Rhee (United States, 1995); *Brotherhood of Murder,* directed by Martin Bell (United States, 1999).

17. Steve Neale, *Genre and Hollywood* (New York: Routledge, 2000), 112–18.

18. *American History X,* directed by Tony Kaye (United States, 1998); Slane, *A Not So Foreign Affair,* 188–210.

19. Rand C. Lewis, *The Neo-Nazis and German Unification* (Westport, CT: Praeger, 1996).

20. Meredith W. Watts, *Xenophobia in United Germany: Generations, Modernization, and Ideology* (New York: St. Martin's Press, 1997); Jeffrey Kaplan and Leonard Weinberg, *The Emergence of a Euro-American Radical Right* (New Brunswick, NJ: Rutgers University Press, 1998).

21. *Terror 2000,* directed by Christoph Schlingensief (Germany, 1992).

22. *Stau-jetzt-gehts los,* directed by Thomas Heise (Germany, 1992); *Beruf Neo-Nazi,* directed by Winfried Bonengel (Germany, 1993); David Bathrick, "Anti-Neonazism as Cinematic Practice: Bonengel's *Beruf Neo-Nazi,*" *New German Critique* 67 (Winter 1996): 133–46; John E. Davidson, "In der Führer's Face: Undermining Reflections in *Beruf-Neonazi,*" *Arachne* 32 (Fall 1997): 67–92.

23. *The Parrot,* directed by Ralf Huettner (Germany, 1992).

24. *Neues Deutschland,* directed by Philip Gröning, Uwe Janson, Gerd Kroske, Dani Levi, and Maris Pfeiffer (Germany, 1993).

25. *Rosenzweig's Freedom,* directed by Liliane Targownik (Germany, 1998).

26. Linda E. Feldman, "Zapping Jews, Zapping Turks: Microchip Murder and Identity Slippage in a Neo-Nazi Hate Game," in *Evolving Jewish Identities in German Culture: Borders and Crossings,* ed. Linda E. Feldman and Diana Orendi (Westport, CT: Praeger, 2000), 167–78.

27. Liliane Targownik, personal communications, August 22 and September 13, 2002.

28. "Awards and Honors," *Rosenzweig's Freedom,* at www.imdb.com; Avi Obiligenarz, "*Rosenzweig's Freedom* Premiered on German TV," *Indic Media News* (February 12, 1999): www.indic.co.il (accessed September 3, 2002).

29. Liliane Targownik, personal communication, August 22, 2002.

30. Sabine Hake, *German National Cinema* (New York: Routledge, 2002), 186–92.

31. Gary Weissman, *Fantasies of Witnessing: Postwar Efforts to Experience the Holocaust* (Ithaca, NY: Cornell University Press, 2004), 188.

32. Alvin H. Rosenfeld, "The Americanization," in *Thinking about the Holocaust after Half a Century,* ed. Alvin H. Rosenfeld (Bloomington: University of Indiana Press, 1997), 137–47.

33. Pitirim Sorokin, *Altruistic Love: A Study of American "Good Neighbors" and Christian Saints* (Boston: Beacon Press, 1950); Pitirim Sorokin, *Explorations in Altruistic Love and Behavior: A Symposium* (Boston: Beacon Press, 1950).

34. Eric H. Boehm, *We Survived: The Stories of 14 of the Hidden and Hunted of Nazi Germany as Told to Eric H. Boehm* (New Haven, CT: Yale University Press, 1949); Aage Bertelsen, *October '43,* trans. Milly Lindholm and Willy Agtby (New York: Putnam and Sons, 1954); Philip Friedman, *Their Brothers' Keepers* (New York: Crown Publications, 1957).

35. Harold M. Schulweis, "After the Trial—What?" *National Jewish Monthly* (July/August, 1961); Samuel P. Oliner, "The Heroes of the Nazi Era: A Plea for Recognition," *Reconstructionist* 48 (June 1982): 7–14.

36. Samuel P. Oliner and Pearl M. Oliner, *The Altruistic Personality: Rescuers of Jews in Nazi Europe* (New York: Free Press, 1988); Nechama Tec, *When Light Pierced the Darkness: Christian Rescue of Jews in Nazi-Occupied Poland* (New York: Oxford University Press, 1986).

37. *The Last Chance,* directed by Leopold Lindtberg (Switzerland, 1945); *Monastero di Santa Chiara,* directed by Mario Sequi (Italy, 1949); *Conspiracy of Hearts,* directed by Robert Mulligan (United States, 1956); *Conspiracy of Hearts,* directed by Ralph Thomas (United Kingdom, 1960).

38. *Ich weiss, wofür ich lebe,* directed by Paul Verhoeven (West Germany, 1955).

39. *The Two of Us,* directed by Claude Berri (France, 1966).

40. Insdorf, *Indelible Shadows,* 258–75.

41. Per Anger, *With Raoul Wallenberg in Budapest* (New York: Holocaust Library, 1981); John Bierman, *Righteous Gentile: The Story of Raoul Wallenberg, Missing Hero of the Holocaust* (New York: Viking Press, 1981); Elenore Lester, *Wallenberg: The Man in the Iron Web* (Englewood Cliffs, NJ: Prentice Hall, 1982); Kati Marton, *Wallenberg* (New York: Random House, 1982); Harvey Rosenfeld, *Raoul Wallenberg: Angel of Rescue* (Buffalo, NY: Prometheus Books, 1982); Frederick E. Werbell and Thurston Clarke, *Lost Hero: The Mystery of Raoul Wallenberg* (New York: McGraw-Hill, 1982). The documentaries were *Raoul Wallenberg: Buried Alive,* directed by David Harel (United States, 1983), and *Raoul Wallenberg: Between the Lines,* directed by Karin Altmann (United States, 1985).

42. Tom Lantos, "Proclaiming Raoul Wallenberg to Be an Honorary Citizen of the United States," *Committee on Foreign Affairs and Its Subcommittees on Europe and the Middle East and on Human Rights and International Organizations of the House of Representatives,* 97th Cong., 1st Sess., H. R. Resolution 220 (June 4 and 9, 1981), 23–28.

43. Ronald Reagan, "Remarks Proclaiming Honorary US Citizenship for Raoul Wallenberg of Sweden, Appendix 2," *Update on Raoul Wallenberg Hearing before the Subcommittee on Human Rights and International Organizations of the Committee of Foreign Affairs,* U.S. House of Representatives, 98th Congress (August 3, 1983), 96.

44. Edward T. Linenthal, *Preserving History: The Struggle to Create America's Holocaust Museum* (New York: Viking Press, 1995), 88–91.

45. *Wallenberg: A Hero's Story,* directed by Lamont Johnson (United States, 1985).

46. Poster and "Guide for Viewers," *Wallenberg: A Hero's Story,* April 8–9, 1985; Elie Wiesel, "*Wallenberg: A Hero's Story:* The Brave Christians Who Saved Jews from the Nazis," *TV Guide* (April 6–12, 1985): 2–3.

47. Susan Jeffords, *The Remasculization of America: Gender and the Viet Nam War* (Bloomington: Indiana University Press, 1989), 144–86.

48. James Pallot, "*Good Evening Mr. Wallenberg,*" *Motion Picture Guide 1994 Annual,* ed. James Pallot (New York: Cine Books, 1994), 110.

49. *God afton, Herr Wallenberg,* directed by Kjell Grede (Sweden, 1990).

50. *Life for Life—Maximilian Kolbe,* directed by Krzysztof Zanussi (France, Germany, Poland, 1991); *The Hill of a Thousand Children,* directed by Jean-Louis Lorenzi (France, 1996); *Rescuers: Stories of Courage—Two Women,* directed by Peter Bogdanovich (United States, 1997); *Rescuers: Stories of Courage—Two Families,* directed by Tim Hunter and Tony Bill (United States, 1997); *Rescuers: Stories of Courage—Two Couples,* directed by Tim Hunter and Lynne Litman (United States, 1998).

51. *Warszawa, Année 5703,* directed by Janusz Kijowski (France, Germany, Poland, 1993).

52. *Les Misérables,* directed by Claude Lelouche (France, 1995).

53. *The Ogre,* directed by Volker Schlöndorff (Germany, France, United Kingdom, 1996).

54. Kurt Grossman, "He Cheated Hitler," *Jewish Digest* (January 1960): 7–11; Moshe Bejski, "The Righteous among the Nations and Their Part in the Rescue of the Jews," *Rescue Attempts during the Holocaust: Proceedings of the Second Yad Vashem International Historical Conference, April 1974,* ed. Yisrael Gutman and Efraim Zuroff (Jerusalem: Yad Vashem, 1977), 642–45.

55. "*Schindler's List,*" *Kirkus Reviews,* Part 2 (August 15, 1982): 952–53.

56. Stephen Schiff, "Seriously Spielberg," in *Steven Spielberg: Interviews,* ed. Lester D. Friedman and Brent Notbohm (Jackson: University Press of Mississippi, 2000), 170–73; Ian Freer, *The Complete Spielberg* (London: Virgin Publishing Ltd., 2001), 220–35.

57. Omer Bartov, "Spielberg's Oskar: Hollywood Tries Evil," in *Spielberg's Holocaust: Critical Perspectives on Schindler's List,* ed. Yosefa Loshitzky (Bloomington: Indiana University Press, 1997), 50; Bryan Cheyette, "The Uncertain Certainty of *Schindler's List,*" in Loshitzky, *Spielberg's Holocaust,* 235–37; Caroline Joan Picart and David Frank, "*Schindler's List*: History, Horror, and the Monstrous," in Caroline Joan Picart, *The Holocaust Film Sourcebook* (Westport, CT: Praeger, 2004), 1:330–42.

58. Neale, *Genre and Hollywood,* 154–55.

59. Susan Royal, "*Schindler's List:* An Interview with Steven Spielberg," *Inside Film Magazine Online,* at www.insidefilm.com/spielberg.html (accessed June 16, 2003).

60. Bartov, "Spielberg's Oskar," 46.

61. Moshe Bejski, "*Schindler's List*: Fact or Fiction," 10th Annual Rabbi Israel Goldstein Holocaust Lecture, Center for Conservative Judaism, Jerusalem, April 18, 1994.

62. Stephen J. Whitfield, *In Search of American Jewish Culture* (Hanover, NH: Brandeis University Press, 1999), 188–89.

63. Weissman, *Fantasies of Witnessing*, 159; Picart and Fank contend that the slower scene is voyeuristic and could leave the impression that the gassing of Jews never happened at Auschwitz. See Picart and Frank, "*Schindler's List*," in Picart, *Holocaust Film Sourcebook*, 1:332–35.

64. Jeffrey Shandler, "Schindler's Discourse: America Discusses the Holocaust and Its Mediation from NBCs Miniseries to Spielberg's Film," in Loshitzky, *Spielberg's Holocaust*, 161.

65. David Brenner, "Working through the Holocaust Blockbuster: *Schindler's List* and *Hitler's Willing Executioners*, Globally and Locally," *Germanic Review* 75, no. 4 (Fall 2000): 299.

66. Judith Doneson, *The Holocaust in American Film*, 2nd ed. (Syracuse, NY: Syracuse University Press, 2001), 203–15; Sara R. Horowitz, "But Is It Good for the Jews? Spielberg's Schindler and the Aesthetics of Atrocity," in Loshitzky, *Spielberg's Holocaust*, 124–35.

67. Miriam Bratu Hansen, "*Schindler's List* Is Not *Shoah:* The Second Commandment, Popular Modernism, and Public Memory," in Loshitzky, *Spielberg's Holocaust*, 85–86.

68. Alan Mintz, *Popular Culture and the Shaping of Holocaust Memory in America* (Seattle: University of Washington Press, 2001), 127–49.

69. Art Spiegelman quoted in "*Schindler's List:* Myth, Movie, and Memory," *Village Voice*, (March 23–29, 1994), 30.

70. Lawrence Baron, "Teaching about the Rescuers of Jews," in *Methodology in the Academic Teaching of the Holocaust*, ed. Zev Garber, Alan L. Berger, and Richard Libowitz (Lanham, MD: University Press of America, 1988), 143–54.

71. Moshe Bejski, quoted in Eric Silver, *The Book of the Just: The Unsung Heroes Who Rescued Jews from Hitler* (New York: Grove Press, 1992), 148.

72. Lawrence A. Blum, *Moral Perception and Particularity* (New York: Cambridge University Press, 1994), 171–86; Luitgard N. Wundheiler, "Oskar Schindler's Moral Development during the Holocaust," *Humboldt Journal of Social Relations* 13, nos. 1, 2 (1986): 333–55; David M. Crowe, *Oskar Schindler: The Untold Account of His Life, Wartime Activities, and the True Story behind the List* (Boulder, CO: Westview Press, 2004).

73. Alan L. Berger, "Oskar Schindler: The Moral Complexity of Rescue," *Literature and Belief* 18, no. 1 (1998): 144.

74. Lawrence Baron, "Holocaust Awareness and Denial in the United States: The Hype and the Hope," in *Lessons and Legacies*, Vol. III, ed. Peter Hayes (Evanston, IL: Northwestern University Press, 1999); Lynn Rapaport, "Hollywood's Holocaust: *Schindler's List* and the Construction of Memory," *Film and History* 32, no. 1 (2002): 55–62.

75. Bartov, "Spielberg's Oskar." 46.

76. Charles R. Acland, *Screen Traffic: Movies, Multiplexes, and Global Culture* (Durham, NC: Duke University Press, 2003), 77, 198–228, 253–55.

77. Tom W. Smith, *Holocaust Denial: What the Survey Data Reveal* (New York: American Jewish Committee, 1995), 46.

78. Reeve Robert Brenner, *The Faith and Doubt of Holocaust Survivors* (Northvale, NJ: Jason Aronson, Inc., 1997), 104, 115; Aaron Hass, *The Aftermath: Living with the Holocaust* (New York: Cambridge University Press, 1995), 143–60.

79. *The Juggler*, directed by Edward Dmytryk (United States, 1953); *Singing in the Dark*, directed by Max Nosseck (United States, 1956).

80. *The Pawnbroker,* directed by Sidney Lumet (United States, 1965); Frank R. Cunningham, *Sidney Lumet: Film and Literary Vision* (Lexington: University of Kentucky Press, 2001), 157–85.

81. Mintz, *Popular Culture,* 107–25.

82. Raul Hilberg, *The Destruction of the European Jews* (New York: Quadrangle Books, 1961); Hannah Arendt, *Eichmann in Jerusalem: A Report on the Banality of Evil* (New York: Viking Press, 1963).

83. Bruno Bettelheim, *The Informed Heart: Autonomy in a Mass Age* (Glencoe, IL: Free Press, 1960); Terrence Des Pres, *The Survivor: An Anatomy of Life in the Death Camps* (New York: Oxford University Press, 1976).

84. Dorothy Rabinowitz, *New Lives: Survivors of the Holocaust Living in America* (New York: Knopf, 1976).

85. Doneson, *The Holocaust,* 143–96; Shandler, *While America Watches,* 155–81.

86. Linenthal, *Preserving Memory.*

87. Oren Baruch Stier, *Committed to Memory: Cultural Mediations of the Holocaust* (Amherst: University of Massachusetts Press, 2003), 67–148; Weissman, *Fantasies of Witnessing,* 89–139.

88. *Harold and Maude,* directed by Hal Ashby (United States, 1971); *The Night Porter,* directed by Liliana Cavani (Italy, 1974).

89. *Sophie's Choice,* directed by Alan J. Pakula (United States, 1982); *The Murderers among Us: The Story of Simon Wiesenthal*, directed by Brian Gibson (United States, 1989).

90. *The Summer of Aviya,* directed by Eli Cohen (Israel, 1988); *Under the Donim Tree,* directed by Eli Cohen (Israel, 1995); *Shine,* directed by Scott Hicks (Australia, 1996); *The Substance of Fire,* directed by Daniel Sullivan (United States, 1997); Insdorf, *Indelible Shadows,* 293–99.

91. Alan Berger, *Children of Job: American Second-Generation Witnesses to the Holocaust* (Albany: State University of Press of New York, 1997); Helen Epstein, *Children of the Holocaust: Conversations with Sons and Daughters of Survivors* (New York: G. P. Putnam Sons, 1979); Hass, *The Aftermath*; Aaron Hass, *In the Shadow of the Holocaust: The Second Generation* (Ithaca, NY: Cornell University Press, 1990), 25–50; William Helmreich, *Against All Odds: Holocaust Survivors and the Successful Lives They Made in America* (New York: Simon and Schuster, 1992).

92. *Never Forget,* directed by Joseph Sargent (United States, 1991); *The Truce,* directed by Francesco Rosi (Italy, 1997).

93. *The Quarrel,* directed by Eli Cohen (Canada, 1990).

94. Chaim Grade, "My Quarrel with Hersh Rasseyner," trans. Milton Himmelfarb, in *A Treasury of Yiddish Stories,* ed. Irving Howe and Eliezer Greenberg (New York: Viking Press, 1953), 579–606.

95. "Telushkin: The Accidental Star," *Atlanta Jewish Times,* March 3, 2000, at www.atjewishtimes.com/archives/2000/030300cs.htm (accessed June 16, 2003).

96. Saul Rubinek, *So Many Miracles* (New York: Viking Press, 1988).

97. Grade, "My Quarrel," 583–606.

98. Jennifer L. Koosed, "Joseph and His Brothers: Quarreling after the Holocaust," in *Imag(in)ing Otherness: Filmic Visions of Living Together,* ed. S. Brent Plate and David Jasper (Atlanta: Scholars Press, 1999), 37–46.

99. *The Quarrel*, videotape (New York: BMG Entertainment, 1996).

100. Alan L. Berger, *Crisis and Covenant: The Holocaust in American Jewish Fiction* (Albany: State University of New York Press, 1985), 39–150; Berger, *Children of Job*, 35–182.

101. Irving Greenberg, quoted in "*The Quarrel*," National Center for Jewish Film, at www.jewishfilm.org/quarrel.html (accessed January 8, 2003). Also see Omer Bartov, *The "Jew" in Cinema: From the Golem to Don't Touch My Holocaust* (Bloomington: Indiana University Press, 2005), 241–46.

102. "Awards" and "Box Office and Business," *The Quarrel*, at www.us.imdb.com.

103. Mark R. Leeper, "*The Quarrel*," http://us.imdb.com/Reviews/20/2092 (accessed January 26, 2003).

104. Hass, *In the Shadow of the Holocaust*, 46.

105. Insdorf, *Indelible Shadows*, 208–10.

106. Epstein, *Children of the Holocaust*.

107. *Breaking the Silence: The Generation after the Holocaust*, directed by Edward Mason (United States, 1984); *A Generation Apart*, directed by Jack Fisher and Danny Fisher (United States, 1984); *Kaddish*, directed by Steven Brand (United States, 1984); *Dark Lullabies*, directed by Abbey Jack Neidik and Irene Lilienheim Angelico (Canada, 1985).

108. *Out of Evil*, directed by Joseph Krumgold (Israel, 1950).

109. *Sandra*, directed by Luchino Visconti (Italy, 1965); Insdorf, *Indelible Shadows*, 125–27.

110. *Yesterday Girl*, directed by Alexander Kluge (West Germany, 1966).

111. *And Now My Love*, directed by Claude Lelouche (France, 1974); *Make Room for Tomorrow*, directed by Peter Kassovitz (France, 1979).

112. *Germany, Pale Mother*, directed by Helma Sanders-Brahms (West Germany, 1980).

113. *Marianne and Juliane*, directed by Margarethe von Trotta (West Germany, 1981). Also see *Wundkanal*, directed by Thomas Harlan (France, West Germany, 1985).

114. *Malou*, directed by Jeanine Meerapfel (West Germany, 1982); *In the Country of My Parents*, directed by Jeanine Meerapfel (West Germany, 1982).

115. *Bastille*, directed by Rudolf van den Berg (Netherlands, 1985).

116. Insdorf, *Indelible Shadows*, 293–98; *The Summer of Aviya*, directed by Eli Cohen (Israel, 1988); *Shine*, directed by Scott Hicks (Australia, 1996); *The Substance of Fire*, directed by Daniel Sullivan (United States, 1997).

117. *I Love You, I Love You Not*, directed by Billy Hopkins (United States, 1997); *A Call to Remember*, directed by Jack Bender (United States, 1997).

118. Insdorf, *Indelible Shadows*, 238–39, 298.

119. Roger Ebert, "*Left Luggage*," *Chicago Sun-Times*, May 11, 2001, at www.imdb.com.

120. Harvey S. Karten, "*Left Luggage*," at www.imdb.com.

121, Carl Friedman, *The Shovel and the Loom*, trans. Jeanette K. Ringold (New York: Persea Books, 1996); Carl Friedman, *Nightfather*, trans. Arnold Pomerans and Erica Pomerans (New York: Persea Books, 1994).

122. Anna Elisabeth Rosmus, *Against the Stream: Growing Up Where Hitler Used to Live*, trans. Imogen von Tannenberg (Columbia, SC: University of South Carolina Press, 2002), 3.

123. Alexander Mitscherlich and Margarethe Mitscherlich, *The Inability to Mourn: Principles of Collective Behavior*, trans. Beverley R. Placzek (New York: Grove Press, 1975).

124. Nicholas Balabkins, *West German Reparations to Israel* (New Brunswick, NJ: Rutgers University Press, 1971).

125. Mary Fulbrook, *German National Identity after the Holocaust* (Cambridge, UK: Polity Press, 1999). For the most recent work on German attitudes toward the Holocaust, see *Thinking about the Holocaust 60 Years Later* (New York: American Jewish Committee, 2005), 2–13.

126. *The White Rose,* directed by Michael Verhoeven (West Germany, 1982).

127. Insdorf, *Indelible Shadows,* 185.

128. John Willett, ed. and trans., *Brecht on Theatre: The Development of an Aesthetic* (New York: Hill and Wang, 1964).

129. David Denby, quoted in Insdorf, *Indelible Shadows,* 277.

130. Roger Ebert, "*The Nasty Girl*," *Chicago Sun-Times,* March 8, 1991.

131. Roy Grundmann, "*The Nasty Girl*," *Cineaste* 18, no. 2 (1991): 49.

132. Caroline Wiedmer, *The Claims of Memory: Representations of the Holocaust in Contemporary Germany and France* (Ithaca, NY: Cornell University Press, 1999), 87–103.

133. Rosmus, *Against the Stream,* 116.

134. Rosmus, *Against the Stream,* 134–41.

135. George Tabori, *My Mother's Courage,* trans. Jack Zipes, *Theatre* 29, no. 2 (1999): 109–29; *My Mother's Courage*, directed by Michael Verhoeven (Austria, Germany, Ireland, United Kingdom: 1995); Anat Feinberg, *Embodied Memory: The Theatre of George Tabori* (Iowa City: University of Iowa, 1999).

136. David Bathrick, "Rescreening 'The Holocaust': The Children's Stories," *New German Critique* 80 (Spring/Summer 2000): 55–57.

137. "Awards," *The Nasty Girl,* at www.imdb.com.

138. *The Nasty Girl,* videotape (United States: Miramax Film and HBO Video, 1990).

• 8 •

Projecting the Holocaust into the Twenty-first Century

> While stakes and strategies may differ profoundly they do have one thing in common—the recognition that the features of conventional genre films subjected to such intensive re-articulation are not the mere detritus of exhausted cultures past—those icons, scenarios, visual conventions continue to carry with them some sort of cultural "charge" or resonance that must be reworked according to the exigencies of the present.[1]
>
> —Jim Collins

Holocaust educators and survivors fear that the murder of six million Jews by the Third Reich will be forgotten when the last survivor dies. The proliferation of Holocaust archives, articles, books, college courses, films, monuments, museums, and public school units should dispel this fear.[2] No eyewitnesses can confirm that the Roman Empire fell or the Civil War occurred, but major upheavals like these have earned their place in history just as the Holocaust has, assuring their relevance to the present.

What changes over time are the interpretations and representations of such epochal events. A film like *Glory* (1989), which chronicles the combat of an African American battalion fighting for the Union, shows the Civil War in a different light than earlier movies like *The Birth of a Nation* (1915).[3] Who is cast as the protagonists of these films reflects transformations in what race and slavery mean to Americans at different times in their nation's history.

In much of today's world, the Holocaust has become the "master moral paradigm" about the potential dangers of bigotry, bureaucracy, demagoguery, nationalism, propaganda, science, technology, and warfare.[4] Rather than being a traumatic subject that the mass media avoids, the Holocaust exerts a greater spell today on filmmakers than it did when the first footage of the liberated

239

concentration camps served as evidence at the Nuremberg Trials in 1946.[5] The storehouse of images and ideas associated with the Shoah has grown exponentially as mass culture reaches us not just through print media, movie theaters, museums, and network television, but also via cable channels, DVDs, film festivals, the Internet, and videos.[6] New films draw on a rich source of previous movie plotlines and images. Since this repertoire of "cultural mediations" permeates contemporary collective memory, filmmakers presume that these images and themes will be familiar to viewers of their movies.[7]

HUMANIZING HITLER—THE DICTATOR AS A YOUNG MAN: *MAX, HITLER: THE RISE OF EVIL,* AND *THE DOWNFALL*

> Hitler still poses a nearly insoluble puzzle, but by obsessively focusing on him, filmmakers apparently hope to insure that his like will never rise again.[8]
>
> —Charles P. Mitchell

Since 2000, biopics have remained the most common genre of Holocaust feature films. The biopic allows directors to dramatize how individuals affected or responded to policies whose scope was vast and whose causes were manifold. Biography creates a sense of human agency in the face of impersonal forces that otherwise seem overwhelming[9] (see table 8.1). Human cogs controlling or crushed by the machinery of mass death generally do not make for compelling cinema. Even films about the bureaucratic aspects of the Holocaust, like *The Wannsee Conference* or its American remake *Conspiracy* (2001), endow their characters with distinct personalities to avoid degenerating into dull verbal exchanges.[10]

Hitler's charismatic appeal and ideological obsessions continue to attract directors. Both *Max* (2002) and the TV miniseries *Hitler: The Rise of Evil* (2003) turn back to the formative years of Hitler's political career. *Max* provides a conjectural premise for understanding Hitler. Rather than the vanquished leader

Table 8.1.   Holocaust Feature Films, 2000–2004

Most Common	Genre	Theme	National Origin
1st	Biopic (22)	Rescue (15)	Multinational (39)
2nd	Action (15)	Postwar survival (13)	United States (19)
3rd	Romance (13)	Perpetratation/Nazi collaboration (10)	Germany (8)
4th	Comedy (10)	Second generation (8)	France (8)

ranting in the bunker, the Hitler of *Max* is an aspiring painter and disgruntled army veteran residing in Munich. He blames the Entente's triumph over Germany on Jewish and communist traitors. Max, a Jewish art dealer, empathizes with Hitler's alienation because he lost an arm in World War I. Unlike the Jew who really sold Hitler's paintings in Vienna,[11] Max organizes exhibitions of dadaist and expressionist works that condemn imperialism, militarism, and nationalism for plunging Europe into war. He encourages Hitler to channel his wounded patriotism into drawings that mirror his inner turmoil. Instead, Hitler taps into this outrage to mesmerize demobilized soldiers with political tirades. At this stage in his life, Hitler has not decided which calling he will heed. Responding to criticism that the film humanizes Hitler, John Cusack, who plays Max, retorted, "The fact that the man is human doesn't make him less culpable, it makes him more culpable. If he's not human, then he's beyond human reckoning."[12]

The young Hitler chooses between characters who vie for his soul and the forms of expression his discontent will take. The poles of art and politics are symbolized by Max and Capt. Karl Mayr. Mayr encourages Hitler to be a tribune for his nation's "betrayed" veterans.[13] Max reminds his colleagues of the horrors of World War I by exhibiting the satiric drawings of George Grosz and staging a performance in which he shouts the patriotic slogans of 1914 as his body is pulverized by a meat grinder symbolizing the war.[14] Hitler evolves from sketching portraits and landscapes to designing models of buildings and swastika banners. He sways crowds by blaming Jews, the Versailles Treaty, and the Weimar Republic for Germany's problems.

Applauded by crowds for his interpretation of German history as an eternal struggle between noble Aryans and deceitful Jews, Hitler feels he has found his purpose in life. Despite knowing that Max is one of one hundred thousand German Jews who served in the German army during World War I, Hitler labels Jews "vampires" who feed on the blood of their hosts. His closing speech against the Jews incites a mob to attack Max. Bleeding to death in the snow, Max glances at graffiti that reads, "Stabbed in the back!" The camera ascends above his body, reducing it to a speck on the screen. Thus, Max becomes the first casualty of Hitler's anti-Semitism.

Hitler: The Rise of Evil surveys how Hitler developed the ideas and ruthlessness that paved the way for him to become the führer of the Third Reich. Unfortunately, it condenses his childhood, artistic aspirations, and combat experiences during World War I into a twenty-minute sequence whose brevity obscures more than it illuminates.

After Hitler delivers his first political speech in Munich, he quickly develops into the consummate demagogue, who demonizes the Jews and the Weimar Republic and idealizes the Aryan race. The remainder of the movie traces Hitler's exploitation of the endemic instability of Germany's fledgling democracy to amass popular support while outflanking or killing his political rivals. His lust for power manifests itself in his domineering relationships with his niece, Geli Raubal, and fawning mistress, Eva Braun. The depiction of Hitler as a rabble-rouser and wicked leader never reveals any redeeming ideals or traits. Indeed, the movie is not all that different from *The Hitler Gang* (1944), which likened the ascendant Hitler to a mobster.[15]

Every unscrupulous villain deserves a virtuous foe. Fritz Gerlich, a reporter for a conservative Munich daily, picked up the gauntlet tossed down in defiance of the Weimar Republic by Hitler in the Beer Hall Putsch. In article after article, Gerlich alerted his readers to Hitler's dictatorial ambitions, incendiary anti-Semitism, and militarism. He did not desist when the Nazis threatened to murder him and his wife. After Hitler assumed power, he ordered Gerlich's arrest. Gerlich died at Dachau a year later. Although Gerlich merits remembrance, the movie's portrayal of him is as one-dimensional as its depiction of Hitler. Moreover, it reduces the opposition to Hitler to one man's crusade rather than to the leftist and centrist political parties that retained the support of nearly half of the German electorate before Hitler became chancellor in 1933.

Ian Kershaw, the historian whose biography of Hitler served as the basis for the script, disassociated himself from the production because it abandoned historical accuracy to enhance dramatic impact.[16] "The Guide for Educators" that accompanies the movie devotes half a page to the Holocaust but concludes that "no one knows for certain why Adolf Hitler hated the Jews."[17] A majority of the scholars who responded to an Internet forum about the miniseries faulted its hectic pacing and simplistic interpretations of Weimar politics and Hitler's pathological personality.[18] The selection of Christian Duguay, best known for making action adventure movies, as the film's director indicates that the network sought someone skilled in editing visually powerful scenes and writing snappy dialog to prevent the miniseries from dragging. This cinematic style precludes character development and historical analysis.[19]

Since Hitler epitomizes political evil in the twentieth century,[20] movies deviating from this image are vulnerable to the charge of glossing over his inhumanity. The controversy they generate does not appear to lure moviegoers into buying tickets to see a sanitized version of Hitler. Produced on a modest budget of $11 million, *Max* recouped little more than $500,000 dollars in ticket sales. Despite the star power of Cusack, it was booked at only 37 theaters nationally.[21] By contrast, CBS broadcast *Hitler: The Rise of Evil* during May Sweeps week. It did remarkably well in that competitive period of programming, placing eighteenth in the Nielsen Ratings and drawing an audience of 13.6 million viewers.[22] Alvin Rosenfeld's fear that humanizing Hitler in popular culture will "ultimately erase" his "fingerprints from a history of mass murder" ignores how deeply ingrained the public's negative perceptions of Hitler have become.[23]

The release of Oliver Hirschbiegel's *The Downfall* (2004) broke the postwar taboo against German productions about Hitler. Hirschbiegel returns to the bunker where Hitler is on the verge of defeat and suicide. His characterization of Hitler as a vanquished but unremorseful fanatic contains nothing that might inspire today's Germans to take up the cudgels of national socialism again. The film does, however, spend an inordinate amount of time on scenes showing the victimization of decent Berliners by barbaric Soviet soldiers. Conversely, there is only a passing reference to the destruction of European Jewry.

As an effective remake of a well-documented story, *The Downfall* excels, but it blazes no new cinematic trails. As Hitler biographer Ian Kershaw has averred, "A focus on the grotesque events in the bunker, at their center the physical and mental wreck of a man about to kill himself as his world collapses in ruins, can in itself do little to explain how it had come to this."[24]

THE SOLOIST: *THE PIANIST*
Directed by Roman Polanski
(France, Germany, Poland, United Kingdom, United States: Agencja Produkcji Filmowej, Beverly Detroit/Canal + Polska, Filmfernseh Fonds Bayern, Filmboard Berlin-Brandenburg, Filmförderungsanstalt/Héritage Films, Interscope Communications/Le Studio Canal, Mainstream S.A./R.P. Productions, Runteam Ltd./Studio Babelsberg, Telewizja Polska S.A., 2002)

> At first I had a home, parents, two sisters, and a brother. Then we had no home of our own any more, but we were together. Later I was alone, but surrounded by other people. And now I was lonelier, I supposed, than anyone else in the world. Even Defoe's creation, Robinson Crusoe, the prototype of the ideal solitary, could hope to meet another human being. . . . I had to be alone, entirely alone, if I wanted to live.[25]
>
> —Władysław Szpilman

Recent biographical films about Jewish victims and survivors of the Holocaust outnumber those depicting the lives of the Gentiles who conceived of this genocidal policy, implemented it, or condoned it (see table 8.2). This reflects interrelated developments: (1) the recognition of Jews as the primary targets of Hitler's racism, (2) the heightened public awareness of the discrimination and victimization encountered by various minority groups, and (3) the corresponding

Table 8.2.   Protagonists of Holocaust Biopics 2000–2004

Types of Protagonists	Number of Films
Jewish victims and survivors	8
Perpetrators and collaborators	5
Rescuers of Jews	4
Neo-Nazis	2
Resisters	2
Gentile victim of Nazism	1

directorial preference for dramatizing the lives of ordinary people who prevail against disadvantages, prejudices, and persecution.[26]

Not since *Schindler's List* (1993) has a feature film containing as many graphic scenes of Nazi atrocities and carnage as Roman Polanski's *The Pianist* (2002) enjoyed such international box-office success and critical acclaim. Many factors contributed to this phenomenon: the lurid popular fascination with Polanski's notoriety, his taut directorial style, Adrien Brody's restrained performance, the multinational perspectives brought to the movie by the diverse studios and people involved in its production, and the triumphant story of a gifted musician who perseveres to play his instrument once again.

Moreover, Polanski's survival as a boy hiding from the Germans in occupied Poland after being separated from his mother, who died at Auschwitz, and his father, who was incarcerated at Mauthausen, adds credibility to his cinematic reconstruction of Jewish life within and outside the Warsaw ghetto.[27] Steven Spielberg tried in vain to persuade Polanski in the 1980s to direct the movie based on Thomas Keneally's book about Oskar Schindler shortly after he purchased the film rights to the story.[28] After reading Władysław Szpilman's memoir, Polanski found its descriptions accorded with his own wartime memories.[29]

The Pianist borrows liberally from familiar images from Nazi newsreel footage, wartime photographs of the Warsaw ghetto, and previous documentaries and feature films about the ghettos. This renders what once was shocking more palatable. The DVD version of the film features a stunning sequence of crosscuts between actual movies and photographs of the Warsaw ghetto and Polanski's re-creations of these scenes. His shots of Jews carrying their belongings in suitcases or on carts, nude corpses strewn on the pavement, the bricking of the ghetto wall, German cameramen filming Jews herded into the ghetto, and Jews crossing the bridge connecting the two parts of the ghetto lend historical authenticity to Polanski's representation of the ghetto. Viewers who have watched the original German newsreels or other feature films about ghettos like *Korczak* (1990), *Schindler's List*, and *Uprising* (2001), may find these images derivative.[30]

Familiarity does not necessarily breed audience contempt. The stock images from the Warsaw ghetto contextualize the deteriorating conditions the Szpilman family endured. The idyllic footage of prewar Warsaw precedes the bombardment of the city while Szpilman performs at a Polish radio station until an artillery shell explodes and knocks him off his stool. After German troops march into the city, the members of the Szpilman family debate where they should hide their money. The period of normalcy abruptly ends when Władysław reads a decree posted on the door of his favorite restaurant forbidding Jews from dining there. His family must sell its piano for a pittance of its real value. The before and after shots of Jews evicted from their residences into the ghetto contrast the comfort they once enjoyed with the deprivation they now endure.

Polanski combs Szpilman's memoir for graphic incidents that symbolize the ubiquitous danger and deprivation Jews confronted in the ghetto. Audiences may have seen the Nazi newsreel of a Jewish boy frisked by German guards for concealed food that tumbles into a mound around his feet. Polanski subjects them to witnessing a young smuggler caught by his feet and beaten so brutally by his captors on the Aryan side of the wall that he is dead by the time Szpilman pulls him over to the Jewish side.[31] Another haunting scene shows a character nicknamed the "grabber" trying to snatch a can of soup from a woman. When it spills on the ground, he voraciously licks the liquid off the pavement.[32] The Szpilmans impotently watch a Gestapo squad push an elderly man in a wheelchair over the ledge of his balcony and execute the Jews who gather around his corpse. Positioned from the perspective of a window in the Szpilmans' apartment, this camera shot foreshadows Władysław's observer status when he goes into hiding.[33]

Amid the anguish, panic, or resignation of Jews awaiting deportation at the *Umschlagplatz*, Polanski interjects his childhood memories into the story. Determined to stay with his family, Szpilman is unexpectedly yanked out of line by a Jewish policeman who prevents him from joining them. In the memoir, Szpilman darts away as quickly as he can.[34] In Polanski's case, he asked a Polish guard if he could fetch some food for the journey. The guard warned him not to run but to walk slowly so that he wouldn't attract attention. Polanski retains Szpilman's rescue by a Jewish policeman but adds the advice about not running. Szpilman sobs as he walks through a boulevard littered with cadavers, furniture, suitcases, and falling feathers from ripped-open comforters and pillows.[35]

Hiding in an apartment furnished by Polish friends, Szpilman hangs onto his sanity by silently fingering a real keyboard as if he were playing it. He eventually suffers from malnutrition and jaundice when his Polish contact fails to supply him with food on a regular basis. Brody, with his gaunt face, unkempt beard, and lengthy periods of silence, resembles Tom Hanks when shipwrecked in *Cast Away* (2000).[36] Angling the camera down upon the action at street level and shooting through curtains and window cracks, Polanski reduces Szpilman to a passive spectator of the Warsaw Ghetto Uprising in 1943 and the Polish Revolt of 1944. This visual distancing diminishes the heroic stature posterity has conferred on these armed struggles. Contrast Polanski's approach with Jon Avnet's in *Uprising* (2001). The latter glorifies the Jewish resisters with close-up, straight-on, or low-angle camera shots as they plan and mount their rebellion.[37]

What prevents *The Pianist* from grinding to a dramatic halt at this point is the metamorphosis of Szpilman from a sedentary observer into an escape artist. When the German troops crush the Polish revolt, Szpilman is at the epicenter of their assault. Suddenly, he must dodge the blasts from flamethrowers, bazookas, and machine guns that seem to divine his location although they are fired at Poles who rush into the apartment building and deserted hospital that shelter him. Staying one step ahead of spectacular explosions creates a segment that looks and feels more like an action movie.[38] Polanski changes the tone of *The Pianist* by tracking Szpilman's perilous close calls into the cavernous ruins of the ghetto. Polanski replicated this barren landscape by razing an abandoned Soviet army base in the former East Germany.[39]

The upbeat ending of *The Pianist* undercuts the gloomy mood pervading the rest of the movie. When Szpilman clumsily tries to open a can of pickles, the container falls from of his hands and rolls to the feet of an on-looking Wehrmacht captain. In a curt exchange, the German officer, whose name was Wilm Hosenfeld, learns that the scraggly scavenger had been a pianist before the war. He asks him to play something on a piano in the next room. Szpilman plays a Chopin nocturne. His bony fingers stiffly strike the keys at first, but as they regain dexterity, the music flows expressively, with the camera alternating between close-ups of Szpilman's hands and the transfigured faces of the two men. After the officer departs, Szpilman weeps as his former self reawakens. Instead of arresting him, the captain brings him bread and jam. When Szpilman confesses that he does not know how to thank him, Hosenfeld responds, "Thank God, not me. He wants us to survive. Well, that's what we have to believe." Retreating with his troops, the captain makes one final gesture of kindness by giving Szpilman his coat. Wearing a Wehrmacht coat, Szpilman narrowly escapes execution by Russian soldiers, who at first mistake him for a German soldier. Interned by the Russians, Captain Hosenfeld attempts to contact Szpilman to vouch for his act of mercy. The closing scene juxtaposes Szpilman's resumption of his musical career with a postscript that Hosenfeld died in Soviet captivity.

Polanski presents Hosenfeld as an enigmatic figure whose benevolence appears to be situational rather than ethical. Did he spare Szpilman because he loved music? Did he feel he had no reason to kill Szpilman since the war was lost? Did he want Szpilman to testify before a Soviet tribunal that he had treated him decently? Appalled by Nazi brutality against Polish civilians, particularly Jews, the real Hosenfeld saved a number of them during the war. In his memoir, Szpilman records Hosenfeld's reply to being asked if he was a German: "Yes, I am! And ashamed of it, after everything that's been happening." Szpilman volunteered to testify that Hosenfeld merited lenient treatment.[40]

Polanski perceived the story as a "tribute to the power of music" and downplayed Hosenfeld's altruistic motivations, even though Polanski was clearly aware of them. *The Pianist* exhibits the double-narrative structure employed by many of the films discussed in this book. The majority of the Jews in these motion pictures perish, but central characters survive. The original tagline for *The Pianist* assured viewers that "survival was his masterpiece." The liner notes for the DVD and video proclaim the film "follows Szpilman's heroic and inspirational journal of survival," evincing "both the power of hope and the resiliency of the human spirit." Omer Bartov astutely observes that Polanski celebrates the triumph of Szpilman the musician more than his survival as a Jew.[41]

The Pianist also capitalized on its multinational origins. It was coproduced by studios from five countries. Polanski's cinematic career has involved him in making movies for American, British, French, German, Italian, Polish, and Spanish companies. In Randall Halle's opinion, the international appeal of such movies stems from their emphasis on "action, music, and effects (emotional, visual, and special)" and deemphasis of dialog because it always poses the problems of rendering the dubbing imperceptible or the subtitles accurate for each national market.[42] *The Pianist* exhibits these characteristics and accordingly won major film awards in five countries.[43]

In keeping with Szpilman's cosmopolitanism, the script avoids stereotyping Germans, Jews, or Poles. Indeed, when stopped by Russian soldiers, Szpilman identifies himself as a Pole in the memoir and the film. Polanski incorporates a spectrum of Jewish characters from black marketers to resisters and of Polish ones from the embezzler of Szpilman's food money to his loyal rescuers. Once again, Polish–Jewish animosities colored the reception of the movie. Ignoring at least two instances of Poles' betraying Szpilman in the film, novelist Thane Rosenbaum categorized the film "as a valentine to Polanski's Poland," which distorted the historical record by depicting Gentile Poles "only as freedom fighters."[44] Offended by Rosenbaum's generalization that "most Poles were either complicit or indifferent to the fate of their Jewish neighbors," critic Robert Strybel endorsed the film as a "must see" for Polish Americans not because it idealized Poles but because it reflected Szpilman's dispassionate account of survival in wartime Warsaw.[45]

A news report about a German audience laughing at scenes of Jews being shot in *The Pianist* overshadowed the Polish–Jewish dispute it had sparked.[46] While this appears to have been an isolated incident, the failure of *The Pianist* to receive any German film awards may have resulted from its having an excellent German competitor that year, *Nowhere in Africa*.[47]

DOUBLY DISPLACED: *NOWHERE IN AFRICA*
Directed by Caroline Link
(Germany: Bavarian Film/Constantin Film/MTM Cineteve, 2001)

> We were Jews—in our home country in fear for our lives, in Kenya "bloody refugees," and after the outbreak of the second world war "enemy aliens."[48]
>
> —Stephanie Zweig

> The story of the Redlich family is a refugee story. The relationship between blacks and whites is consequently different. And the movie has a strong black major character: Owuor. I wanted to make sure that his perspective was presented by giving him a conspicuous role in the film.[49]
>
> —Caroline Link

When Caroline Link's *Nowhere in Africa* took home the Oscar for Best Foreign Language Film of 2002, it became the first German feature film to win this prize since Volker Schlöndorff's *The Tin Drum* in 1979. Link's first two movies, *Beyond Silence* (1996) and *Annaluise and Anton* (1999), had been commercial hits in Germany and won film awards there and abroad.[50] *Beyond Silence* garnered a nomination for Best Foreign Language Film from the Academy of Motion Picture Arts and Sciences, an auspicious beginning for a novice director.[51] Stefanie Zweig's autobiographical novel provided the basis for Link's dramatically engrossing and visually impressive movie about how a German Jewish family fleeing Hitler found asylum in Kenya.[52]

In Germany, the movie benefited from the recent wave of "heritage" films like *The Harmonists*, which mourn the dispersion and destruction of German Jewry.[53] Keeping the Holocaust in the background, the plotline of *Nowhere in Africa* revolves around personal issues that are complicated by political developments. The flight of the Redlich family to rural Kenya exacerbates marital tensions between the husband and wife and accelerates the coming of age of their daughter, who adapts more rapidly to her new surroundings than her parents. National, racial, and religious affiliations assume new meanings when the

British intern German Jewish refugees immediately after the outbreak of World War II. The unpretentious kindness of the indigenous populace and the allure of tribal customs gradually overcome the smug superiority Jettel Redlich feels toward a society she considers more primitive than the one she has left.[54]

For audiences outside of Germany, *Nowhere in Africa* combined several popular themes: the Holocaust, marital strife, the psychological growth of a once shallow female character, the immigrant experience, pioneering in a harsh environment, and the coming of age of an adolescent girl. By transferring familiar plotlines into an exotic setting, the movie puts a new spin on them.

The film opens by crosscutting scenes of an African messenger boy riding a bicycle across the Kenyan plains with Jettel and her daughter, Regina, playing in the snow in Germany. The difficulty the Redlichs will have in adjusting to Kenya is visually conveyed by the contrast between these radically different climates and topographies. The African scene radiates the heat of the tropical sun and depicts the Kenyan lowlands as spacious but sparsely vegetated. The German scene has an icy blue hue that appears more inhospitable than its African counterpart. After the boy on the bicycle delivers the letter he is carrying in his mouth, another bicycle violently knocks Jettel down into the snow. A German boy with impeccable Aryan looks offers to help her up. A small red swastika flag noticeably sticks out of his pants' pocket.

In a voice-over, Regina recollects, "I was always afraid. I remember Germany as a dark place." She recalls how the government had banned her father from practicing law and her grandfather from owning a hotel. When she questioned her parents about why their situation was worsening, they told her, "Because we are Jews, Regina, that's why." Climbing the staircase to her parent's apartment, Regina meets two boys she knows. One says hello, but the other chides him for speaking to a Jew. Jettel receives a letter from her husband, Walter, urging Regina and her to join him in Kenya. Although Walter's father, Max, remains because he believes the persecution of the Jews will soon end, Jettel packs for the journey. The last glimpse of Germany shows Regina waiting for her mother to board a taxi. Three swastika banners hang ominously close to where their cab is standing.

Whereas Germany's political malaise threatens the security of the Redlichs, Kenya beckons to them as an unlikely haven. The first glimpse of Walter shows him stricken by malaria. He fails to respond to the quinine doled out to him by a fellow German Jew, Süsskind, but recovers from a mixture of herbs prepared by his native cook, Owuor. Walter, who oversees the farm for a British landlord, accepts the role reversal that has occurred in his life. As a token of appreciation, he gives his judicial robe to Owuor to signify that his Kenyan caretaker is the more learned man in the bush. When the truck transporting Jettel and Regina is a speck on the horizon, Owuor detects their presence

long before Walter. As Regina stands awkwardly alone while her mother and father embrace, Owuor warmly welcomes her by lifting her above his shoulders.

Jettel attempts to segregate her daughter from the local children, whom
she deems dirty and disease ridden. Consequently, Owuor introduces Regina
to them and allows her to explore the area beyond the boundaries set by her
mother. Owuor gives Regina a fawn. When it is killed by a predator, she
blames herself for not affording it sufficient protection. Despite her bad memories of attack dogs in Germany, Regina accepts the dog Owuor bestows on
her to replace the fawn and overcomes her fears.

Jettel clings to her former lifestyle. Instead of bringing the ice chest Walter had requested, she stuffs her trunks with Rosenthal china and buys an expensive evening gown. Both are impractical in the remote corner of Kenya that
has become her home. She insists that Owuor speak German and resists learning Kiswaheli, which her daughter and husband use to communicate with him.
Jettel wonders if surviving under such spartan conditions is really preferable to
staying in Germany. Walter remarks that her attitudes toward Owuor and the
natives are not very different from those of the Nazis toward the Jews. Jettel's
spirits are buoyed when the British intern Regina and her in a posh hotel
whose management will not compromise on the quality of its food and lodg-
ing even though its guests are "enemy aliens." There Jettel has an affair with a
British officer, who reciprocates by securing Walter's release from the detention center where he is being held. When Walter enlists in the British Army
to fight Germany, Jettel learns how to manage the farm by herself.

As Jettel grows to respect the natives and appreciate the stark beauty of
the Kenyan landscape, the camera captures her changing attitudes. Jettel blends
into her surroundings by wearing khaki outfits and going topless when her
husband asks her to imitate the local women. Spectacular panoramic shots sup-
plant earlier scenes of the bush portrayed as "rough and dry."[55] Until this turning point, Jettel had been oblivious to the relevancy of Heinrich Heine's *The
Lorelei*, which Walter reads to Regina at bedtime. The sirens of German culture sang beautifully, but lured sailors' boats to sink on the shoals of the
Rhine.[56]

Link dwells on the importance of kinship and ritual among the Kenyans
and draws parallels with their significance for Jewish identity. Upon their arrival
in Kenya, Süsskind partakes of the Sabbath with the Redlichs. As he joins in the
kindling of the candles and blessings over the challah and wine, Walter admits
that he never felt the need for God before. Jettel comments that she doesn't remember when she last observed the Sabbath. Later in the movie, Süsskind accuses Walter of not really feeling he is a Jew. It is the communal solidarity and
religious ceremonies of the natives that provide an antidote to the anomie Jettel and Walter experience as uprooted and assimilated Jews. When a drought

threatens their crops, the local Kikuyu tribe slaughters a lamb to appease their ancestors and the god Ngai who resides atop Mount Kenya. Like the Jews in ancient Egypt, the Redlichs are in exile in Africa. The sacrifice of the lamb recalls how the Jews enslaved by Pharaoh daubed sheep's blood on their doors to alert God to pass over their homes and spare their firstborn sons.

Jettel orders Owuor to bring an old woman who is dying beneath a tree back to her hut. Owuor explains that this woman prefers to die outside near the spirits of her ancestors rather than to contaminate the hut of the living. Although the film contains no footage of Nazi atrocities, choosing to die serenely under a tree seems far more humane than the anonymous burial or incineration of Jewish cadavers in trenches or crematoria. Jettel attends an initiation ceremony for a Pokot boy in which a cow is sacrificed. Jettel wears her evening gown to attend what she now regards as an occasion as special as the cocktail parties she once hosted in Germany.

The most overt biblical analogy in the movie comes toward the end. Upon hearing of Germany's surrender, Walter accepts an appointment as a judge in Germany. Neither Jettel nor Regina wants to leave the land each has come to cherish. As Walter departs, a swarm of locusts descends upon the cornfields. Seeing the infestation, he returns. Members of the local tribe help Jettel, Regina, and Walter drive the insects away by flailing their arms, making noise, swinging sticks, and waving torches. Just as the plague of locusts preceded the Jewish exodus, the victory over the vermin reunites the Redlichs as a family ready to return to their homeland and participate in the building of a just society there. Regina's voice-over at the end of the movie announces that Jettel gave birth to the Redlichs's first son in Germany in 1947. Tracing her brother's multicultural lineage, she credits the Kenyan god Ngai for endowing him with strength and confirms his Jewish ancestry by noting he was named after his deceased grandfather.

Kristin Kopp has criticized Link for obscuring German guilt for the Holocaust by portraying the British as the anti-Semitic oppressors and referring to the fate of the Jews in Europe only indirectly via radio broadcasts and the reading of letters.[57] She discerns a visual resemblance between the camp where Walter is interned and German concentration camps. She likens the scene of the Jewish women departing for the hotel on a lorry to images of Eastern European Jews carted off on trucks headed for the death camps. When the men are arrested, however, Süsskind assures Walter that the British will treat them humanely. Although some of the women in the former are wearing babushkas, others, including Jettel, are wearing safari hats. The ride to the hotel appears more like a picturesque tour of Kenya than a trip to a death camp. The British soldiers treat the internees politely. Regina exclaims, "What a nice prison!" when she and her mother enter the hotel where the German Jewish women are held. The British boarding school Regina attends excludes the Jewish girls from religious instruction and teaches them that Jews killed Christ. Its headmaster admires Regina's academic achievements but attributes her success to innate Jewish ambitiousness and cleverness.

Yet, these are all rather minor instances of discrimination compared to the letters and radio reports the Redlichs receive about what is happening to the Jews under Nazi rule. After learning about the *Kristallnacht* pogrom, they conclude, "The Nazis no longer see us as human." A letter from the Red Cross informs Jettel that her mother and sister have been deported to Poland. Walter instinctively knows that "Poland means death." After Victory in Europe Day, he receives word from a former teacher that his father was killed by the SS and his sister was gassed at Belzec. Walter's decision to accept the judgeship in Germany is triggered by watching newsreels of the war-crimes trials at Nuremberg. Jettel fears that many Nazis remain in Germany.

Kopp insists that the Holocaust should be more visible in the movie because she assumes audiences have little familiarity with the event. Link recognizes how widespread awareness of the Holocaust has become. Producer Peter Herrmann concedes that Link and he avoided showing graphic images from the Holocaust because they expected the audience's preconceived notions about the Jewish genocide to be "stronger than showing the reality."[58] Critic Donald Munro astutely asserted, "The Holocaust is so deeply imprinted on our culture that director Caroline Link, working from her own screenplay, uses it like shorthand. . . . This cultural shorthand frees us up to ponder more tender plot possibilities—marital nuances, for example—that tend to get trampled in Holocaust dramas by the heavy horrors of genocide."[59]

Kopp argues that the film never denounces the colonial oppression of Africa and the privileged position whites occupied there.[60] This charge ignores the thematic focus of the film, namely the struggle of German Jews to find a haven in a remote corner of the British Empire. Must every picture that uses Africa as a setting contain an analysis of imperialism and racism? In the film, the "cultured" Germans murder Jews; the "liberal" British suspect them of being spies; and only the "primitive" Kenyans deal with them kindly.[61] By highlighting the latter's hospitality, Link implicitly discredits the arrogant justification that Africans needed Europeans to civilize them. Jettel confides to her daughter that Kenya taught her "how valuable differences are." When a Kenyan woman tries to sell bananas to the passengers on the train leaving the country, Jettel apologizes for not buying one by saying she is as poor as a monkey. The woman graciously gives Jettel a banana to feed her monkey.

The Pianist and *Nowhere in Africa* popularize lesser-known stories from the Holocaust. This trend parallels the approach taken in many recent works on the subject. Elsewhere I have compared the evolving image of the Holocaust to a "pointillist painting" in which each new account of "different aspects of the Holocaust fills a small space on a canvas, which, when viewed from a distance, reveals the contours and details of Germany's attempt to eradicate the Jews of Europe, as well as the spectrum of Jewish and Gentile responses to state-sponsored genocide."[62]

The German heritage films remember forgotten instances of German Jewish reciprocity. Such stories represent exceptions to exclusionary and then murderous rule. When Levi's wagon fades into the dark of night at the end of *Jew Boy Levi*, the audience knows he is doomed to become a victim of the Nazis.[63] The Jewish members of *The Harmonists* must leave the land where they enjoyed their greatest popularity.[64] Despite Lilly's love for Felice, it is Felice who is arrested and killed. These movies individualize the collective suffering inflicted on German Jewish citizens through disenfranchisement, discrimination, deportation, and for those who shared Felice's fate, liquidation.[65] For German Jews, who felt so attached to German culture, immigrating to "nowhere" in Africa was preferable to being deported to "somewhere" in Poland. This narrative strategy does not evade national guilt but rather indicts the Third Reich for the personal tragedies that resulted from its genocidal policies.

THE LIMITS OF REALISM: *THE GREY ZONE*
Directed by Tim Blake Nelson
(United States: Goatsingers, Killer Films,
Martien Holdings, Millennium Films, 2001)

> We do not believe in the most obvious and facile deduction: that man is fundamentally brutal, egotistic and stupid in his conduct once every civilized institution is taken away and the *Häftling* is consequently nothing but a man without inhibitions. We believe, rather, that the only conclusion to be drawn is that in the face of driving necessity and physical disabilities many social habits and instincts are reduced to silence.[66]
>
> —Primo Levi

Based on Miklòs Nyiszli's Auschwitz memoir and Primo Levi's seminal essay "The Gray Zone," Tim Blake Nelson's *The Grey Zone* constitutes the most graphic cinematic portrayal of the gassing facility at Birkenau to date.[67] Dr. Nyiszli occupied a privileged position among the camp's inmates in exchange for performing autopsies on twins who died as a result of Josef Mengele's experiments. As a reward for his services, Nyiszli obtained permission to transfer his wife and daughter to a work camp. The beneficiaries of ample food and living quarters, the Hungarian Jews of the Twelfth *Sonderkommando* postponed their deaths for four month by supervising the stripping of Jews before their executions, removing cadavers from the gas chambers, and incinerating them in open pits or crematoria. Although coerced to perform these repugnant tasks, the "special squadron" and the doctor survived by enabling Auschwitz-Birkenau to function like an efficient death-mill factory and medical-research clinic.

Nelson's metaphor of the camp as a factory pervades the film. A grayish layer of ashen emissions from the crematoria chimneys darkens the drab colors of the heaps of bodies, the uniforms of the guards and inmates, and the interiors of the undressing rooms and gas chambers. The main characters employ industrial euphemisms about their heinous duties to shield themselves from the reality that they are killing and burning human beings.[68] Nelson deleted panoramic shots of the camp to capture the sense of entrapment the members of the Sonderkommando felt as they abetted the liquidation of Jews.[69] The ambient noise consists of the roar and crackling of fires, occasional gunshots in the background, the hum of electrical generators, and the air rushing through exhaust fans removing gas fumes from the chambers. These sounds remind the characters that they are "inside the very organs of the most massively lethal killing apparatus ever assembled."[70]

The Grey Zone plunges its audience into the netherworld of loathsome choices facing the privileged Jewish prisoners of Birkenau. A handheld camera guides the viewer through dimly lit corridors, tracing the steps of Nyiszli rushing to treat a comatose man. Later in the film, a flashback recalls the chain of events that preceded this scene. The man once belonged to the Sonderkommando and carted corpses to the crematorium. Dumping a load of bodies in front of the grate, he recognizes his wife and daughter in the pile. Bereft of his family, he attempts suicide. Other Sonderkommando workers resent that the doctor tries to revive someone who no longer possesses the will to live. While one of them physically restrains Nyiszli, another smothers the man with a pillow. A third comments, "It's what he wanted, that's all." Was the doctor right to prolong the life of a man who had chosen to die? Were the Sonderkommando members murderers because they had honored his wish? Nelson refrains from judging either.[71]

After showing the disintegration of moral standards at Auschwitz, Nelson introduces the sights and sounds of a typical workday in the camp. Tossed over the shoulder of a former comrade, the suffocated man is carried down to the furnaces. The roar of the fires gets louder as he approaches the ovens. An outdoor shot of the chimneys brightens the night sky. Juxtaposed with this iconographic image is a daytime picture of an innocuous-looking brick building, which houses the machinery of death. The lawn in front of the structure is green, neatly manicured, and well watered by sprinklers. Most of the people walking around its perimeter wear civilian clothing, not striped uniforms. Pieces of furniture await collection and storage in the camp's warehouses. Inside a gas chamber, inmates hose away the blood, excrement, and urine left behind by the last group of Jews poisoned there. Other prisoners scrub and repaint the walls in preparation for the next trainload of Jews. In his office, Mengele compliments Nyiszli on his professionalism and informs him that the "volume" of their research will be increasing soon.

A transport carrying the next shipment of Jews rumbles toward the camp. The camera focuses on the frightened eyes of a Jewish girl inside a cattle car. As she looks around at the faces of the other Jews in there, the camera replicates her gaze. They look more dazed than scared. In the Union Munitions Plant at Auschwitz, the women workers are smuggling gunpowder out of the factory. They hide it on the bodies of dead Jews for the Sonderkommando to find and store. The conspirators realize that their clandestine activity jeopardizes the lives of all the women in their work detail. Their calloused leader, Rosa Robota, cavalierly remarks, "What's the fucking difference when you're dead anyway?"

Meanwhile the cycle of death and disposal continues. Two SS men empty a canister of Zyklon B into a slot in the gas chamber's roof. Muffled screams follow. Jews in long lines calmly file down the steps to their demise to the strains of a Strauss waltz played by an orchestra consisting of inmates. Although such orchestras entertained the SS, greeted Jewish transports, and performed for inmates marching to work, they never played background music for Jews descending into gas chambers.[72] An aerial shot reveals the chimneys out of which flames and the smoke from burning corpses are rising. The crematorium room looks like a foundry with the Sonderkommando feeding its fires with human carcasses. A truck dumps the ashes of the incinerated Jews, which then are shoveled into a nearby river. Nyiszli diagnoses Commandant Muhsfeldt's headaches and heavy drinking as a reaction to the recent increase in the level of "cargo."

The film then segues into a scene of the Sonderkommando feasting upon food and liquor confiscated from the new arrivals. Several prisoners discuss whether they should use the weapons and gunpowder they have procured to blow up the crematoria or to escape to testify about the atrocities they have seen. A younger inmate, Hoffman, pointedly asks, "Do you want to look anyone in the face, if any of your family is even alive, and tell them what you have done for a little more life, for vodka and bed linens?" Nelson artificially heightens the suspense by having the SS torture Dina to force her to disclose what she knows about the plot to bomb the crematoria. The interrogations and the hanging of the women implicated in the plot actually occurred after the revolt.[73]

The transport finally pulls into Auschwitz. The camera again serves as a proxy for the eyes of the girl on the cattle car. Ordered to undress and put their clothes and shoes on numbered hooks so they can locate their belongings after showering, they seem oblivious to their fate until an agitated man demands that Hoffman admit that they will be gassed. Hoffman does not comply, and the man calls him a "Nazi liar." When Hoffman notices the man is wearing a wristwatch, he commands him to surrender it. Filled with rage, Hoffman pummels the man into a bloody pulp in front of the man's hysterical wife. An SS guard kills her and smiles as he hands the watch to Hoffman. The girl watches in astonishment. Hoffman crouches on the floor, ashamed and shocked by his act of brutality.

The camera returns to the girl's gaze as she enters the gas chamber. Panic sets in among the doomed. The door is shut. The screams of the victims thunder in the ears of the distraught Hoffman. As his work crew hauls away bodies, Hoffman detects that the girl is still breathing. Somehow she has survived in an air pocket on the wet floor. A subsequent flashback replicates what she sees as she lies choking at the bottom of a pile of corpses. Saving her becomes Hoffman's chance to redeem himself.

As her face becomes visible for the first time, the audience cannot help but perceive that she bears a resemblance to Anne Frank. In his director's notes, Nelson indicates that reading Primo Levi convinced him that people are not "good at heart," as Anne Frank hoped.[74] Casting an actress who looks like Anne Frank may have been a means of discrediting the optimism Anne clung to before she was deported.

The leaders of the Sonderkommando argue over whether keeping the girl alive is a "distraction" from the uprising or proof that they are not murderers. The story of the girl who survived a gassing is true, but Nelson inserted it as a factor in the impending rebellion to heighten "dramatic tension."[75] Prior to the insurrection, Muhsfeldt had rejected Nyiszli's pleas to spare the girl and summarily shot her in the back of the neck about a half hour after learning of her existence.[76] In the movie, Muhsfeldt forces the girl to witness the reprisal executions of the Sonderkommando. Hoffman and Max console themselves by thinking "they did something." Driven to despair, the girl runs toward the electrified fence, but is shot before she can reach it.

Ironically, the most moving scene in *The Grey Zone* jettisons the film's graphic realism in favor of a more stylized look and poetic monologue. Members of the new Sonderkommando carry the girl's body to the crematorium. Filmed at a slightly slower speed with a soft focus, the figures bearing her and pushing her into the furnace look like robots burning an inanimate object. The girl stoically describes her own incineration:

> I catch fire quickly. The first part of me rises in dense smoke that mingles with the smoke of others. Then there are the bones, which settle in ash, and

these are swept up to be carried to the river, and the last bits of our dust, that simply float there in air around the working of the new group. These bits of dust are grey. We settle on their shoes and on their faces, and in their lungs, and they begin to get so used to us that soon they don't cough and they don't brush us away. At this point, they're just moving. Breathing, and moving, like anyone else still alive in that place. And this is how the work continues.[77]

The Grey Zone received mixed reviews.[78] Even its critics conceded that it was a well-intentioned attempt to dramatize the moral dilemma faced by the Sonderkommandos. What distinguished the positive from negative reviews was whether the critic believed that the depths of human depravity manifested in the operation of the extermination camp could ever be authentically represented. Roger Ebert gave the movie four stars for its devastating realism: "I have seen a lot of films about the Holocaust, but I have never seen one so immediate, unblinking, and painful in its materials." Elsewhere he opines that "there cannot be a happy ending except that the war eventually ended."[79]

Manohla Dargis of the *Los Angeles Times* doubted that any movie could convey what transpired at Auschwitz. She contended, "It isn't just that there's something unsettling about a film that aestheticizes a crematorium; it's that there's something trivializing about the very effort." She declared that "the crimes committed at Auschwitz . . . were beyond what cinema entertainment, which demands realism but not necessarily truth, can show us." Not distinguishing between audiences apt to go to films like *The Grey Zone* and those who attend teenage slasher movies, Dargis questioned the casting of David Arquette as Hoffman because he had starred in Wes Craven's *Scream* and its two sequels (1996, 1997, 2000).[80]

Dargis finds flaws in the casting, filming, and scripting of *The Grey Zone* because she shares Claude Lanzmann's belief that the Holocaust can never be adequately captured in fictional representations. Nelson anticipated this sort of criticism. In the preface to his screenplay, he states, "Of course, those in the Lanzmann camp will claim there are no events like the Holocaust, that it stands alone. It most certainly does. Yet to extend sanctimoniously the place it occupies to an area so far beyond that of other tragedies that it becomes untouchable for certain forms of artistic expression is not only self-righteous, but also self-defeating."[81] Nelson acknowledges that his "jagged and hard realism" is not the only way to depict the Holocaust and refers to the differing approaches taken by Roberto Benigni in *Life Is Beautiful* (1998) and Spielberg in *Schindler's List*.[82]

Whether the movie compels the viewer to think, this is how it must have been,[83] or to dismiss it for being nowhere horrible enough,[84] its assault on the emotional, moral, and visual sensibilities of its audience destined the film for

box-office failure. It never got booked widely and quickly disappeared from release.[85] Ads for the movie did not conceal its grim subject matter. The poster
tagline, which read, "the story you haven't seen," appeared beneath a close-up
of the haunting face of the girl. The trailer began with this voice-over: "We
can't know what we're capable of, any of us. How can you know what you'd
really do to stay alive, until you're asked? I know now that the answer for most
of us is anything."[86]

The videotape and DVD of *The Grey Zone* marketed it as a movie about
resistance despite Nelson's explicit wish that it not be construed as a heroic
film.[87] On its jacket, the recognizable faces of actors Harvey Keitel, Mira
Sorvino, David Arquette, and Steve Buscemi hover above the tagline, "While
the world was fighting . . . a secret battle was about to erupt." The narrator of
the trailer declares, "Their freedom was lost; their hope was shattered, until the
sight of one girl inspired a people to rebel."[88] Such ads deceptively implied that
The Grey Zone was a tribute to the brave defiance of the Twelfth Sonderkommando rather than about its moral debasement.

REFERENTIAL TREATMENT—THE
HOLOCAUST AS POP METAPHOR: *X-MEN*
Directed by Bryan Singer
(United States: Bad Hat Harry, Digital Domain, Donner/Schuler/Donner, Ge-
netics Productions, Marvel Entertainment, Springwood, 20th Century Fox:
2000)

> One could argue that the Holocaust is not appropriate subject
> matter for an action movie based on a comic book, but having
> talked to some *X-Men* fans, I believe that in their minds the
> medium is as deep and portentous as say, *Sophie's Choice*.[89]
>
> —Roger Ebert

The Holocaust and its contemporary repercussions lend themselves to being
filmed as action movies. This genre easily accommodates stories about resistance, rescue, suppressing neo-Nazi conspiracies, and tracking down German
war criminals. Since 2000, action movies rank as the second most popular
genre of Holocaust films. The best-known recent Holocaust thrillers were
Charlotte Gray (2001), *Uprising* (2001), and *The Statement* (2003). In the adaptation of Tom Clancy's *The Sum of All Fears* (2003), neo-Nazis resort to nuclear
terrorism to provoke a war between the United States and Russia. After September 11, 2001, vilifying neo-Nazis was an evasion of the recent assault on
America perpetrated by Islamic fundamentalists.[90]

Bryan Singer's *X-Men* establishes more substantial connections to the Holocaust to clarify the motivations of its leading villain and draw parallels between it and contemporary prejudices. The opening scene recapitulates a shot from *Schindler's List* when Schindler's female workers arrive in Auschwitz. After emerging from real showers, they see less fortunate Jews walking down a stairway into the room where they will disrobe before entering the gas chambers. The camera pans to the smoke and flames rising out of the crematoria chimney. In *X-Men*, the Germans separate a teenage Jewish boy named Erik Lehnsherr from his parents at the entrance to a death camp. A caption informs viewers that the place and time are somewhere in Poland in 1944. The numbers on the arms of some inmates and the Jewish stars on the coats of the new inmates identify them as Jews. As Lehnsherr struggles to rejoin his parents, the guards restrain him. At that moment, he generates a jolt of magnetic energy that twists the iron bars of the camp's gate. Then, Singer focuses the camera on the crematorium chimney, panning halfway up it before the dissolve. By editing the frame this way, he presumes viewers can complete the tracking of the camera on their own.

Lehnsherr represents a new species, whose members possess superhuman powers as a result of a genetic mutation or exposure to radiation. Their superpowers manifest themselves initially when they are under great stress or going through puberty. As fears arise that mutants pose a danger to national security, an American senator named Kelly rallies public opinion and Congress to mandate the registration of all mutants for surveillance. At the hearing on the Mutant Registration Act, Magneto (a.k.a. Lehnsherr) listens to arguments for a bill that reminds him of the Nazi laws that disenfranchised Jews as the prelude to their destruction. Convinced that a war between mutants and human beings cannot be averted, Magneto has invented a process to mutate the genes of humans and thereby homogenize the world's population. Singer expects audiences to find Magneto's fear of an imminent mutant holocaust credible.[91]

Dr. Charles Xavier is Magneto's nemesis. Played by Patrick Stewart of *Star Trek: The Next Generation* (1987–1994) fame, Dr. X brings an aura of moral rectitude to the part. The son of a nuclear technician, he developed tremendous telepathic powers when he was exposed to radiation as a child. Although mentally superior, Xavier lost the use of his legs in a childhood accident. Although not a Jew, Dr. X fits a traditional stereotype of Jewish males whose intellectuality compensates for a lack of physical prowess.[92] In the comic book series, Dr. X had befriended Magneto in Israel, where the latter worked in a psychiatric hospital for Holocaust survivors. Xavier envisages a world in which mutants and humans can live in harmony. Magneto believes humans "will fear what they do not understand and destroy what they fear." To advance his dream of peaceful coexistence between humans and mutants, Dr. X runs a boarding school to train teenage mutants how to harness their powers to benefit society.

A volatile loner nicknamed Wolverine provides the movie's other link to the Holocaust. Since his body can heal from any injury, the Canadian Army selected Wolverine to undergo experimental surgery that grafted an unbreakable alloy onto his bones and retractable claws onto his hands. Flashbacks of the excruciating operation enter momentarily into his consciousness. The jump-cut frames of X-ray negatives, electrodes, and physicians hovering over him conjure up images of Nazi medical experiments. In the film's sequel *X2: X-Men United* (2003), Wolverine returns to the abandoned compound where this occurred. The barbed wire on its dilapidated fence appears first in sharp and then soft focus as is often done in documentaries and feature films with exterior shots of German concentration camps. At the site, Wolverine learns that General Stryker, who headed the project that operated on him, is preparing to destroy all mutants.[93] Only the most avid fans of the comic book series will recognize that Stryker is based on SS war-crimes fugitive Baron von Strucker, who kidnapped Dr. X's Israeli paramour Gabrielle Haller, a survivor of Dachau.[94]

Singer draws parallels between the genocide survived by Magneto and those chapters in American history when mass hysteria has led to egregious violations of the civil liberties of political radicals and minority groups. On a website posted in conjunction with the release of the film, Senator Kelly warns Americans that it is their patriotic duty to report suspected mutants. Surveying developments throughout the United States, the site features news stories about the Boy Scouts denying membership to mutants, health insurance companies withholding coverage from them, and a superintendent banning them from enrolling in the schools in his district.[95] Kelly convenes a U.N. meeting on Ellis Island, the gateway to America for past generations of immigrants, to coordinate efforts against the mutants. Without disrupting the flow of his action-driven film, Singer implies that the dynamics of prejudice operate similarly against those who differ from mainstream Americans, whether they are communists, gays, immigrants, Jews, or people afflicted with AIDS.

Some critics denounced *X-Men* for trivializing the Holocaust. Chuck Rudolph fumed, "Opening with a scene set in Auschwitz, *X-Men* progresses to draw distinct and subversive parallels between its battling groups of mutant superheroes and real-world relations with race and ethnicity, both past and present, homegrown and worldwide—parallels that are dangerously shallow and exploitive."[96] Others were impressed by the serious themes the movie raised. David Denby advised audiences to see the film a second time "to sort out the thickly allusive texture of references."[97] James Brundage cited the historical precedents for the movie's political scenario: "Magneto and the like offer one degree of Social Darwinism (I'd say Nazism, but I would get flamed) . . . that the mutants are a super race. Humans offer McCarthyism, that mutants should be registered. However, let's not forget that Jewish registration eventually led to the Holocaust."[98]

Singer's entertaining mixture of science fiction action with socially significant themes has its roots in the original Marvel comic books. Jack Kirby and Stan Lee, the creators of the series, were the American-born children of Jews who immigrated to the United States before World War II. Their own social mobility, the rise of Nazism, and the advent of world war, the McCarthy Hearings, and the civil rights movement provided the formative experiences that validated their faith in American democratic ideals and fear of charismatic demagogues. Kirby designed the cover page for the first issue of *Captain America* in March 1941. It featured the patriotic superhero punching Hitler in the face. Similarly, Lee's first comic strip character was the Destroyer, a superhero dedicated to defeating the Third Reich.[99]

The two developed the *X-Men* series during the height of the American civil rights movement in 1963. In a 1965 "soapbox" column, Lee declared, "We believe that man has a divine destiny, and an awesome responsibility of treating all who share this wondrous world of ours with tolerance and respect—judging each fellow human on his own merit, regardless of race, creed, or color."[100]

In the 1970s, Marvel writer Chris Claremont changed Magneto into a Holocaust survivor, transforming him into a "tragic figure who wants to save his people"[101]

Born in 1966, director Singer grew up in the era when the Holocaust increasingly entered American consciousness. His adaptation of Stephen King's novella *Apt Pupil* (1998) consists of a series of intense exchanges between a teenage boy and a Nazi war criminal residing in his neighborhood. The boy is so curious to learn firsthand about the Final Solution that he prefers interrogating the former SS commandant about the atrocities he perpetrated to turning him over to the police.[102] When asked what attracted him to King's story, Singer replied that it was "that this terrible, awful thing that happened so many years ago, so many decades ago in Europe . . . would somehow have crept up, across the ocean, through time, and into this beautiful southern California suburban neighborhood and this seemingly normal, all American, young man."[103]

Singer's use of the Holocaust as a plot device in a fantasy action movie may strike scholars and survivors of the event as tasteless and trivial. Yet, it illustrates how the Shoah symbolizes the essence of evil to the average viewer. This is why it has become such an inviting topic to reference in films about human intolerance. If Art Spiegelman can be acclaimed for presenting the Holocaust as a conflict between Jewish mice and Nazi cats, then why is it inappropriate for a cinematic allegory about the fear and persecution of genetic mutants to draw parallels with the Holocaust?[104] Pragmatically, one might consider that *X-Men* and its sequel grossed over \$157 and \$214 million in American box-office sales alone. The first film not only swept the Saturn Awards conferred by the Academy of Science Fiction, Fantasy, and Horror Films, but it earned a nomination from the Political Film Society for the Best Picture on Human Rights and Peace.[105] As a stimulus to increase interest in the Holocaust, *X-Men* has a better chance of reaching younger audiences than most movies.[106]

HOLOCAUST CINEMA AS PROSTHETIC MEMORY

> The mass cultural technologies that enable the production and dissemination of prosthetic memories are incredibly powerful; rather than disdain and turn our backs on these technologies, we must instead recognize their power and political potential.[107]
>
> —Alison Landsberg

Like the particles of dust filling the air in *The Grey Zone*, images and themes from the Holocaust permeate popular culture. I hope this survey of recent representations of the Holocaust in feature films dispels the fear frequently expressed by survivors of the Shoah that nobody remembers the event that shattered their lives. The sheer quantity of such movies and the diverse lessons drawn from the Holocaust raise new concerns. If the topic becomes too familiar, will it eventually lose its ability to outrage? If it stands as the benchmark for measuring the severity of other state crimes, will the public minimize the suffering of other groups persecuted for ethnic, political, or racial reasons in the past or the present.[108] Barbie Zelizer argues that the Holocaust is "overused because it reconfigures not only what we see versus what we remember, but also what we remember of the events of yore versus what we need to see of the events of now."[109]

Returning to the metaphor from *The Grey Zone*, the issue could be posed in a different way. Perhaps we will never become inured to the Holocaust by seeing it on the screen. It may stick in the throats of viewers, alerting them to how bigotry, human rights abuses, and modern warfare can escalate into genocide. Prosthetic memories, to use Alison Landsberg's term, are those experienced vicariously through their reenactment in cinema or other mass media. Presenting serious themes as a form of entertainment may rob them of their social impact, but if done well, it can also make the historical and current injustices endured by diverse groups accessible to audiences anywhere and "might be instrumental in generating empathy and articulating an ethical relation to the other."[110]

Filmmakers assist audiences in making these empathic leaps into allegedly "unimaginable" circumstances by employing familiar genres, images, or themes that render what is portrayed something not entirely alien to them. The biopic has emerged as the most common genre of Holocaust movie precisely because it encourages viewers to experience vicariously a spectrum of individual responses to the vast historical forces that thrust Hitler into power and transformed Europe into a charnel house for Jews. Through the attentive eyes and stunned silence of Władysław Szpilman, audiences glimpse some semblance of what it was like to witness the deprivation and deportation of an entire community and to feel vulnerable as a Jew in hiding. Moviegoers may avoid films that make this cinematic encounter with dehumanization and systematic mass murder too personally disturbing and visceral, as the dismal box-office record of *The Grey Zone* indicates. Relocating a family like the Redlichs to a remote place that seems like "nowhere" from a Eurocentric perspective conveys the sense of disorientation all refugees feel when they must flee their homelands and assume new identities as aliens. For adolescents first learning about the Shoah, embedding it in an action movie like *X-Men* may spark an interest in it and other instances of genocide and political repression.

As the Holocaust recedes into the past, the current rate of Holocaust film production probably cannot be sustained. Nevertheless, pictures that do get made can allude to a wealth of images and themes conveyed by books, educational courses, the Internet, movies, museums, television, videos, and DVDs. I expect critics of my book will doubt that the public possesses this level of familiarity with the event. Yet, would a commercially savvy director like Bryan Singer include such plot and visual references in *X-Men* without checking to see whether they resonated with audience focus groups. Similarly, *Anne B. Real* (2003) assumes African American teenagers know enough about *The Diary of Anne Frank* to recognize why a black girl who struggles to break out of the slum on Amsterdam Avenue in New York by composing rap music identifies with Anne Frank's aspirations to become a famous writer under the most adverse conditions.[111]

The meanings wrested from the Shoah will change over time, relating it to current events and the roles it plays in the histories of particular countries. Given both the quantity and quality of Holocaust feature movies, particularly over the past two decades, we should cease posing the outdated question, Can the Holocaust be represented in feature films? and ask instead, Which cinematic genres and themes will be used to represent it and render it relevant to future audiences?

NOTES

1. Jim Collins, *Architecture of Excess: Cultural Life in the Information Age* (New York: Routledge, 1995), 147–48.

2. Lawrence Baron, "Holocaust Awareness and Denial in the United States: The Hype and the Hope," in *Memory, Memorialization, and Denial*, Vol. 3 of *Lessons and Legacies*, ed. Peter Hayes (Evanston, IL: Northwestern University Press, 1999), 225–38.

3. Robert Brent Toplin, *Reel History: In Defense of Hollywood* (Lawrence: University of Kansas Press, 2002), 8–9, 26–28, 59–69, 184–88, 196–205.

4. Jeffrey Shandler, *While America Watches: Televising the Holocaust* (New York: Oxford University Press, 1999), 211–56.

5. Lawrence Baron, "Remembering the Holocaust in American Life: 1945–1960," *Holocaust and Genocide Studies* 16, no. 4 (Spring 2003): 62–88.

6. Charles R. Acland, *Screen Traffic: Movies, Multiplexes, and Global Culture* (Durham, NC: Duke University Press, 2003), 198–246; Mark Jancovich and Lucy Faire with Sarah Stubbins, *The Place of the Audience* (London: BFI Publishing, 2003), 183–250.

7. Oren Baruch Stier, *Committed to Memory: Cultural Mediations of the Holocaust* (Amherst: University of Massachusetts Press, 2002); John Storey, *Inventing Popular Culture: From Folklore to Globalization* (Malden, MA: Blackwell Publishing, 2003), 70–73.

8. Charles P. Mitchell, *The Hitler Filmography: Worldwide Feature Films and Television Miniseries Portrayals, 1940–2000* (Jefferson, NC: McFarland and Co., 2002), 9.

9. Carolyn Anderson and Jon Lupo, "Hollywood Lives: The State of the Biopic at the Turn of the Century," in *Genre and Contemporary Hollywood*, ed. Steve Neale (London: British Film Institute, 2002), 92.

10. *Conspiracy,* directed by Frank Pierson (United States, 2001).

11. Ian Kershaw, *Hitler: 1889–1936: Hubris* (New York: W. W. Norton and Co., 1999), 63–67.

12. *Max,* directed by Menno Meyjes (Canada, Germany, Hungary, 2002). Max Gross, "Portrait of the Führer as a Young Man," *Forward* (December 20, 2002): 13; Rebecca Murray and Fred Topel, "John Cusack Talks about *Max,*" at http://movies.about.com/library/weekly/aamaxinta.htm (accessed June 16, 2005).

13. Kershaw, *Hubris,* 122–29 and 153–54.

14. Anthony Wood and Frank Whitford, eds., *The Berlin of George Grosz: Drawings, Watercolors, and Prints, 1912–1930* (New Haven, CT: Yale University Press, 1997).

15. *The Hitler Gang,* directed by John Farrow (United States, 1944).

16. Robin Young, "Historian Abandons Hitler TV Series," *London Times*, March 17, 2003.

17. "*Hitler: The Rise of Evil*: Guide for Educators," at www.kidsnet.org.pdf.riceofevil_edguide.pdf (accessed June 16, 2005).

18. "H-German Media Forum on the Miniseries: *Hitler: The Rise of Evil,*" at www.hnet.org/~german/discuss/hitlerminiseries/Hitler_miniseries_index.html (accessed July 10, 2003).

19. "Christian Duguay," at www.northernstars.ca/directorsal/duguay.html (accessed August 13, 2003).

20. "The History News Network, Tracks Hitler Analogies Made by Politicians, Journalists, and Polemicists," "Hitler Watch," October 19, 2003, at http://hnn.us/articles/1412.html (accessed October 19, 2003).

21. "Box Office and Business," *Max*, at www.imdb.com.

22. Joel Ryan, "'Friends' Wins Big: CBS Wins Bigger," May 20, 2003, at www.eonline.com (accessed May 20, 2003).

23. Alvin Rosenfeld, *Imagining Hitler* (Bloomington: Indiana University Press, 1985), 104–5.

24. Ian Kershaw, "The Human Hitler," *Guardian*, September 17, 2004, at www.guardian.co.uk (accessed October 1, 2004). Also, see *The Downfall*: The Official Movie Website, at www.downfallthefilm.com (accessed June 17, 2005).

25. Władysław Szpilman, *The Pianist: The Extraordinary True Story of One Man's Survival in Warsaw, 1939–1945*, trans. Anthea Bell (New York: Picador, 2000), 182.

26. Peter Novick, *The Holocaust in American Life* (Boston: Houghton Mifflin, 1999), 189–203, 234–38; George F. Custen, *Bio/Pics: How Hollywood Constructed Public History* (New Brunswick, NJ: Rutgers University Press, 1992), 214–25.

27. Roman Polanski, *Roman* (New York: William Morrow and Co., 1984), 17–59.

28. Joseph McBride, *Steven Spielberg* (New York: Simon and Schuster, 1997), 424–26.

29. "A Story of Survival: Behind the Scenes of *The Pianist*," *The Pianist*, DVD (Universal City, CA: Focus Features, 2003).

30. Barbie Zelizer, *Remembering to Forget: Holocaust Memory through the Camera's Eye* (Chicago: University of Chicago Press, 1998), 213–20.

31. Szpilman, *The Pianist*, 13.

32. Szpilman, *The Pianist*, 79–80.

33. Szpilman, *The Pianist*, 73–74.

34. Szpilman, *The Pianist*, 106.

35. Polanski, *Roman*, 33; "A Story of Survival," *The Pianist*, DVD.

36. *Cast Away*, directed by Robert Zemeckis (United States, 2000).

37. *Uprising*, directed by Jon Avnet (United States, 2001).

38. The cover of the DVD quotes Rex Reed praising *The Pianist*, as "a riveting adventure story!"

39. "A Story of Survival," *The Pianist*, DVD.

40. "Extracts from the Diary of Captain Wilm Hosenfeld," and Wolf Biermann, "Epilogue: A Bridge between Władysław Szpilman and Wilm Hosenfeld," in Szpilman, *The Pianist*, 176–81, 193–222.

41. See the blurbs on the case for *The Pianist*, DVD. Omer Bartov, *The "Jew" in Cinema: From the Golem to Don't Touch My Holocaust* (Bloomington: Indiana University Press, 2005), 142–44.

42. Randall Halle, "German Film, Aufgehoben: Ensembles of Transnational Cinema," *New German Critique* 87 (Fall 2002): 21–28.

43. "Awards and Nominations," *The Pianist*, at www.imdb.com.

44. Thane Rosenbaum, "A Skewed Vision: What's Wrong with Holocaust Movies," *Wall Street Journal*, January 9, 2003; Also see Bartov, *The "Jew" in Cinema*, 144–45.

45. Robert Strybel, "Polanski's *Pianist*, a 'Must See' for Every Polish American," *The Summit Times* 10, no. 29 (2003); The National Polish-American-Jewish Council, Letter to Paul E. Stiger, January 21, 2003, at www.npajac.org/press/20030121_wsj_pianist .html (accessed December 10, 2004).

46. William Grim, "The Pianist Plays Germany," *Congress Monthly* (January–February 2003), 17–18.

47. "Awards and Nominations," *Nowhere in Africa*, at www.imdb.com. Eight of the sixteen film awards that *Nowhere in Africa* received were from German organizations.

48. Stephanie Zweig, "Strangers in a Strange Land," *Guardian* (March 21, 2003).

49. Caroline Link, "Der Geruch Afrikas," in *Abenteuer Afrika: Erlebnisse, Geschichten, und Bilder*, ed. Caroline Link and Peter Herrmann (Munich: Langen Müller, 2002), 29.

50. *Beyond Silence*, directed by Caroline Link (Germany, 1997); *Annaluise and Anton*, directed by Caroline Link (Germany, 1997).

51. Daniel Rosenthal, "Screen Time for Hitler," *Times*, April 3, 2003, Features, 18.

52. Stefanie Zweig, *Nirgendwo in Afrika* (Munich: Langen Müller, 1995); Stephanie Zweig, *Nowhere in Africa: An Autobiographical Novel*, trans. Marlies Comjean (Madison: University of Wisconsin Press, 2002); Stefanie Zweig, "Brief an Sidede Onyulo," in *Abenteuer Afrika*, 9–25.

53. Lutz Koepnick, "Reframing the Past: Heritage Cinema and Holocaust in the 1990s," *New German Critique* 87 (Fall 2002): 47–82.

54. Juliane Köhler, "Ich war Jettel," in *Abenteuer Afrika*, 72–82.

55. Caroline Link, quoted in Matthew Ross, "The Perils of Escape; Caroline Link Discusses *Nowhere in Africa*," at www.indiewire.com/people/people_030307link.html (accessed July 24, 2003).

56. Heinrich Heine, "Die Heimkehr," in *Heine* (Baltimore: Penguin Books, 1967), 40–41.

57. Kristen Kopp, "Exterritorialized Heritage in Caroline Link's *Nowhere in Africa*," *New German Critique* 87 (Fall 2002): 112–15.

58. Peter Herrmann, quoted in David Rosenthal, "Screen Time for Hitler," 2–3.

59. Donald Munro, "Not Just Another Holocaust Movie," *Fresno Bee*, July 11, 2003.

60. Kopp, "Exterritorialized," 115–26.

61. Link, "Der Geruch Afrikas," in *Abenteuer Afrika*, 27–29; Peter Herrmann, "Es Regnet," in *Abenteuer Afrika*, 49–50.

62. Lawrence Baron, "Experiencing, Explaining, and Exploiting the Holocaust," *Judaism: A Quarterly Journal of Jewish Life and Thought* 50, no. 2 (Spring 2001): 158.

63. Johannes von Moltke, "Heimat and History: *Viehjud Levi*," *New German Critique* 87 (Fall 2002): 82–105.

64. Lutz Koepnick, "Honor Your German Masters: History, Memory, and National Identity in Joseph Vilsmaier's *Comedian Harmonists*," in *Light Motives: German Popular Film in Perspective*, ed. Randalle Halle and Margaret McCarthy (Detroit, MI: Wayne State University Press, 2003), 349–79.

65. von Moltke, "Heimat and History," 99–105.

66. Primo Levi, *Survival in Auschwitz*, trans. Stuart Woolf (New York: Collier Books, 1961), 79.

67. Primo Levi, "The Gray Zone," in *The Drowned and the Saved*, trans. Raymond Rosenthal (New York: Summit Books, 1988), 36–69; Miklos Nyiszli, *Auschwitz: A Doc-*

tor's Eyewitness Account, trans. Tibere Kremer and Richard Seaver (Greenwich, CT: Fawcett Crest, 1960).

68. Tim Blake Nelson, *The Grey Zone: Director's Notes and Screenplay* (New York: Newmarket Press, 2003), 145.

69. "Deleted Scenes," *The Grey Zone,* DVD (United States: Lions Gate Home Entertainment, 2003).

70. Nelson, *The Grey Zone,* 165.

71. Nelson, *The Grey Zone,* 141.

72. Danuta Czech, "The Auschwitz Prisoner Administration," in *Anatomy of the Auschwitz Death Camp*, ed. Yisrael Gutman and Michael Berenbaum (Bloomington: Indiana University Press, 1994), 367–68.

73. Nelson, *The Grey Zone,* 157–58; Hermann Langbein, "The Auschwitz Underground," in *Anatomy of the Auschwitz Death Camp,* 502.

74. Nelson, *The Grey Zone,* ix.

75. Nelson, *The Grey Zone,* 155–56.

76. Nyiszli, *Auschwitz,* 88–92.

77. Nelson, *The Grey Zone,* 120–21.

78. "*The Grey Zone*," at www.metacritic.com. *The Grey Zone* received a rating of 61 out of 100.

79. Roger Ebert, "*The Grey Zone*," October 25, 2002, at www.suntimes.com.

80. Manohla Dargis, "Meticulous Details Add Up to Holocaust Trivia in *Zone*," October 18, 2002, at www.caldendarlive.com, 1–2.

81. Nelson, *The Grey Zone,* xii.

82. Nelson, *The Grey Zone,* 163.

83. Joe Leydon, "Shades of Grey," *San Francisco Examiner*, October 25, 2002.

84. Dargis, "Meticulous," 1.

85. "Box Office and Business Data," *The Grey Zone,* www.imdb.com.

86. See "Posters" and "Trailers" for *The Grey Zone* at www.imdb.com; also see Bartov, *The "Jew" in Cinema*, 146–47.

87. Nelson, *The Grey Zone,* 158–59.

88. *The Grey Zone,* DVD (United States: Lion's Gate Home Entertainment, 2003).

89. Roger Ebert, "*X-Men*," at www.suntimes.com.

90. Roger Ebert, "*The Sum of All Fears*," *Chicago Sun-Times*, May 31, 2002.

91. Kathrin Bower, "Holocaust Avengers: Fact and (Science) Fiction" (paper presented at the German Studies Association, October 2002, San Diego, CA).

92. Sander Gilman, *The Jews' Body* (New York: Routledge, 1991); Sander Gilman, *Smart Jews: The Construction of the Image of Jewish Superior Intelligence* (Lincoln: University of Nebraska Press, 1996), 175–206.

93. *X2: X-Men United*, directed by Bryan Singer (United States, 2003).

94. "Baron von Strucker," at www.marveldirectory.com.

95. "A Word from Senator Kelly," at www.mutantwatch.com.

96. Chuck Rudolph, "X-Men," *Matinee Magazine*, at www.rottentomatoes.com; also see Peter Travers, "X-Men: Geek Movie of the Year," *Rolling Stone* 887 (August 17, 2000): 119–20.

197. David Denby, "Dazzled: Mutants and the Human Problem," *The New Yorker* (July 24, 2000): 86–87.

98. James Brundage, "The Good Nazi," August 9, 2000, at www.epinions.com.

99. Lawrence Baron, "X-Men as J-Men: The Jewish Subtext of a Comic Book Movie," in *Shofar: An Interdisciplinary Journal of Jewish Studies* 22, no. 1 (Fall 2003): 44–52; Ronin Ro, *Tales to Astonish: Jack Kirby, Stan Lee, and the American Comic Book Revolution* (New York: Bloomsbury, 2004), 1–48.

100. Stan Lee, "Stan's Soapbox," reprinted in Les Daniels, *Marvel: Five Fabulous Decades of the World's Greatest Comics* (New York: Harry N. Abrams, 1991), 107.

101. Arie Kaplan, "Kings of Comics—How Jews Transformed the Comic Book Industry; Part II: The Silver Age (1956–1978)," *Reform Judaism* 32, no. 2 (Winter 2003): 12–13.

102. *Apt Pupil*, directed by Bryan Singer (United States, 1998); Claudia Eppert, "Entertaining History: (Un)heroic Identifications, Apt Pupils, and an Ethical Imagination," *New German Critique* 86 (Summer 2002): 71–73; Caroline Joan Picart and Jason Grant McKahan, "Sexuality, Power, and Holocaust Film Spectatorship in *Apt Pupil*," in Caroline Joan Picart, *The Holocaust Film Sourcebook* (Westport, CT: Praeger, 2004), 1:22–40.

103. Bryan Singer, quoted in Eddie Cockrell, "One Good Hard Step beyond Innocence: A Few Moments with Bryan Singer," at www.nitrateonline.com/faptpupil.html (accessed June 16, 2005).

104. Art Spiegelman, *My Father Bleeds History*, Vol. 1 of *Maus: A Survivor's Tale* (New York: Pantheon, 1986); Art Spiegelman, *And Here My Troubles Began*, Vol. 2 of *Maus: A Survivor's Tale* (New York: Pantheon, 1991).

105. "Awards and Honors," *X-Men* and *X2: X Men United*, directed by Bryan Singer (United States, 2003), at www.imdb.com.

106. Peter Hanson, *The Cinema of Generation X* (Jefferson, NC: McFarland and Co., 2002), 123–25.

107. Alison Landsberg, "Prosthetic Memory: The Ethics and Politics of Memory in an Age of Mass Culture," in *Memory and Popular film*, ed. Paul Grange (Manchester, UK: Manchester University Press, 2003), 158.

108. Novick, *The Holocaust in American Life*, 239–63.

109. Zelizer, *Remembering to Forget*, 227.

110. Landsberg, "Prosthetic Memory," 149.

111. *Anne B. Real*, directed by Lisa France (United States, 2003).

Selected Bibliography

FILM AND POPULAR CULTURE

Acland, Charles R. *Screen Traffic: Movies, Multiplexes, and Global Culture.* Durham, NC: Duke University Press, 2003.

Altman, Rick. *Film/Genre.* London: British Film Institute, 1999.

Balio, Tina, ed. *Hollywood in the Age of Television.* Boston: Unwin Hyman, 1990.

Browne, Nick, ed. *Refiguring American Film Genres.* Berkeley: University Press of California, 1998.

Collins, Jim. *Architectures of Excess: Cultural Life in the Information Age.* New York: Routledge, 1995.

Custin, George F. *Bio/Pics: How Hollywood Constructed Public History.* New Brunswick, NJ: Rutgers University Press, 1992.

Dixon, Wheeler Winston, ed. *Film Genre 2000.* Albany: State University Press of New York, 2000.

Doherty, Thomas. *Teenagers and Teenpics: The Juvenalization of American Movies in the 1950s.* London: Unwin Hyman, 1988.

Ferro, Marc. *Cinema and History,* trans. Naomi Greene. Detroit, MI: Wayne State University Press, 1988.

Fowkes, Katherine A. *Giving Up the Ghost: Spirits, Ghosts, and Angels in Mainstream Comedy Films.* Detroit, MI: Wayne State University Press, 1998.

Gehring, Wes D., ed. *Handbook of American Film Genres.* Westport, CT: Greenwood Press, 1988.

———. *Parody as Film Genre: "Never Give a Saga an Even Break."* Westport, CT: Greenwood Press, 1999.

Grange, Paul, ed. *Memory and Popular Film.* Manchester, UK: Manchester University Press, 2003.

Grant, Barry Keith, ed. *Film Genre Reader II.* Austin: University of Texas Press, 1995.

Hanson, Peter. *The Cinema of Generation X.* Jefferson, NC: McFarland and Co., 2002.

Hill, John, and Pamela Church Gibson, ed. *Film Studies: Critical Approaches*. New York: Oxford University Press, 2000.

Horton, Andrew, and Stuart Y. McDougal, eds. *Play It Again, Sam: Retakes on Remakes*. Berkeley: University of California Press, 1998.

Jancovich, Marv, and Lucy Faire with Sarah Stubbings. *The Place of the Audience: Cultural Geographies of Film Consumption*. London: British Film Institute, 2003.

Jeffords, Susan. *Hard Bodies: Hollywood Masculinity in the Reagan Era*. New Brunswick, NJ: Rutgers University Press, 1994.

Kaminsky, Stuart M. *American Film Genres*, 2nd ed. Chicago: Nelson-Hall, 1985.

Kaplan, Ann. *Feminism and Film*. New York: Oxford University Press, 2000.

King, Geoff. *New Hollywood Cinema: An Introduction*. New York: Columbia University Press, 2002.

Kuhn, Annette. *Women's Pictures: Feminism and Cinema*, 2nd ed. New York: Verso, 1994.

Lewis, Jon, ed. *The End of Cinema as We Know It*. New York: New York University Press, 2001.

Lipkin, Steven N. *Real Emotional Logic: Film and Television Docudrama as Persuasive Practice*. Carbondale: Southern Illinois University Press, 2002.

Mathijs, Ernest, and Xavier Mendik, eds. *Alternative Europe: Eurotrash and Exploitation Cinema Since 1945*. London: Wallflower Press, 2004.

Mayne, Judith. *Cinema and Spectatorship*. New York: Routledge, 1993.

Mitchell, Charles P. *The Hitler Filmography: Worldwide Feature Film and Miniseries Portrayals, 1940 through 2000*. Jefferson, NC: McFarland and Company, 2002.

Monaco, James. *How to Read a Film*, 3rd ed. New York: Oxford University Press, 2000.

Morris, Tim. *You're Only Young Twice: Children's Literature and Film*. Urbana: University of Illinois Press, 2000.

Naficy, Hamid, ed. *Home, Exile, Homeland: Film, Media, and the Politics of Place*. New York: Routledge. 1999.

Naremore, James. *Film Adaptation*. New Brunswick, NJ: Rutgers University Press, 2000.

Neale, Steve. *Genre and Hollywood*. New York: Routledge, 2000.

———, ed. *Genre and Contemporary Hollywood*. London: British Film Institute, 2002.

Neale, Steve, and Frank Krutnik. *Popular Film and Television Comedy*. New York: Routledge, 1990.

Platte, S. Brent, and David Jasper, eds. *Imagining Otherness: Filmic Visions of Living Together*. Atlanta: Scholars Press, 1999.

Pomerance, Murray, ed. *Bad: Infamy, Darkness, Evil and Slime on Screen*. Albany: State University Press of New York, 2004.

Rosenstone, Robert A. *Visions of the Past: The Challenge of Film to Our Idea of History*. Cambridge, MA: Harvard University Press, 1995.

Rosenthal, Alan, ed. *Why Docudrama: Fact-Fiction on Film and TV*. Carbondale: Southern Illinois University Press, 1999.

Ruffles, Tom. *Ghost Images: Cinema of the Afterlife*. Jefferson, NC: MacFarland and Co., 2004.

Schatz, Thomas. *Hollywood Genres: Formulas, Filmmaking, and the Studio System*. New York: Random House, 1981.

Sorlin, Pierre. *The Film in History: Restaging the Past*. Totowa, NJ: Barnes and Noble Books, 1980.

Staiger, Janet. *Interpreting Films: Studies in the Historical Reception of American Cinema*. Princeton, NJ: Princeton University Press, 1992.

Staples, Terry. *All Pals Together: The Story of Children's Cinema*. Edinburgh, Scotland: Edinburgh University Press, 1997.

Storey, John. *Inventing Popular Culture: From Folklore to Globalization*. Malden, MA: Blackwell, 2003.

Street, Douglas, ed. *Children's Novels and the Movies*. New York: Frederick Ungar, 1983.

Toplin, Robert Brent. *Reel History: In Defense of Hollywood*. Lawrence: University of Kansas Press, 2002.

Turim, Maureen. *Flashbacks in Film*. New York: Routledge, 1989.

Turner, Graeme. *The Film as Social Practice*, 3rd ed. New York: Routledge, 1999.

———, ed. *The Film Cultures Reader*. New York: Routledge, 2002.

Wartenberg, Thomas. *Unlikely Couples: Movie Romance as Social Criticism*. Boulder, CO: Westview Press, 1990.

Wasko, Janet. *Hollywood in the Information Age*. Austin: University of Texas Press, 1994.

Wojcik-Andres, Ian. *Children's Films: History, Ideology, Pedagogy, Theory*. New York: Garland, 2000.

NATIONAL CINEMAS

Bergfelder, Tim, Erica Carter, and Deniz Goturk, eds. *German Cinema Book*. London: British Film Institute, 2003.

Bondanella, Donald. *Italian Cinema,* 3rd ed. New York: Continuum, 2001.

Cavenaugh, Carole, and Dennis Washburn, eds. *Word and Image in Japanese Cinema*. New York: Cambridge University Press, 2001.

Conrad, Peter. *Orson Welles: The Stories of His Life*. London: Faber and Faber, 2003.

Corrigan, Timothy. *New German Cinema*. Bloomington: Indiana University Press, 1994.

Cunningham, John. *Hungarian Cinema: From Coffee House to Multiplex*. London: Wallflower Press, 2004.

Dalla Vacche, Angela. *The Body in the Mirror: Shapes of History in Italian History*. Princeton, NJ: Princeton University Press, 1992.

Davidson, John. *Deterritorializing the New German Cinema*. Minneapolis: University of Minnesota Press, 1999.

Desser, David, and Lester D. Friedman. *American Jewish Filmmakers*, 2nd ed. University of Illinois Press, 2004.

Elsaesser, Thomas. *New German Cinema*. New Brunswick, NJ: Rutgers University Press, 1989.

Elsaesser, Thomas, and Michael Wedel, eds. *The BFI Companion to German Cinema*. London: British Film Institute, 1999.

Erens, Patricia. *The Jew in American Cinema*. Bloomington: Indiana University Press, 1984.

Ford, Charles, and Robert Hammond. *Polish Film: A Twentieth-Century History.* Jefferson, NC: McFarland and Co., 2005.

Friedman, Lester. *Jewish Image in American Film: 70 Years of Hollywood's Vision of Jewish Characters and Themes.* Secaucus, NJ: Citadel Press, 1987.

Fehrenbach, Heide. *Cinema in Democratizing Germany.* Chapel Hill: University of North Carolina Press, 1995.

Finney, Angus. *The State of European Cinema: A New Dose of Reality.* New York: Cassell, 1996.

Goldman, Eric A. *Visions, Images, and Dreams: Yiddish Film Past and Present.* Teaneck, NJ: Ergo, 1988.

Goric, Goran. *The Cinema of Emir Kustrica: Notes from the Underground.* London: Wallflower Press, 2001.

Greene, Naomi. *Landscapes of Loss: The National Past in Postwar French Cinema.* Princeton, NJ: Princeton University Press, 1999.

Gunsberg, Maggie. *Italian Cinema.* New York: Palgrave Macmillan, 2005.

Hake, Sabine. *German National Cinema.* New York: Routledge, 2002.

Haltof, Marek. *Polish National Cinema.* New York: Berghahn, 2001.

Hoberman, John. *Bridge of Light: Yiddish Film between Two Worlds.* Philadelphia: Temple University Press, 1995.

Iordanova, Dina. *Cinema of Flames: Balkan Film, Culture, and the Media.* London: British Film Institute, 2001.

———. *Cinema of the Other Europe: The Industry and Artistry of East Central European Film.* London: Wallflower Press, 2003.

Jewish Film Directory: A Guide to More Than 1,200 Films of Jewish Interest from 32 Countries over 85 Years. Westport, CT: Greenwood Press, 1992.

Knight, Julia. *New German Cinema: The Images of a Generation (Short Cuts).* London: Wallflower Press, 2004.

Kuzniar, Alice. *The Queer German Cinema.* Palo Alto, CA: Stanford University Press, 2000.

Landy, Marcia. *Italian Cinema.* New York: Cambridge University Press, 2000.

Liehm, Antonin J. *Closely Watched Films: The Czechoslovakian Experience.* White Plaines, NY: International Arts and Science Press, 1974.

Loshitzsky, Yosefa. *Identity Politics on the Israeli Screen.* Austin: University of Texas Press, 2002.

Marcus, Millicent. *Filmmaking by the Book: Italian Cinema and Literary Adaptation.* Baltimore: Johns Hopkins University Press, 1993.

———. *After Fellini: National Cinema in the Postmodern Age.* Baltimore: Johns Hopkins University Press, 2002.

Michalek, Boleslaw, and Frank Turaj, *The Modern Cinema of Poland.* Bloomington: Indiana University Press, 1988.

Moss, Marilyn Ann. *Giant: George Stevens, a Life on Film.* Madison, WI: Terrace Books, 2004.

Napier, Susan J. *Anime from Akira to Princess Mononoke: Experiencing Contemporary Japanese Animation.* New York: Palgrave, 2001.

Orr, John, and Elzbieta Ostrowska, eds. *The Cinema of Andrzej Wajda: The Art of Irony and Defiance*. London: Wallflower Press, 2003.

Powrie, Phillip, ed. *French Cinema in the 1990s*. New York: Oxford University Press, 1996.

Santner, Eric. *Stranded Objects: Mourning, Memory, and Film in Postwar Germany*. Ithaca, NY: Cornell University Press, 1990.

Silberman, Marc. *German Cinema: Texts in Context*. Detroit, MI: Wayne State University Press, 1995.

Slocum, J. David, ed. *Violence and American Cinema*. New York: Routledge, 2001.

Shandley, Robert R. *Rubble Films: German Cinema in the Shadow of the Third Reich*. Philadelphia: Temple University Press, 2001.

Soila, Tytti, ed. *Nordic National Cinemas*. New York: Routledge, 1998.

Sorlin, Pierre. *Italian National Cinema from 1896–1996*. New York: Routledge, 1997.

Taylor, Richard, ed. *BFI Companion to Eastern European and Russian Cinema*. London: British Film Institute, 2001.

Temple, Michael, and Michael Witt, eds. *The French Cinema Book*. London: British Film Institute, 2004.

Williams, Alan, ed. *Film and Nationalism*. New Brunswick, NJ: Rutgers University Press, 2002.

Wright, Rochelle. *The Visible Wall: Jews and Other Ethnic Outsiders in Scandinavian Film*. Carbondale: Southern Illinois University, 1998.

Zinnemann, Fred. *A Life in the Movies: An Autobiography*. New York: Charles Scribner's Sons, 1992.

THE HOLOCAUST IN FILM, LITERATURE, AND NATIONAL MEMORY

Amishai-Maises, Ziva. *Depiction and Interpretation: The Influence of the Holocaust on the Visual Arts*. New York: Pergamon Press, 1993.

Avisar, Ilan. *Screening the Holocaust*. Bloomington: Indiana University Press, 1988.

Bartov, Omer. *The "Jew" in Cinema: From the Golem to Don't Touch My Holocaust*. Bloomington: Indiana University Press, 2005.

———. *Germany's War and the Holocaust: Disputed Histories*. Ithaca, NY: Cornell University Press, 2003.

———. *Mirrors of Destruction: War, Genocide, and Modern Identity*. New York: Oxford University Press, 2000.

———. *Murder in Our Midst: The Holocaust: Industrial Killing and Representation*. New York: Oxford University Press, 1996.

Berger, Alan. *Children of Job: American Second-Generation Witnesses to the Holocaust*. Albany: State University of Press of New York, 1997.

———. *Crisis and Covenant: The Holocaust in American Jewish Fiction*. Albany: State University Press of New York, 1985.

Bernard-Donals, Michael, and Richard Glejzer. *Between Witness and Testimony: The Holocaust and the Limits of Representation.* Albany: State University Press of New York, 2001.

———. *Witnessing the Disaster: Essays on Representation and the Holocaust.* Madison: University of Wisconsin, 2003.

Burama, Ian. *The Wages of Guilt: Memories of War in Germany and Japan.* New York: Farrar, Straus, and Giroux, 1994.

Celli, Carlo. *The Divine Comic: The Cinema of Roberto Benigni.* Lanham, MD: Scarecrow Press, 2001.

Clendinnen, Inga. *Reading the Holocaust.* New York: Cambridge University Press, 1999.

Cole, Tim. *Selling the Holocaust.* New York: Routledge, 2000.

Colombat, Andre Pierre. *The Holocaust in French Film.* Metuchen, NJ: Scarecrow Press, 1993.

Cooper, Leo. *In the Shadow of the Polish Eagle: Poles, the Holocaust, and Beyond.* New York: Palgrave Macmillan, 2000.

Davies, Fred. *Film, History, and the Holocaust.* Portland, OR: Frank Cass, 2005.

Dean, Carolyn J. *The Fragility of Empathy after the Holocaust.* Ithaca, NY: Cornell University Press, 2004.

Doneson, Judith. *The Holocaust in American Film,* 2nd ed. Syracuse, NY: Syracuse University Press, 2001.

Ezrahi, Sidra. *By Words Alone: The Holocaust in Literature.* Chicago: University of Chicago Press, 1980.

Epstein, Julia, and Lori Hope, eds. *Shaping Losses: Cultural Memory and the Holocaust.* Urbana: University of Illinois Press, 2001.

Erens, Patricia, and Mary Johnson. *Perspectives on the Holocaust: A Course for Adolescents.* New York: Jewish Media Fund, 1997.

Felman, Shoshana, and Dori Laub. *Testimony: The Crises of Witnessing in Literature, Psychoanalysis, and History.* New York: Routledge, 1992.

Finkelstein, Norman. *The Holocaust Industry: Reflections on the Exploitation of Jewish Suffering.* New York: Verso Press, 2000.

Flanzbaum, Hilene, ed. *The Americanization of the Holocaust.* Baltimore: Johns Hopkins University Press, 1999.

Fox, Thomas. *Stated Memory: East Germany and the Holocaust.* Rochester, NY: Camden House, 1999.

Friedländer, Saul, ed. *Probing the Limits of Representation: Nazism and the "Final Solution."* Cambridge, MA: Harvard University Press, 1992.

———. *Reflections of Nazism: An Essay on Kitsch and Death,* trans. Thomas Wehr. New York: Harper and Row, 1984.

Fuchs, Esther, ed. *Women and the Holocaust: Narrative and Representation.* Lanham, MD: University Press of America. 1999.

Fulbrook, Mary. *German National Identity after the Holocaust.* Malden, MA: Blackwell, 1999.

Gittelman, Zvi. *Bitter Legacy: Confronting the Holocaust in the USSR.* Bloomington: Indiana University Press, 1997.

Haggith, Toby. *The Holocaust and the Moving Image.* London: Wallflower Press, 2005.

Hartman, Geoffrey, ed. *Holocaust Remembrance:The Shapes of Memory.* Oxford: Blackwell, 1994.

———. *The Longest Shadow: In the Aftermath of the Holocaust.* Bloomington: Indiana University Press, 1996.

Herf, Jeffrey. *Divided Memory:The Nazi Past in the Two Germanys.* Cambridge, MA: Harvard University Press, 1997.

Hirsch, Joshua. *Afterimage: Film, Trauma, and the Holocaust.* Philadelphia: Temple University Press, 2004.

Hirsch, Marianne, and Irene Kacandes, eds. *Teaching the Representation of the Holocaust.* New York: Modern Languages Association of America, 2004.

Horowitz, Sara. *Voicing the Void: Muteness and Memory in Holocaust Fiction.* Albany: State University Press of New York, 1997.

Hungerford, Amy. *The Holocaust of Texts: Genocide, Literature, and Personification.* Chicago: University of Chicago Press, 2003.

"Images of Romanies (Gypsies) in International Cinema: Special Issue," *Framework:The Journal of Film and Media* 42:2 (2003).

Insdorf, Annette. *Indelible Shadows: Film and the Holocaust,* 3rd ed. New York: Cambridge University Press, 2003.

Kaes, Anton. *From Heimat to Hitler.* Cambridge, MA: Harvard University Press, 1989.

Kassenoff, Miriam Klein, and Anita Meyer Meinbach. *Studying the Holocaust through Film and Literature: Human Rights and Social Responsibility.* Norwood, MA: Christopher-Gordon, 2004.

Kertzer, Adrienne. *My Mother's Voice: Children, Literature, and the Holocaust.* Petersborough, Canada: Broadview Press, 2002.

Kleeblatt, Norman, ed. *Mirroring Evil: Nazi Imagery/Recent Art.* New Brunswick, NJ: Rutgers University Press, 2002.

LaCapra, Dominick. *Representing the Holocaust: History, Theory, Trauma.* Ithaca, NY: Cornell University Press, 1994.

Lang, Berel. *Holocaust Representation:Art within the Limits of History and Ethics.* Baltimore: Johns Hopkins University Press, 2000.

Langer, Lawrence. *Admitting the Holocaust: Collected Essays.* New York: Oxford University Press, 1996.

———. *The Holocaust and the Literary Imagination.* New Haven, CT: Yale University Press, 1977.

———. *Holocaust Testimonies: The Ruins of Memory.* New Haven, CT: Yale University Press, 1991.

———. *Preempting the Holocaust.* New Haven, CT: Yale University Press, 2000.

Liss, Andrea. *Trespassing through Shadows: Memory, Photography, and the Holocaust.* Minneapolis: University of Minnesota Press, 1998.

Loshitzky, Yosefa, ed. *Spielberg's Holocaust: Critical Perspectives on Schindler's List.* Bloomington: Indiana University Press, 1997.

Mintz, Alan. *Popular Culture and the Shaping of Holocaust Memory in America.* Seattle: University of Washington Press, 2001.

Mitchell, Charles P. *The Hitler Filmography:Worldwide Feature Films and Television Miniseries Portrayals, 1940–2000.* Jefferson, NC: McFarland and Co., 2002.

Niv, Kobi. *Life Is Beautiful but Not for Jews: Another View of the Film by Benigni,* trans. Jonathan Beyrak Lev. Lanham, MD: Scarecrow Press, 2003.

Niven, Bill. *Facing the Nazi Past: United Germany and the Legacy of the Third Reich.* New York: Routledge, 2002.

Novick, Peter. *The Holocaust in American Life.* Boston: Houghton Mifflin, 1999.

Patraka, Vivian M. *Spectacular Suffering: Theatre, Fascism, and the Holocaust.* Bloomington: Indiana University Press, 1999.

Picart, Caroline Joan, ed. *The Holocaust Film Sourcebook,* Vols. 1 and 2. Westport, CT: Praeger, 2004.

Raphael, Marc Lee, ed. *The Representation of the Holocaust in Literature and Film.* Williamsburg, VA: College of William and Mary, 2003.

Ravetto, Kriss. *The Unmaking of Fascist Aesthetics.* Minneapolis: University of Minnesota Press, 2001.

Reimer, Robert C., and Carol J. Reimer. *Nazi-Retro Film: How German Narrative Cinema Remembers the Past.* New York: Twayne, 1992.

Reiter, Andrea. *Narrating the Holocaust.* New York: Continuum, 2000.

Rosenfeld, Alvin. *Imagining Hitler.* Bloomington: Indiana University Press, 1985.

———, ed. *Thinking about the Holocaust: After Half a Century.* Bloomington: Indiana University Press, 1997.

Rosenfeld, Gavriel. *The World Hitler Never Made: Alternate History and the Memory of Nazism.* New York: Cambridge University Press, 2005.

Rothberg, Michael. *Traumatic Realism: The Demands of Holocaust Representation.* Minneapolis: University of Minnesota Press, 2000.

Schwartz, Daniel. *Imagining the Holocaust.* New York: St. Martin's Press, 1999.

Shandler, Jeffrey. *While America Watches: Televising the Holocaust.* New York: Oxford University Press, 1999.

Skirball, Sheba F. *Films of the Holocaust: An Annotated Filmography of the Collections in Israel.* New York: Garland Publishers, 1990.

Skloot, Robert. *The Darkness We Carry: The Drama of the Holocaust.* Madison: University of Wisconsin Press, 1988.

Slane, Andrea. *A Not So Foreign Affair: Fascism, Sexuality, and the Cultural Rhetoric of American Democracy.* Durham, NC: Duke University Press, 2001.

Steinlauf, Michael. *Bondage to the Dead: Poland and the Memory of the Holocaust.* Syracuse: Syracuse University Press, 1997.

Stier, Oren Baruch. *Committed to Memory: Cultural Mediations of the Holocaust.* Amherst: University of Massachusetts Press, 2003.

Sullivan, Edward T. *The Holocaust in Literature for Youth: A Guide and Resource Book.* Lanham, MD: Scarecrow Press, 1999.

"The Holocaust on Film: Special Issues," *Film and History: An Interdisciplinary Journal of Film and Television Studies* 32 nos. 1 and 2, 2002.

Totten, Samuel, and Stephen Feinberg, eds. *Teaching and Studying the Holocaust.* Boston: Allyn and Bacon, 2001.

Walker, Janet. *Trauma Cinema: Documenting Incest and the Holocaust.* Berkeley: University of California Press, 2005.

Weissman, Gary. *Fantasies of Witnessing: Postwar Efforts to Experience the Holocaust.* Ithaca, NY: Cornell University Press, 2004.

Wiedmer, Caroline. *The Claims of Memory: Representations of the Holocaust in Contemporary France and Germany.* Ithaca, NY: Cornell University Press, 1999.

Wolf, Joan B. *Harnessing the Holocaust: The Politics of Memory in France.* Palo Alto, CA: Stanford University Press, 2004.

Young, James. *At Memory's Edge: After-Images of the Holocaust in Contemporary Art and Architecture.* New Haven, CT: Yale University Press, 2000.

———. *The Texture of Memory: Holocaust Memorials and Meaning.* New Haven, CT: Yale University Press, 1993.

Wyman, David, and Charles H. Rosenzveig, eds. *The World Reacts to the Holocaust.* Baltimore: Johns Hopkins University Press, 1996.

Zelizer, Barbie. *Remembering to Forget: Holocaust Memory through the Camera's Eye.* New Brunswick, NJ: Rutgers University Press, 2000.

———, ed. *Visual Culture and the Holocaust.* New Brunswick, NJ: Rutgers University Press, 2001.

Zimmerman, Joshua, ed. *Contested Memories: Poles and Jews during the Holocaust and Its Aftermath.* New Brunswick, NJ: Rutgers University Press, 2003.

Filmography: 1990–2004

THE NAZIFICATION OF GERMAN SOCIETY

Leo and Claire. Germany, 2001. D: Joseph Vilsmaier. The trial of Leo Katzenberger for "racial defilement" of an Aryan girl.

> *Background:* Christiane Kohl. *The Maiden and the Jew*, trans. John S. Barrett. Hanover, NH: Steerforth Press, 2004.

My Heart Is Mine Alone. Germany, 1997. D: Helma Sanders-Brahms. The doomed love affair between the poets Else Lasker-Schüler and the pro-Nazi Gottfried Benn.

> *Background:* Hans W. Cohn. *Else Lasker-Schüler: The Broken World.* New York: Cambridge University Press, 1974.

The Ninth Day. Germany and Luxembourg, 2004. D: Volker Schlöndorff. A priest interned in a concentration camp is released for nine days to persuade his bishop to endorse Nazi racial policies.

> *Source:* Jean-Jacques Bernard. *The Camp of Slow Death,* trans. Edward Owen Marsh. London: Victor Gallanz, 1945.

Taking Sides. Austria, France, Germany, and the United Kingdom, 2001. D: Istvan Szabó. The postwar trial of orchestra conductor Wilhelm Furtwängler.

> *Background:* Fred Prieberg. *Trial of Strength: Wilhelm Furtwängler in the Third Reich*, trans. Christopher Dolan. Boston: Northeastern University Press, 1994.

Three Days in April. Germany, 1994. D: Oliver Storz. The reactions of Germans in a village to an abandoned cattle car of starving Gypsies, Jews, and Poles.

> *Background:* David Bankier. *The Germans and the Final Solution: Public Opinion under Nazism.* Cambridge, MA: Blackwell, 1992.

NAZI PERPETRATORS

After the Truth. Germany and the United States, 1997. D: Roland Suso Richter. An elderly Josef Mengele stands trial for experimenting on and killing Jews.

    Background: Gerald L. Posner and John Ware. *Mengele: The Complete Story.* New York: McGraw Hill, 1985.

Conspiracy. United Kingdom and United States, 2001. D: Frank Pierson. A reenactment of the Wannsee Conference where German officials planned the "Final Solution."

    Background: Steven Lehrer. *Wannsee House and the Holocaust.* Jefferson, NC: McFarland and Co., 2000.

Conversation with the Beast. Germany and the United States, 1996. D: Armin Mueller-Stahl. An elderly Hitler is discovered and interviewed by a historian.

    Background: Alvin R. Rosenfeld. *Imagining Hitler.* Bloomington: Indiana University Press, 1985.

The Downfall. Austria, Germany, and Italy, 2004. D: Oliver Hirschbiegel. Hitler's final days in the bunker.

    Background: Hugh R. Trevor Roper. *The Last Days of Hitler.* New York: Macmillan, 1947.

COLLABORATION

Hamsun. Denmark, Germany, Norway, and Sweden, 1996. D: Jan Troell. The support of Quisling and Hitler by Knut Hamsum, Norway's greatest novelist.

    Background: Robert Ferguson. *Enigma: The Life of Knut Hamsun.* New York: Farrar, Straus, and Giroux, 1987.

The Ogre. France, Germany, and the United Kingdom, 1996. D: Volker Schlöndorff. The story of a captured French simpleton who kidnaps German boys to serve in the army.

    Source: Michael Tournier. *The Ogre,* trans. Barbara Bray. Garden City, NY: Doubleday, 1972.

Pétain. France, 1993. D: Jean Marboeuf. The collaboration of the leaders of Vichy France with Germany in the implementation of German anti-Semitic policies.

    Background: Paul Webster. *Pétain's Crime: The Full Story of French Collaboration in the Holocaust.* London: Macmillan, 1990.

Rabbit Hunt. Austria and Germany, 1994. D: Andreas Gruber. Austrians assist the Germans in hunting Soviet POWs who have escaped from Mauthausen.

Background: Gordon J. Horwitz. *In the Shadow of Death: Living outside the Gates of Mauthausen.* New York: Free Press, 1990.

EINSATZGRUPPEN MASSACRES

Babij Jar. Belarus and Germany, 2003. D: Jeff Kanew. Reenactment of the Babi Yar massacre.

    Background: A. Anatoli (Kuznetsov). *Babi Yar,* trans. David Floyd. New York: Farrar, Straus, and Giroux, 1970.

Die Grube. Germany, 1995. D: Karl Fruchtmann. Jewish children witness and survive the killing of their families.

    Background: Richard Rhodes. *The SS Einsatzgruppen and the Invention of the Holocaust.* New York: Alfred A. Knopf, 2002.

Ladies' Tailor. USSR, 1990. D: Leonid Gorovets. Jews await mass shootings at Babi Yar.

    Background: Judith Kornblatt. "Why a Ladies' Tailor: *Ladies' Tailor* and the End of Soviet Jewry," *Jewish Social Studies* 5(3) (1999): 180–95.

DEPORTATION

My Mother's Courage. Austria, Germany, Ireland, and the United Kingdom, 1995. D: Michael Verhoeven. A woman on a deportation train persuades an SS officer to let her go.

    Source: George Tabori. *My Mother's Courage,* trans. Jack Zipes, *Theatre* 92(2) (1999): 109–29.

GHETTOS

In the Presence of Mine Enemies. United States, 1997. D: Joan Micklin Silver. The crisis of faith of a rabbi in the Warsaw Ghetto.

    Background: Irving J. Rosenbaum. *The Holocaust and Halakhah.* New York: KTAV, 1976.

The Last Butterfly. Czechoslovakia, France, and the United Kingdom, 1991. D: Karel Kochyna. Mime stages a play to warn children of their deportation from Theresienstadt.

    Source: Michael Jacot. *The Last Butterfly.* New York: Bobbs-Merrill, 1974.

The Last Letter. France and the United States, 2002. D: Frederick Wiseman. A Jewish mother recalls life under the German occupation as she reads her son's last letter.

   Source: Vasilii Semenovich Grossman. *Life and Fate,* trans. Robert Chandler. London: Collins Harvill, 1985.

Uprising. United States, 2001. D: Jon Avnet. Jewish responses to the worsening conditions in the Warsaw Ghetto, culminating in the Warsaw Ghetto Uprising of 1943.

   Background: Yisrael Gutman. *Resistance: The Warsaw Ghetto Uprising.* Boston: Houghton Mifflin, 1994.

DEATH CAMPS

Jonah Who Lived in the Whale. France and Italy, 1994. D: Robert Faenza. A twelve-year-old Jewish boy survives a death camp but is traumatized by his ordeal.

   Source: Jona Oberski. *Childhood,* trans. Ralph Manheim. Garden City, NY: Doubleday, 1983.

Out of the Ashes. United States, 2003. D: Joseph Sargent. Gisella Perl serves as a doctor in Auschwitz and faces a postwar trial for aiding the Germans.

   Source: Gisella Perl, *I Was a Doctor in Auschwitz.* New York: International Universities Press, 1948.

Sidonie. Austria, 1990. D: Karin Brandauer. A Gypsy girl's experiences in Auschwitz.

   Source: Erich Hackl. *Farewell to Sidonia,* trans. Edna McCown. New York: Fromm, 1991.

HIDING AND PASSING

The Diary of Anne Frank. Japan, 1995. D: Akinori Nagaoke. The Japanese anime version of *The Diary of Anne Frank.*

   Source: Anne Frank. *The Diary of a Young Girl,* trans. B. M. Mooyaart. New Modern Library, 1952.

Anne Frank: The Whole Story. United States, 2001. D: Robert Dornhelm. Anne Frank's life.

   Source: Melissa Müller. *Anne Frank: The Biography,* trans. Rita and Robert Kimber. New York: Metropolitan Books, 1998.

Farewell to Maria. Poland, 1993. D: Filip Zylber. A Jewish girl escapes from the ghetto and tries to pass as an Aryan in German-occupied Poland.

Source: Tadeusz Borowski. "Farewell to Maria," trans. Tadeusz Pióri. In *Holocaust Poetry*, ed. Hilda Schiff. New York: St. Martin's Griffin, 1995.

Hidden in Silence. United States, 1996. D: Richard A. Colla. A true story about a Polish maid who helps and hides Jews during the German occupation.

Background: Nechama Tec, *When Light Pierced the Darkness: Christian Rescue of Jews in Nazi-Occupied Poland*. New York: Oxford University Press, 1986.

ESCAPING TO SAFETY

All My Loved Ones. Czech Republic, 1999. D: Mazey Minac. Nicholas Winton's efforts to bring German-Jewish children to England.

Background: Muriel Emanuel and Vera Gissing. *Nicholas Winton and the Rescued Generation: Save One Life, Save the World*. Portland, OR: Valentine Mitchell, 2002.

The Aryan Couple. The United Kingdom and United States, 2004. D: John Daly. A Jewish industrialists bargains with the SS to gain passage for his family to Palestine.

Background: Yehuda Bauer. *Jews for Sale: Nazi-Jewish Negotiations*. New Haven, CT: Yale University Press, 1994.

Varian's War. Canada, the United Kingdom, and the United States, 2000. D: Lionel Chetwynd. Varian Fry's rescue network for getting intellectual and political refugees out of southern France.

Source: Varian Fry. *Surrender on Demand*. New York: Random House, 1945.

REFUGEES

Haven. Canada and the United States, 2001. D: John Gray. The story of 982 European refugees, mostly Jews, interned in the United States from 1944 until 1946.

Source: Ruth Gruber. *Haven: The Unknown Story of 1,000 World War Two Refugees*. New York: Coward, McCann, and Geoghegan, 1983.

Journey to Jerusalem. Bulgaria and Germany, 2003. D: Ivan Nitchev. A group of Bulgarians helps two German-Jewish boys evade capture and gain passage to Palestine.

Background: Frederick B. Chary. *The Bulgarian Jews and the Final Solution, 1940–1944*. Pittsburgh, PA: University of Pittsburgh Press, 1972.

Transit. France, 1991. D: René Allio. German refugees in France during the 1930s.

Source: Anna Seghers. *Transit,* trans. James A. Galston. Boston: Little, Brown, 1944.

RESCUE

A Day in October. Denmark and the United States. D: Kenneth Madsen. The rescue of Jews in Denmark in October of 1943.

   Background: Emmy E. Werner. *A Conspiracy of Decency: The Rescue of Danish Jews during World War Two.* Boulder, CO: Westview, 2002.
Divided We Fall. Czech Republic, 2000. D: Jan Hrebejk. Comedy about a Czech couple who hide a Jewish man despite a collaborator's romantic interest in the wife.

   Background: The Jews of Czechoslovakia, Vol. 3, ed. Avignor Dagan. Philadelphia: Jewish Publication Society, 1984.
The Hill of a Thousand Children (a.k.a. *Le Chambon*). France, 1994. D: Jean-Louis Lorenzi. The villagers of Le Chambon shelter Jews from the Germans.

   Background: Phillip Paul Hallie. *Lest Innocent Blood Be Shed: The Story of the Village of Le Chambon and How Goodness Happened There.* New York: Harper and Row, 1979.
Les Misérables. France, 1995. D: Claude Lelouche. The story of a rescuer of Jews whose life parallels that of Victor Hugo's character Jean Valjean.

   Source: Victor Hugo. *Les Misérables: A New Unabridged Translation,* trans. Norman MacAfee. New York: Signet, 1987.
Lucie Aubrac. France, 1997. D: Claude Berri. A woman in the French Resistance saves her imprisoned Jewish husband.

   Source: Lucie Aubrac. *Outwitting the Gestapo,* trans. Konrad Bieber. Lincoln: University of Nebraska Press, 1993.
Monsieur Batignole. France, 2002. D: Gerard Jugnot. Comedy about a French man who rescues the children of a Jewish couple he betrayed.

   Background: Susan Zucotti. *The Holocaust, the French, and the Jews.* New York: Basic Books, 1993.
Perlasca: An Italian Hero. Italy, Hungary, France, and Sweden, 2002. D: Alberto Negrin. True story of an Italian diplomat who posed as the Spanish ambassador to Hungary to rescue Jews.

   Source: Enrico Deaglio. *The Banality of Goodness: The Story of Giorgio Perlasca,* trans. Gregory Conti. Notre Dame, IN: University of Notre Dame Press, 1998.
The Visas That Saved Lives. Japan, 1992. D: Katsumi Obyama. The Japanese consul in Lithuania disobeys orders and issues transit visas for Jews fleeing Europe.

Background: Hillel Levine. *In Search of Sugihara, the Elusive Japanese Diplomat Who Risked His Life to Rescue 10,000 Jews from the Holocaust.* New York: Free Press, 1996.

RESISTANCE

Amen. France, Germany, United States, 2002. D: Costa-Gavras. An SS officer leaks the secret about the "Final Solution" to persuade the Vatican to condemn it.
    Source: Rolf Hochhuth. *The Deputy*, trans. Richard and Clara Winston. New York: Grove Press, 1964.

Edelweiss Pirates. Germany, Luxembourg, Netherlands, Switzerland, 2004. D: Niko von Glasow. True story of a group of teenagers in Cologne, who engage in anti-Nazi activities.
    Background: Sally Rogow. *Faces of Courage: Young Heroes of World War II.* Vancouver, Canada: Glenville Island Publishing, 2003, 31–42.

The Plot to Kill Hitler. United States and Yugoslavia, 1990. D: Lawrence Schiller. The conspiracy to assassinate Hitler in July of 1944.
    Background: Joachim C. Fest. *Plotting Hitler's Death: The Story of the German Resistance.* New York: Metropolitan Books, 1996.

Rosenstrasse. Germany and the Netherlands, 2003. D: Magarethe von Trotta. Gentile wives of Jewish men demonstrate in Berlin to prevent the deportation of their husbands.
    Background: Nathan Stoltzfus. *Resistance of the Heart: Intermarriage and the Rossenstrasse Protest in Nazi Germany.* New York: W. W. Norton, 1996.

Witness against Hitler. United Kingdom, 1996. D: Betsan Morris Evans. Helmuth James Von Moltke's participation in the plot to assassinate Hitler.
    Background: Michael Balfour and Julian Frisby. *Helmuth von Moltke: A Leader against Hitler.* London: MacMillan, 1972.

A Woman at War. Belgium, France, and the United Kingdom. D: Edward Bennett. The story of how Helene Moszkiewiez infiltrated Gestapo headquarters in Belgium.
    Source: Helene Moszkiewiez. *Inside the Gestapo: A Jewish Woman's Secret War.* Toronto: Macmillan of Canada, 1985.

PERSECUTION OF HOMOSEXUALS

The Einstein of Sex. Germany and the Netherlands. 1999. D: Rosa von Praunheim. The life of Magnus Hirschfeld, the founder of the gay right's movement in Germany.

Background: Charlotte Wolff. *Magnus Hirschfeld: A Portrait of a Pioneer in Sexuality.* London: Quartet, 1986.

I Am My Own Woman. Germany, 1992. D: Rosa von Praunheim. The persecution and resistance of a transvestite in the Third Reich and East Germany.

    Source: Charlotte von Mahlsdorf. *I Am My Own Woman: The Outlaw Life of Charlotte von Mahlsdorf, Berlin's Most Distinguished Transvestite,* trans. Jean Hollander. Pittsburgh, PA: Cleis Press, 1995.

GENERATIONAL SAGAS: JEWISH FAMILIES DURING THE TWENTIETH CENTURY

House of the Generals. United States, 2000 D: Dan Spigal. The fate of Jews in the Ukraine from the overthrow of the czar until the end of World War II.

    Background: Karl Berkhoff. *Harvest of Despair: Life and Death in the Ukraine under Nazi Rule.* Cambridge, MA: Belnap Press, 2004.

The Man Who Cried. France and the United Kingdom, 2000. D: Sally Potter. A Jewish woman's odyssey from Czarist Russia to England, France, and the United States.

    Source: Sally Potter. *The Man Who Cried.* London: Faber and Faber, 2001.

Sunshine. Austria, Canada, Germany, and Hungary, 1999. D: Istvan Szabó. A Jewish family from the Austro-Hungarian Empire through the fall of communism in Hungary.

    Background: Raphael Patai. *The Jews of Hungary: History, Culture, Psychology.* Detroit, MI: Wayne State University Press, 1996.

JEWISH REPATRIATION AFTER WORLD WAR II

Almost Peaceful. France, 2002. D: Michel Deville. Survivors return to Paris in 1946.

    Background: Maud Mandel. *In the Aftermath: Armenians and Jews in 20th Century France.* Durham, NC: Duke University Press, 2003.

Burial of a Potato. Poland, 1991. D: Jan Kolski. A concentration camp survivor returns to Poland and encounters anti-Semitism from Poles who think he is Jewish.

    Background: Jan Marek Chodakiewicz. *Polish-Jewish Conflict in the Wake of World War Two.* New York: Columbia University Press, 2003.

From Hell to Hell. Belarus and Germany, 1997. D: Dmitri Astrakhan, A dramatization of the Kielce pogrom against returning Jews in 1946.

Background: Michael Steinlauf. *Bondage to the Dead: Poland and the Memory of the Holocaust.* Syracuse, NY: Syracuse University Press, 1997.

The Truce. France, Germany, Italy, and Switzerland. D: Francesco Rosi. Primo Levi's journey back to Italy after the liberation of Poland.

　　Source: Primo Levi. *The Reawakening: A Liberated Prisoner's Long March Home through East Europe,* trans. Stuart Woolfe. Boston: Little, Brown, 1965.

HOLOCAUST SURVIVORS AND MEMORY IN ISRAEL

The Kastner Trial. Israel, 1994. D: Uri Barbash. The trial of Rudolf Kastner for collaborating with the Germans to spare Labor Zionists in Hungary.

　　Background: Tom Segev. *The Seventh Million: Israelis and the Holocaust,* trans. Haim Watzman. New York: Henry Holt, 2000.

Kedma. France, Israel, and Italy. D: Amos Gitai. Holocaust survivors illegally enter Palestine during the 1948 War of Independence.

　　Background: Idith Zertal. *From Catastrophe to Power: Holocaust Survivors and the Emergence of Israel.* Berkeley: University of California Press, 1998.

Newland. Israel, 1994. D: Orna Ben-Dor Niv. Child survivors search for parents in Israel.

　　Background: Hanna Yablonka. *Survivors of the Holocaust: Israel after the War,* trans. Ora Cummings. New York: New York University Press, 1999.

Under the Donim Tree. Israel, 1994. D: Eli Cohen. Teenage Holocaust survivors on an Israeli kibbutz in the 1950s.

　　Source: Gila Almagor. *Under the Donim Tree,* trans. Hillel Schenker. New York: Simon and Schuster for Young Readers, 1995.

HOLOCAUST SURVIVORS

Birch Tree Meadow. France, Germany, and Poland, 2003. D: Marceline Loridan-Ivens. A survivor returns to Auschwitz and shares her memories with a German tourist.

　　Compare: D. Peter Morley. *Kitty: A Return to Auschwitz.* United Kingdom, 1979.

Bronstein's Children. Germany and Poland, 1990. D: Jerzy Kawalerowicz. Survivor secretly keeps an SS guard imprisoned after the war.

　　Source: Jurek Becker. *Bronstein's Children,* trans. Leila Vennewitz. Chicago: University of Chicago Press.

Miss Rose White. United States, 1992. D: Joseph Sargent. A survivor is re-united with her sister, who immigrated to the United States before the Holocaust.

  Source: Barbara Lebow. *A Shayna Maidel.* New York: New American Library, 1988.

Voyages. France, 1999. D: Emanuel Finkiel. Three woman survivors recall how the Holocaust affected their subsequent lives.

  Background: Aaron Hass. *The Aftermath: Living with the Holocaust.* New York: Cambridge University Press, 1995.

SECOND GENERATION
(CHILDREN OF HOLOCAUST SURVIVORS)

Anna's Summer. Germany, Greece, and Spain, 2001. D: Jeanine Meerapfel. Granddaughter learns about her grandmother's fate in the Holocaust.

  Background: Rebecca Camhi Fromer. *The House by the Sea: A Portrait of the Holocaust in Greece.* San Francisco: Mercury House, 1998.

A Call to Remember. United States, 1997. D: Jack Bender. Children of survivors cope with their mother's learning that a son she presumed dead has been located.

  Compare: A Generation Apart. United States, 1984. D: Jack and Danny Fisher.

Shine. Australia, 1996. D: Scott Hicks. Survivor father mentally and physically abuses his son, who becomes a mentally unstable, but brilliant, concert pianist.

  Sources: Gillian Helfgott with Alissa Tanskaya. *Love You to Bits and Pieces: Life with David Helfgott.* New York: Penguin, 1996. Margaret Helfgott with Tom Gross. *Out of Tune: The Myth of Shine.* New York: Warner Books, 1998.

The Substance of Fire. United States, 1997. D: Daniel Sullivan. Survivor father clashes with his children over his plans to publish a costly book on Auschwitz.

  Source: Jon Robin Baitz. *The Substance of Fire and the Film Society: Two Plays.* Garden City, NY: Fireside Theatre, 1991.

WAR CRIMINALS IN HIDING OR ON TRIAL

Apt Pupil. United States, 1998. D: Bryan Singer. High-school student blackmails a Nazi war criminal into telling him what it was like to commit genocide.

Source: Stephen King. "Apt Pupil." In *Different Season.* New York: Viking, 1982.

Nuremberg. Canada, 2000. D: Yves Simoneau. Docudrama of the first Nuremberg trial.

Source: Joseph E. Persico. *Nuremberg: Infamy on Trial.* New York: Viking, 1994.

The Man Who Captured Eichmann. United States, 1996. D: William Graham. The tracking and capture of Adolf Eichmann by the Israeli Mossad.

Source: Peter Malkin and Harry Stein. *Eichmann in My Hands.* New York: Warner Books, 1990.

The Statement. Canada and France, 2003. D: Norman Jewison. The hunt for a French collaborator who has evaded arrest with help from the Catholic Church.

Source: Brian Moore. *The Statement.* New York: Dutton, 1996.

NEO-NAZIS AND HOLOCAUST DENIERS

The Believer. United States, 2001. D: Henry Bean. A Jewish man becomes a neo-Nazi to protest what he perceives as Jewish theological fatalism and passivity during the Holocaust.

Source: Henry Bean. *The Believer: Confronting Jewish Self-Hatred.* New York: Thunder's Mouth Press, 2002.

Führer-Ex. Germany and Italy, 2002. D: Winfried Bonengel. A German neo-Nazi recants his racist views and violent acts.

Source: Ingo Hasselbach with Tom Reiss. *Führer-Ex: Memoirs of a Former Neo-Nazi.* New York: Random House, 1996.

The Infiltrator. United States, 1995. D: John McKenzie. An Israeli–American reporter infiltrates a German neo-Nazi group.

Source: Yaron Svoray and Nick Taylor. *In Hitler's Shadow: An Israeli's Amazing Journey inside Germany's Neo-Nazi Movement.* New York: Nan A. Talese, 1994.

Never Forget. United States, 1991. D: Joseph Sargent. Survivor sues Holocaust denial group for failing to pay him for proving that Jews were gassed at Auschwitz.

Background: Alex Grobman and Michael Shermer. *Denying History: Who Says the Holocaust Never Happened and Why Do They Say It.* Berkeley: University of California Press, 2000.

Not In This Town. United States, 1997. D: Donald Wrye. The citizens of Billings, Montana, demonstrate their solidarity with the victims of neo-Nazi hate crimes.

Background: Janice Cohn. *The Christmas Menorahs: How a Town Fought Hate.* Morton Grove, IL: Albert Whitman, 2000.

Internet Resources

Annotated Videography, United States Holocaust Memorial Museum: www.ushmm.org/education/foreducators/resource/videography.pdf.

Catalogue of the Collection of Holocaust Film and Video, Joan Sourasky-Constantiner Holocaust Multimedia Research Center, Center of the Israel Film Archive: www.jer-cin.org.il.filmholo.htm.

Cinematography of the Holocaust, Fritz Bauer Institute: www.cine-holocaust .de.html.

Ergo Jewish Video Catalog, Ergo Media (for purchase of videos): www .jewishvideo.com.

Facets Multimedia (for purchase or rental of videos): www.facets.org.

Felix Posen Bibliographic Project on Anti-Semitism, Vidal Sassoon International Center for the Study of Anti-Semitism: www.sicsa.huji.ac.il.bibear.html.

Film and Photo Department of the Yad Vashem Archive: www.yad-vashem.org/ about yad/departments/archives/photo archive.html.

Films on the Holocaust, Simon Wiesenthal Center: www.motic.wiesenthal.com/ text/X01/xm0113.html.

German Cinema on DVD and Video, Moffit Library, University of California, Berkeley: www.lib.berkeley.edu/MRC/germanfilmresources.html.

German Films: www.german-cinema.de.

Internet Movie Database: www.imdb.com.

Jewish Film Archive: www.jewishfilm.com.

Jewish Heritage Video Collection: www.jhvc.org.

Kinoeye: New Perspectives on European Film: www.kinoeye.org.

Movies Dealing with the Holocaust and Catholics or Other Christians, Hiatt Holocaust Collection, Denand Library, College of the Holy Cross: www.holy cross.edu/departments/history/vlpomar/hiatt/movies.htm.

National Center for Jewish Film, Brandeis University: www.brandeis.edu/jewish-film.

Steven Spielberg Jewish Film Archive, Hebrew University in Jerusalem: www.spielbergfilmarchive.org.il.

UCLA Film and Television Archive: www.cinema.ucla.edu.

Videography: A Teacher's Guide to the Holocaust, Florida Center for Instructional Technology, University of South Florida: www.fcit.coedu.usf.edu/holocaust/resource/film.htm.

World War II and Holocaust Filmography, University of North Carolina-Chapel Hill: www.lib.unc.edu/house.mrc/films/genre._php?genre_id=65.

Index

Page numbers in italics refer to tables.

About the Author

Lawrence Baron has served as the Abraham Nasatir Professor of Modern Jewish History and the director of the Lipinksy Institute for Judaic Studies at San Diego State University since 1988. He received his Ph.D. from the University of Wisconsin in 1974 and taught at St. Lawrence University between 1975 and 1988. He has authored a biography of the German-Jewish anarchist Erich Mühsam, coedited four anthologies, and acted as the consulting historian for Sam and Pearl Oliner's *The Altruistic Personality: Rescuers of Jews in Nazi Europe*. He is the founder and current president of the Western Jewish Studies Association and a member of the board of directors of the Association for Jewish Studies.